Debbie Mumm's
Country Quilts
for All Occasions

120 Quilts, Decorations and Accessories You Can Make Using Easy, Timesaving Techniques

RODALE

WE INSPIRE AND ENABLE PEOPLE TO IMPROVE THEIR LIVES AND THE WORLD AROUND THEM

This book is a compilation of *Debbie Mumm's Quick Country Quilts for Every Room* (© 1998 Debbie Mumm) and *Quick Country Christmas Quilts* (© 1995 Debbie Mumm), previously published by Rodale Inc.

The author and editors who compiled this book have tried to make all of the contents as accurate and as correct as possible. Illustrations, photographs, and text have all been carefully checked and cross-checked. However, due to the variability of materials, personal skill, and so on, neither the author nor Rodale Inc. assumes any responsibility for any damages or other losses incurred that result from the material presented herein. All instructions and diagrams should be carefully studied and clearly understood before beginning any project.

Printed in the United States of America
Rodale Inc. makes every effort to use acid-free ∞, recycled paper ♻ .

Cover Designer: Rita Baker Design
Cover Photographer: Mitch Mandel

ISBN 1–57954–434–7 hardcover

2 4 6 8 10 9 7 5 3 1 hardcover

Quick

Country
Quilts

for Every Room

CONTENTS

INTRODUCTION

I am stating the obvious when I say that I love decorating with quilts! Doing this book has been a wonderful experience—I have enjoyed creating the room settings to go along with the quilt projects that I designed. This really shows off how beautiful the projects can look in your home.

I enjoy many different styles of decorating, and I love themes. It was fun to pick themes that would match up well with a room and inspire a variety of project ideas. Of course, there were always many more project ideas than we could fit in the book! By redecorating and showcasing some of the rooms in my own home, I was able to have free reign to take a theme as far as I wanted.

A definite highlight was designing the romantic renaissance environment in my bedroom—a fun departure from my typical country style. The process was certainly challenging, but the results were stunning. I love to see the astonished looks on the faces of friends when I show them the room. They feel

as if they have walked into another world. It was also satisfying to use my home-decorator fabrics to create this fusion of classic and country looks.

Another high point of the book was planning, sketching, and painting the pages for "Country Decorating with Debbie Mumm." This special section is a visual interpretation of favorite decorating ideas culled from a notebook that I kept for more than a year. As I planned how to translate my notes and inspirations into watercolor illustrations, I always kept in mind that I wanted this section to be visually fun while providing useful tips and ideas to spark your imagination. This entire process involved a great deal of planning and coordination, but ultimately, it became what I had envisioned. I am very pleased with the results, and I hope you enjoy looking at the pages as much as I enjoyed painting them.

The process of doing this book has given me plenty of insights into decorating and redecorating. Here are my tips.

Debbie's Decorating Checklist

✓ Pick a room. Focus on one room at a time.

✓ Scour decorating books and magazines for inspiration. Start a scrapbook for all your clippings, notes, and thoughts.

✓ Choose a theme and a color scheme.

✓ Do a brainstorming of ideas. Rally your creative friends for ideas and help.

✓ Estimate the costs and develop a budget.

✓ Hold a yard sale to get rid of the old and raise money for the new.

✓ Look for refurbishing possibilities—chairs and sofas to be reupholstered, furniture to be painted.

✓ Start the hunt for accessories to carry out your theme. Hit the flea markets and thrift stores first for frugal finds. Then move on to antique stores, catalogs, craft shows, gift shops, and interior design stores.

✓ Decide on wall treatments. Some options include fresh paint, faux or sponge texturing, wallpaper, and stenciled borders.

✓ Consider your floors. Look for a new area rug or a painted floor cloth. Maybe the hardwood floors are ready for refinishing.

✓ Select three or four fabrics in a variety of scales and textures for window treatments and room accessories.

✓ Choose a design or pattern for a quilt to hang or drape.

✓ Come up with a schedule and get started. Do the walls first, floors next, and then furniture, windows, and accessories.

Remember that it usually takes a little longer and costs a little more than you plan on. Ouch!

Whatever you choose to do, have fun and try not to get stressed out about the process!

I designed the quilts and projects in this book around room themes, but most of them can be mixed and matched or used in other rooms. This is the first time that I have included bed quilts, and that was a welcome change of pace for me. Now you can get a total look for a room all in one book. To get inspiration, study the photos. There are plenty of accessories and ideas that you can apply to decorating your own home.

As you thumb through the book, you'll see a "Weekender" stamp on some of the project photos. These are especially suited to start and finish in a weekend. You'll also notice I've scattered tips of all kinds throughout the pages. Be sure to look for these box logos.

This box contains quick and easy decorating tips and ideas or notes from me.

 Look for creative options and suggestions for varying the basic projects in these boxes.

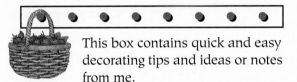

This is the cue that you'll find an important helpful hint for making the project here.

I hope you have fun making the quilts and displaying them in your home. Happy Quilting and Happy Decorating!

Debbie Mumm

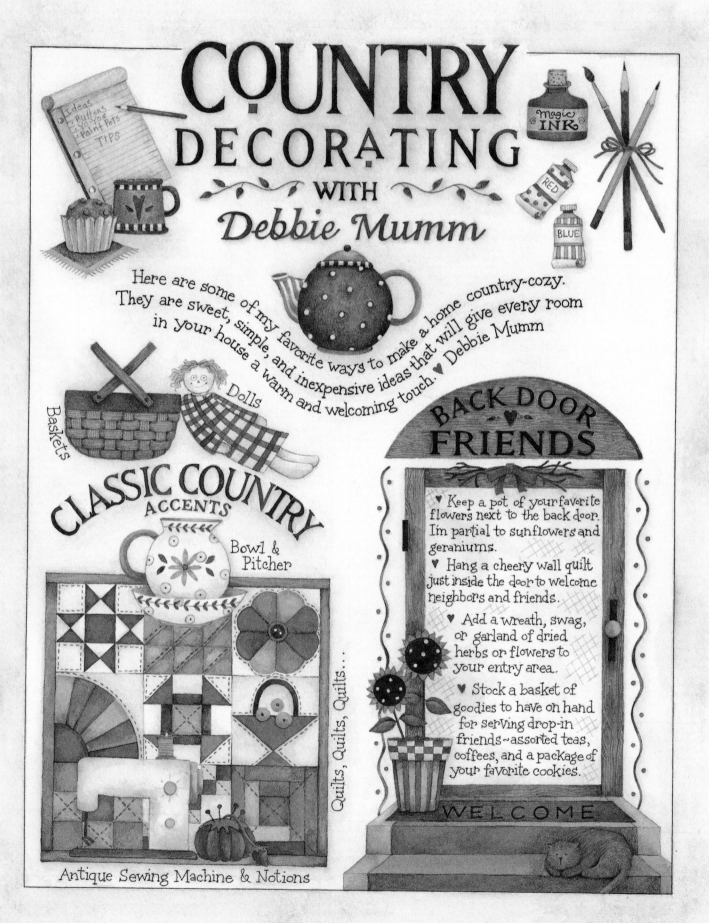

COUNTRY DECORATING
WITH
Debbie Mumm

Here are some of my favorite ways to make a home country-cozy. They are sweet, simple, and inexpensive ideas that will give every room in your house a warm and welcoming touch. ♥ Debbie Mumm

Baskets

Dolls

CLASSIC COUNTRY ACCENTS

Bowl & Pitcher

Quilts, Quilts, Quilts...

Antique Sewing Machine & Notions

BACK DOOR FRIENDS

♥ Keep a pot of your favorite flowers next to the back door. I'm partial to sunflowers and geraniums.

♥ Hang a cheery wall quilt just inside the door to welcome neighbors and friends.

♥ Add a wreath, swag, or garland of dried herbs or flowers to your entry area.

♥ Stock a basket of goodies to have on hand for serving drop-in friends ~ assorted teas, coffees, and a package of your favorite cookies.

WELCOME

Stack up comfy pillows and tie them with a pretty ribbon.

HOMESPUN TOUCHES

ABUNDANCE OF BUTTONS

FRAME 'EM & HANG 'EM

Hang framed quilt blocks with other prints and pictures on a decorative drapery rod. Interesting finials add a fun touch.

Fill baskets, mason jars, pots, tins or well-worn wooden drawers with buttons. Sew them on your quilts~to the corners, around the borders, and to the blocks. Decorate pillows, fragrant sachets, lampshades, and pots. Buttons add dimension and charm to everyday items.

QUILTS MAKE IT FEEL LIKE HOME

COZY COMFORTS

Blanket stitch fabric or felt motifs and simple appliqué shapes to a plain, purchased knit or fleece throw.

PILLOWS WITH PIZZAZZ

Stitch yo-yos, buttons, tassels or appliqué designs to a plain, purchased pillow to create a unique, one-of-a-kind accent.

SOFT LIGHTS

Decoupage lamp shades with fabric shapes, buttons, stickers, gift wrap, greeting cards, sports cards, yo-yos, and quilt block designs cut from colored paper.

GREAT SPOTS FOR QUILTS

Hanging from the mantel, draping out of a basket, folded and stacked in a hutch on an end table or dining table, draped over the back of a sofa or chair, over the stair railing.

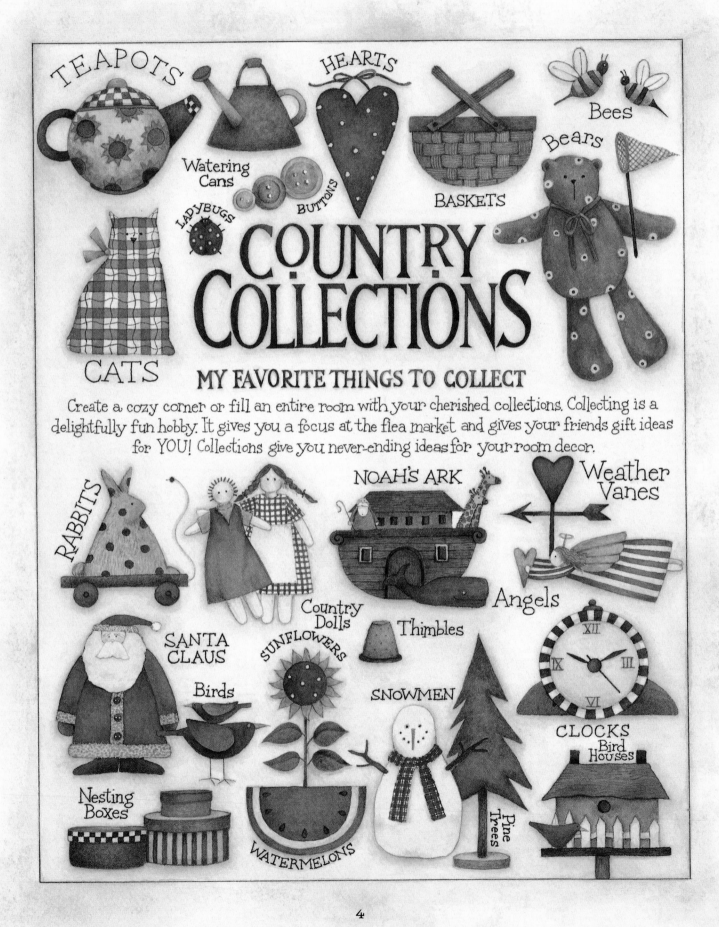

TEAPOTS

HEARTS

Watering Cans

BASKETS

Bees

Bears

LADYBUGS

BUTTONS

CATS

COUNTRY COLLECTIONS

MY FAVORITE THINGS TO COLLECT

Create a cozy corner or fill an entire room with your cherished collections. Collecting is a delightfully fun hobby. It gives you a focus at the flea market and gives your friends gift ideas for YOU! Collections give you never-ending ideas for your room decor.

RABBITS

NOAH'S ARK

Weather Vanes

Angels

Country Dolls

Thimbles

SANTA CLAUS

SUNFLOWERS

Birds

SNOWMEN

CLOCKS
Bird Houses

Nesting Boxes

WATERMELONS

Pine Trees

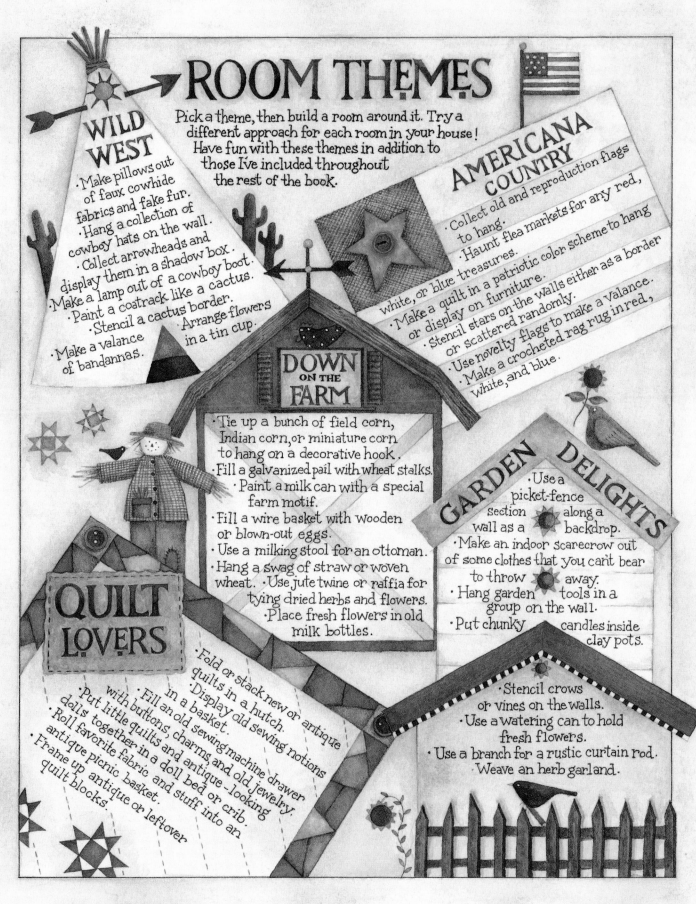

ROOM THEMES

Pick a theme, then build a room around it. Try a different approach for each room in your house! Have fun with these themes in addition to those I've included throughout the rest of the book.

WILD WEST

· Make pillows out of faux cowhide fabrics and fake fur.
· Hang a collection of cowboy hats on the wall.
· Collect arrowheads and display them in a shadow box.
· Make a lamp out of a cowboy boot.
· Paint a coatrack like a cactus.
· Stencil a cactus border.
· Arrange flowers in a tin cup.
· Make a valance of bandannas.

AMERICANA COUNTRY

· Collect old and reproduction flags to hang.
· Haunt flea markets for any red, white, or blue treasures.
· Make a quilt in a patriotic color scheme to hang or display on furniture.
· Stencil stars on the walls either as a border or scattered randomly.
· Use novelty flags to make a valance.
· Make a crocheted rag rug in red, white, and blue.

DOWN ON THE FARM

· Tie up a bunch of field corn, Indian corn, or miniature corn to hang on a decorative hook.
· Fill a galvanized pail with wheat stalks.
· Paint a milk can with a special farm motif.
· Fill a wire basket with wooden or blown-out eggs.
· Use a milking stool for an ottoman.
· Hang a swag of straw or woven wheat.
· Use jute twine or raffia for tying dried herbs and flowers.
· Place fresh flowers in old milk bottles.

GARDEN DELIGHTS

· Use a picket-fence section along a wall as a backdrop.
· Make an indoor scarecrow out of some clothes that you can't bear to throw away.
· Hang garden tools in a group on the wall.
· Put chunky candles inside clay pots.
· Stencil crows or vines on the walls.
· Use a watering can to hold fresh flowers.
· Use a branch for a rustic curtain rod.
· Weave an herb garland.

QUILT LOVERS

· Fold or stack new or antique quilts in a hutch.
· Display old sewing notions in a basket.
· Fill an old sewing machine drawer with buttons, charms, and antique jewelry.
· Put little quilts and antique-looking dolls together in a doll bed or crib.
· Roll favorite fabric and stuff into an antique picnic basket.
· Frame up antique or leftover quilt blocks.

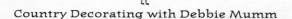
THE COUNTRY DECORATOR

MURPH'S TURF

GO!

Decoupage sports cards onto a used or unfinished bedside stand. For knobs and feet, drill baseballs into place.

COOL!

DINOSAURS · SPACE · SPORTS

TIME FOR TEA

To decorate a hutch, gather all your tea goodies together to create a pleasing arrangement.

YELLOWSTONE

OLD FAITHFULL

1

COZY

NOOKS & CRANNIES ♥

Stack three vintage suitcases for an end table. Store games and puzzles inside.

FAMILY-ROOM RETREAT

- Make a collage out of family memorabilia and souvenirs from trips.
- Build a cabin out of Lincoln Logs and display it with a miniature Log Cabin quilt.
- Collect leaves from the yard or park and spray them with metallic gold, copper, or silver paint. Add them to wreaths or show them off in a bowl or basket.
- Use old wagons to display vintage dolls and stuffed animals with companion quilts.
- Place soft-sculpture snowmen in a wreath for a wintertime accessory.
- Fill a basket with pinecones, nuts, and faux fruit.

- Group wooden toys together for a nostalgic yet functional display.

THE BIRD BATH

~ Stitch fun fabric borders to the edge of bathroom linens to create custom~ trimmed towels.

~ Purchase and paint small wooden birdhouses for finials on your curtain rod.

~ Stencil a sisal mat with birdhouses.

HOLIDAY FRONT DOOR

Fun finds from the flea market make for a welcoming front door:
- Vintage coal or snow shovel
- Pail of Christmas greenery
- Antique skis & snowshoes
- Old mittens
- Old sled
- Ice skates

FOR A SPECIAL GIRL

Create a stuffed Heart Garland to hang on her door or above her headboard. Put one letter from her name on each heart.

FRUITY KITCHEN

COVERED BOXES

Use purchased papier~mâché boxes and decorate with fabrics and buttons.

DEBBIE'S RECIPE

FOR A COUNTRY KITCHEN
- Bright red, golden, and green apples ·
- Pears in tan and gold ·
- Cheery red cherries ·

Mix the fruits together with plenty of red and natural checkerboards. Add a hint of black for accent. Throw in a handful of green leaves and sprinkle liberally around your kitchen. Enjoy immediately!

Decoupage apple shapes to a purchased serving tray~ A perfect way to serve pie and coffee.

©Debbie Mumm

COZY COUNTRY DINING ROOM

Tea lovers, rejoice! The world's most popular beverage gets its just reward as the main feature in this coordinated dining room grouping. The delightful tea theme will set the mood for pleasant conversation no matter what you prefer in your cup! For a peek at the same room done up for Christmas, see page 31.

TEAPOT TABLE QUILT

These teapots take their color cue from the rich reds and browns of antique Staffordshire pottery. English potters in the late seventeenth century capitalized on the rising popularity of tea with the creation of teapots, cups, and saucers. Today's quilter can capitalize on easy patchwork and quick-fuse appliqué to make this totally up-to-date Teapot Table Quilt. But don't reserve this just for teatime—teapots around the table are also the perfect accompaniment for breakfast, lunch, or dinner.

Finished Size: 34 inches square   **Finished Teapot Block: 9 × 7 inches**

MATERIALS

(Obvious directional prints are not recommended.)

■ ¼ yard red-and-black print for teapots

■ ¼ yard light tan print for background

■ ¼ yard tan-and-black print for block centers

■ ⅝ yard green print for lattice and binding

■ ¼ yard black print for patchwork border

■ ¼ yard red print for patchwork border and corner squares

■ ⅛ yard gold print for patchwork border

■ ⅝ yard multicolor check for border

1⅛ yards fabric for backing

1⅛ yards cotton batting

Scraps, or ⅛-yard pieces, of several coordinated fabrics for appliqué pieces

Lightweight, sewable fusible web

Embroidery floss

4 assorted ⅝-inch buttons

CUTTING

Prewash and press all of your fabrics. Using a rotary cutter, see-through ruler, and cutting mat, prepare the pieces as described below. Measurements for all pieces include ¼-inch seam allowances.

FABRIC	FIRST CUT		SECOND CUT	
Color	No. of Pieces	Dimensions	No. of Pieces	Dimensions
Red-and-black print	**Teapots**			
	4	5½-inch squares	No second cut	
Light tan print	**Background**			
	3	2½ × 42-inch strips	4	2½ × 9½-inch pieces
			8	2½ × 5½-inch pieces
			16	1½-inch squares
Tan-and-black print	**Block centers**			
	1	6½-inch square	No second cut	
	4	5½-inch squares	No second cut	
Green print	**Lattice**			
	7	1 × 42-inch strips	2	1 × 25½-inch strips
			4	1 × 24½-inch strips
			2	1 × 9½-inch strips
			6	1 × 7½-inch strips
			2	1 × 6½-inch strips
	Binding			
	4	2¾ × 42-inch strips	No second cut	
Black print	**Patchwork border**			
	4	1½ × 42-inch strips	8	1½ × 14-inch strips
Red print	**Patchwork border**			
	2	1½ × 42-inch strips	4	1½ × 14-inch strips
	Corner squares			
	4	4½-inch squares	No second cut	
Gold print	**Patchwork border**			
	2	1½ × 42-inch strips	4	1½ × 14-inch strips
Multicolor check	**Border**			
	4	4½ × 25½-inch strips	No second cut	

Making the Teapot Blocks

You will be making four teapot blocks. Refer to "Making Quick Corner Triangles" on page 269 for instructions on making the corner triangle units. Refer to "Assembly Line Piecing" on page 268 for in- structions on making the corner triangle units for all four blocks at the same time. Press the seams to- ward the triangle just added.

STEP 1. Sew four 1½-inch light tan print squares to each of the four 5½-inch red-and-black print squares. See **Diagram 1**. Press.

DIAGRAM 1

STEP 2. Using ¼-inch seams, sew the four units from Step 1 between the eight 2½ × 5½-inch light tan print pieces. Press, following the arrows in **Diagram 2**.

DIAGRAM 2

STEP 3. Sew the four 2½ × 9½-inch light tan print pieces to the four units from Step 2. See **Diagram 3**. Press. Each block will now measure 9½ × 7½ inches.

DIAGRAM 3

Appliqué

The appliqué pieces were added to the teapot blocks using the technique described in "Blanket Stitch Appliqué" on page 272. You can machine appliqué with either a satin stitch or blanket stitch if you prefer. Refer to "Machine Appliqué" on pages 271–272 for instructions on these techniques. Use a lightweight, sewable fusible web for all of these techniques.

STEP 1. Refer to "Quick-Fuse Appliqué" on pages 270–271. Trace four spouts, handles, lids, and daisies from the appliqué patterns on page 17.

STEP 2. Position and fuse the appliqué pieces to the teapots, referring to **Diagram 4** for placement.

DIAGRAM 4

STEP 3. Use two strands of embroidery floss to blanket stitch around the edges of the appliqué pieces.

Making the Center Block

STEP 1. Sew the 1 × 6½-inch lattice strips to the top and bottom of the 6½-inch tan-and-black print square. See **Diagram 5**. Press the seams toward the lattice.

DIAGRAM 5

Blanket Stitch First

It is a good idea to complete the blanket stitch for each block before you assemble the Teapot Table Quilt. That way, your blocks will be portable—you can work on them whenever you find a few spare minutes.

STEP 2. Sew one 1 × 7½-inch lattice strip to each side, as shown in **Diagram 6**. Press.

DIAGRAM 6

STEP 3. Arrange four 1½ × 14-inch patchwork border strips (two black print, one red print, and one gold print) in the order shown in **Diagram 7**. Sew the strips together to make a 4½ × 14-inch strip set. Change sewing direction with each strip sewn, and press the seams toward the black print as you go. Cut this strip set into halves, approximately 7 inches each.

DIAGRAM 7

STEP 4. Resew the halves together to make an 8½ × 7-inch strip set. Using a rotary cutter and ruler, cut four 1½ × 8½-inch strips from this strip set. There should be eight squares in each strip. See **Diagram 8.**

8½"

7"

1½"

DIAGRAM 8

STEP 5. For the top and bottom borders, use a seam ripper to remove one black print square from each of two 1½ × 8½-inch patchwork border strips to make two strips with seven squares each. Set aside the black print squares for use in Step 6. Compare the strips to the top and bottom of the center block unit. You may need to take in or let out a few seams (⅟₁₆ inch or less) to make them fit. Referring to **Diagram 9** for placement, pin and sew the 1½ × 7½-inch patchwork border strips to the top and bottom. Press the seams toward the lattice.

7½"

DIAGRAM 9

STEP 6. Sew one 1½-inch black print square removed in Step 5 to the red print end of each remaining 1½ × 8½-inch patchwork border strip. See **Diagram 10.** Press.

1½"   8½"

1½"   1½"

DIAGRAM 10

STEP 7. Referring to **Diagram 11** for placement, fit, pin, and sew the 1½ × 9½-inch patchwork border strips to the sides. Press. The center block will now measure 9½ inches square.

1½"   7½"   1½"

9½"   9½"

DIAGRAM 11

Making the Corner Blocks

STEP 1. Arrange five 1½ × 14-inch patchwork border strips (two black print, one red print, and two gold print) in the order shown in **Diagram 12.** Sew the strips together to make a 5½ × 14-inch strip set. Change sewing direction with each strip sewn, and press the seams toward the black print as

you go. Using a rotary cutter and ruler, cut eight 1½ × 5½-inch strips from this strip set. There should be five squares in each strip.

5½"

1½"

14"

DIAGRAM 12

STEP 2. Fit, pin, and sew the 1½ × 5½-inch patchwork border strips to the tops and bottoms of the four 5½-inch tan-and-black print squares. See **Diagram 13.** Press the seams toward the square.

5½"

1½"

5½"

1½"

DIAGRAM 13

STEP 3. Arrange the seven remaining 1½ × 14-inch patchwork border strips (four black print, two red print, and one gold print) in the order shown in **Diagram 14.** Sew the strips together to make a 7½ × 14-inch strip set. Change sewing direction with each strip sewn, and press the seams toward the black print as you go. Using a rotary cutter and ruler, cut eight 1½ × 7½-inch strips from this strip set. There should be seven squares in each strip.

DIAGRAM 14

STEP 4. Fit, pin, and sew the 1½ × 7½-inch patchwork border strips to the sides, as shown in **Diagram 15**. Press. Each corner block will now measure 7½ inches square.

DIAGRAM 15

Assembling the Top

STEP 1. Sew two 7½-inch corner blocks, two 1 × 7½-inch lattice strips, and one 9½ × 7½-inch teapot block together in the order shown in **Diagram 16**. Press. Repeat to make a second unit.

STEP 2. Sew the 1 × 24½-inch lattice strips to the tops and bottoms of the two units from Step 1. See **Diagram 17**. Press.

STEP 3. Sew the remaining two 9½ × 7½-inch teapot blocks, the two 1 × 9½-inch lattice strips, and the 9½-inch center block together in the order shown in **Diagram 18**. Press.

STEP 4. Sew the two units from Step 2 and the unit from Step 3 together in the order shown in **Diagram 19** on page 16. Press.

STEP 5. Sew the 1 × 25½-inch lattice strips to the sides. Press the seams toward the lattice.

STEP 6. Sew one 4½ × 25½-inch border strip each to the top and bottom. Press the seams toward the border.

STEP 7. Sew a 4½-inch red print square to each end of the remaining two 4½ × 25½-inch border strips. Press the seams toward the border. Pin and sew the border strips to the sides. Press.

Layering the Quilt

Arrange and baste the backing, batting, and top together, following the directions in "Layering the Quilt" on page 275. Trim the batting and backing to ¼ inch from the raw edges of the quilt top.

Make 2
DIAGRAM 16

DIAGRAM 17

DIAGRAM 18

Step 2
Unit

Step 3
Unit

Step 2
Unit

DIAGRAM 19

34"

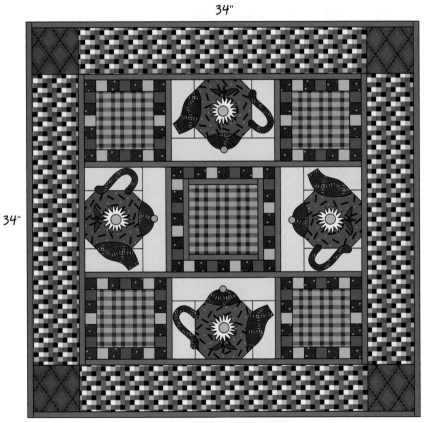

34"

TABLE QUILT LAYOUT

Binding the Quilt

Using the four 2¾ × 42-inch binding strips, follow the directions for "Binding the Quilt" on pages 275–276.

Finishing Stitches

Machine or hand quilt in the seam lines of the teapots, lattice, corner squares, and patchwork border squares. Outline the appliqué designs by quilting ¹⁄₁₆ inch from the edges. Using a commercial quilting template, quilt a flower in the center block and each corner block. Quilt a 1¼-inch diagonal grid in each teapot block background and a 2-inch diagonal grid in the border. Sew a button to the lid of each teapot.

Fresh Flowers

Brighten up the table with a bouquet of fresh daisies in your favorite vase or teapot.

DAISY
PATTERN

TEAPOT
SPOUT
PATTERN

TEAPOT LID PATTERN

TEAPOT
HANDLE PATTERN

APPLIQUÉ PATTERN KEY

———— Tracing line

- - - - - Tracing line
(will be hidden behind
other fabric)

WEEKENDER

TEAPOT TRIO

Whether it's breakfast tea in the morning, low tea in the afternoon,

or high tea in the evening, any time is teatime when you have this captivating

trio of teapots hanging in your dining room. Craft your pots of folk art reds,

blacks, and golds, as shown in the photo, or choose lovely springtime florals

if that's more your cup of tea. (See the **Color Option** on page 21.)

Whatever your preference, the quick and easy techniques will have you

displaying your teapot colors in record time!

Finished Size: 18 × 32 inches   **Finished Teapot Block: 9 × 7 inches**

MATERIALS

(Obvious directional prints are not recommended.)

 ⅙ yard, or 5½-inch square, *each* of black, red, and multicolor prints for teapots

⅛ yard *each* of 3 tan prints for background

▮ ½ yard green print for lattice and binding

⅛ yard, or 1½ to 2½ × 32-inch strip, *each* of 7 fabrics for scrap border

⅔ yard fabric for backing

⅔ yard lightweight batting

Scraps, or ⅛-yard pieces, of several coordinated fabrics for appliqué pieces

Lightweight, sewable fusible web

Embroidery floss

3 assorted ⅝- to ¾-inch buttons

CUTTING

Prewash and press all of your fabrics. Using a rotary cutter, see-through ruler, and cutting mat, prepare the pieces as described below. Measurements for all pieces include ¼-inch seam allowances.

FABRIC	FIRST CUT		SECOND CUT	
Color	No. of Pieces	Dimensions	No. of Pieces	Dimensions
Black, red, and multicolor prints	**Teapots**—from *each* of the 3 fabrics, cut the following:			
	1	5½-inch square	No second cut	
Tan prints	**Background**—from *each* of the 3 fabrics, cut the following:			
	1	2½ × 42-inch strip	1	2½ × 9½-inch piece
			2	2½ × 5½-inch pieces
			4	1½-inch squares
Green print	**Lattice**			
	3	1½ × 42-inch strips	2	1½ × 25½-inch strips
			4	1½ × 9½-inch strips
	Binding		Cut *1* strip into the following:	
	3	2¾ × 42-inch strips	2	2¾ × 21-inch strips
Border fabrics	**Scrap border**			
	7	32-inch-long strips that vary in width from 1½ to 2½ inches	No second cut	

Making the Blocks

You will be making three teapot blocks, one each of three different fabric combinations. Before you start sewing, coordinate the fabrics for all combinations. Keep track of the combinations as you sew.

Refer to "Making the Teapot Blocks" and "Appliqué" on pages 12–13 to make three teapot blocks without daisies.

Assembling the Top

STEP 1. Using ¼-inch seams, sew one 1½ × 9½-inch lattice strip to the top of each block. See **Diagram 1**. Press the seams toward the lattice.

9½"
1½"

DIAGRAM 1

STEP 2. Sew the three blocks together and press. Sew the remaining 1½ × 9½-inch lattice strip to the bottom. See **Diagram 2**. Press.

STEP 3. Sew the 1½ × 25½-inch lattice strips to the sides. Press the seams toward the lattice.

1½"
9½"

DIAGRAM 2

Making the Scrap Border

STEP 1. Sew the seven 32-inch strips (one each of seven different fabrics) together to make an 11½ × 32-inch strip set. Change sewing direction with each strip sewn, and press the seams in one direction as you go. Using a rotary cutter and ruler, cut eight 3½ × 11½-inch strips from this strip set. See **Diagram 3**.

11¹/₂"

3¹/₂"

32"

DIAGRAM 3

STEP 2. Pin and sew 3½ × 11½-inch scrap border strips to the top and bottom. Press the seams toward the lattice.

STEP 3. For the sides, sew two sets of three 3½ × 11½-inch scrap border strips together to make two 3½ × 33½-inch strips. Pin and sew the scrap border strips to the sides. Trim the excess length and press.

Layering the Quilt

Arrange and baste the backing, batting, and top together, following the directions in "Layering the Quilt" on page 275. Trim the batting and backing to ¼ inch from the raw edges of the quilt top.

Binding the Quilt

Using the two 2¾ × 21-inch binding strips for the top and bottom and the two 2¾ × 42-inch binding strips for the sides, follow the directions for "Binding the Quilt" on pages 275–276.

Finishing Stitches

Machine or hand quilt in the seam lines of the teapots, lattice, and scrap border pieces. Outline the appliqué designs by quilting ¹⁄₁₆ inch from the edges. Quilt a 1¼-inch diagonal grid in each block background. Sew a button to the lid of each teapot.

A Teacup Label

Use the teacups appliqué pattern from the Tea Sampler on page 26 to make a label for the back of your Teapot Trio quilt. Use a Pigma pen or Identipen to write your sentiment, name, and date on the cups. Fuse or appliqué the label to the back of the quilt.

18"

32"

QUILT LAYOUT

COLOR OPTION

Using florals and prints in shades of blue, pink, lavender, and peach can give your teapot quilt a springtime flavor.

WEEKENDER

TEA SAMPLER

The sipping of tea with guests as a sociable activity and token

of friendship has a long history—nearly 4,000 years. In celebration of the

enduring appeal of this beverage, make this sweet Tea Sampler and hang it

in a cozy nook to make your guests feel welcome in your home.

Finished Size: 15 × 14½ inches

MATERIALS AND CUTTING

Prewash and press all of your fabrics. Using a rotary cutter, see-through ruler, and cutting mat, prepare the pieces as described below. Measurements for all pieces include ¼-inch seam allowances.

FABRIC	YARDAGE	NO. OF PIECES	DIMENSIONS
Light to medium tan prints for background	⅛ to ¼ yard *each* of 5 fabrics	1	3 × 3½-inch piece (Block #1)
		1	3½-inch square (Block #2)
		1	3 × 3½-inch piece (Block #3)
		1	4 × 5½-inch piece (Block #4)
		1	5½-inch square (Block #5)
Green print for lattice	⅛ yard (cut into two 1 × 42-inch strips)	2	1 × 10-inch strips
		3	1 × 9½-inch strips
		1	1 × 5½-inch strip
		2	1 × 3½-inch strips
Red prints for border	⅛ yard *each* of 2 fabrics	1	2½ × 10½-inch strip *each*
Black prints for border	⅛ yard *each* of 2 fabrics	1	2½ × 14-inch strip *each*
Black solid for binding	⅛ yard (cut into two 1 × 42-inch strips)	2	1 × 15-inch strips
		2	1 × 14½-inch strips
Backing fabric	½ yard	—	—
Lightweight batting	½ yard	—	—
Several coordinated fabrics for appliqué pieces	Scraps, or ⅛-yard pieces	—	—
Lightweight, sewable fusible web; embroidery floss; ½-inch button			

Assembling the Background

Assemble the wallhanging top before adding the appliqué pieces. Refer to **Diagrams 1** through **3** for the measurements of the background blocks. Use ¼-inch seams and press the seams toward the lattice after each sewing step.

STEP 1. Sew background Block #2 between the two 1 × 3½-inch lattice strips. See **Diagram 1**. Press.

DIAGRAM 1

STEP 2. Sew the unit from Step 1 between background Blocks #1 and #3, as shown in **Diagram 2**. Press.

DIAGRAM 2

STEP 3. Sew the 1 × 5½-inch lattice strip between background Blocks #4 and #5. See **Diagram 3**. Press.

DIAGRAM 3

STEP 4. Sew one 1 × 9½-inch lattice strip between the units from Steps 2 and 3. See **Diagram 4**. Press.

DIAGRAM 4

STEP 5. Sew the remaining 1 × 9½-inch lattice strips to the top and bottom of the unit from Step 4. Press seams toward the lattice.

STEP 6. Sew the 1 × 10-inch lattice strips to the sides. Press.

STEP 7. Sew the 2½ × 10½-inch border strips to the top and bottom. Press the seams toward the border.

STEP 8. Sew the 2½ × 14-inch border strips to the sides. Press.

STEP 9. Sew the 1 × 14½-inch binding strips to the top and bottom. Press the seams toward the binding.

STEP 10. Sew the 1 × 15-inch binding strips to the sides. Press.

Appliqué

STEP 1. Refer to "Quick-Fuse Appliqué" on pages 270–271. Trace the teapot, teakettle, teacups, sugar bowl, and tea bag from the appliqué patterns on pages 25–26. Trace the lettering onto the tea bag tag before fusing.

STEP 2. Quick-fuse each appliqué design to the center of its corresponding background piece.

Position and fuse one design at a time, referring to the **Wallhanging Layout** on the opposite page for placement.

STEP 3. Use two strands of embroidery floss to stem stitch the lettering on the tea bag tag. Use one strand of embroidery floss to stem stitch the string and line on the tea bag and the steam lines on the teakettle. See "Decorative Stitches" on page 272 for instructions on stem stitching.

Flavored by Fabrics

For a totally different look, make this Tea Sampler with your favorite Japanese or batik fabrics.

Finishing Stitches

STEP 1. Position the top and backing with right sides together. Lay both pieces on top of the batting, with the backing next to the batting. Pin all three layers together. Using ¼-inch seams, sew around the edges, leaving a 3- to 4-inch opening for turning. Trim the backing and batting to the same size as the top. Trim the corners, turn the wallhanging right side out, hand stitch the opening closed, and press.

STEP 2. Machine or hand quilt in the seam lines of the lattice and binding. Outline the appliqué designs by quilting ¹⁄₁₆ inch from the edges. Quilt a 1¼-inch diagonal grid in the border. Sew the button to the lid of the teapot.

15"

14 1/2"

WALLHANGING LAYOUT

Stem stitch embroider this line

Tea

Lettering

TEA BAG PATTERN FOR BLOCK #3

SUGAR BOWL PATTERN FOR BLOCK #1

Button

TEAPOT PATTERN FOR BLOCK #5

APPLIQUÉ PATTERN KEY

——————— Tracing line

- - - - - - - Tracing line
(will be hidden behind other fabric)

Stitching lines

TEA KETTLE PATTERN
FOR BLOCK #2

TEACUPS PATTERN
FOR BLOCK #4

TEATIME ACCESSORIES

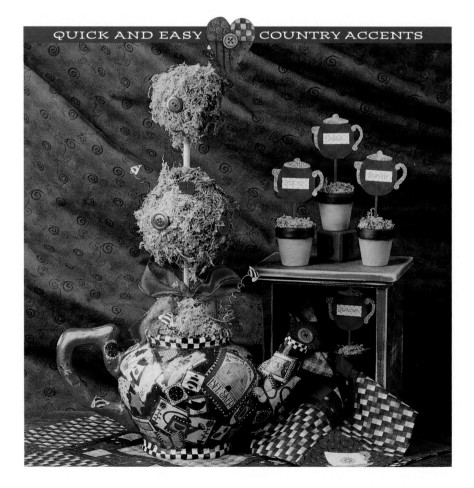

QUICK AND EASY   COUNTRY ACCENTS

Create your own tea ceremony, and from the moment they arrive, enchant your guests with this spirited Teapot Topiary, coordinating Teatime Napkins, Napkin Rings (directions on page 30), and Teapotted Place Cards (page 30). Make these accessories in folk art colors, as shown in the photo, or coordinate them with your favorite teapot or cups and saucers.

TEAPOT TOPIARY

Height: 18 inches

Materials

Papier-mâché teapot
Acrylic paint
Decoupage finish
Assorted fabric or paper motifs
Matte-finish spray varnish
Antiquing medium
Floral foam
3½-inch Styrofoam ball
2½-inch Styrofoam ball
¼-inch dowel, 16 inches long, stained
Tacky glue
Sheet moss
Assorted buttons
Medium-gauge wire
Glue gun and glue sticks
1 yard wire-edged ribbon

Assembly

STEP 1. Refer to "Decorative Painting" on page 53. Paint the papier-mâché teapot with acrylic paint and allow the paint to dry. (I painted the body of the teapot black and the handle red.) Add decorative painting touches, such as dots and checkerboards, as desired, and let dry.

STEP 2. Decoupage fabric or paper motifs to the teapot as directed on the container. Allow the decoupage to dry.

STEP 3. Spray the teapot with matte-finish varnish, and allow the varnish to dry thoroughly.

STEP 4. To antique the teapot, apply antiquing medium as directed on the container. Allow the medium to dry, and spray the teapot with a second coat of matte-finish varnish.

STEP 5. Fill the teapot with floral foam. Push the Styrofoam balls onto the dowel, leaving 1½ inches of space between them, and glue them in place with tacky glue. Insert the dowel into the teapot.

STEP 6. Coat the balls and the top of the floral foam base with tacky glue. Cover the glued areas with sheet moss.

STEP 7. Decorate the topiary with buttons and twisted wire pokes. Use the glue gun to add the buttons. To form twisted wire pokes, twist the medium-gauge wire around a dowel or pencil. Glue fabric or paper motifs to the ends of the wires.

STEP 8. Tie a bow of wire-edged ribbon around the stem of the topiary.

17"

17"

TEATIME NAPKINS

Finished Size: 17 inches square

(See the napkins in the photo on pages 8–9.)

Materials

To make 4 napkins:

¼ yard tan-and-black plaid for center square
⅓ yard green print for accent border
¼ yard black print for patchwork border
⅛ yard red print for patchwork border
⅛ yard gold print for patchwork border
¾ yard multicolor print for outer border
⅓ yard red-and-black print for corner squares
1⅛ yards fabric for backing
Scraps, or ⅛-yard pieces, of several coordinated fabrics for appliqué pieces
Lightweight, sewable fusible web
Embroidery floss

Assembling the Napkins

STEP 1. See "Cutting" on page 28. Using ¼-inch seams, sew the 1 x 6½-inch accent border strips to the tops and bottoms of the

C U T T I N G

Prewash and press all of your fabrics. Using a rotary cutter, see-through ruler, and cutting mat, prepare the pieces as described below. Measurements for all pieces include ¼-inch seam allowances.

FABRIC	FIRST CUT		SECOND CUT	
Color	No. of Pieces	Dimensions	No. of Pieces	Dimensions
Tan-and-black plaid	**Center square**			
	4	6½-inch squares	No second cut	
Green print	**Accent borders**			
	8	1 × 42-inch strips	8	1 × 10½-inch strips
			8	1 × 9½-inch strips
			8	1 × 7½-inch strips
			8	1 × 6½-inch strips
Black print	**Patchwork border**			
	4	1½ × 28-inch strips	No second cut	
Red print	**Patchwork border**			
	2	1½ × 28-inch strips	No second cut	
Gold print	**Patchwork border**			
	2	1½ × 28-inch strips	No second cut	
Multicolor print	**Outer border**			
	6	4 × 42-inch strips	16	4 × 10½-inch strips
Red-and-black print	**Corner squares**			
	2	4 × 42-inch strips	16	4-inch squares
Backing fabric	4	17½-inch squares	No second cut	

four 6½-inch tan-and-black plaid center squares. See **Diagram 1**. Press seams toward the accent border.

DIAGRAM 1

STEP 2. Sew the 1 × 7½-inch accent border strips to the sides, as shown in **Diagram 2**. Press.

DIAGRAM 2

STEP 3. Arrange the eight 1½ × 28-inch patchwork border strips (four black print, two red print, and two gold print) in the order shown in **Diagram 3** on the following page. Sew the strips together to make an 8½ × 28-inch strip set. Change sewing direction with each strip sewn, and press the seams toward the black print as you go. Using a rotary cutter and ruler, cut sixteen 1½ × 8½-

inch strips from this strip set. There should be eight squares in each strip.

DIAGRAM 3

STEP 4. For the top and bottom borders, use a seam ripper to remove one black print square from each of eight 1½ × 8½-inch patchwork border strips to make eight strips with seven squares each. Set aside the black print squares for use in Step 5. Compare the strips to the tops and bottoms of the units from Step 2. You may need to take in or let out a few seams (¹⁄₁₆ inch or less) to make them fit. Referring to **Diagram 4** for placement, pin and sew the 1½ × 7½-inch patchwork border strips to the tops and bottoms of the units from Step 2. Press.

DIAGRAM 4

STEP 5. Sew one 1½-inch black print square removed in Step 4 to the red print end of each of the remaining eight 1½ × 8½-inch

patchwork border strips. See **Diagram 5**. Press.

DIAGRAM 5

STEP 6. Referring to **Diagram 6** for placement, fit, pin, and sew the 1½ × 9½-inch patchwork border strips to the sides of the units from Step 4. Press.

DIAGRAM 6

STEP 7. Sew the 1 × 9½-inch accent border strips to the tops and bottoms of the units from Step 6. Press the seams toward the accent border.

STEP 8. Sew the 1 × 10½-inch accent border strips to the sides. Press.

STEP 9. Sew 4 × 10½-inch outer border strips to the tops and bottoms of the units from Step 8. Press the seams toward the outer border.

STEP 10. Sew one 4-inch red-and-black print corner square to each end of the remaining eight 4 × 10½-inch outer border strips. Press the seams toward the outer border. Pin and sew the outer border strips to the sides. Press.

Appliqué

The appliqué pieces were added to the napkins using the technique described in "Blanket Stitch Appliqué" on page 272. You can machine appliqué with either a satin stitch or blanket stitch if you prefer. Refer to "Machine Appliqué" on pages 271–272. Use a lightweight, sewable fusible web for all of these techniques.

STEP 1. Refer to "Quick-Fuse Appliqué" on pages 270–271. Trace four teacups from the appliqué pattern on page 30.

STEP 2. Position and fuse a teacup to one corner square of each napkin, referring to the napkin layout on page 27 for placement. Be sure to allow for the ¼-inch seam allowances on the two raw edges of the corner squares when positioning the teacups.

STEP 3. Use two strands of embroidery floss to blanket stitch around the edges of the appliqué pieces.

Finishing

For each napkin, position the top and backing with right sides together. Using ¼-inch seams, sew around the edges, leaving a 3- to 4-inch opening for turning. Trim the corners, turn the napkin right side out, hand stitch the opening closed, and press.

NAPKIN RINGS

(See the napkin ring in the photo on pages 8–9.)

Materials

To make 4 napkin rings:

2½ × 30-inch strip red print
　for rings
2½ × 30-inch strip felt for backing
Lightweight, sewable fusible web
Embroidery floss
Four ⅞-inch buttons

Assembly

STEP 1. Refer to "Quick-Fuse Appliqué" on pages 270–271. Fuse the wrong side of the red print to the felt backing.

STEP 2. With a rotary cutter and ruler, cut four 1½ × 7-inch napkin ring strips.

STEP 3. Using two strands of embroidery floss, blanket stitch (page 272) around the edges of each napkin ring.

STEP 4. Sew a button to one end of each napkin ring. To make the buttonhole, cut a 1-inch slit in the opposite end of each napkin ring. Use two strands of embroidery floss to blanket stitch around each slit. Slip the button through the buttonhole to form a ring.

APPLIQUÉ PATTERN KEY
_____ Tracing line
- - - - - Tracing line (will be hidden behind other fabric)

TEAPOTTED PLACE CARDS

Height: 5¼ inches

(See the place cards in the photo on page 26.)

Materials

To make 4 place cards:

Scraps, or ⅛-yard pieces, of
　several coordinated fabrics for
　appliqué pieces and backing
Fusible web
Permanent fine-point felt pen
Four 2-inch clay pots
Acrylic paint
Matte-finish spray varnish
Antiquing medium
Floral foam
Tacky glue
Sheet moss
⅛-inch dowel, at least 16
　inches long

Assembly

STEP 1. Refer to "Quick-Fuse Appliqué" on pages 270–271 and follow Steps 1 through 4. Use the teapot appliqué pattern below. Position and fuse the teapots to the wrong side of the backing fabric. Cut out along the edges of the fused teapots. Use the permanent felt pen to write a name on each.

STEP 2. Refer to "Decorative Painting" on page 53. Make sure the clay pots are clean and dry. Paint the outside of each pot and inside the rim with acrylic paint. Spatter-paint if desired.

STEP 3. Spray the pots with matte-finish varnish and let dry. Apply antiquing medium as directed on the container. Allow to dry, and spray the pots with a second coat of varnish.

STEP 4. Fill each pot with floral foam. Glue sheet moss to the top.

STEP 5. Cut four 4-inch lengths from the dowel. Paint the dowels with acrylic paint. Insert one dowel into each clay pot. Glue the teapots to the dowels with tacky glue.

TEACUP APPLIQUÉ PATTERN

TEAPOT PLACE CARD PATTERN

ANGELS ALL AROUND

Angels and stars are my very favorite Christmas theme. I love to fill my home with them and let them work their holiday magic. I've designed this set of projects to make it easy to transform your dining room into a heavenly scene for Christmas. But you can keep these angels on display year-round for a heaven-sent touch of charm.

CHRISTMAS ANGELS

These rag-doll–like angels are an irresistible duo that begs to be made.

The star-studded Angel Quilt hanging in the window is perfect for angel lovers

or anyone who likes to decorate for Christmas. (For a look that works year-

round, see the **Color Option** on page 37.) Checkerboards, stars, and angels

make the Angel Table Runner at the lower left (directions on page 38) extra

appealing. Your dining room will glimmer with warmth and good cheer.

Angel Quilt

Finished Size: 28 × 21½ inches   **Finished Angel Block: 8 × 12 inches**

MATERIALS

(Obvious directional prints are not recommended.)

▢ ⅛ yard tan solid for heads, arms, and legs

▨ ¼ yard tan-and-black print for background

▨ ▨ ⅛ yard *each* of 2 gold prints for wings

▨ ▨ ⅙ yard, or 4½ × 8½-inch piece, *each* of 2 red prints for dresses

▨ ⅙ yard red print for lattice

▨ ¾ yard black print for border and binding

¾ yard fabric for backing

¾ yard lightweight batting

Scraps, or ⅛-yard pieces, of several gold prints for appliqué stars

Fusible web

Yarn for hair (See "Quilting by Mail" on page 280 for ordering information.)

Embroidery floss

CUTTING

Prewash and press all of your fabrics. Using a rotary cutter, see-through ruler, and cutting mat, prepare the pieces as described below. Measurements for all pieces include ¼-inch seam allowances.

FABRIC	FIRST CUT		SECOND CUT	
Color	No. of Pieces	Dimensions	No. of Pieces	Dimensions
Tan solid	**Heads, arms, and legs**			
	1	2½ × 10-inch piece (heads)	No second cut	
	2	1½ × 15-inch pieces (arms)	No second cut	
	4	1 × 2½-inch pieces (legs)	No second cut	
Tan-and-black print	**Background**			
	2	2½ × 42-inch strips	2	2½ × 8½-inch pieces
			4	2½ × 3⅝-inch pieces
			4	2½ × 3½-inch pieces
			4	2½-inch squares
			2	2½ × 1¼-inch pieces
			4	1½-inch squares
	2	1 × 42-inch strips	4	1 × 13-inch strips
			2	1 × 8½-inch strips
Gold prints	**Wings**—from *each* of the 2 fabrics, cut the following:			
	1	2½ × 42-inch strip	2	2½ × 5½-inch pieces
			2	1½ -inch squares
Red prints	**Dresses**—from *each* of the 2 fabrics, cut the following:			
	1	4½ × 8½-inch piece	No second cut	
Red print	**Lattice**			
	3	1½ × 42-inch strips	2	1½ × 19½-inch strips
			2	1½ × 15-inch strips
			1	1½ × 13-inch strip
Black print	**Border**			
	4	3½ × 42-inch strips	2	3½ × 21½-inch strips
			2	3½ × 21-inch strips
	Binding			
	4	2¾ × 42-inch strips	No second cut	

Making the Heads and Arms

STEP 1. Make a template for the angel heads from the pattern on page 41.

STEP 2. Fold the 2½ × 10-inch tan solid piece in half crosswise with right sides together. Draw around the template to make two heads, leaving a generous ½-inch space between the heads. See **Diagram 1**.

Fold ⎯ 2½"

5"

DIAGRAM 1

STEP 3. Sew on each drawn line, leaving the bottom edge open for turning. See **Diagram 2.** Cut out each head approximately ⅛ inch from the sewing line. Clip or pink the curves, turn the heads right side out, and press.

Fold

Leave open

DIAGRAM 2

STEP 4. To make the arms, fold each 1½ × 15-inch tan solid piece in half lengthwise with right sides together. Sew a ¼-inch seam on the edge opposite the fold, as shown in **Diagram 3.** Turn each tube right side out, press it, and cut it in half. You will now have four arms that measure ½ × 7½ inches each.

Fold

¾" ⎓ 15"

DIAGRAM 3

Turning Help

Use a bow whip or narrow loop turner to help turn the arms right side out. See "Quilting by Mail" on page 280 for ordering information.

Quick Corner Triangles

You will be making two angel blocks, one each of two different fabric combinations. Before sewing, coordinate the gold and red prints for the two combinations. The background is the same for both. Keep track of the combinations as you sew.

Refer to "Making Quick Corner Triangles" on page 269 for instructions on making the corner triangle units. Press the seams toward the triangle just added.

STEP 1. For the left wings, sew one 1½-inch and one 2½-inch tan-and-black print square to each of two 2½ × 5½-inch gold print pieces (one each of the two gold prints). See **Diagram 4.** Press.

LEFT WINGS
2½"

5½"

DIAGRAM 4

STEP 2. For the right wings, sew one 1½-inch and one 2½-inch tan-and-black print square to each of two 2½ × 5½-inch gold print pieces (one each of the two gold prints). Press. These corner triangles are sewn in the opposite direction from those in Step 1. See **Diagram 5** for proper placement.

RIGHT WINGS
2½"

5½"

DIAGRAM 5

STEP 3. With the arms centered and sandwiched between, sew two 1½-inch gold print squares to each of two 4½ × 8½-inch red print pieces (one each of the two different fabric combinations). See **Diagram 6.** Press.

4½"

8½"

DIAGRAM 6

Assembling the Blocks

Refer to "Assembly Line Piecing" on page 268 for instructions on completing the same steps for both angel blocks at the same time. Pay close attention that the corner triangle units are positioned as shown in the diagrams. Be sure to use ¼-inch seams and to press after each sewing step. Follow the arrows in the diagrams for pressing direction.

STEP 1. For the left wings, sew two 2½ × 5½-inch corner triangle units to two 2½ × 3½-inch tan-and-black print pieces. See **Diagram 7.** Press.

LEFT WINGS
2½"

5½"

3½"

DIAGRAM 7

STEP 2. For the right wings, sew two 2½ × 5½-inch corner triangle units to two 2½ × 3½-inch tan-and-black print pieces. See **Diagram 8**. Press.

RIGHT WINGS

DIAGRAM 8

STEP 3. Sew the 4½ × 8½-inch corner triangle units between the units from Step 1 and the units from Step 2. See **Diagram 9**. Press.

DIAGRAM 9

STEP 4. Sew two 3⅝ × 2½-inch tan-and-black print pieces, two 1 × 2½-inch tan solid pieces, and one 1¼ × 2½-inch tan-and-black print piece together in the order shown in **Diagram 10**. Press. Repeat to make two units.

DIAGRAM 10

STEP 5. Sew the two units from Step 3 to the two units from Step 4. See **Diagram 11**. Press.

DIAGRAM 11

STEP 6. Baste the angel heads to the centers of the two 8½ × 2½-inch tan-and-black print pieces. See **Diagram 12**.

DIAGRAM 12

STEP 7. Sew the two units from Step 6 to the two units from Step 5. See **Diagram 13**. Press. Each angel block will now measure 8½ × 12½ inches.

DIAGRAM 13

STEP 8. Sew a 1 × 8½-inch tan-and-black print strip to the top of each block, as shown in **Diagram 14**. Press.

DIAGRAM 14

STEP 9. Sew the 1 × 13-inch tan-and-black print strips to the sides of each block. See **Diagram 15**. Press. Each angel block will now measure 9½ × 13 inches.

DIAGRAM 15

Assembling the Top

STEP 1. Sew the 1½ × 13-inch lattice strip between the two blocks. Press the seams toward the lattice.

STEP 2. Sew the 1½ × 19½-inch lattice strips to the top and bottom. Press.

STEP 3. Sew the 1½ × 15-inch lattice strips to the sides. Press.

STEP 4. Sew the 3½ × 21½-inch border strips to the top and bottom. Press the seams toward the border.

STEP 5. Sew the 3½ × 21-inch border strips to the sides. Press.

Appliqué

STEP 1. Refer to "Quick-Fuse Appliqué" on pages 270–271. Trace five large stars and six small stars from the appliqué patterns on page 41.

STEP 2. Quick-fuse the stars to the border, referring to the **Quilt Layout** for placement.

Layering the Quilt

Arrange and baste the backing, batting, and top together, following the directions in "Layering the Quilt" on page 275. Trim the batting and backing to ¼ inch from the raw edges of the quilt top.

Binding the Quilt

Using the four 2¾ × 42-inch binding strips, follow the directions for "Binding the Quilt" on pages 275–276.

Star-Studded Details

For a celestial decorating theme, fuse stars to embellish your curtains or valances. Stencil or sponge stars on furniture, walls, ceilings, or floors.

Finishing Stitches

STEP 1. Machine or hand quilt in the seam lines of the wings, dresses, legs, lattice, and border. Quilt vertical lines ¾ inch apart in the dresses. Quilt a 1¼-inch diagonal grid in the background and random lines in the border. Outline the appliqué stars by quilting 1/16 inch from the edges.

STEP 2. Use yarn to add hair to the heads. Make French-knot eyes with embroidery floss, referring to "Decorative Stitches" on page 272 for instructions. Hand sew the heads in place. Tie a knot in the end of each arm and sew the arms in place.

28"

21½"

QUILT LAYOUT

COLOR OPTION

Use pastels for a soft, ethereal look. This quilt could hang year-round.

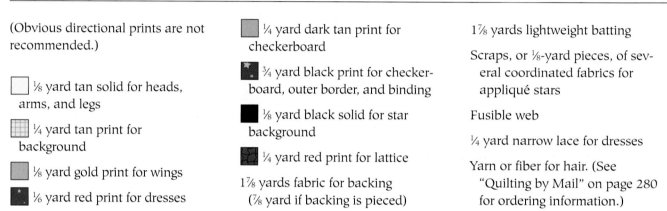

Angel Table Runner

Finished Size: 13 × 61 inches
Finished Angel Block: 8 × 12 inches

(See the table runner in the photo on page 32.)

MATERIALS

(Obvious directional prints are not recommended.)

☐ ⅛ yard tan solid for heads, arms, and legs

▦ ¼ yard tan print for background

☐ ⅛ yard gold print for wings

■ ⅙ yard red print for dresses

☐ ¼ yard dark tan print for checkerboard

☐ ¾ yard black print for checkerboard, outer border, and binding

■ ⅛ yard black solid for star background

☐ ¼ yard red print for lattice

1⅞ yards fabric for backing (⅞ yard if backing is pieced)

1⅞ yards lightweight batting

Scraps, or ⅛-yard pieces, of several coordinated fabrics for appliqué stars

Fusible web

¼ yard narrow lace for dresses

Yarn or fiber for hair. (See "Quilting by Mail" on page 280 for ordering information.)

Embroidery floss

CUTTING

Prewash and press all of your fabrics. Using a rotary cutter, see-through ruler, and cutting mat, prepare the pieces as described below. Measurements for all pieces include ¼-inch seam allowances.

FABRIC	FIRST CUT			SECOND CUT	
Color	No. of Pieces	Dimensions	No. of Pieces	Dimensions	
Tan solid ☐	**Heads, arms, and legs**				
	1	2½ × 10-inch piece (heads)	No second cut		
	2	1½ × 15-inch pieces (arms)	No second cut		
	4	1 × 2½-inch pieces (legs)	No second cut		
Tan print ▦	**Background**				
	2	2½ × 42-inch strips	2	2½ × 8½-inch pieces	
			4	2½ × 3⅝-inch pieces	
			4	2½ × 3½-inch pieces	
			4	2½-inch squares	
			2	2½ × 1¼-inch pieces	
			4	1½-inch squares	

FABRIC	FIRST CUT		SECOND CUT	
Color	No. of Pieces	Dimensions	No. of Pieces	Dimensions
Gold print	**Wings**			
	1	2½ × 42-inch strip	4	2½ × 5½-inch pieces
			4	1½-inch squares
Red print	**Dresses**			
	2	4½ × 8½-inch pieces	No second cut	
Dark tan print	**Checkerboard**			
	4	1½ × 27-inch strips	No second cut	
Black print	**Checkerboard**			
	4	1½ × 27-inch strips	No second cut	
	Outer border		Cut 2 strips into the following:	
	4	2 × 42-inch strips	2	2 × 9½-inch strips
			2	2 × 21-inch strips
	Binding		Cut 2 strips into the following:	
	4	2¾ × 42-inch strips	2	2¾ × 14-inch strips
			2	2¾ × 26-inch strips
Black solid	**Star background**			
	1	3½ × 42-inch strip	4	3½ × 8½-inch pieces
Red print	**Lattice**		Cut 4 strips into the following:	
	7	1 × 42-inch strips	14	1 × 8½-inch strips

Making the Blocks

Refer to "Making the Heads and Arms" on pages 34–35 and "Quick Corner Triangles" on page 35 for instructions. You will be making two identical angel blocks.

Refer to "Assembling the Blocks" on pages 35–36 for instructions. Follow Steps 1 through 7. After assembly, each angel block will measure 8½ × 12½ inches.

Assembling the Top

STEP 1. To make the checkerboard, alternate the two colors and sew the eight 1½ × 27-inch checkerboard strips together to make an 8½ × 27-inch strip set. Change sewing direction with each strip sewn, and press the seams toward the darker fabric as you go. Using a rotary cutter and ruler, cut fourteen 1½ × 8½-inch checkerboard strips from this strip set. See **Diagram 16.**

8½"

1½"

27"

DIAGRAM 16

STEP 2. Sew eight 1½ × 8½-inch checkerboard strips together in the order shown in **Diagram 17.** Press the seams, following the direction of the arrows in the diagram. The checkerboard unit will now measure 8½ inches square.

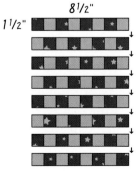

8½"

1½"

DIAGRAM 17

STEP 3. Sew the 8½-inch checker-board unit, fourteen 1 × 8½-inch lattice strips, four 3½ × 8½-inch black solid star background pieces, six 1½ × 8½-inch checkerboard strips, and two angel blocks together as shown in **Diagram 18.** Press seams toward the lattice.

STEP 4. Cut one 1 × 42-inch lattice strip in half to make two 1 × 21-inch strips. Sew one 1 × 21-inch strip to each of the remaining two 1 × 42-inch lattice strips to make two strips approximately 1 × 63 inches each. Press. Sew the lattice strips to the sides. Trim the excess length and press.

STEP 5. Sew the 2 × 9½-inch outer border strips to the short ends of the table runner. Press the seams toward the outer border.

STEP 6. Sew one 2 × 21-inch outer border strip to each of the remaining two 2 × 42-inch outer border strips to make two strips approximately 2 × 63 inches each. Press. Sew the outer border strips to the sides. Trim the excess length and press.

Appliqué

STEP 1. Refer to "Quick-Fuse Appliqué" on pages 270–271. Trace 12 stars from the appliqué pattern on the opposite page.

STEP 2. Quick-fuse the stars to the star backgrounds, referring to the **Table Runner Layout** on the opposite page for placement.

DIAGRAM 18

Layering

Arrange and baste the backing, batting, and top together, following the directions in "Layering the Quilt" on page 275. Trim the batting and backing to ¼ inch from the raw edges of the table runner top.

Binding

Sew one 2¾ × 26-inch binding strip to each of the two 2¾ × 42-inch binding strips to make two strips approximately 2¾ × 68 inches each. Using the two 2¾ × 14-inch binding strips for the short ends and the two 2¾ × 68-inch binding strips for the sides, follow the directions for "Binding the Quilt" on pages 275–276.

Finishing Stitches

STEP 1. Machine or hand quilt in the seam lines of the wings, dresses, legs, checkerboards, lattice, and outer border. Quilt vertical lines ¾ inch apart in the dresses, or let your fabric suggest a quilting design. Quilt a 1¼-inch diagonal grid in the background of each angel block. In the outer border, quilt straight lines, approximately 2 inches apart, from the lattice to the binding. Outline the appliqué stars by quilting ¹⁄₁₆ inch from the edges.

STEP 2. Hand sew the lace to the bottoms of the dresses. Use yarn or fiber to add hair to the heads. Make French-knot eyes with embroidery floss, referring to "Decorative Stitches" on page 272. Hand sew the heads in place. Tie a knot in the end of each arm and sew the arms in place.

13"

61"

TABLE RUNNER LAYOUT

ANGEL HEAD
PATTERN

STAR PATTERNS FOR QUILT

STAR PATTERN FOR TABLE RUNNER

CELESTIAL NAPKINS, NAPKIN RINGS, AND TRAY

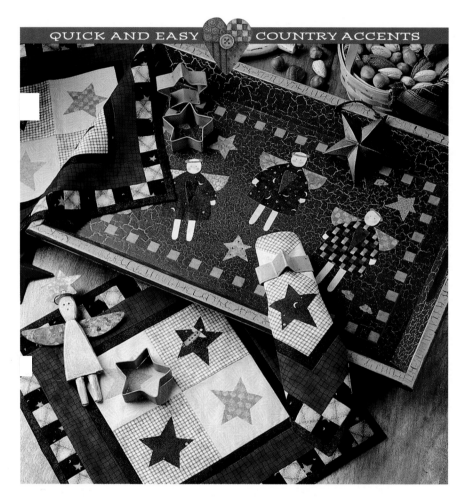

QUICK AND EASY • COUNTRY ACCENTS

Stars and Angels Forever could be your entertaining motto with these Starry Napkins, Stellar Napkin Rings (directions on page 44), and Angelic Decoupage Tray (page 45). You'll have fun painting cookie cutters to transform them into napkin rings, and you can try both painting and decoupage on the wooden tray. The angels are made of fabric that is fused to the tray. (For a smaller version of the tray, see the photos on page 32 and the **Small Tray Layout** on page 45.)

STARRY NAPKINS

Finished Size: 15 inches square

Materials

To make 4 napkins:

⅙ yard *each* of 2 tan prints for background

⅓ yard black solid for accent border and binding

⅓ yard red plaid for wide border

⅓ yard dark tan print for checkerboard

⅓ yard black print for checkerboard

1 yard fabric for backing

Scraps, or ⅛-yard pieces, of several coordinated fabrics for appliqué stars

Lightweight, sewable fusible web

Embroidery floss

Assembling the Background

STEP 1. Using a ¼-inch seam, sew the two 4½ × 42-inch tan print background strips together to make an 8½ × 42-inch strip set. Press. Using a rotary cutter and ruler, cut eight 4½ × 8½-inch pieces from this strip set. See **Diagram 1** on the opposite page.

CUTTING

Prewash and press all of your fabrics. Using a rotary cutter, see-through ruler, and cutting mat, prepare the pieces as described below. Measurements for all pieces include ¼-inch seam allowances.

FABRIC	FIRST CUT		SECOND CUT	
Color	No. of Pieces	Dimensions	No. of Pieces	Dimensions
Tan prints	**Background**—from *each* of the 2 fabrics, cut the following:			
	1	4½ × 42-inch strip	No second cut	
Black solid	**Accent border and binding**			
	10	1 × 42-inch strips	8	1 × 15½-inch strips (binding)
			8	1 × 14½-inch strips (binding)
			8	1 × 9½-inch strips (accent border)
			8	1 × 8½-inch strips (accent border)
Red plaid	**Wide border**			
	5	2 × 42-inch strips	8	2 × 12½-inch strips
			8	2 × 9½-inch strips
Dark tan print	**Checkerboard**			
	6	1½ × 32-inch strips	No second cut	
Black print	**Checkerboard**			
	6	1½ × 32-inch strips	No second cut	
Backing fabric	4	15½-inch squares	No second cut	

8½"

4½"

42"

DIAGRAM 1

STEP 2. Sew the 4½ × 8½-inch background pieces together in pairs to make four background units, as shown in **Diagram 2**. Press, following the direction of the arrow in the diagram.

8½"

4½"

DIAGRAM 2

STEP 3. Sew the 1 × 8½-inch accent border strips to the tops and bottoms of the four background units from Step 2. Press the seams toward the accent border.

STEP 4. Sew the 1 × 9½-inch accent border strips to the sides. Press.

STEP 5. Sew the 2 × 9½-inch wide border strips to the tops and bottoms. Press the seams toward the border.

STEP 6. Sew the 2 × 12½-inch wide border strips to the sides. Press.

Making the Checkerboard

STEP 1. Alternating the two colors, sew the twelve 1½ × 32-inch checkerboard strips together to make a 12½ × 32-inch strip set. Change sewing direction with each strip sewn, and press the seams toward the darker fabric as you go. Using a rotary cutter and ruler, cut eighteen 1½ × 12½-inch checkerboard strips from this strip set. There should be 12 squares in each strip. See **Diagram 3.**

DIAGRAM 3

STEP 2. Compare eight 1½ × 12½-inch checkerboard strips to the tops and bottoms of the background units. You may need to take in or let out a few seams (1/16 inch or less) to make them fit. Pin and sew the checkerboard strips to the tops and bottoms of the background units. Press the seams toward the wide border.

STEP 3. Using a seam ripper, separate two 1½ × 12½-inch checkerboard strips into eight sets of 2 squares each. Sew one set of 2 squares to each of the remaining eight 1½ × 12½-inch checkerboard strips to make eight strips with 14 squares each. Press.

STEP 4. Fit, pin, and sew the 1½ × 14½-inch checkerboard strips to the sides. Press.

Appliqué

The stars were added to the napkins using the technique described in "Blanket Stitch Appliqué" on page 272. You can machine appliqué with either a satin stitch or blanket stitch if you prefer. Refer to "Machine Appliqué" on pages 271–272 for instructions on either technique. Be sure to use a lightweight, sewable fusible web for all of these appliqué techniques.

STEP 1. Refer to "Quick-Fuse Appliqué" on pages 270–271. Trace 16 stars from the appliqué pattern on page 46.

STEP 2. Position and fuse the stars to the napkins, referring to the **Napkin Layout** below for placement.

STEP 3. Use two strands of embroidery floss to blanket stitch around the edges of the stars.

Finishing

STEP 1. Sew the 1 × 14½-inch binding strips to the tops and bottoms of the napkins. Press the seams toward the binding.

STEP 2. Sew the 1 × 15½-inch binding strips to the sides. Press.

STEP 3. For each napkin, position the top and backing with right

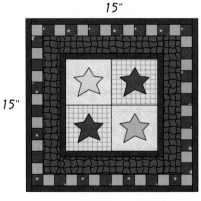

NAPKIN LAYOUT

sides together. Using ¼-inch seams, sew around the edges, leaving a 3- to 4-inch opening for turning. Trim the corners, turn the napkin right side out, hand stitch the opening closed, and press.

STELLAR NAPKIN RINGS

(See the napkin rings in the photo on page 42.)

Materials

To make 4 napkin rings:

4 star-shaped cookie cutters (approximately 2¾ inches each)
Spray primer
Acrylic paint
Matte-finish spray varnish
Antiquing medium

Assembly

STEP 1. Refer to "Decorative Painting" on page 53. Spray the cookie cutters with primer and allow the primer to dry thoroughly.

STEP 2. Paint with acrylic paint and allow the paint to dry. Apply a second coat if needed.

STEP 3. Spatter the cookie cutters with a contrasting paint, if desired, and allow the paint to dry.

STEP 4. Spray with matte-finish varnish and let dry.

STEP 5. Apply antiquing medium as directed on the container. Allow it to dry, and spray the cookie cutters with a second coat of matte-finish varnish.

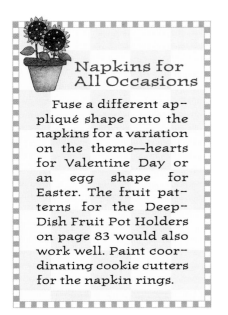

Napkins for All Occasions

Fuse a different appliqué shape onto the napkins for a variation on the theme—hearts for Valentine Day or an egg shape for Easter. The fruit patterns for the Deep-Dish Fruit Pot Holders on page 83 would also work well. Paint coordinating cookie cutters for the napkin rings.

ANGELIC DECOUPAGE TRAY

(See the tray in the photo on page 42.)

Materials

21 × 14-inch wooden tray
Acrylic paint
Crackle medium
Scraps, or ⅛-yard pieces, of several coordinated fabrics for appliqué pieces
Fusible web
Permanent fine-point felt pen
Red colored pencil
Bristle or foam brush
Decoupage finish
Matte-finish spray varnish
Press cloth

21"

14"

LARGE TRAY LAYOUT

Assembly

STEP 1. Refer to "Decorative Painting" on page 53. Paint the wooden tray with acrylic paint, and allow the paint to dry thoroughly.

STEP 2. Apply crackle medium and a second coat of paint as directed on the container. Allow the paint to dry thoroughly. Add decorative painting touches, such as checkerboards and contrasting borders, as desired, and let dry.

STEP 3. Refer to "Quick-Fuse Appliqué" on pages 270–271. Trace three angels, five small and/or large flying hearts, and three small and/or large stars from the appliqué patterns on page 46. Cover the appliqué pieces with a press cloth while quick-fusing them to the tray. Add eyes to the angels with the permanent felt pen and lightly blush the cheeks with the red colored pencil.

STEP 4. Use a bristle or foam brush to spread decoupage finish over the surface of the tray. Allow the finish to dry, and apply a second coat. When the second coat is dry, spray the tray with matte-finish varnish and let dry thoroughly.

13½"

10"

SMALL TRAY LAYOUT

Make a small angelic tray, like the one shown in the photo on page 32, to pair with the large tray.

APPLIQUÉ PATTERN KEY

——— Tracing line

- - - - Tracing line
(will be hidden behind
other fabric)

ANGEL PATTERN

SMALL STAR

LARGE STAR

STAR PATTERNS FOR TRAYS

FLYING HEART PATTERNS

Top

STAR PATTERN FOR NAPKINS

ANGEL TOPIARIES

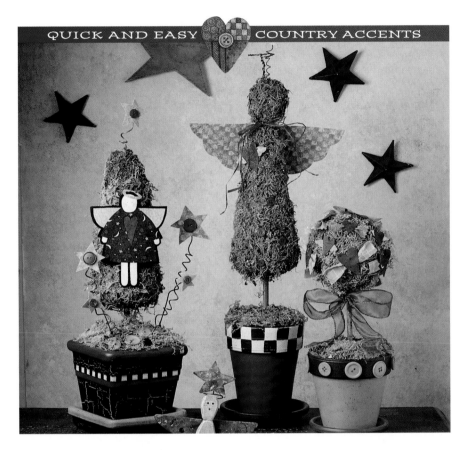

QUICK AND EASY COUNTRY ACCENTS

These fun and easy-to-make angel topiaries will be stellar additions to your collection of Christmas decorations. They coordinate with the Christmas Angels quilt and table runner on page 32 and can also function as decorations in their own right, adorning a mantel, table, or hutch with holiday or year-round cheer. I display the topiaries in my bedroom, where I can enjoy them all year long.

Materials

To make all 3 topiaries:

3 clay pots
Acrylic paint
Antiquing medium
Crackle medium
Matte-finish spray varnish
Floral foam
2 Styrofoam cones, each 9" tall
2 Styrofoam balls, measuring 1½" and 4" in diameter
Three ¼-inch dowels, stained (one 14" long or two 5" long for Large Angel Topiary; 5" long for Small Angel Topiary; 6" long for Traditional Topiary Topiary)
Tacky glue

Sheet moss
Scraps of several coordinated fabrics and felt
Fusible web
Assorted buttons, raffia, and wire-edged ribbon
Medium-gauge wire
Glue gun and glue sticks
Permanent fine-point felt pen
Red colored pencil

Topiary Assembly

The assembly instructions for all three topiaries are the same. The specifics for decorating each topiary are listed after these steps.

STEP 1. Refer to "Decorative Painting" on page 53. Make sure the clay pot is clean and dry. Paint the pot with acrylic paint and allow to dry. Add decorative painting. Spray with matte-finish varnish and let dry.

STEP 2. Fill the pot with floral foam. Insert the dowel into the foam. Push the Styrofoam cone and/or ball onto the dowel, and glue in place with tacky glue.

STEP 3. Coat the topiary shape and the top of the floral foam base with tacky glue. Cover the glued areas with sheet moss.

STEP 4. Use a glue gun to decorate the topiary with fused shapes, buttons, bows, and twisted wire pokes.

LARGE ANGEL TOPIARY

Height: 21 inches

STEP 1. Refer to "Topiary Assembly" on page 47. Paint a checkerboard on the rim of the clay pot, spatter the pot with a contrasting color, and antique it.

STEP 2. Trace the angel wings, large flying heart, and small star from the appliqué patterns on the opposite page. Refer to Steps 1 through 4 in "Quick-Fuse Appliqué" on pages 270–271. To make two-sided shapes, position and fuse the designs to the wrong side of the backing fabric. Cut out along the edges of the fused shapes. Use the glue gun to glue the angel wings and flying heart to the topiary.

STEP 3. To form a wire poke, twist medium-gauge wire around a dowel or pencil. Use the glue gun to glue the star to one end of the wire, and insert the wire into the top of the topiary. Twist two pieces of wire together to form a halo, and insert the wire into the top of the topiary. Add a raffia bow to the neck, and glue buttons to the topiary.

SMALL ANGEL TOPIARY

Height: 18 inches

STEP 1. Refer to "Topiary Assembly" on page 47. Paint a checkerboard around the clay pot, spatter the pot with a contrasting color, apply crackle medium, and antique it.

STEP 2. Trace two of each of the stars from the appliqué patterns on the following page. Trace one large star from the appliqué patterns for the tray on page 46. Refer to Steps 1 through 4 in "Quick-Fuse Appliqué" on pages 270–271. To

make two-sided stars, position and fuse the stars to the wrong side of the backing fabric. Cut out along the edges of the fused stars.

STEP 3. To form five wire pokes, twist medium-gauge wire around a dowel or pencil. Use the glue gun to glue a star and button to one end of each wire. Insert one wire into the top of the topiary and the remaining wires into the pot.

STEP 4. Trace the angel from the appliqué pattern on page 46. Fuse to the back of the angel fabrics. Position and fuse the angel to the felt background. Cut around the angel approximately ⅛ inch from the edges. Add eyes to the angel with the permanent felt pen and lightly blush the cheeks with a red colored pencil. Glue the angel and assorted buttons to the topiary.

TRADITIONAL TOPIARY

Height: 12 inches

STEP 1. Refer to "Topiary Assembly" on page 47. Spatter the clay pot with a contrasting color and antique it. Use the glue gun to glue buttons to the rim.

STEP 2. Trace 12 to 15 hearts from the appliqué patterns below. Refer to Steps 1 through 4 in "Quick-Fuse Appliqué" on pages 270–271. To make two-sided hearts, position and fuse the hearts to the wrong side of the backing fabric. Cut out along the edges of the fused hearts. Add fused fabric wings to the hearts, or make dimensional wings by tearing small fabric strips, approximately 1 × 2½ inches each. Gather the center of each strip and glue one strip to the back of each fused heart.

STEP 3. Glue the hearts to the topiary. Tie a bow around the dowel with wire-edged ribbon.

STAR PATTERNS

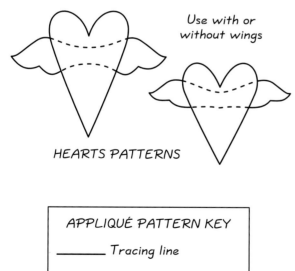

Use with or without wings

HEARTS PATTERNS

ANGEL WINGS PATTERN

APPLIQUÉ PATTERN KEY

———— Tracing line

- - - - - Tracing line (will be hidden behind other fabric)

SHELF DOILIES

QUICK AND EASY • COUNTRY ACCENTS

Adorn your shelves or furniture with doilies handmade quickly from purchased napkins or hankies. This is a perfect way to immortalize vintage linens. For the Angel Doily, *bottom,* Flying Angel Doily, *middle* (directions on page 51), and Button Doily, *top* (page 52), I used border fabrics in colors that coordinate with the Christmas Angels quilt and table runner shown on page 32.

MATERIALS AND CUTTING *(for Angel Doily)*

Prewash and press all of your fabrics. Using a rotary cutter, see-through ruler, and cutting mat, prepare the pieces as described below. Measurements for all pieces include ¼-inch seam allowances.

FABRIC	YARDAGE	NO. OF PIECES	DIMENSIONS
Light-color fabric for background square	⅓ yard, or 1 fat quarter	1	8½-inch square
Multicolor print for border	⅛ yard	4	3 × 8½-inch strips
Corner squares	⅛ yard	4	3-inch squares
Backing fabric	½ yard, or 1 fat quarter	1	13½-inch square
Several coordinated fabrics for appliqué pieces	Scraps, or ⅛-yard pieces	—	—
9½-inch napkin or hankie; lightweight, sewable fusible web; embroidery floss; 4 assorted ⁹⁄₁₆- to ¾-inch buttons			

13"

13"

ANGEL DOILY

Finished Size: 13 inches square

Assembling the Doily

See "Materials and Cutting" on page 50.

STEP 1. Sew one 3 × 8½-inch border strip each to the top and bottom of the 8½-inch light-color background square. Press the seams toward the border.

STEP 2. Sew a 3-inch corner square to each end of the remaining two 3 × 8½-inch border strips. Press the seams toward the border. Pin and sew the border strips to the sides. Press.

STEP 3. Position the top and backing with right sides together. Using ¼-inch seams, sew around the edges, leaving a 3- to 4-inch opening for turning. Trim the corners, turn the doily right side out, hand stitch the opening closed, and press.

Appliqué

The appliqué pieces were added to the 9½-inch napkin using the technique described in "Blanket Stitch Appliqué" on page 272. Be sure to use a lightweight, sewable fusible web.

STEP 1. Refer to "Quick-Fuse Appliqué" on pages 270–271. Trace the angel from the appliqué pattern on page 46.

STEP 2. Position and fuse the appliqué pieces to the napkin, referring to the illustration at left for placement.

STEP 3. Use two strands of embroidery floss to blanket stitch around the edges of the angel. Using two strands of embroidery floss, add hair by tying five knots around the top of the head and clipping the ends to ⅜ inch in length. Make French-knot eyes with embroidery floss, referring to "Decorative Stitches" on page 272.

Finishing

Center the napkin over the background square and pin it securely. Use three strands of embroidery floss to make a running stitch around the edges of the napkin through all layers. Sew one button to each corner of the napkin.

Size Variations

The napkin used for the Angel Doily measures 13 inches square. However, you can adapt the instructions to fit any size napkin or hankie. Start by cutting the background square 1 inch smaller than the measurement of the napkin or hankie. Then adjust the border and backing to fit.

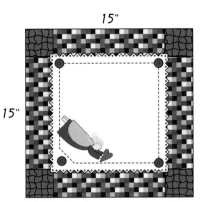

15"

15"

FLYING ANGEL DOILY

Finished Size: 15 inches square

(See the doily on the middle shelf in the photo on the opposite page.)

Assembling the Doily

See "Materials and Cutting" on page 52.

STEP 1. Sew one 3 × 10½-inch border strip each to the top and bottom of the 10½-inch light-color background square. Press the seams toward the border.

STEP 2. Sew a 3-inch corner square to each end of the remaining two 3 × 10½-inch border strips. Press the seams toward the border. Pin and sew the border strips to the sides. Press.

STEP 3. Position the top and backing with right sides together. Using ¼-inch seams, sew around the edges, leaving a 3- to 4-inch opening for turning. Trim the corners, turn the doily right side out, hand stitch the opening closed, and press.

Appliqué

The appliqué pieces were added to the 11½-inch napkin using the

MATERIALS AND CUTTING *(for Flying Angel Doily)*

Prewash and press all of your fabrics. Using a rotary cutter, see-through ruler, and cutting mat, prepare the pieces as described below. Measurements for all pieces include ¼-inch seam allowances.

FABRIC	YARDAGE	NO. OF PIECES	DIMENSIONS
Light-color fabric for background square	⅓ yard, or 1 fat quarter	1	10½-inch square
Multicolor print for border	¼ yard	4	3 × 10½-inch strips
Corner squares	⅛ yard	4	3-inch squares
Backing fabric	½ yard, or 1 fat quarter	1	15½-inch square
Several coordinated fabrics for appliqué pieces	Scraps, or ⅛-yard pieces	—	—

11½-inch napkin or hankie; lightweight, sewable fusible web; embroidery floss; 4 assorted ¾- to ⅞-inch buttons

technique described in "Blanket Stitch Appliqué" on page 272. Be sure to use a lightweight, sewable fusible web.

STEP 1. Refer to "Quick-Fuse Appliqué" on pages 270–271. Trace the flying angel from the appliqué pattern on page 53.

STEP 2. Position and fuse the appliqué pieces to the napkin, referring to the Flying Angel Doily illustration on page 51 for placement.

STEP 3. Use two strands of embroidery floss to blanket stitch around the edges of the flying angel. Backstitch the hair with two strands of embroidery floss, and make a French-knot eye with embroidery floss. See "Decorative Stitches" on page 272.

Finishing

Center the napkin over the background square and pin it securely. Use three strands of embroidery

floss to make a running stitch around the edges of the napkin through all layers. Sew one button to each corner of the napkin.

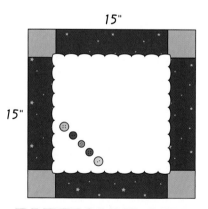

15"

15"

BUTTON DOILY

Finished Size: 15 inches square

(See the doily on the top shelf in the photo on page 50.)

Making the Doily

The materials, cutting directions, and assembly instructions for the Button Doily are the same as those for the Flying Angel Doily on page 51, except that the

Button Doily does not require appliqué fabrics and uses five assorted buttons.

Finishing

Center the napkin over the background square and pin it securely. Hand stitch the edges of the napkin to the doily. Sew the buttons across one corner of the napkin, referring to the illustration at left for placement.

Use Sentimental Buttons

Snip the buttons off children's outgrown clothing, and sew them on a special keepsake doily. Select novelty print fabrics for the borders.

FLYING ANGEL PATTERN

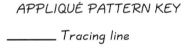

APPLIQUÉ PATTERN KEY

—————— Tracing line

- - - - - Tracing line
(will be hidden behind other fabric)

ANGEL PATTERN

Decorative Painting

Decorative painting can be done on almost any surface. Sand wood surfaces before painting and between coats with a fine-grit sandpaper. Always allow paint to dry thoroughly between steps.

STEP 1. Apply a base coat of acrylic paint. Many surfaces require two coats. Clay pots and papier-mâché are best painted with inexpensive foam brushes.

STEP 2. Add surface textures, such as sponging, spattering, or crackling. To sponge, apply contrasting color with a textured sponge. To spatter, apply contrasting color by running your thumb over a paint-filled toothbrush. To crackle, purchase a commercial crackle medium and follow the manufacturer's instructions.

STEP 3. Add detail painting, such as checkerboards, flowers, or hearts. To make checkerboards, use a commercial stencil or draw a graph for a checkerboard with a ruler. Paint every other square in contrasting colors.

STEP 4. Spray or brush on a coat of matte-finish varnish.

STEP 5. Add antiquing medium. Many products are available in both oil-base and latex formulas. Follow the manufacturer's instructions for best results.

STEP 6. Add a final coat of varnish in either matte, satin, or gloss finish.

HARVEST KITCHEN

There's nothing more comforting to me than a kitchen brimming with the harvest of fall's colorful bounty. The red apples, golden pears, and eye-catching checkerboard designs on these quilts and accessories will keep your kitchen filled with a warm country glow all through the year. Add country collectibles or accents from your garden for a look to call your own.

APPLE
TABLE QUILT

Bright and bold red apples on the table make the perfect accompaniment
to a home-cooked meal or an apple pie. The striking graphic accents in the
blocks make this quilt irresistible whether you use it on your table or hang it
on the wall. Keep an image of shiny Red Delicious apples in your head as
you select the red print for the apple portion of the blocks.

Finished Size: 35 inches square   **Finished Apple Block: 4 × 6 inches**

MATERIALS

½ yard red print for apples

⅞ yard light tan print for background, four patches, and border

⅛ yard brown print for stems

¼ yard green print for triangles, corner squares, and center block

¼ yard tan print for triangles

¾ yard black solid for four patches, center block, lattice, and binding

 ⅛ yard red print for pieced blocks and center block

1⅛ yards fabric for backing

1⅛ yards cotton batting

Scraps of green print for appliqué leaves

Lightweight, sewable fusible web

Embroidery floss

CUTTING

Prewash and press all of your fabrics. Using a rotary cutter, see-through ruler, and cutting mat, prepare the pieces as described below. Measurements for all pieces include ¼-inch seam allowances.

FABRIC	FIRST CUT		SECOND CUT	
Color	No. of Pieces	Dimensions	No. of Pieces	Dimensions
Red print	**Apples**			
	3	4½ × 42-inch strips	20	4½-inch squares
Light tan print	**Background and four patches**			
	3	2¼ × 42-inch strips	40	2¼ × 2½-inch pieces (background)
	4	1½ × 42-inch strips	1	1½ × 30-inch strip (four patches)
			80	1½-inch squares (background)
	2	1½ × 42-inch strips (four patches)	No second cut	
	Border			
	4	2½ × 30½-inch strips	No second cut	
Brown print	**Stems**			
	2	1 × 42-inch strips	20	1 × 2½-inch pieces
Green print	**Triangles, corner squares, and center block**			
	3	2½ × 42-inch strips	32	2½-inch squares (triangles)
			4	2½-inch squares (corner squares)
			4	2½ × 1½-inch pieces (center block)
Tan print	**Triangles**			
	2	2½ × 42-inch strips	32	2½-inch squares
Black solid	**Four patches and center block**		Cut *1* strip into the following:	
	3	1½ × 42-inch strips (use *2* for four patches)	1	1½ × 30-inch strip (four patches)
			4	1½-inch squares (center block)
	Lattice			
	8	1 × 42-inch strips	2	1 × 30½-inch strips
			4	1 × 29½-inch strips
			2	1 × 16½-inch strips
			4	1 × 6½-inch strips
	Binding			
	4	2¾ × 42-inch strips	No second cut	
Red print	**Pieced blocks and center block**			
	1	2½ × 42-inch strip	9	2½-inch squares

Piecing the Blocks

You will be making 20 apple blocks, 8 pieced blocks, and 1 center block. Refer to "Making Quick Corner Triangles" on page 269 and "Assembly Line Piecing" on page 268. It is more efficient to do the same step for all blocks at the same time than to piece an entire block together at one time. Be sure to press after each sewing step, following the direction of the arrows in the diagrams unless instructed otherwise.

Making the Apple Blocks

STEP 1. Sew four 1½-inch light tan print squares to each of the twenty 4½-inch red print squares. See **Diagram 1**. In 12 of the units, press the seams toward the light tan print (Apple #1 Blocks). Press the seams in the remaining 8 units toward the red print (Apple #2 Blocks).

DIAGRAM 1

Be Creative with Extra Blocks

Stitch up some extra apple blocks to decorate kitchen towels, appliance covers, or an apron. You could also create chair cushions or place mats.

STEP 2. Using ¼-inch seams, sew the twenty 1 × 2½-inch brown print pieces between the forty 2¼ × 2½-inch light tan print pieces. See **Diagram 2**. Press.

DIAGRAM 2

STEP 3. Sew the 20 units from Step 2 to the 20 corner triangle units from Step 1, as shown in **Diagram 3**. Press the seams in the 12 Apple #1 Blocks toward the stems. Press the seams in the 8 Apple #2 Blocks toward the apples. Each apple block will now measure 4½ × 6½ inches.

Step 2 Unit

Step 1 Unit

DIAGRAM 3

Appliqué

The leaves were added to the apple blocks using the technique described in "Blanket Stitch Appliqué" on page 272. Be sure to use a lightweight, sewable fusible web.

STEP 1. Refer to "Quick-Fuse Appliqué" on pages 270–271. Trace 40 leaves from the appliqué pattern on page 62.

STEP 2. Allowing for ¼-inch seam allowances around the apple blocks, position and fuse the leaves in place.

Stitch the Leaves First

It is a good idea to complete the blanket stitch for each block before you assemble the Apple Table Quilt. The blocks will be easier to handle.

STEP 3. Use two strands of embroidery floss to blanket stitch around the edges of the leaves.

Making the Pieced Blocks

STEP 1. To make the green-and-tan corner triangle units, sew the thirty-two 2½-inch green print squares to the thirty-two 2½-inch tan print squares. See **Diagram 4**. Press the seams toward the green print.

DIAGRAM 4

STEP 2. To make the four patches, use ¼-inch seams. Sew two 1½ × 42-inch light tan print strips and two 1½ × 42-inch black solid strips together in pairs to make two 2½ × 42-inch strip sets. Press the seams toward the black fabric. Using a rotary cutter and ruler, cut twenty-five 1½ × 2½-inch segments from each strip set. See **Diagram 5**.

DIAGRAM 5

STEP 3. Sew the 1½ × 30-inch light tan print strip to the 1½ × 30-inch black solid strip to make a 2½ × 30-inch strip set. Press the seam toward the black fabric. Using a rotary cutter and ruler, cut fourteen 1½ × 2½-inch segments from this strip set. See **Diagram 6.**

DIAGRAM 6

STEP 4. Sew the tan/black segments from Steps 2 and 3 together in pairs to make 32 four-patch units. See **Diagram 7.** Press.

DIAGRAM 7

STEP 5. Sew 16 of the four-patch units from Step 4 between the 32 corner triangle units from Step 1, as shown in **Diagram 8.** Press.

DIAGRAM 8

STEP 6. Sew eight 2½-inch red print squares between the remaining 16 four-patch units from Step 4. See **Diagram 9.** Press.

DIAGRAM 9

STEP 7. Sew the 8 units from Step 6 between the 16 units from Step 5, as shown in **Diagram 10.** Press. Each pieced block will now measure 6½ inches square.

DIAGRAM 10

Making the Center Block

STEP 1. Sew two 2½ × 1½-inch green print pieces between the four 1½-inch black solid squares. See **Diagram 11.** Press.

DIAGRAM 11

STEP 2. Sew the remaining 2½-inch red print square between the two remaining 1½ × 2½-inch green print pieces. See **Diagram 12.** Press.

DIAGRAM 12

STEP 3. Sew the unit from Step 2 between the two units from Step 1, as shown in **Diagram 13.** Press. The center block will now measure 4½ inches square.

DIAGRAM 13

Assembling the Top

STEP 1. Referring to **Diagram 14** for placement, sew two Apple #1 Blocks between four pieced blocks. Press.

DIAGRAM 14

STEP 2. Sew the center block between two Apple #1 Blocks. See **Diagram 15.** Press.

DIAGRAM 15

STEP 3. Sew the unit from Step 2 between the two units from Step 1. See **Diagram 16** on the opposite page. Press.

STEP 4. Alternating Apple #1 and Apple #2 Blocks, sew blocks together to make four rows with four blocks each. See **Diagram 17** on the opposite page. Press.

STEP 5. Sew the 1 × 6½-inch lattice strips to both ends of two rows of apples from Step 4. Press the seams toward the lattice.

STEP 6. Referring to **Diagram 18** on the opposite page for placement, sew the two units from Step 5 between the four remaining pieced blocks. Press.

STEP 7. Sew the 1 × 16½-inch lattice strips to the tops of the two remaining rows of apples from Step 4. Press.

STEP 8. Sew the unit from Step 3 between the two units from Step 7. See **Diagram 19**. Press.

STEP 9. Sew the 1 × 29½-inch lattice strips to the tops and bottoms of the two units from Step 6. Press.

STEP 10. Sew the unit from Step 8 between the two units from Step 9. See **Diagram 20** on page 62. Press.

STEP 11. Sew the 1 × 30½-inch lattice strips to the sides. Press.

STEP 12. Sew one 2½ × 30½-inch border strip each to the top and bottom. Press the seams toward the border.

STEP 13. Sew one 2½-inch green print corner square to each end of the remaining two 2½ × 30½-inch border strips. Press the seams toward the border. Pin and sew the border strips to the sides. Press.

Layering the Quilt

Arrange and baste the backing, batting, and top together, following the directions in "Layering the

Easing Extra Length

If one unit is slightly longer than the other, keep the longer unit on the bottom when stitching. The action of the feed dogs will help to ease in the longer piece to fit.

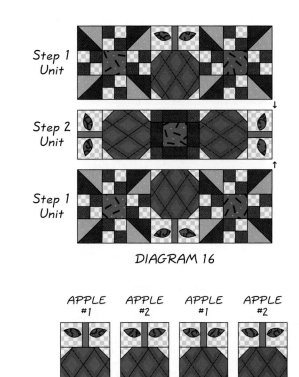

Step 1 Unit

Step 2 Unit

Step 1 Unit

DIAGRAM 16

APPLE #1   APPLE #2   APPLE #1   APPLE #2

DIAGRAM 17

Step 5 Unit

DIAGRAM 18

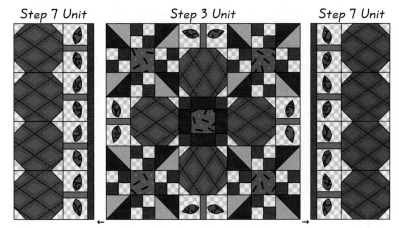

Step 7 Unit   Step 3 Unit   Step 7 Unit

DIAGRAM 19

Step 9
Unit

Step 8
Unit

Step 9
Unit

DIAGRAM 20

35"

35"

TABLE QUILT LAYOUT

Quilt" on page 275. Trim the batting and backing to ¼ inch from the raw edges of the quilt top.

Binding the Quilt

Using the four 2¾ × 42-inch binding strips, follow the directions for "Binding the Quilt" on pages 275–276.

Finishing Stitches

Machine or hand quilt in the seam lines of the apples, stems, pieced blocks, center block, lattice, and corner squares. Outline the appliqué leaves by quilting ¹⁄₁₆ inch from the edges. Quilt an × in the center squares of the pieced blocks and in each corner square. Quilt a 1-inch diagonal grid in each apple. Quilt a 1¼-inch diagonal grid in the border.

LEAF
PATTERN

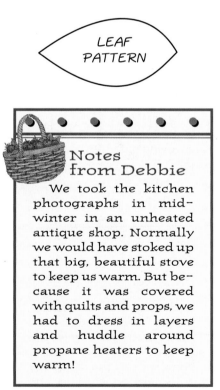

Notes
from Debbie
We took the kitchen photographs in mid-winter in an unheated antique shop. Normally we would have stoked up that big, beautiful stove to keep us warm. But because it was covered with quilts and props, we had to dress in layers and huddle around propane heaters to keep warm!

FOUR-APPLE QUILT

Turn the page for a quilt that may bring back warm memories of home or Grandma's kitchen. Maybe you remember helping to peel apples for pie or snitching slices when no one was looking! One of my favorite taste treats when helping my mom bake was to roll out the excess piecrust, top it with cinnamon and sugar, and bake it for about ten minutes. Yummm! This quilt would be sweet in any country kitchen. (If Granny Smith is your favorite apple, see the **Color Option** on page 66.)

Finished Size: 22 inches square   **Finished Apple Block: 4 × 6 inches**

MATERIALS

⅙ yard red print for apples

¼ yard light tan print for background and four patches

⅛ yard, or 1 × 12-inch strip, brown print for stems

⅙ yard gold print for triangles and center block

⅛ yard green print for triangles

½ yard black solid for four patches, center block, and binding

⅙ yard red print for block centers and accent border

¼ yard green plaid for outer border

¾ yard fabric for backing

¾ yard lightweight batting

Scraps of green print for appliqué leaves

Lightweight, sewable fusible web

Embroidery floss

CUTTING

Prewash and press all of your fabrics. Using a rotary cutter, see-through ruler, and cutting mat, prepare the pieces as described below. Measurements for all pieces include ¼-inch seam allowances.

FABRIC	FIRST CUT		SECOND CUT	
Color	No. of Pieces	Dimensions	No. of Pieces	Dimensions
Red print	**Apples**			
	4	4½-inch squares	No second cut	
Light tan print	**Background and four patches**			
	1	2¼ × 42-inch strip	8	2¼ × 2½-inch pieces (background)
	2	1½ × 42-inch strips	2	1½ × 28-inch strips (four patches)
			16	1½-inch squares (background)
Brown print	**Stems**			
	4	1 × 2½-inch pieces	No second cut	
Gold print	**Triangles**			
	1	2½ × 42-inch strip	16	2½-inch squares
	Center block			
	1	1½ × 42-inch strip	4	1½ × 2½-inch pieces
Green print	**Triangles**			
	1	2½ × 42-inch strip	16	2½-inch squares
Black solid	**Four patches and center block**			
	2	1½ × 42-inch strips	2	1½ × 28-inch strips (four patches)
			4	1½-inch squares (center block)
	Binding			
	4	2¾ × 42-inch strips	No second cut	
Red print	**Block centers**			
	5	2½-inch squares	No second cut	
	Accent border			
	2	1 × 42-inch strips	2	1 × 17½-inch strips
			2	1 × 16½-inch strips
Green plaid	**Outer border**			
	2	2½ × 42-inch strips	2	2½ × 21½-inch strips
			2	2½ × 17½-inch strips

Making the Apple Blocks

You will be making four apple blocks. Refer to "Making Quick Corner Triangles" on page 269 for instructions on making the corner triangle units. Refer to "Assembly Line Piecing" on page 268 for instructions on making the same corner triangle units for all four blocks at the same time.

STEP 1. Follow Steps 1 through 3 under "Making the Apple Blocks" on page 59 to make four apple blocks. Press the seams in Step 1 toward the light tan print. Press the seams in Step 3 toward the apples.

STEP 2. Refer to "Appliqué" on page 59 to add the leaves to the apple blocks.

Making the Pieced Blocks

Refer to "Making the Pieced Blocks" on page 59 to make four pieced blocks. Use the sixteen 2½-inch gold print squares and the sixteen 2½-inch green print squares to make 16 gold-and-green corner triangle units. To make the four patches, use the two 1½ × 28-inch light tan print strips and the two 1½ × 28-inch black solid strips to make two strip sets. Cut these strip sets into thirty-two 1½ × 2½-inch segments. Follow the directions in Steps 5 through 7 to finish making four pieced blocks.

Making the Center Block

Refer to "Making the Center Block" on page 60 to make one center block. You will be using the gold print in place of the green print.

Assembling the Top

STEP 1. Follow Steps 1 through 3 under "Assembling the Top" on page 60.

STEP 2. Sew the 1 × 16½-inch accent border strips to the top and bottom. Press the seams toward the accent border.

STEP 3. Sew the 1 × 17½-inch accent border strips to the sides. Press.

STEP 4. Sew the 2½ × 17½-inch outer border strips to the top and bottom. Press the seams toward the outer border.

STEP 5. Sew the 2½ × 21½-inch outer border strips to the sides. Press.

Layering the Quilt

Arrange and baste the backing, batting, and top together, following the directions in "Layering the Quilt" on page 275. Trim the batting and backing to ¼ inch from the raw edges of the quilt top.

Binding the Quilt

Using the four 2¾ × 42-inch binding strips, follow the directions for "Binding the Quilt" on pages 275–276.

Finishing

Machine or hand quilt in the seam lines of the apples, stems, pieced blocks, center block, and accent border. Outline the appliqué leaves by quilting ¹⁄₁₆ inch from the edges. Quilt a 1-inch diagonal grid in each apple. In the outer border, quilt lines perpendicular to the binding, approximately 1 inch apart.

QUILT LAYOUT

COLOR OPTION

Here's a Granny Smith version of the quilt that will delight those who love the combination of blue, green, and gold.

FRESH FRUIT IN SEASON

The orchard-fresh Fruit Sampler and Apple Valance window dressing

on the next page look as if they've come straight from your favorite roadside

stand. The Fruit Sampler goes together easily with quick-fuse appliqué.

The Apple Valance (directions on page 71) is easy as apple pie

to make and can be adapted to fit any size window.

Fruit Sampler

Finished Size: 19 × 18 inches

MATERIALS AND CUTTING

Prewash and press all of your fabrics. Using a rotary cutter, see-through ruler, and cutting mat, prepare the pieces as described below. Measurements for all pieces include ¼-inch seam allowances.

FABRIC	YARDAGE	NO. OF PIECES	DIMENSIONS
Tan, green, and red prints for background (See Dimensions at right.)	⅛ to ¼ yard *each* of 7 fabrics	1	4 × 3½-inch piece *each* of 2 tan fabrics for cherries
		1	4 × 4½-inch piece *each* of 2 green fabrics for pears
		1	4 × 5½-inch piece *each* of 2 red fabrics for pineapples
		1	5½ × 7½-inch piece of tan print for apple basket
Tan print for checkerboard	⅛ yard	1	1½ × 24-inch strip
Black print for checkerboard	⅛ yard	1	1½ × 24-inch strip
Black solid for lattice	⅛ yard (cut into three 1 × 42-inch strips)	4	1 × 13½-inch strips
		2	1 × 12½-inch strips
		2	1 × 5½-inch strips
Gold prints for corner squares	⅛ yard, or 2½-inch square, *each* of 4 fabrics	1	2½-inch square *each*

(continued)

WEEKENDER

MATERIALS AND CUTTING – continued

FABRIC	YARDAGE	NO. OF PIECES	DIMENSIONS
Red prints for border	⅛ yard, or 2½ × 15-inch strip, *each* of 4 fabrics	1	2½ × 14½-inch strip *each* of 2 fabrics for sides
		1	2½ × 13½-inch strip *each* of 2 fabrics for top and bottom
Black solid for binding	⅛ yard (cut into two 1 × 42-inch strips)	4	1 × 18½-inch strips
Backing fabric	⅝ yard	—	—
Lightweight batting	⅝ yard	—	—
Several coordinated fabrics for appliqué pieces	Scraps, or ⅛-yard pieces	—	—
Fusible web			

Assembling the Background

Assemble the wallhanging top before adding the appliqué pieces. Referring to the **Wallhanging Layout** on page 71, lay out the background pieces in a pleasing arrangement. Keep track of your layout while sewing the background together. Be sure to use ¼-inch seams and to press after each sewing step.

STEP 1. For Row #1, sew one 4 × 4½-inch green pear background piece between one 4 × 3½-inch tan cherries background piece and one 4 × 5½-inch red pineapple background piece, as shown in **Diagram 1**. Press the seams, following the arrows in the diagrams.

ROW #1

4"

3½"

4½"

5½"

DIAGRAM 1

STEP 2. For Row #2, sew the 1 × 5½-inch lattice strips to the top and bottom of the 5½ × 7½-inch tan apple basket background piece. See **Diagram 2**. Press.

ROW #2

5½"

1"

7½"

1"

DIAGRAM 2

STEP 3. Sew the two 1½ × 24-inch checkerboard strips together to make a 2½ × 24-inch strip set. Press the seam toward the darker fabric. Cut this strip set into thirds, approximately 8 inches each. See **Diagram 3**.

2½"

8"

24"

8"

8"

DIAGRAM 3

STEP 4. Resew the thirds together to make a 6½ × 8-inch strip set. Using a rotary cutter and ruler, cut four 1½ × 6½-inch strips from this strip set. There should be six squares in each strip. See **Diagram 4**. Use a seam ripper to remove one black square from two strips to make two 1½ × 5½-inch strips that begin and end with a tan square. Remove one tan square from the remaining two strips to make two 1½ × 5½-inch strips that begin and end with a black square.

6½"

1½"

8"

DIAGRAM 4

STEP 5. Compare the 1½ × 5½-inch strips to the top and bottom of the unit from Step 2. You may need to take in or let out a few seams (1/16 inch or less) to make them fit. Make adjustments before you sew the checkerboard strips together into pairs. If you do make adjustments, make them in the same place on each strip so that the strips will still match up. Refer to "Fitting Pieced Borders" on page 274 for further instructions. Sew the checkerboard strips together in pairs, and press.

STEP 6. Referring to **Diagram 5** for placement of the light and dark squares, pin and sew the checkerboard to the unit from Step 2. Press.

STEP 7. For Row #3, sew the remaining 4 × 5½-inch red pineapple background piece between the 4 × 4½-inch green pear background piece and the 4 × 3½-inch tan cherries background piece, as shown in **Diagram 6**. Press.

STEP 8. Sew one 1 × 12½-inch lattice strip to each side of Row #2. Press the seams toward the lattice.

STEP 9. Sew Row #2 between Rows #1 and #3. Press the seams toward the lattice.

STEP 10. Sew one 1 × 13½-inch lattice strip each to the top and bottom. Press the seams toward the lattice.

STEP 11. Sew the two remaining 1 × 13½-inch lattice strips to the sides. Press.

ROW #2

Step 2 Unit

DIAGRAM 5

ROW #3
4"
4½"
5½"
3½"

DIAGRAM 6

Border and Binding

STEP 1. Lay out your border strips and corner squares in a pleasing arrangement. Keep track of your layout while sewing on the border. Sew the 2½ × 13½-inch border strips to the top and bottom. Press the seams toward the border.

STEP 2. Sew a 2½-inch corner square to each end of the 2½ × 12½-inch border strips. Press the seams toward the border. Pin and sew the border strips to the sides. Press.

Checkerboard Tips

The key to a successful checkerboard is selecting fabrics with good contrast. Making a scrap checkerboard is an option to give a different look to the Fruit Sampler wallhanging.

STEP 3. Sew one 1 × 18½-inch binding strip each to the top and bottom. Press the seams toward the binding.

STEP 4. Sew the two remaining 1 × 18½-inch binding strips to the sides. Press.

Appliqué

STEP 1. Refer to "Quick-Fuse Appliqué" on pages 270–271. Trace two clusters of cherries, two pears, two pineapples, and one apple basket from the appliqué patterns on pages 74–75.

STEP 2. Quick-fuse each appliqué design to the center of its corresponding background piece. Position and fuse one design at a time, referring to the photo on page 68 for placement.

Finishing Stitches

STEP 1. Position the top and backing with right sides together. Lay both pieces on top of the batting, with the backing next to the batting. Pin all three layers together. Using ¼-inch seams, sew around the edges, leaving a 3- to 4-inch opening for turning. Trim the backing and batting to the same size as the top. Trim the corners, turn the wallhanging right side out, hand stitch the opening closed, and press.

STEP 2. Machine or hand quilt in the seam lines of the lattice, checkerboard squares, corner squares, and binding. Outline the appliqué designs by quilting ¹⁄₁₆ inch from the edges. Quilt a 1¼-inch diagonal grid in the border.

19"

18"

WALLHANGING LAYOUT

Apple Valance

Finished Size: 6 × 10 inches

(See the valance in the photo on page 68.)

MATERIALS

You will need to measure your window(s) to determine how many 6-inch-wide valance panels you need to make. I used four panels in each of the two windows shown in the photo on pages 54–55. The following Materials list gives fabric requirements for both a single valance panel and a group of eight panels. Before buying fabric, use the Cutting directions on page 72 to customize the Materials list to fit your needs.

To make 1 valance panel:

☐ ¼ yard, or 6 × 8-inch piece, light tan print for background

■ ⅛ yard, or 1½ × 42-inch strip, green print for border

▦ ⅛ yard, or 1½ × 18-inch piece, tan print for checkerboard

■ ⅛ yard, or 1½ × 18-inch piece, red print for checkerboard

▨ ⅛ yard green plaid for tabs

¼ yard, or 8 × 12-inch piece, fabric for backing

Scraps, or ⅛-yard pieces, of several coordinated fabrics for appliqué pieces

Fusible web

To make 8 valance panels:

☐ ⅜ yard light tan print for background

■ ⅓ yard green print for border

▦ ⅙ yard tan print for checkerboard

■ ⅙ yard red print for checkerboard

▨ 1 yard green plaid for tabs

¾ yard fabric for backing

Scraps, or ⅛-yard pieces, of several coordinated fabrics for appliqué pieces

Fusible web

CUTTING

Prewash and press all of your fabrics. Using a rotary cutter, see-through ruler, and cutting mat, prepare the pieces as described below. Measurements for all pieces include ¼-inch seam allowances (to make 1 valance panel).

FABRIC	FIRST CUT		SECOND CUT	
Color	No. of Pieces	Dimensions	No. of Pieces	Dimensions
Light tan print	**Background**			
	1	Make a template for the background from the pattern on page 75	No second cut	
Green print	**Border**			
	1	1½ × 42-inch strip	2	1½ × 8-inch strips
			2	1½ × 6-inch strips
			1	1½ × 4½-inch strip
Tan print	**Checkerboard**			
	3	1½ × 5-inch strips	No second cut	
Red print	**Checkerboard**			
	3	1½ × 5-inch strips	No second cut	
Green plaid	**Tabs**			
	2	2 × 30-inch strips	No second cut	

Valance Assembly

STEP 1. Using a ¼-inch seam, sew the 1½ × 4½-inch border strip to the top of the light tan print background piece, as shown in **Diagram 7**. Press.

STEP 2. Sew one 1½ × 6-inch border strip to the lower left edge of the background piece. Press the seam toward the border. Trim the excess length from the border. See **Diagram 8**.

STEP 3. Sew the remaining 1½ × 6-inch border strip to the lower right edge of the background piece. Press. Trim, as shown in **Diagram 9**.

STEP 4. Sew the 1½ × 8-inch border strips to the sides. Press and trim. See **Diagram 10**.

STEP 5. Alternating the two colors, sew the six 1½ × 5-inch checkerboard strips together to make a 6½ × 5-inch strip set. Press the seams toward the darker

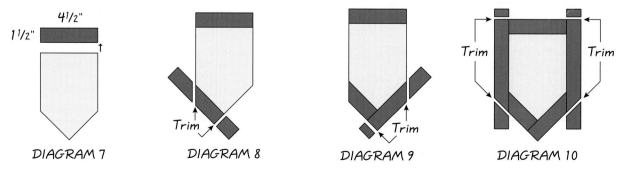

DIAGRAM 7   DIAGRAM 8   DIAGRAM 9   DIAGRAM 10

fabric as you go. Using a rotary cutter and ruler, cut two 1½ × 6½-inch strips from this strip set. See **Diagram 11**.

DIAGRAM 11

STEP 6. Compare the 1½ × 6½-inch strips to the top of the unit from Step 4. You may need to take in or let out a few seams (¹⁄₁₆ inch or less) to make them fit. Make adjustments before you sew the checkerboard strips together. If you do make adjustments, make them in the same place on each strip so that the strips will still match up. Refer to "Fitting Pieced Borders" on page 274 for further instructions. Sew the checker-board strips together and press.

STEP 7. Referring to the **Valance Layout** for placement of the light and dark squares, pin and sew the checkerboard to the unit from Step 4. Press toward the green border.

Appliqué

STEP 1. Refer to "Quick-Fuse Appliqué" on pages 270–271. Trace one apple from the appliqué pattern on page 74.

STEP 2. Quick-fuse the apple to the center of the background piece, referring to the photo on page 68 for placement.

Finishing

STEP 1. To make the hanging tabs, fold each 2 × 30-inch green plaid tab strip in half lengthwise with right sides together. Sew a ¼-inch seam along the edge opposite the fold. Turn the tab right side out and press.

STEP 2. Fold the tabs in half and pin them in place, keeping the folds even with the top edge of the valance. The outside edge of each tab should line up with the seam of the first checkerboard square. Baste the tabs in place. They will be sewn into the seam when the valance is finished. See **Diagram 12**.

DIAGRAM 12

Try Other Fruits

If you like, substitute a pear or cherries on your valance, using the appliqué patterns for the Fruit Sampler on pages 74–75. You can also mix and match fruits within the window valance.

STEP 3. Position and pin the top and backing with right sides together. Make sure the tabs are tucked inside the valance so that they will not get caught in the seams. Using ¼-inch seams, sew around the edges, leaving a 3-inch opening for turning. Trim the backing to the same size as the top. Trim the corners, turn the valance right side out, hand stitch the opening closed, and press.

VALANCE LAYOUT

PEAR PATTERN

APPLE BASKET PATTERN

APPLE PATTERN

APPLIQUÉ PATTERN KEY

—————— Tracing line

- - - - - - Tracing line
(will be hidden behind
other fabric)

BACKGROUND PATTERN

CHERRIES PATTERN

PINEAPPLE PATTERN

75

ORCHARD TRIO

Apples, pears, and plaids, oh my! This quilt and these two plaid towels make a perfect trio. Make the Fruitful Towel Holder and Fruit Tea Towels (directions on page 81) in a jiffy in your sewing room—you don't have to go to the orchard to pick these fruits. Just pick your favorite plaids, whip up some easy, quick-sew checkerboards, and quick-piece some fresh apples and pears.

Fruitful Towel Holder

Finished Size: 19 × 11 inches   **Finished Block: 4 × 6 inches**

MATERIALS

(Obvious directional prints are not recommended.)

⅙ yard, or 4½-inch square, *each* of 2 red prints for apples

¼ yard light tan print for background, tabs, and checkerboard

⅛ yard, or 1 × 2½-inch piece, *each* of 2 brown prints for apple stems

⅙ yard, or 4½ × 6½-inch piece, gold print for pear

⅛ yard, or 1 × 1½-inch piece, brown print for pear stem

⅛ yard green print for lattice

⅛ yard black print for checkerboard

⅛ yard black solid for binding

⅜ yard fabric for backing

⅜ yard lightweight batting

Scraps of green print for appliqué leaves

Lightweight, sewable fusible web

Green embroidery floss

½-inch wooden dowel, 19 inches long

CUTTING

Prewash and press all of your fabrics. Using a rotary cutter, see-through ruler, and cutting mat, prepare the pieces as described below. Measurements for all pieces include ¼-inch seam allowances.

FABRIC	FIRST CUT		SECOND CUT	
Color	**No. of Pieces**	**Dimensions**	**No. of Pieces**	**Dimensions**
Red print	**Apples**—from *each* of the 2 fabrics, cut the following:			
	1	4½-inch square	No second cut	
Light tan print	**Background, tabs, and checkerboard**			
	1	2½ × 42-inch strip	1	2½ × 12-inch strip (tabs)
			4	2½ × 2¼-inch pieces (apple background)
	2	1½ × 42-inch strips	1	1½ × 30-inch strip (checkerboard)
			2	1½ × 2½-inch pieces (pear background)
			2	1½ × 2¼-inch pieces (pear)
			8	1½-inch squares (apple)
			4	1½-inch squares (pear)
			2	1-inch squares (pear)
	1	1½ × 42-inch strip (checkerboard)	No second cut	
Brown print	**Apple stems**—from *each* of the 2 fabrics, cut the following:			
	1	1 × 2½-inch piece	No second cut	
Gold print	**Pear**			
	1	4½ × 3½-inch piece	No second cut	
	1	2½-inch square	No second cut	
Brown print	**Pear stem**			
	1	1 × 1½-inch piece	No second cut	
Green print	**Lattice**			
	2	1½ × 42-inch strips	2	1½ × 14½-inch strips
			2	1½ × 8½-inch strips
			2	1½ × 6½-inch strips
Black print	**Checkerboard**			
	1	1½ × 42-inch strip	No second cut	
	1	1½ × 30-inch strip	No second cut	
Black solid	**Binding**			
	2	1 × 42-inch strips	2	1 × 18½-inch strips
			2	1 × 11½-inch strips

Making the Blocks

You will be making two apple blocks, one each of two different apple and stem combinations. Before you start sewing, coordinate the fabrics for the two combinations. Keep track of the combinations as you sew. You will also be making one pear block.

Refer to "Making Quick Corner Triangles" on page 269. For each apple and pear block, the corner triangle units are made first and then the block is pieced. Pay close attention that the corner triangle units are positioned as shown in the diagrams. Press the seams toward the triangle just added.

STEP 1. Follow Steps 1 through 3 under "Making the Apple Blocks" on page 65 to make two apple blocks. Press the seams in Steps 1 and 3 toward the apples.

STEP 2. Refer to "Appliqué" on page 59 to add the leaves to the apple blocks.

STEP 3. To make the pear block, sew the four 1½-inch light tan print squares to the 4½ × 3½-inch gold print piece. See **Diagram 1**. Press.

DIAGRAM 1

STEP 4. Sew the two 1-inch light tan print squares to the 2½-inch gold print square, as shown in **Diagram 2**. Press.

DIAGRAM 2

STEP 5. Using ¼-inch seams, sew the corner triangle unit from Step 4 between the two 1½ × 2½-inch light tan print pieces. See **Diagram 3**. Press the seams, following the arrows in the diagram.

DIAGRAM 3

STEP 6. Sew the 1 × 1½-inch brown print piece between the two 2¼ × 1½-inch light tan print pieces. See **Diagram 4**. Press.

2¼"   1"   2¼"
1½" ▢▮▢ 1½"

DIAGRAM 4

STEP 7. Sew the unit from Step 5 between the units from Steps 6 and 3, as shown in **Diagram 5**. Press. The pear block will now measure 4½ × 6½ inches.

DIAGRAM 5

Adding the Lattice

STEP 1. Sew the pear block between two 1½ × 6½-inch lattice strips. Press toward the lattice.

STEP 2. Sew the unit from Step 1 between the two apple blocks. Press.

STEP 3. Sew the 1½ × 14½-inch lattice strips to the top and bottom. Press.

STEP 4. Sew the 1½ × 8½-inch lattice strips to the sides. Press.

Making the Checkerboard

STEP 1. For the top and bottom, sew the two 1½ × 42-inch checkerboard strips together to make a 2½ × 42-inch strip set. Press the seam toward the darker fabric. Cut this strip set into halves, approximately 21 inches each. See **Diagram 6**.

DIAGRAM 6

STEP 2. Resew the halves together to make a 4½ × 21-inch strip set. Cut this strip set into fourths, approximately 5 inches each. See **Diagram 7**.

DIAGRAM 7

STEP 3. Resew the quarters together to make a 16½ × 5-inch strip set. Using a rotary cutter and ruler, cut two 1½ × 16½-inch strips from this strip set. There should be 16 squares in each strip. See **Diagram 8.**

DIAGRAM 8

STEP 4. Compare the 1½ × 16½-inch strips to the top and bottom of the apple-pear unit. You may need to take in or let out a few seams (⅟₁₆ inch or less) to make them fit. Referring to the **Towel Holder Layout**, pin and sew the checkerboard strips to the top and bottom. Press the seams toward the lattice.

STEP 5. For the sides, sew the two 1½ × 30-inch checkerboard strips together to make a 2½ × 30-inch strip set. Press the seam toward the darker fabric. Cut this strip set into halves approximately 15 inches each. See **Diagram 9.**

DIAGRAM 9

STEP 6. Resew the halves together to make a 4½ × 15-inch strip set. Cut this strip set in thirds, approximately 5 inches each. See **Diagram 10.**

DIAGRAM 10

STEP 7. Resew the thirds together to make a 12½ × 5-inch strip set. Using a rotary cutter and ruler, cut two 1½ × 12½-inch strips from this strip set. See **Diagram 11**. Use a seam ripper to remove two squares from each strip to make two strips with 10 squares each.

DIAGRAM 11

STEP 8. Fit, pin, and sew the checkerboard strips to the sides. Press.

Binding

STEP 1. Sew the 1 × 18½-inch binding strips to the top and bottom. Press the seams toward the binding.

STEP 2. Sew the 1 × 11½-inch binding strips to the sides. Press.

Finishing Stitches

STEP 1. To make hanging tabs, fold the 2½ × 12-inch light tan print strip in half lengthwise with right sides together. Sew a ¼-inch seam along the raw edges. Turn the tab right side out, press, and cut into three 1 × 3½-inch pieces.

STEP 2. On the right side of the quilt top, space the tabs evenly across the bottom of the quilt. Position the tabs with the raw edges even with the raw edge of the quilt. Pin and then baste the tabs in place. They will be sewn into the seam when the quilt is finished.

STEP 3. Position the top and backing with right sides together. Lay both pieces on top of the batting, with the backing next to the batting. Pin all three layers together. Using ¼-inch seams, sew around the edges, leaving a 3- to 4-inch opening for turning. Trim the backing and batting to the same size as the top. Trim the corners, turn the towel holder right side out, hand stitch the opening closed, and press.

STEP 4. Machine or hand quilt in the seam lines of the apples, pear, lattice, checkerboard squares, and binding. Outline the appliqué leaves by quilting ⅟₁₆ inch from the edges. Paint the dowel and insert it through the hanging tabs.

TOWEL HOLDER LAYOUT

Fruit Tea Towels

(See the towels in the photo on page 76.)

MATERIALS

To make 1 tea towel:

These instructions are written for a tea towel that measures approximately 18 × 27 inches. You may have to adjust the length of your checkerboard and accent border to fit the size of your towel.

Purchased tea towel

⅛ yard gold or tan print for checkerboard

⅛ yard black print for checkerboard

⅛ yard, or 1 × 42-inch strip, red or green print for accent border

⅛ yard fabric for checkerboard backing

Scraps, or ⅛-yard pieces, of several coordinated fabrics for appliqué pieces

Lightweight, sewable fusible web

Embroidery floss

CUTTING

Prewash the tea towel and all of your fabrics. Press the fabrics. Using a rotary cutter, see-through ruler, and cutting mat, prepare the pieces as described below. Measurements for all pieces include ¼-inch seam allowances.

FABRIC	FIRST CUT		SECOND CUT	
Color	No. of Pieces	Dimensions	No. of Pieces	Dimensions
Gold or tan print	**Checkerboard**			
	2	1½ × 42-inch strips	3	1½ × 15-inch strips
Black print	**Checkerboard**			
	2	1½ × 42-inch strips	3	1½ × 15-inch strips
Red or green print	**Accent border**			
	2	1 × 18½-inch strips	No second cut	
Backing fabric	**Checkerboard backing**			
	1	3½ × 18½-inch piece	No second cut	

Assembling the Checkerboard

STEP 1. Alternating the two colors, sew the six 1½ × 15-inch checkerboard strips together to make a 6½ × 15-inch strip set. Press the seams toward the darker fabric as you go. Cut this strip set into thirds, approximately 5 inches each. See **Diagram 12.**

6½"

5"

15"

5"

5"

DIAGRAM 12

STEP 2. Resew the thirds together to make an 18½ × 5-inch strip set. Using a rotary cutter and ruler, cut two 1½ × 18½-inch strips from this strip set. There should be 18 squares in each strip. See **Diagram 13** on the following page.

18½"

5"

1½"

DIAGRAM 13

STEP 3. Compare the checkerboard to the tea towel. The sides of the checkerboard should extend ¼ inch beyond the sides of the tea towel. You may need to take in or let out a few seams (¹⁄₁₆ inch or less) to make them fit. Make adjustments before you sew the checkerboard strips together. See "Fitting Pieced Borders" on page 274 for further instructions. Sew the checkerboard strips together and press.

STEP 4. Sew the checkerboard from Step 3 between the two 1 × 18½-inch accent border strips. Press the seams toward the accent border.

STEP 5. Position the unit from Step 4 and the 3½ × 18½-inch backing strip with right sides together. Pin them together, keeping the raw edges even. (Remember to adjust the backing if you made a different-size checkerboard and accent border.) Using ¼-inch seams, sew around the edges, leaving a 3- to 4-inch opening for turning. Trim the corners, turn the checkerboard right side out, hand stitch the opening closed, and press.

STEP 6. Position the checkerboard approximately 3 inches up from the bottom edge of the towel. Pin it in place and topstitch around all the edges.

Appliqué

The appliqué pieces were added to the tea towels using the technique described in "Blanket Stitch Appliqué" on page 272. Be sure to use a lightweight, sewable fusible web.

Make Your Own Tea Towel

To make a tea towel, cut a fabric rectangle 1 inch larger than the desired finished size and narrow hem the edges.

STEP 1. Refer to "Quick-Fuse Appliqué" on pages 270–271. Trace three apples or two pears from the appliqué patterns below.

STEP 2. Position and fuse the apples or pears to the tea towel, referring to the photo on page 76 for placement.

STEP 3. Use two strands of embroidery floss to blanket stitch around the edges of the apples or pears.

18"

27"

TOWEL LAYOUT

PEAR PATTERN

APPLE PATTERN

APPLE LEAF PATTERN

APPLIQUÉ PATTERN KEY

——— Tracing line

- - - - - Tracing line (will be hidden behind other fabric)

DEEP-DISH FRUIT POT HOLDERS

QUICK AND EASY • COUNTRY ACCENTS

Mix and match your favorite fruits to hang as decorative accents or to use as practical but pretty pot holders. Stitch several to have on hand for hostess gifts after a backyard barbecue or picnic. And what could be better for a summer birthday gift than a cherry pie accompanied by a pair of cherry pot holders!

Finished Size: 7 inches square

Assembling the Background

See "Materials and Cutting" on the following page. Assemble the pot holder top before adding the appliqué pieces. Be sure to use ¼-inch seams and to press after each sewing step.

STEP 1. Sew the two 1½ × 24-inch checkerboard strips together to make a 2½ × 24-inch strip set. Press the seam toward the darker fabric. Cut this strip set into thirds, approximately 8 inches each. See **Diagram 1.**

STEP 2. Resew the thirds together to make a 6½ × 8-inch strip set. Using a rotary cutter and ruler, cut four 1½ × 6½-inch strips

from this strip set. There should be six squares in each strip. See **Diagram 2.**

DIAGRAM 1

DIAGRAM 2

STEP 3. For the top and bottom, use a seam ripper to remove two squares each from two of the strips. Compare the strips to the top and bottom of the 4½-inch background square. You may need to take in or let out a few seams (¹⁄₁₆ inch or less) to make them fit.

MATERIALS AND CUTTING

Prewash and press all of your fabrics. Using a rotary cutter, see-through ruler, and cutting mat, prepare the pieces as described below. Measurements for all pieces include ¼-inch seam allowances (to make 1 pot holder).

FABRIC	YARDAGE	NO. OF PIECES	DIMENSIONS
Background square	⅙ yard	1	4½-inch square
Light tan print for checkerboard	⅛ yard	1	1½ × 24-inch strip
Red print for checkerboard	⅛ yard	1	1½ × 24-inch strip
Black solid for binding and tab	⅛ yard	2	1 × 7½-inch strips (binding)
		2	1 × 6½-inch strips (binding)
		1	1 × 4½-inch strip (tab)
Backing fabric	¼ yard	1	8-inch square
Cotton batting (See Note below.)	¼ yard	1	8-inch square
Several coordinated fabrics for appliqué pieces	Scraps, or ⅛-yard pieces	—	—

Fusible web

Note: If you plan to use your pot holder, use two layers of cotton batting. Use a lightweight, sewable fusible web and secure the edges of the appliqué pieces with machine or hand stitching.

STEP 4. Referring to **Diagram 3**, pin and sew the 1½ × 4½-inch checkerboard strips to the background square. Press the seams toward the background square.

DIAGRAM 3

STEP 5. Fit, pin, and sew the remaining 1½ × 6½-inch checker-board strips to the sides, as shown in **Diagram 4**. Press.

DIAGRAM 4

STEP 6. Sew the 1 × 6½-inch binding strips to the top and bottom. Press the seams toward the binding.

STEP 7. Sew the 1 × 7½-inch binding strips to the sides. Press.

Teakettle Revival

I picked up an old teakettle at a thrift shop, primed it with a spray primer, painted it with acrylic paint, antiqued it, and then sealed it with a spray sealer. It is **decorative** only!

Appliqué

STEP 1. Refer to "Quick-Fuse Appliqué" on pages 270–271. Trace an apple or a cluster of cherries from the appliqué patterns below or a pear from the Fruit Sampler patterns on page 74.

STEP 2. Quick-fuse the appliqué pieces to the center of the background square. If you plan to use your pot holder, remember to finish the edges of the appliqué pieces using machine appliqué (page 271) or hand blanket stitch (page 272).

7"

7"

POT HOLDER LAYOUT

Finishing Stitches

STEP 1. To make the hanging tab, fold the 1 × 4½-inch black tab strip in half lengthwise with wrong sides together. Press. Open the fabric and fold each long edge into the center fold. Press again. Topstitch along the open folded edges of the fabric strip. Fold the tab in half. Position and baste the tab to the top corner of the pot holder. See **Diagram 5.**

Basting stitches

DIAGRAM 5

STEP 2. Position the top and backing with right sides together. Lay both pieces on top of the batting, with the backing next to the batting. Pin all three layers together. Using ¼-inch seams, sew around the edges, leaving a 3-inch opening for turning. Trim the backing and batting to the same size as the top. Trim the corners, turn the pot holder right side out, hand stitch the opening closed, and press.

STEP 3. Machine or hand quilt in the seam lines of the center square, checkerboard, and binding. Outline the appliqué design by quilting ¹⁄₁₆ inch from the edges. If you plan to use your pot holder, do not machine quilt with a nylon monofilament thread, as it will melt.

CHERRIES PATTERN

APPLE PATTERN

APPLIQUÉ PATTERN KEY

———— Tracing line

- - - - - Tracing line
(will be hidden behind
other fabric)

THE BIRD BATH

Welcome to the Bird Bath, where all my favorite outdoor objects have found a cozy indoor home! I transformed the guest bathroom in my home by using birds and birdhouses, flowers and flowerpots, plus watering cans and picket fences. Fill your bath with gardening cheer all year-round.

BIRD BATH
SHOWER CURTAIN

You'll almost hear the birds singing when you shower behind this

colorful curtain decked out with birds and birdhouses, as shown in the

photo on pages 86–87. I love the big, bold birdhouse shapes, and they're

easy to cut and fuse. With the addition of country checkerboard borders,

you can create a wonderfully refreshing look for your bath.

Finished Size: 76 × 72 inches

MATERIALS FOR LARGE APPLIQUÉ PIECES

Refer to the **Shower Curtain Layout** on page 92 for the birdhouse and panel numbers.

¼ yard red print for House #1

⅓ yard black print for House #2

¼ yard gold print for Roof #2

¼ yard red print for House #3

¼ yard gold print for House #4

⅓ yard green print for House #5

⅓ yard black-and-tan check for House #6

¼ yard red print for Roof #6

½ yard, or 1 fat quarter, green print for watering can

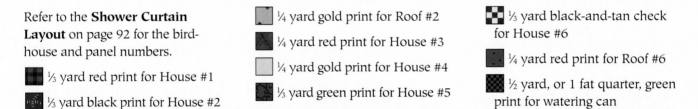

MATERIALS AND CUTTING

Prewash and press all of your fabrics. Using a rotary cutter, see-through ruler, and cutting mat, prepare the pieces as described below. Measurements for all pieces include ¼-inch seam allowances. (Obvious directional prints are not recommended.)

FABRIC	YARDAGE	NO. OF PIECES	DIMENSIONS
Light tan print for background and outer border	5 yards		Cut these first from the length of the fabric:
		2	3½ × 80-inch strips (outer border)
		1	26½ × 56½-inch piece (background Panel #2)
		2	25½ × 56½-inch pieces (background Panels #1 and #3)

FABRIC	YARDAGE	NO. OF PIECES	DIMENSIONS
■ Black print for accent border	⅓ yard	8	1 × 42-inch strips
▪ Gold print for checkerboard	⅝ yard	7	2½ × 42-inch strips
■ Green print for checkerboard	⅝ yard	7	2½ × 42-inch strips
Green print for ties	¾ yard	12	2 × 36½-inch strips
Lining fabric	4½ yards	—	—
Several coordinated fabrics for yo-yos and small appliqué pieces	Scraps, or ⅛-yard pieces	—	—
6½ yards lightweight, sewable fusible web; thread to match appliqué pieces; 6½ yards Tear-Away fabric stabilizer; embroidery floss			

Appliqué

STEP 1. Refer to "Quick-Fuse Appliqué" on pages 270–271. Be sure to use a lightweight, sewable fusible web. Trace the shapes from the appliqué patterns on pages 93–100 onto the paper side of the fusible web.

STEP 2. For the remaining appliqué shapes, draw the following rectangles on the paper side of the fusible web, leaving at least ½ inch between the rectangles. Label the rectangles as you go.

Birdhouse #1
House	9 × 11-inch rectangle
Roof	Two 1 × 8½-inch rectangles
Perch	½ × 3½-inch rectangle
Base	1 × 11-inch rectangle
Pole	1 × 13-inch rectangle

Birdhouse #2
House	11½ × 9-inch rectangle

Roof	13 × 6-inch rectangle
Windows	Two 1 × 3-inch rectangles
Door frame	Four ¾ × 5-inch rectangles
Door	3 × 5-inch rectangle
Base	1 × 13-inch rectangle
Pole	2 × 24-inch rectangle
	Two 1½ × 6-inch rectangles

Birdhouse #3
House	7 × 18-inch rectangle
Roof	Two 1 × 6½-inch rectangles
Base	1 × 9-inch rectangle
Pole	2 × 20-inch rectangle

Birdhouse #4
House	8 × 10-inch rectangle
Roof	Two 1½ × 8-inch rectangles
Pole	1 × 13-inch rectangle

Birdhouse #5
House	8 × 19-inch rectangle

Roof	Two 1½ × 8-inch rectangles
Base	1½ × 10-inch rectangle
Pole	2 × 26-inch rectangle
	Two 1½ × 5-inch rectangles

Birdhouse #6
House	15 × 11-inch rectangle
Roof	17 × 5-inch rectangle
Chimneys	Two 1 × 5-inch rectangles
Fence rail	1½ × 15-inch rectangle
Base	1 × 17-inch rectangle
Pole	3 × 23-inch rectangle

STEP 3. Fuse the traced shapes and drawn rectangles to the wrong side of your selected fabrics. Cut out each shape on the drawn line. As you cut, organize the appliqué pieces according to the birdhouse numbers. Remove the paper backing; a thin film will remain on the fabric.

STEP 4. Trim five of the rectangles, as shown in **Diagrams 1** through **5**, to create rooflines.

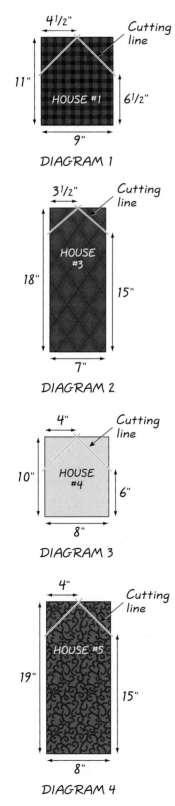

DIAGRAM 1

DIAGRAM 2

DIAGRAM 3

DIAGRAM 4

DIAGRAM 5

STEP 5. Position and fuse the appliqué pieces to the light tan print background panels, allowing for the ¼-inch seam allowances on the raw edges of the background panels. Refer to the **Shower Curtain Layout** on page 92 for placement. The roofs on Houses #1, #3, #4, and #5 are created by placing one end of the first rectangle over one end of the second rectangle, as shown in **Diagram 6**.

DIAGRAM 6

STEP 6. Referring to "Machine Appliqué" on pages 271–272, machine appliqué the pieces to the background panels. Use the Tear-Away fabric stabilizer on the wrong sides of the background panels for an even machine stitch. Remove the stabilizer after stitching.

Adding the Borders

STEP 1. Using ¼-inch seams, sew background Panels #1, #2, and #3 together. Refer to the **Shower Curtain Layout** on page 92 for placement. Press the seams open.

STEP 2. Sew the eight 1 × 42-inch accent border strips together in pairs to make four strips approximately 1 × 84 inches each. Press. Sew one 1 × 84-inch accent border strip each to the top and bottom of the shower curtain. Trim the excess length, and press the seams toward the accent border.

STEP 3. Alternating the two colors, sew the fourteen 2½ × 42-inch checkerboard strips together to make a 28½ × 42-inch strip set. Change sewing direction with each strip sewn, and press the seams toward the darker fabric as you go. Using a rotary cutter and ruler, cut twelve 2½ × 28½-inch strips from this strip set. There should be 14 squares in each strip. See **Diagram 7**.

DIAGRAM 7

Add a Touch of Rustic Authenticity

I added a long branch above my traditional curtain rod. I tied the Bird Bath Shower Curtain to this branch and used the regular rod for the plastic shower curtain liner.

STEP 4. Sew eight 2½ × 28½-inch checkerboard strips together in pairs to make four 2½ × 56½-inch checkerboard strips.

STEP 5. Sew the four remaining 2½ × 28½-inch checkerboard strips to the four checkerboard strips made in Step 4. You will now have four 2½ × 84½-inch checkerboard strips.

STEP 6. Using a seam ripper, remove 4 squares from each checkerboard strip to make four 2½ × 76½-inch strips with 38 squares each.

STEP 7. Compare the strips to the top and bottom of the shower curtain. You may need to take in or let out a few seams (¹⁄₁₆ inch or less) to make them fit. Make adjustments before you sew the checkerboard strips together in pairs. If you do make adjustments, make them in the same place on each strip so that the strips will still match up. Refer to "Fitting Pieced Borders" on page 274 for further instructions. Sew the strips together in pairs and press.

STEP 8. Pin and sew the checkerboards to the top and bottom of the shower curtain. Press the seams toward the accent border.

STEP 9. Sew the two remaining 1 × 84-inch accent border strips to the top and bottom of the shower curtain. Trim the excess length, and press the seams toward the accent border.

STEP 10. Sew the 3½ × 80-inch outer border strips to the top and

bottom of the shower curtain. Trim the excess length, and press the seams toward the accent border.

Assembly

STEP 1. Refer to "Making Yo-yos" on pages 272–273. Make two yo-yos flowers from the pattern on page 93. Sew the yo-yos above the bird standing on the pot in Panel #1, referring to the **Shower Curtain Layout** on page 92 for placement. Use six strands of embroidery floss to stem stitch bird legs and flower stems. Make French-knot eyes on the birds with embroidery floss. See "Decorative Stitches" on page 272.

STEP 2. Cut the 4½-yard piece of lining fabric into two 2¼-yard

lengths. Trim the selvage edges off both lining pieces. With right sides together, sew the halves together to make one piece approximately 80 × 81 inches. Press the seams open.

STEP 3. With right sides together, position and pin the shower curtain top and lining together. Using ¼-inch seams, sew around the edges, leaving an 8- to 10-inch opening for turning. Trim the lining to the same size as the top. Trim the corners, turn the shower curtain right side out, hand stitch the opening closed, and press.

STEP 4. Mark placement and make twelve 1-inch buttonholes ½ inch down from the top edge. The first and last buttonholes are spaced 1 inch from the sides, and

Debbie's Decorating Diary

The Bird Bath, shown in the photo on pages 86–87, was created from a very ordinary guest bathroom, right off my home art studio. Because the room is small, the custom vanity was pared down in size with a bar-size brass sink. Slate countertops add an outdoorsy feel. The mirror is surrounded by shutters, a window box, a peaked roof, and outdoor lighting fixtures.

We laid green carpet down and stenciled it with brown and terra-cotta brick shapes to look like a patio with moss growing around stone pavers. The floor cloth was painted on pretreated canvas and was antiqued before varnishing. The walls and ceiling are faux painted with blue sky and billowy clouds. A picket fence lines the walls of the room throughout.

The storage cupboards to the right of the shower represent gardeners' cupboards, with hook-and-eye latches mimicking old-fashioned screen doors. Chicken wire that was spray painted green adds an interesting texture to these cupboard doors.

What you can't see in the corner is our updated outhouse, complete with roof, shelves on the wall, and a carved moon.

the remaining ten buttonholes are spaced approximately 6½ inches apart.

STEP 5. To make the ties, fold the twelve 2 × 36½-inch strips in half lengthwise with right sides together. Sew a ¼-inch seam on the edge opposite the fold and on one short side on each tie. Trim the corners, turn the ties right side out, and press. Fold in the remaining end and stitch the opening closed. Topstitch the edges.

STEP 6. Insert the ties through the buttonholes and tie them in bows, attaching the curtain to the shower curtain rod.

Time-Saver

A bow whip or narrow loop turner will make turning the long, narrow tubes of fabric for the shower curtain ties much easier. See "Quilting by Mail" on page 280 for ordering information.

SHOWER CURTAIN LAYOUT

STAR PATTERN
FOR HOUSE #4

YO-YO PATTERN

APPLIQUÉ PATTERN KEY

——————— Tracing line

- - - - - - Tracing line
(will be hidden behind
other fabric)

CHIMNEY PATTERN
FOR HOUSE #1

NEST PATTERN
FOR HOUSE #1

MOON
PATTERN
FOR
HOUSE #5

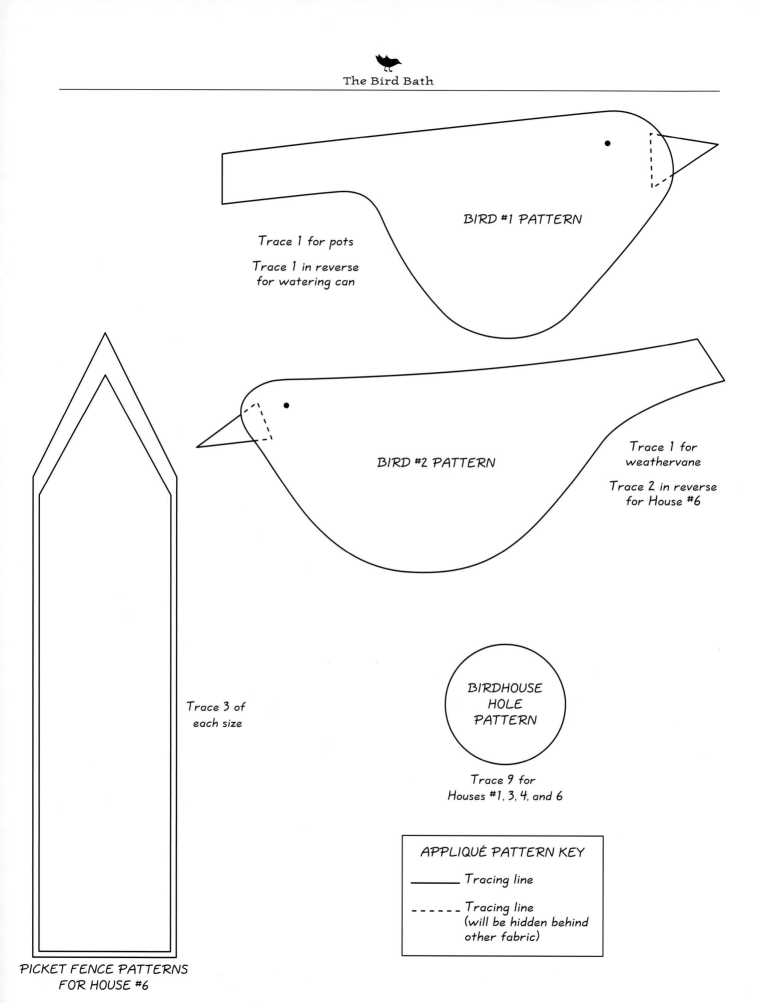

BIRD #1 PATTERN

Trace 1 for pots

Trace 1 in reverse
for watering can

BIRD #2 PATTERN

Trace 1 for
weathervane

Trace 2 in reverse
for House #6

Trace 3 of
each size

BIRDHOUSE
HOLE
PATTERN

Trace 9 for
Houses #1, 3, 4, and 6

APPLIQUÉ PATTERN KEY

———— Tracing line

- - - - - Tracing line
(will be hidden behind
other fabric)

PICKET FENCE PATTERNS
FOR HOUSE #6

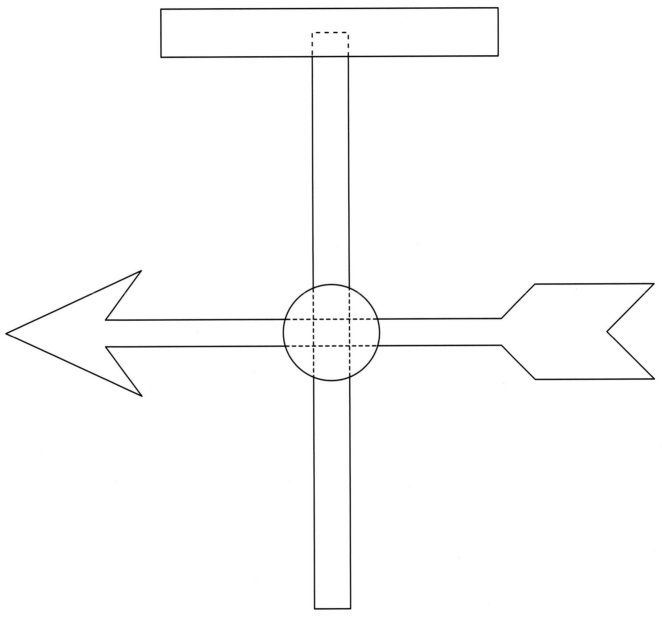

WEATHERVANE PATTERN FOR HOUSE #2

FLOWERPOT PATTERNS

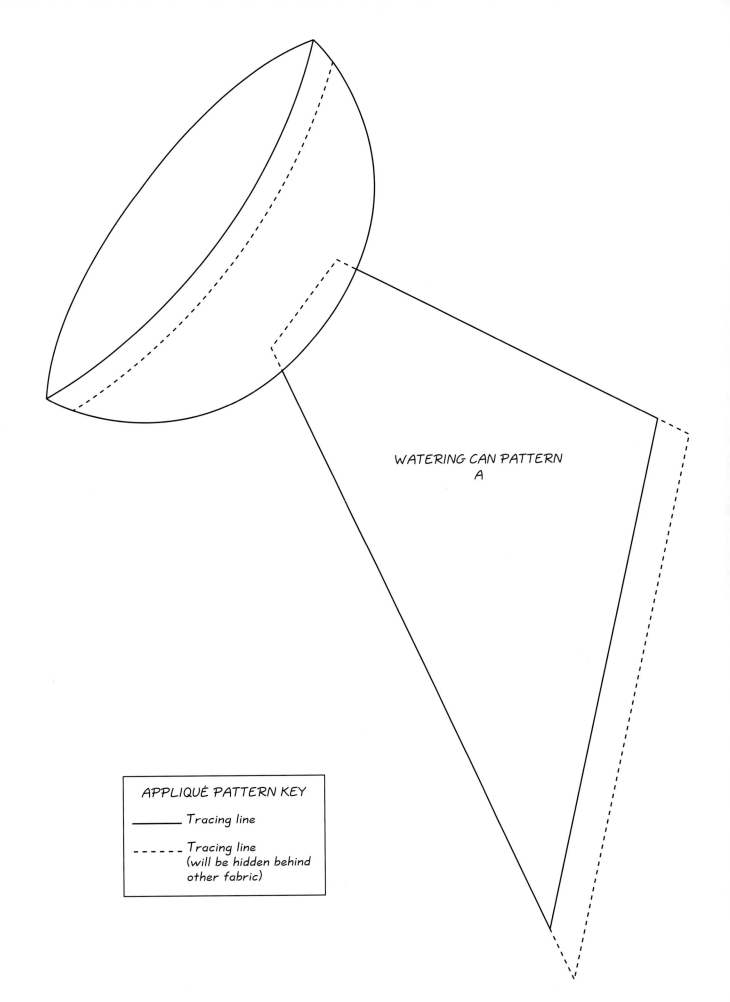

WATERING CAN PATTERN
A

APPLIQUÉ PATTERN KEY

———— Tracing line

- - - - Tracing line
(will be hidden behind
other fabric)

Watering Can Pattern D goes here

Watering Can Pattern A goes here

WATERING CAN PATTERN
B

Align with red line of Watering Can Pattern C

WATERING CAN PATTERN
C

Align with red line of Watering Can Pattern B

BIRDHOUSE #5
DOOR PATTERN

Watering Can
Pattern E
goes here

APPLIQUÉ PATTERN KEY

———— Tracing line

- - - - Tracing line
(will be hidden behind
other fabric)

WATERING CAN PATTERN
D

Align with blue line of
Watering Can Pattern E

APPLIQUÉ PATTERN KEY

———— Tracing line

- - - - Tracing line
(will be hidden behind
other fabric)

Align with blue line of
Watering Can Pattern D

D

A

B   C

E

WATERING CAN
ASSEMBLY DIAGRAM

WATERING CAN PATTERN
E

WATERING CAN WALLHANGING

Watering cans are so quaint and picturesque. I love their shape

and like to collect all sizes of antique and reproduction versions. The

wallhanging you see on the next page is perfect for a gardening friend and

would be right at home in any room, nook, or hallway. (For a more

summery look, see the **Color Option** on page 104.)

Finished Size: 19 × 21 inches

MATERIALS AND CUTTING			
Prewash and press all of your fabrics. Using a rotary cutter, see-through ruler, and cutting mat, prepare the pieces as described below. Measurements for all pieces include ¼-inch seam allowances.			

FABRIC	YARDAGE	NO. OF PIECES	DIMENSIONS
Tan plaid for background	½ yard	1	15½ × 18½-inch piece
Black print for accent border and binding	⅙ yard (cut into three 1 × 42-inch strips)	2	1 × 18½-inch strips (accent border)
		2	1 × 21½-inch strips (binding)
		2	1 × 18½-inch strips (binding)
Gold print for checkerboard	¼ yard	3	1½ × 24-inch strips
Green print for checkerboard	¼ yard	3	1½ × 24-inch strips
Backing fabric	⅔ yard	—	—
Lightweight batting	⅔ yard	—	—

(continued)

WEEKENDER

MATERIALS AND CUTTING—CONTINUED			
FABRIC	**YARDAGE**	**NO. OF PIECES**	**DIMENSIONS**
Green print for appliqué watering can	12 × 16-inch piece	—	—
Several coordinated fabrics for remaining appliqué pieces and dimensional leaves	Scraps, or ⅛- to ¼-yard pieces	—	—
Lightweight, sewable fusible web; embroidery floss; 11 assorted buttons			

Assembling the Background

Assemble the wallhanging top before adding the appliqué pieces. Be sure to use ¼-inch seams and to press after each sewing step.

STEP 1. Sew the 1 × 18½-inch accent border strips to the top and bottom of the 18½ × 15½-inch tan plaid background piece. Press the seams toward the accent border.

STEP 2. Alternating the two colors, sew the six 1½ × 24-inch checkerboard strips together to make a 6½ × 24-inch strip set. Change sewing direction with each strip sewn, and press the seams toward the darker fabric as you go. Cut this strip set into thirds, approximately 8 inches each. See **Diagram 1**.

6½"

24" *8"* *8"* *8"*

DIAGRAM 1

STEP 3. Resew the thirds together to make an 18½ × 8-inch strip set. Using a rotary cutter and ruler, cut four 1½ × 18½-inch strips from this strip set. There should be 18 squares in each strip. See **Diagram 2**.

18½"

8" *1½"*

DIAGRAM 2

STEP 4. Compare the strips to the top and bottom of the wallhanging. You may need to take in or let out a few seams (1/16 inch or less) to make them fit. Make adjustments before you sew the checkerboard strips together into pairs. If you do make adjustments, make them in the same place on each strip so that the strips will still match up. Refer to "Fitting Pieced Borders" on page 274 for further instructions. Sew the checkerboard strips together in pairs and press.

STEP 5. Pin and sew the checkerboards to the top and bottom of the wallhanging. Press the seams toward the accent border.

STEP 6. Sew the 1 × 18½-inch binding strips to the top and bottom. Press the seams toward the binding.

STEP 7. Sew the 1 × 21½-inch binding strips to the sides. Press.

Appliqué

The appliqué pieces were added to the background using the technique described in "Blanket Stitch Appliqué" on page 272. You can machine appliqué with either a satin stitch or blanket stitch if you prefer. Refer to "Machine Appliqué" on pages 271–272 for instructions on either technique. Be sure to use a lightweight, sewable fusible web for all of these appliqué techniques.

STEP 1. Refer to "Quick-Fuse Appliqué" on pages 270–271. Trace the watering can from the appliqué pattern on pages 97–100 and trace 11 flowers from the appliqué pattern on page 104.

STEP 2. Position and fuse the appliqué pieces to the background, referring to the **Wallhanging Layout** on the following page for placement.

STEP 3. Use two strands of embroidery floss to blanket stitch around the edges of the appliqué pieces. Use six strands of embroidery floss to chain stitch the flower stems, referring to "Decorative Stitches" on page 272 for instructions on chain stitching.

Finishing Stitches

STEP 1. Position the top and backing with right sides together. Lay both pieces on top of the batting, with the backing next to the batting. Pin all three layers together. Using ¼-inch seam allowances, sew around the edges, leaving a 3- to 4-inch opening for turning. Trim the backing and batting to the same size as the top. Trim the corners, turn the wallhanging right side out, hand stitch the opening closed, and press.

STEP 2. Machine or hand quilt in the seam lines of the accent border, checkerboard squares, and binding. Outline the appliqué design by quilting ¹⁄₁₆ inch from the edges. Quilt a 1½-inch grid in the background.

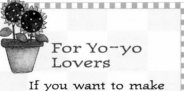

For Yo-yo Lovers

If you want to make the flowers for the wallhanging out of yo-yos, cut circles of fabric at least twice the diameter of the flower appliqué pattern at right. Refer to "Making Yo-yos" on pages 272–273, and use a blanket stitch to attach the yo-yos to the background.

STEP 3. Cut several 1 × 3-inch strips of fabric for the leaves. Tie a knot in the center of each strip. Sew the leaves to the flower stems, and sew a button to the center of each flower.

FLOWER PATTERN

19"

21"

WALLHANGING LAYOUT

COLOR OPTION

Country blues with accents of red, pink, and yellow add a summery touch to the wallhanging.

STACKED CROWS WALLHANGING

Caw, caw, caw! The whimsical and endearing crows on the next page will

win over even the most ardent gardener, despite the raucous reputation of

the real birds. Hearts, a checkerboard border, a star, and a picket fence all

capture the country spirit perfectly, making this wallhanging

suitable for any spot in the house.

Finished Size: 13 × 19 inches

MATERIALS AND CUTTING

Prewash and press all of your fabrics. Using a rotary cutter, see-through ruler, and cutting mat, prepare the pieces as described below. Measurements for all pieces include ¼-inch seam allowances.

FABRIC	YARDAGE	NO. OF PIECES	DIMENSIONS
Tan check for background	⅓ yard	1	9½ × 15½-inch piece
Dark green print for accent border	⅛ yard (cut into two 1 × 42-inch strips)	2	1 × 16½-inch strips
		2	1 × 9½-inch strips
Dark red print for checkerboard	¼ yard	3	1½ × 24-inch strips
Tan print for checkerboard	¼ yard	3	1½ × 24-inch strips
Dark green print for binding	⅛ yard (cut into two 1 × 42-inch strips)	2	1 × 19½-inch strips
		2	1 × 12½-inch strips
Backing fabric	½ yard	—	—
Lightweight batting	½ yard	—	—
Several coordinated fabrics for appliqué pieces	Scraps, or ⅛- to ¼-yard pieces	—	—
Lightweight, sewable fusible web; embroidery floss			

Assembling the Background

Assemble the wallhanging top before adding the appliqué pieces. Be sure to use ¼-inch seams and to press after each sewing step.

STEP 1. Sew the 1 × 9½-inch accent border strips to the top and bottom of the 9½ × 15½-inch tan check background piece. Press the seams toward the accent border.

STEP 2. Sew the 1 × 16½-inch accent border strips to the sides. Press.

STEP 3. Alternating the two colors, sew the six 1½ × 24-inch checkerboard strips together to make a 6½ × 24-inch strip set. Change sewing direction with each strip sewn, and press the seams toward the darker fabric as you go. Cut this strip set into thirds, approximately 8 inches each. See **Diagram 1**.

DIAGRAM 1

STEP 4. Resew the thirds together to make an 18½ × 8-inch strip set. Using a rotary cutter and ruler, cut four 1½ × 18½-inch strips from this strip set. There should be 18 squares in each strip. See **Diagram 2**.

STEP 5. For the top and bottom, use a seam ripper to remove 8 squares from two checkerboard strips to make two strips with 10 squares each. Compare the 1½ × 10½-inch strips to the top and bottom of the wallhanging. You may need to take in or let out a few seams (1/16 inch or less) to make them fit. Referring to the **Wallhanging Layout** on page 108 for placement of the light and dark squares, pin and sew the 1½ × 10½-inch checkerboard strips to the top and bottom. Press the seams toward the accent border.

STEP 6. Fit, pin, and sew the 1½ × 18½-inch checkerboard strips to the sides. Press.

STEP 7. Sew the 1 × 12½-inch binding strips to the top and bottom. Press the seams toward the binding.

STEP 8. Sew the 1 × 19½-inch binding strips to the sides. Press.

Appliqué

The appliqué pieces were added to the background using the technique described in "Blanket Stitch Appliqué" on page 272. Be sure to use a lightweight, sewable fusible web.

STEP 1. Refer to "Quick-Fuse Appliqué" on pages 270–271. Trace the birdhouse, star, fence, birds, and hearts from the appliqué patterns on pages 108–109.

STEP 2. Position and fuse the appliqué pieces to the background, referring to the **Wallhanging Layout** on page 108 for placement.

STEP 3. Use two strands of embroidery floss to blanket stitch around the edges of the appliqué pieces. Using three strands of embroidery floss, stem stitch the legs and make French-knot eyes on the birds. Refer to "Decorative Stitches" on page 272.

Finishing Stitches

STEP 1. Position the top and backing with right sides together. Lay both pieces on top of the batting, with the backing next to the batting. Pin all three layers together. Using ¼-inch seam allowances, sew around the edges, leaving a 3- to 4-inch opening for turning. Trim the backing and batting to the same size as the top. Trim the corners, turn the wallhanging right side out, hand stitch the opening closed, and press.

STEP 2. Machine or hand quilt in the seam lines of the accent border, checkerboard squares, and binding. Outline the appliqué design by quilting 1/16 inch from the edges. Quilt a 1-inch diagonal grid in the background.

DIAGRAM 2

13"

19"

WALLHANGING LAYOUT

BIRD #1 PATTERN

Stem stitch

Align bird #1 legs here

BIRD #2 PATTERN

Stem stitch

Align bird #2 legs here

BIRD #3 PATTERN

Stem stitch

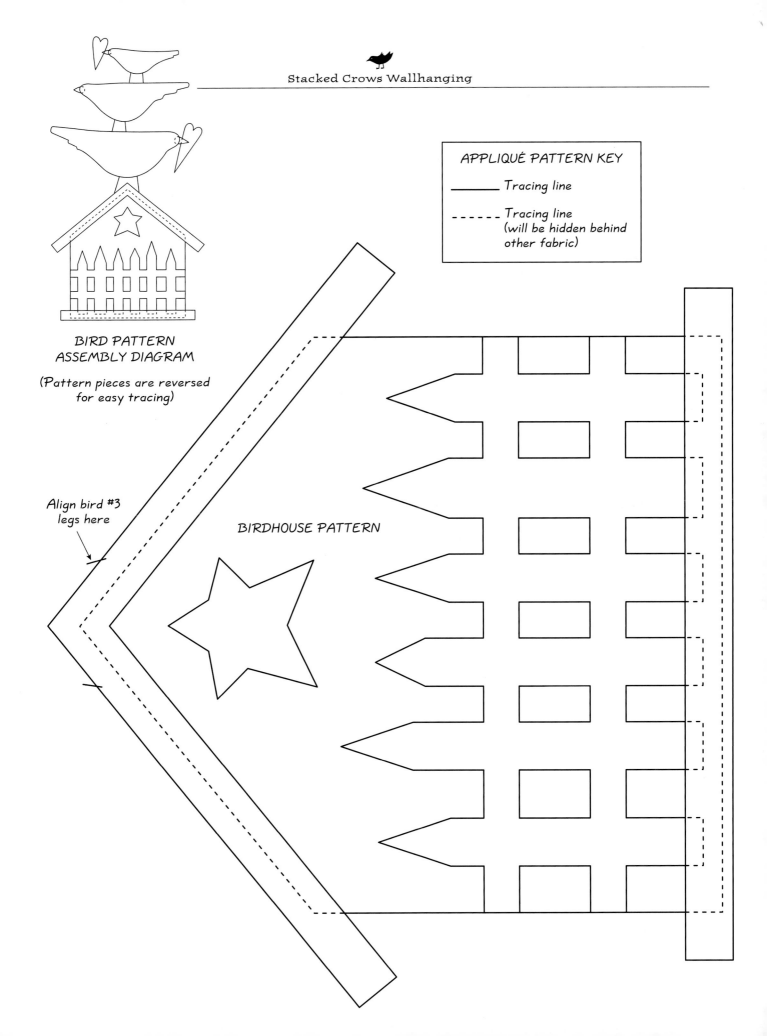

Stacked Crows Wallhanging

APPLIQUÉ PATTERN KEY

——————— Tracing line

- - - - - - - Tracing line
(will be hidden behind
other fabric)

BIRD PATTERN
ASSEMBLY DIAGRAM

(Pattern pieces are reversed
for easy tracing)

Align bird #3
legs here

BIRDHOUSE PATTERN

GARDEN GUEST TOWELS

Complete your birds-in-the-garden theme with these sweet hand towels. The Gardener's Delight Towel, *right*, and the Birdhouse Towel, *left* (directions on page 112), are perfect accessories for any bath, so while you're making a set of your own, make an extra set for a gift, too.

Towel size (unfolded) is 20" × 34"

GARDENER'S DELIGHT TOWEL

These instructions are written for a hand towel that measures approximately 20 × 34 inches. You may have to adjust the length of your checkerboard to fit the size of your towel.

Assembling the Checkerboard

See "Materials and Cutting" on the opposite page.

STEP 1. Sew the two 1½ × 42-inch checkerboard strips together to make a 2½ × 42-inch strip set. Press the seams toward the darker fabric. Using a rotary cutter and ruler, cut twenty 1½ × 2½-inch segments from this strip set. See **Diagram 1**.

2½"

1½"

42"

DIAGRAM 1

MATERIALS AND CUTTING *(for Gardener's Delight Towel)*

Prewash the hand towel and all of your fabrics. Press the fabrics. Using a rotary cutter, see-through ruler, and cutting mat, prepare the pieces as described below. Measurements for all pieces include ¼-inch seam allowances.

FABRIC	YARDAGE	NO. OF PIECES	DIMENSIONS
▢ Gold print for checkerboard	⅛ yard	1	1½ × 42-inch strip
▨ Green print for checkerboard	⅛ yard	1	1½ × 42-inch strip
Backing for checkerboard	⅛ yard	1	2½ × 20½-inch strip
Several coordinated fabrics for appliqué pieces, yo-yos, and dimensional leaves	Scraps, or ⅛-yard pieces	—	—

Purchased hand towel; lightweight, sewable fusible web; thread to match appliqué pieces; Tear-Away fabric stabilizer; embroidery floss

Adjust for Size

It's easy to make adjustments for a smaller hand towel. I cut 20 segments to fit a 20-inch towel. A 17-inch towel would take 17 segments.

STEP 2. Alternating placement of the light and dark squares, sew the 20 checkerboard segments together, as shown in **Diagram 2**. Press the seams in one direction, following the arrows in the diagram.

STEP 3. Compare the checkerboard to the hand towel. The sides of the checkerboard should extend ¼ inch beyond the sides of the towel. You may need to take in or let out a few seams (¹⁄₁₆ inch or less) to make the checkerboard fit.

STEP 4. Position the checkerboard and the 2½ × 20½-inch backing strip with right sides together. Pin them together, keeping the raw edges even. (Remember to adjust the backing if you made a different-size checkerboard.) Using ¼-inch seams, sew around the edges, leaving a 3- to 4-inch opening for turning. Trim the corners, turn the

checkerboard right side out, hand stitch the opening closed, and press.

STEP 5. Position the checkerboard approximately 3 inches up from the bottom edge of the towel. Pin it in place and topstitch around all the edges.

Appliqué

The appliqué pieces were added to the hand towel using the technique described in "Machine Appliqué" on pages 271–272. Be sure to use a lightweight, sewable fusible web.

STEP 1. Refer to "Quick-Fuse Appliqué" on page 270. Trace the flowerpot, bird, and bee from the appliqué patterns on page 115.

STEP 2. Position and fuse the appliqué pieces to the center of the towel, above the checkerboard,

1¹⁄₂"

2¹⁄₂"

DIAGRAM 2

referring to the Gardener's Delight Towel layout on page 110 for placement.

STEP 3. Machine appliqué around the edges of the pieces. Use the Tear-Away fabric stabilizer on the wrong side of the hand towel for an even machine stitch. Remove the stabilizer after stitching.

Finishing

STEP 1. Refer to "Making Yo-yos" on pages 272–273. Make three yo-yo flowers from the pattern on the opposite page. Sew the yo-yos to the towel, above the pot.

STEP 2. Use six strands of embroidery floss to blanket stitch the lower edge of the towel. Use six strands of embroidery floss to stem stitch the bird legs and flower stems and two strands to make a French-knot eye on the bird. See "Decorative Stitches" on page 272. Stitch a meandering bee path, using six strands of embroidery floss.

STEP 3. Cut three 1 × 3-inch strips for leaves. Tie a knot in the center of each strip, and sew one strip to each flower stem.

BIRDHOUSE TOWEL

(See the towel on the left in the photo on page 110.)

See "Materials and Cutting" on the opposite page. These instructions are written for a hand towel that measures approximately 20 × 34 inches. You may have to adjust the length of your border to fit your towel size.

Assembling the Border

STEP 1. Sew the 2 × 20½-inch wide border strip between the two 1 × 20½-inch narrow border strips. Press the seams toward the narrow borders.

STEP 2. Position the border and the 3 × 20½-inch backing strip with right sides together. Pin them together, keeping the raw edges even.

Using ¼-inch seams, sew around the edges, leaving a 3- to 4-inch opening for turning. Trim the corners, turn the border right side out, hand stitch the opening closed, and press.

STEP 3. Position the border approximately 3 inches up from the bottom edge of the towel. Pin it in place and topstitch around all the edges.

Appliqué

The appliqué pieces were added to the hand towel using the technique described in "Machine Appliqué" on pages 271–272. Be sure to use a lightweight, sewable fusible web.

STEP 1. Refer to "Quick-Fuse Appliqué" on pages 270–271. Trace the birdhouses, poles, and birds from the appliqué patterns on page 114.

STEP 2. Position and fuse the appliqué pieces to the center of the towel, above the border, referring to the Birdhouse Towel layout for placement.

STEP 3. Machine appliqué around the edges of the pieces. Use the Tear-Away fabric stabilizer on the wrong side of the hand towel for an even machine stitch. Remove the stabilizer after stitching.

MATERIALS AND CUTTING *(for Birdhouse Towel)*

Prewash the hand towel and all of your fabrics. Press the fabrics. Using a rotary cutter, see-through ruler, and cutting mat, prepare the pieces as described below. Measurements for all pieces include ¼-inch seam allowances.

FABRIC	YARDAGE	NO. OF PIECES	DIMENSIONS
Gold print for wide border	⅛ yard	1	2 × 20½-inch strip
Green print for narrow border	⅛ yard	2	1 × 20½-inch strips
Backing for border	⅛ yard	1	3 × 20½-inch strip
Several coordinated fabrics for appliqué pieces	Scraps, or ⅛-yard pieces	—	—

Purchased hand towel; lightweight, sewable fusible web; thread to match appliqué pieces; Tear-Away fabric stabilizer; embroidery floss; assorted buttons; ceramic buttons (optional). (See "Quilting by Mail" on page 280 for information on ordering ceramic buttons.)

Finishing

Use six strands of embroidery floss to blanket stitch the lower edge of the towel. Use six strands of embroidery floss to stem stitch the bird legs and a vine in the wide border strip (the vine can also be stitched by machine, using a satin stitch). Use two strands to make a French-knot eye on each bird. See "Decorative Stitches" on page 272. Sew assorted buttons to the wide border strip and to the appliqué design.

YO-YO PATTERN

APPLIQUÉ PATTERN KEY

Tracing line

Tracing line
(will be hidden behind
other fabric)

BIRDHOUSE
TOWEL PATTERNS

Button

Button

Stem stitch or satin stitch

Yo-yos

Flower stems and bird legs
are embroidered using stem stitch

Running stitch

Torn fabric strips

GARDENER'S DELIGHT
TOWEL PATTERNS

French knot

Checkerboard border

PINE LODGE FAMILY ROOM

Create a private retreat in your family room
with this relaxing lodge look, whether you live in
the heart of the city or on the edge of the woods.
Use deep, rich, and colorful fabrics to create a
warm, friendly, and inviting hideaway that
you'll escape to every chance you get.
Build a fire, get out the checkers,
relax, and enjoy!

HEARTHSIDE PINEY WOODS

Bring a touch of the pine woods into your home with this quilt for

your mantel. You can just imagine the sunlight filtering down through

the pine boughs in the quiet of the afternoon. (For a more contemporary

look, see the **Color Option** on page 127.) Pair the quilt with the Mantel

Doilies (directions on page 128), or scatter the doilies about the

room on tables, chests, or the backs of chairs.

Piney Woods Quilt

Finished Size: 46½ × 26¾ inches   **Finished Block: 7 inches square**

MATERIALS

(Obvious directional prints are not recommended.)

■ ⅛ yard black print for center squares

■ ⅛ yard brown print for blocks

■ ⅛ yard red print for corner squares

▨ ½ yard dark brown print for blocks, side units, and corner triangle

▨ ⅛ yard multicolor print for corner squares

■ ⅛ yard green print for corner squares

□ ½ yard tan print for blocks, side triangles, and corner triangles

▨ ⅓ yard light brown print for blocks

■ ⅝ yard black solid for accent border and binding

⅛ yard, or 2 to 3 × 40-inch strip, *each* of 7 assorted fabrics for scrap border

1⅜ yards fabric for backing

1⅜ yards lightweight batting

Scraps, or ⅛-yard pieces, of assorted green prints for appliqué trees

Lightweight, sewable fusible web

Embroidery floss

CUTTING

Prewash and press all of your fabrics. Using a rotary cutter, see-through ruler, and cutting mat, prepare the pieces as described below. Measurements for all pieces include ¼-inch seam allowances.

FABRIC	FIRST CUT		SECOND CUT	
Color	No. of Pieces	Dimensions	No. of Pieces	Dimensions
Black print	**Center squares**			
	1	3½ × 42-inch strip	11	3½-inch squares
Brown print	**Blocks**			
	1	3½ × 42-inch strip	1	3½ × 12-inch strip
			6	3½ × 1½-inch strips
Red print	**Corner squares**			
	2	1½ × 42-inch strips	2	1½ × 28-inch strips
			2	1½ × 12-inch strips
Dark brown print	**Blocks**			
	1	5½ × 42-inch strip	1	5½ × 12-inch strip
			6	5½ × 1½-inch strips
	Side triangle units			
	1	6⅞ × 42-inch strip	1	6⅞ × 11-inch strip
			10	6⅞ × 1½-inch strips
	Corner triangle units			
	1	1½ × 42-inch strip	4	1½ × 7⅞-inch strips
Multicolor print	**Corner squares**			
	2	1½ × 42-inch strips	1	1½ × 28-inch strip
			1	1½ × 12-inch strip
			1	1½ × 11-inch strip
Green print	**Corner squares**			
	2	1½ × 42-inch strips	1	1½ × 28-inch strip
			1	1½ × 12-inch strip
			2	1½-inch squares
Tan print	**Blocks**			
	1	3½ × 42-inch strip	1	3½ × 28-inch strip
			6	3½ × 1½-inch strips
	1	1½ × 42-inch strip	10	1½ × 3½-inch strips
	Side triangles and corner triangles			
	1	9¾ × 42-inch strip	2	9¾-inch squares (side triangles)
			2	5½-inch squares (corner triangles)

FABRIC	FIRST CUT		SECOND CUT	
Color	No. of Pieces	Dimensions	No. of Pieces	Dimensions
Light brown print **Blocks**				
	1	5½ × 42-inch strip	1	5½ × 28-inch strip
			7	5½ × 1½-inch strips
	2	1½ × 42-inch strips	9	1½ × 5½-inch strips
Black solid **Accent border**				
	4	1 × 42-inch strips	No second cut	
Binding			Cut 1 strip into the following:	
	5	2¾ × 42-inch strips	2	2¾ × 21-inch strips
Assorted fabrics **Scrap border**				
	7	40-inch-long strips that vary in width from 2 to 3 inches	No second cut	

Piecing the Blocks

You will be making 11 blocks, 3 of Block #1 and 8 of Block #2. For Block #1, use the brown and dark brown print strips. For Block #2, use the tan and light brown print strips. Refer to "Assembly Line Piecing" on page 268. Use ¼-inch seams and press after each sewing step. Follow the arrows in the diagrams for pressing directions.

Making Block #1

STEP 1. Sew three 3½-inch black print center squares between the six 1½ × 3½-inch brown print strips, as shown in **Diagram 1**. Press.

DIAGRAM 1

STEP 2. Sew the 3½ × 12-inch brown print strip between the two 1½ × 12-inch red print strips to make a 5½ × 12-inch strip set. See **Diagram 2**. Press.

DIAGRAM 2

STEP 3. Using a rotary cutter and ruler, cut six 1½ × 5½-inch strips from the strip set made in Step 2. See **Diagram 3**.

STEP 4. Sew the three units from Step 1 between the six units from Step 3, as shown in **Diagram 4**. Press.

DIAGRAM 3

DIAGRAM 4

STEP 5. Sew the three units from Step 4 between the six 1½ × 5½-inch dark brown print strips. See **Diagram 5** on page 122. Press.

DIAGRAM 5

STEP 6. Sew the 5½ × 12-inch dark brown print strip between the 1½ × 12-inch multicolor print strip and the 1½ × 12-inch green print strip to make a 7½ × 12-inch strip set. See **Diagram 6**. Press.

DIAGRAM 6

STEP 7. Using a rotary cutter and ruler, cut six 1½ × 7½-inch strips from the strip set made in Step 6. See **Diagram 7**.

DIAGRAM 7

STEP 8. Sew the three units from Step 5 between the six units from Step 7, referring to **Diagram 8** for placement of the corner

squares. Each Block #1 will now measure 7½ inches square.

BLOCK #1
Step 5 Unit

Step 7 Units
DIAGRAM 8

Making Block #2

STEP 1. Sew the remaining eight 3½-inch black print center squares between the sixteen 1½ × 3½-inch tan print strips. See **Diagram 9**. Press.

DIAGRAM 9

STEP 2. Sew the 3½ × 28-inch tan print strip between the two 1½ × 28-inch red print strips to make a 5½ × 28-inch strip set. See **Diagram 10**. Press.

DIAGRAM 10

STEP 3. Using a rotary cutter and ruler, cut sixteen 1½ × 5½-inch strips from the strip set made in Step 2. See **Diagram 11**.

DIAGRAM 11

STEP 4. Sew the 8 units from Step 1 between the 16 units from Step 3, as shown in **Diagram 12**. Press.

Step 1 Unit

Step 3 Units
DIAGRAM 12

STEP 5. Sew the 8 units from Step 4 between the sixteen 1½ × 5½-inch light brown print strips. See **Diagram 13**. Press.

DIAGRAM 13

STEP 6. Sew the 5½ × 28-inch light brown print strip between the 1½ × 28-inch multicolor print strip and the 1½ × 28-inch green print strip to make a 7½ × 28-inch strip set. See **Diagram 14**. Press.

DIAGRAM 14

STEP 7. Using a rotary cutter and ruler, cut sixteen 1½ × 7½-inch strips from the strip set made in Step 6. See **Diagram 15**.

DIAGRAM 15

STEP 8. Sew the 8 units from Step 5 between the 16 units from Step 7, referring to **Diagram 16** for placement of the corner squares. Each Block #2 will now measure 7½ inches square.

BLOCK #2
Step 5 Unit

Step 7 Units

DIAGRAM 16

Making the Side Triangles

STEP 1. Cut the two 9¾-inch tan print squares in half diagonally in each direction to make eight triangles, as shown in **Diagram 17**.

Cut   9³/₄"   Cut

9³/₄"

Arrows indicate
straight of grain
DIAGRAM 17

STEP 2. Sew one 1½ × 6⅞-inch dark brown print strip to each of

Twiggy Accessories

To bring a bit of the outdoors into your family room, gather interesting branches and twigs to tuck into baskets or crockery. Or bundle the branches together, tie them with raffia, twine, or strips of fabric, and stack them next to your fireplace.

the eight tan print triangles from Step 1. See **Diagram 18**. Press. After pressing, the top of the dark brown strip will be longer than the triangle. It will be trimmed later.

6⁷/₈"   9³/₄"

1½"   6⁷/₈"

DIAGRAM 18

STEP 3. Sew the 1½ × 11-inch multicolor print strip to the 6⅞ × 11-inch dark brown strip to make a 7⅞ × 11-inch strip set. See **Diagram 19**. Press.

1½"   6⁷/₈"

11"   11"

DIAGRAM 19

STEP 4. Using a rotary cutter and ruler, cut six 1½ × 7⅞-inch strips from the strip set made in Step 3. See **Diagram 20**.

7⁷/₈"

1½"

11"

DIAGRAM 20

STEP 5. Sew six units from Step 2 to the six units from Step 4, as shown in **Diagram 21**. Press. These side triangles with the multi-color corner squares will be used for the top and bottom of the quilt.

Step 2 Unit

Step 4 Unit

DIAGRAM 21

STEP 6. Sew the two 1½-inch green print squares to the two remaining 1½ × 6⅞-inch dark brown print strips. See **Diagram 22**. Press.

1½"   6⅞"
1½" ▢   1½"

DIAGRAM 22

STEP 7. Sew the two units from Step 6 to the two remaining units from Step 2, as shown in **Diagram 23**. Press. These side triangles with the green corner squares will be used for the sides of the quilt.

Step 2 Unit

Step 6 Unit

DIAGRAM 23

Making the Corner Triangles

STEP 1. Cut the two 5½-inch tan print squares in half diagonally to make four triangles, as shown in **Diagram 24**.

Don't Stretch the Bias

To avoid stretching the bias edge of the triangle, sew with the triangle on the bottom.

Cut

5½"

5½"

Arrow indicates straight of grain
DIAGRAM 24

STEP 2. Sew the four 1½ × 7⅞-inch dark brown print strips to the four triangles from Step 1, as shown in **Diagram 25**. Press.

5½"   5½"

1½"
7⅞"
DIAGRAM 25

Assembling the Top

The quilt top is sewn together in rows, and then the rows are joined. Pay close attention that the green and multicolor corner squares are positioned as shown in the diagrams. When sewing the side triangles to the blocks, be sure to match the seams of the corner squares. The side triangles will be longer than the blocks; these will be trimmed after the quilt top is assembled. Be sure to use ¼-inch seams throughout.

STEP 1. For Rows #1 and #5, sew one corner triangle to one Block #2. The blocks are slightly smaller than the corner triangles and should be centered on the corner triangles. See **Diagram 26**. Press.

BLOCK #2

DIAGRAM 26

STEP 2. Sew each of the two units from Step 1 between one side triangle with a green corner square and one side triangle with a multicolor corner square, as shown in **Diagram 27**. Press.

ROWS #1 AND #5

Step 1 Unit

Make 2
DIAGRAM 27

STEP 3. For Rows #2 and #4, sew one corner triangle, two Block #2s, one Block #1, and one side triangle with a multicolor corner square together as shown in **Diagram 28** on the opposite page. Press.

STEP 4. For Row #3, sew two side triangles with multicolor corner squares, two Block #2s, and one Block #1 together in the order shown in **Diagram 29**. Press.

STEP 5. Sew the rows together, as shown in **Diagram 30**. Press all the seams in one direction.

STEP 6. The raw edges of the quilt top will be uneven. Use a rotary cutter and ruler to carefully trim the edges ¼ inch from the corner points of the quilt blocks. See **Diagram 31** on the following page.

ROWS #2 AND #4

Block #2

Block #1

Block #2

Make 2
DIAGRAM 28

ROW #3

Block #2

Block #1

Block #2

DIAGRAM 29

Pressed for Time?

Make one tree block, add corner triangles, and frame it for a quick, but heartfelt, gift.

Appliqué

The trees were added to the block centers using the technique described in "Blanket Stitch Appliqué" on page 272. You can machine appliqué with either a satin stitch or blanket stitch if you prefer. Refer to "Machine Appliqué" on pages 271–272. Be sure to use a lightweight, sewable fusible web.

STEP 1. Refer to "Quick-Fuse Appliqué" on pages 270–271. Trace 11 trees from the appliqué pattern on page 127.

ROW #1

ROW #2

ROW #3

ROW #4

ROW #5

DIAGRAM 30

DIAGRAM 33

DIAGRAM 31

STEP 2. Position and fuse the trees to the centers of the black print background squares.

STEP 3. Use two strands of embroidery floss to blanket stitch around the edges of the trees.

Adding the Borders

STEP 1. Sew one 1 × 42-inch accent border strip each to the top and bottom. Trim the excess length, and press the seams toward the accent border.

STEP 2. Sew the two remaining 1 × 42-inch accent border strips to the sides. Trim the excess length and press.

STEP 3. For the scrap border, sew the seven 40-inch strips (one each of seven different fabrics) together to make a 15 × 40-inch strip set. Change sewing direction with each

strip sewn, and press the seams in one direction as you go. Cut this strip set in halves, approximately 20 inches each. See **Diagram 32.**

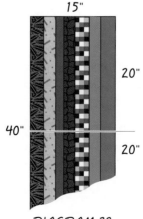

DIAGRAM 32

STEP 4. Resew the halves together to make a 29½ × 20-inch strip set. Using a rotary cutter and ruler, cut six 3 × 29½-inch strips from this strip set. See **Diagram 33.**

STEP 5. For the top and bottom, sew two sets of two 3 × 29½-inch strips together to make two 3 × 58½-inch strips. Pin and sew the scrap border strips to the top and bottom. Trim the excess length, and press the seams toward the accent border.

STEP 6. Pin and sew the remaining two 3 × 29½-inch scrap border strips to the sides. Trim the excess length and press.

Layering the Quilt

Arrange and baste the backing, batting, and top together, following the directions in "Layering the Quilt" on page 275. Trim the batting and backing to ¼ inch from the raw edges of the quilt top.

Binding the Quilt

Sew one 2¾ × 21-inch binding strip to each of two 2¾ × 42-inch binding strips to make two 2¾ × 62½-inch binding strips. Using the two 2¾ × 62½-inch binding strips for the top and bottom and the remaining two 2¾ × 42-inch binding strips for the sides, follow the directions for "Binding the Quilt" on pages 275–276.

46½"

26¾"

QUILT LAYOUT

Try colors of blue, green, purple, and gold with the green trees.

COLOR OPTION

Finishing Stitches

Machine or hand quilt in the seam lines of the blocks, side and corner triangle units, accent border, and scrap border. Outline the appliqué trees by quilting 1/16 inch from the edges. Quilt a 1¼-inch diagonal grid in the side and corner triangles.

TREE
PATTERN

Mantel Doilies

Finished Size: 8 inches square

(See the doilies on the mantel in the photo on page 118.)

MATERIALS

Doilies are made in sets of three. Two sets, each using a different fabric combination, were made for the mantel shown in the photo. Measure your mantle or shelf to determine how many sets you need to make. The doilies measure 11¼ inches from point to point.

To make 3 doilies:

⅛ yard black print for center squares

⅛ yard brown print for border

⅛ yard, or 1½ × 25-inch strip, red print for corner squares

¼ yard dark brown print for outer border

⅛ yard, or 1½ × 12-inch strip, multicolor print for corner squares

⅛ yard, or 1½ × 12-inch strip, green print for corner squares

⅙ yard black print for binding

⅓ yard fabric for backing

CUTTING

Prewash and press all of your fabrics. Using a rotary cutter, see-through ruler, and cutting mat, prepare the pieces as described below. Measurements for all pieces include ¼-inch seam allowances.

FABRIC	FIRST CUT		SECOND CUT	
Color	No. of Pieces	Dimensions	No. of Pieces	Dimensions
Black print	**Center squares**			
	3	3½-inch squares	No second cut	
Brown print	**Border**			
	1	3½ × 42-inch strip	1	3½ × 12-inch strip
			6	3½ × 1½-inch strips
Red print	**Corner squares**			
	1	1½ × 25-inch strip	2	1½ × 12-inch strips
Dark brown print	**Outer border**			
	1	5½ × 42-inch strip	1	5½ × 12-inch strip
			6	5½ × 1½-inch strips
Multicolor print	**Corner squares**			
	1	1½ × 12-inch strip	No second cut	

FABRIC	FIRST CUT		SECOND CUT	
Color	No. of Pieces	Dimensions	No. of Pieces	Dimensions
Green print	**Corner squares**			
	1	1½ × 12-inch strip	No second cut	
Black print	**Binding**			
	3	1 × 42-inch strips	6	1 × 8½-inch strips
			6	1 × 7½-inch strips
Backing fabric	3	8½-inch squares	No second cut	

Making the Doilies

STEP 1. Refer to "Making Block #1" on page 121 for instructions. Follow the directions in Steps 1 through 8 to make three blocks.

STEP 2. Sew the 1 × 7½-inch binding strips to the tops and bottoms of the blocks. Press the seams toward the border.

STEP 3. Sew the 1 × 8½-inch binding strips to the sides. Press.

Finishing

For each doily, position the top and backing with right sides together. Using ¼-inch seams, sew around the edges, leaving a 3- to 4-inch opening for turning. Trim the corners, turn the doily right side out, hand stitch the opening closed, and press. Decorate as desired.

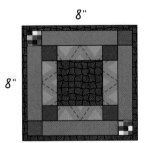

DOILY LAYOUT

8"

8"

Notes from Debbie

We were so thrilled to find such a gorgeous location to photograph the family room projects. The home is a log cabin situated on the beach of beautiful Hayden Lake in Idaho. Many of the photo shoots that I am on are in dark photo studios. This time we lucked out! Not only was the setting spectacular, but we could see the lake through picture windows on one whole side of the home. As we began to shoot, unfortunately we found that there was too much light coming in. We had to cover the windows with huge black blankets—so we were back in the dark again!

CABIN-IN-THE-PINES QUILT

Soften the walls of your family room with this traditional Log Cabin quilt. Or

use it on an overstuffed chair or sofa to cuddle up with on cold autumn and

winter evenings. Of course, it would be equally at home on a bed. The enduring

appeal of this well-loved pattern will guarantee that this quilt will have

a place in your decorating scheme for a long time to come.

Finished Size: 82 inches square   **Finished Block: 13½ inches square**

MATERIALS

⅙ yard gold print for center squares

¼ yard *each* of 18 to 22 red prints for logs

⅛ yard *each* of 30 to 40 assorted prints (no reds or golds) for logs

¾ yard black print for binding

6¼ yards fabric for backing

Lightweight queen-size batting (90 × 108 inches)

C U T T I N G

Prewash and press all of your fabrics. Using a rotary cutter, see-through ruler, and cutting mat, prepare the pieces as described below. Measurements for all pieces include ¼-inch seam allowances.

FABRIC	FIRST CUT		SECOND CUT	
Color	No. of Pieces	Dimensions	No. of Pieces	Dimensions
Gold print	**Center squares**			
	2	2 × 42-inch strips	36	2-inch squares
Red prints	**Logs**			
	36	2 × 12½-inch strips	No second cut	
	36	2 × 11-inch strips	No second cut	
	36	2 × 9½-inch strips	No second cut	

(continued)

131

CUTTING — CONTINUED				
FABRIC	**FIRST CUT**		**SECOND CUT**	
Color	No. of Pieces	Dimensions	No. of Pieces	Dimensions
Red prints— continued	36	2 × 8-inch strips	No second cut	
	36	2 × 6½-inch strips	No second cut	
	36	2 × 5-inch strips	No second cut	
	36	2 × 3½-inch strips	No second cut	
	36	2 × 2-inch squares	No second cut	
Assorted prints	**Logs**			
	36	2 × 14-inch strips	No second cut	
	36	2 × 12½-inch strips	No second cut	
	36	2 × 11-inch strips	No second cut	
	36	2 × 9½-inch strips	No second cut	
	36	2 × 8-inch strips	No second cut	
	36	2 × 6½-inch strips	No second cut	
	36	2 × 5-inch strips	No second cut	
	36	2 × 3½-inch strips	No second cut	
Black print	**Binding**			
	9	2¾ × 42-inch strips	No second cut	

Making the Blocks

You will be making 36 blocks, each with a gold print center square, eight strips of assorted red prints, and eight strips of assorted prints. Pay close attention to the color placement in the diagrams when piecing your blocks. For a scrappy look, try to avoid using the same fabric twice in the same block. Refer to "Assembly Line Piecing" on page 268. Use ¼-inch seams and press after each sewing step, following the direction of the arrows in the diagrams.

STEP 1. Sew one 2-inch red print square to each 2-inch gold print center square. See **Diagram 1**. Press.

DIAGRAM 1

STEP 2. Sew the 2 × 3½-inch red print strips to the units from Step 1, as shown in **Diagram 2**. Press.

DIAGRAM 2

STEP 3. Sew the units from Step 2 to the 3½ × 2-inch assorted print strips. See **Diagram 3**. Press.

DIAGRAM 3

STEP 4. Sew the units from Step 3 to the 2 × 5-inch assorted print strips. See **Diagram 4**. Press.

DIAGRAM 4

STEP 5. Sew the 5 × 2-inch red print strips to the units from Step 4, as shown in **Diagram 5**. Press.

DIAGRAM 5

STEP 6. Sew the 2 × 6½-inch red print strips to the units from Step 5. See **Diagram 6**. Press.

DIAGRAM 6

STEP 7. Sew the units from Step 6 to the 6½ × 2-inch assorted print strips. See **Diagram 7.** Press.

DIAGRAM 7

STEP 8. Sew the units from Step 7 to the 2 × 8-inch assorted print strips, as shown in **Diagram 8.** Press.

DIAGRAM 8

STEP 9. Sew the 8 × 2-inch red print strips to the units from Step 8. See **Diagram 9.** Press.

DIAGRAM 9

STEP 10. Sew the 2 × 9½-inch red print strips to the units from Step 9. See **Diagram 10.** Press.

DIAGRAM 10

STEP 11. Sew the units from Step 10 to the 9½ × 2-inch assorted print strips, as shown in **Diagram 11.** Press.

DIAGRAM 11

STEP 12. Sew the units from Step 11 to the 2 × 11-inch assorted print strips. See **Diagram 12.** Press.

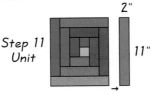

DIAGRAM 12

STEP 13. Sew the 11 × 2-inch red print strips to the units from Step 12. See **Diagram 13.** Press.

DIAGRAM 13

STEP 14. Sew the 2 × 12½-inch red print strips to the units from Step 13, as shown in **Diagram 14.** Press.

DIAGRAM 14

STEP 15. Sew the units from Step 14 to the 12½ × 2-inch assorted print strips. See **Diagram 15.** Press.

DIAGRAM 15

STEP 16. Sew the units from Step 15 to the 2 × 14-inch assorted print strips, as shown in **Diagram 16.** Press. Each Log Cabin block will now measure 14 inches square.

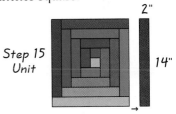

DIAGRAM 16

Assembling the Top

STEP 1. Referring to **Diagram 17** for placement, sew the blocks together in pairs to make 18 two-block units. Press the seams in one way in 9 units; press the seams in the opposite direction in the other 9 units.

DIAGRAM 17

STEP 2. Sew the two-block units from Step 1 together in pairs to make 9 four-block units. See **Diagram 18** on page 134. Press.

DIAGRAM 18

Make 3 rows
DIAGRAM 19

STEP 3. Sew the four-block units from Step 2 together to make three rows, as shown in **Diagram 19.** Press the seams in the middle row in the opposite direction of the seams in the top and bottom rows.

STEP 4. Sew the three rows from Step 3 together and press. The quilt top will now measure 81½ inches square.

Making the Backing

Cut the backing fabric into two 88-inch lengths and one 44-inch length. Remove the selvage edges from all pieces. Cut a 35-inch-wide segment from the entire length of each 88-inch piece. Cut two 20 × 44-inch segments from the 44-inch piece. Sew the two 20 × 44-inch pieces together to make one approximately 20 × 88-inch piece. Sew the pieces together, as shown in **Diagram 20.**

DIAGRAM 20

Layering the Quilt

Arrange and baste the backing, batting, and top together, following the directions in "Layering the Quilt" on page 275.

Finishing Stitches

Machine or hand quilt as desired. The quilt shown in the photo on page 130 was machine quilted in a large overall stipple pattern. Trim the batting and

backing to ¼ inch from the raw edges of the quilt top.

Binding the Quilt

Cut one 2¾ × 42-inch binding strip into four 2¾ × 10-inch strips. Sew one 2¾ × 10-inch binding strip and two 2¾ × 42-inch binding strips together in sets to make four binding strips approximately 2¾ × 94 inches each. Follow the directions for "Binding the Quilt" on pages 275–276.

QUILT LAYOUT

HEARTHSIDE GAMES

Nothing beats a fireside game of checkers and a mug of hot cider on a chilly night. This gameboard (shown on the next page) is a great way to use up scraps and makes a super gift. See the Checkers Storage Bag (page 138) to dye your own buttons for checkers and to make a storage bag. Stitch up quick and easy coordinating Coasters (directions on page 139).

Fireside Checkers Gameboard

Finished Size: 19 × 26 inches

MATERIALS

¼ yard tan print for checkerboard squares

Scrap, or 2½-inch square, *each* of 32 dark fabrics for checkerboard squares

⅜ yard black solid for accent border and binding

Scrap, or 3½ × 4-inch piece, *each* of 12 assorted fabrics for patchwork border

¾ yard fabric for backing

¾ yard lightweight batting

Scraps, or ⅛-yard pieces, of several coordinated fabrics for appliqué pieces

Lightweight, sewable fusible web

Embroidery floss

CUTTING

Prewash and press all of your fabrics. Using a rotary cutter, see-through ruler, and cutting mat, prepare the pieces as described below. Measurements for all pieces include ¼-inch seam allowances.

FABRIC	FIRST CUT		SECOND CUT	
Color	No. of Pieces	Dimensions	No. of Pieces	Dimensions
Tan print	**Checkerboard squares**			
	3	2½ × 42-inch strips	32	2½-inch squares
Dark fabrics	**Checkerboard squares**—from *each* of the 32 fabrics, cut the following:			
	1	2½-inch square	No second cut	

(continued)

135

WEEKENDER

CUTTING —continued				
FABRIC	**FIRST CUT**		**SECOND CUT**	
Color	No. of Pieces	Dimensions	No. of Pieces	Dimensions
Black solid	**Accent border**			
	2	1½ × 42-inch strips	2	1½ × 18½-inch strips
			2	1½ × 16½-inch strips
Binding fabric	**Binding**		Cut *1* strip into the following:	
	3	2¾ × 42-inch strips	2	2¾ × 21-inch strips
Assorted fabrics	**Patchwork border**—from *each* of the 12 fabrics, cut the following:			
	1	3½ × 4-inch piece	No second cut	

Assembly

STEP 1. Alternating the tan print and the dark fabrics, lay out the 2½-inch checkerboard squares in a pleasing arrangement of eight rows with eight squares each. Keep track of your layout while sewing the checkerboard together. Using ¼-inch seams, sew together each of the eight rows of eight squares. See **Diagram 1**. Press the seams toward the dark squares.

STEP 2. Sew the eight rows together to form a 16½-inch-square checkerboard, as shown in **Diagram 2**. Press the seams in one direction.

STEP 3. Sew the 1½ × 16½-inch accent border strips to the top and bottom of the checkerboard. Press the seams toward the accent border.

STEP 4. Sew the 1½ × 18½-inch accent border strips to the sides. Press.

STEP 5. Referring to the photo on the opposite page for placement, lay out the 3½ × 4-inch patchwork border pieces in a pleasing arrangement of two rows of six pieces each. Sew the pieces together to make two 18½ × 4-inch patchwork border strips. See **Diagram 3**. Press the seams in one direction.

STEP 6. Sew the 18½ × 4-inch patchwork border strips to the top and bottom. Press the seams toward the accent border.

Appliqué

The appliqué pieces were added to the patchwork border using the technique described in "Blanket Stitch Appliqué" on page 272. Use a lightweight, sewable fusible web.

STEP 1. Refer to "Quick-Fuse Appliqué" on pages 270–271. Trace six trees from the pattern on page 127 and six stars from the pattern on page 140.

STEP 2. Alternating trees and stars, position and fuse them in place. Be sure to allow for ¼-inch seams on the raw edges of the patchwork border.

DIAGRAM 1

DIAGRAM 2

DIAGRAM 3

STEP 3. Use two strands of embroidery floss to blanket stitch around the edges of the trees and stars.

Layering the Quilt

Arrange and baste the backing, batting, and top together, following the directions in "Layering the Quilt" on page 275. Trim the batting and backing to ¼ inch from the raw edges of the quilt top.

Binding the Quilt

Using the two 2¾ × 21-inch binding strips for the top and bottom and the two 2¾ × 42-inch binding strips for the sides, follow the directions for "Binding the Quilt" on pages 275–276.

Finishing Stitches

Machine or hand quilt in the seam lines of the borders. Outline the trees and stars by quilting ¹⁄₁₆ inch from the edges. Quilt diagonal lines through the checkerboard squares.

19"

26"

GAMEBOARD LAYOUT

Checkers Storage Bag

Finished Size of Bag: approximately 5 × 7 inches

(See the Checkers Storage Bag in the photo on page 136.)

Materials

12 *each* of 2 colors, or 24 light-color, 1⅜-inch plastic buttons
Rit dye (optional)

▪ 7¾ × 10½-inch piece of red print for storage bag

▫ 3½-inch square of gold print for appliqué star

Lightweight, sewable fusible web
Embroidery floss
15-inch-long piece of crochet thread
1⅜-inch buttons—12 *each* of 2 colors, or 24 light-color plastic buttons

Making the Bag

STEP 1. For checkers, use 12 each of two colors of buttons. Or create custom colors by dyeing light-color buttons with Rit dye. See "How to Dye Buttons" on the opposite page.

STEP 2. For the storage bag, make a narrow hem on one 10½-inch edge of the red print piece. Fold ¼ inch to the wrong side, fold another ¼ inch to the wrong side, and stitch along the folded edge.

STEP 3. Fold the bag in half with wrong sides together. Refer to "Quick-Fuse Appliqué" on pages 270–271. Trace one star from the appliqué pattern on page 140. Position and fuse the star to the bottom center of the bag. See **Diagram 4.** Use two strands of embroidery floss to blanket stitch around the edges of the star.

Hemmed edges

Fold

DIAGRAM 4

STORAGE BAG

STEP 4. Fold the bag in half with right sides together. Sew a ¼-inch seam on the bottom and on the edge opposite the fold. Trim the corners, turn the bag right side out, and press.

STEP 5. Use the crochet thread to make a drawstring. Starting above the star, sew a long running stitch 1 inch from the top of the bag.

How to Dye Buttons

Be sure to use an old saucepan, spoon, and strainer. Wear an old shirt or apron and rubber gloves.

STEP 1. Bring approximately 2 cups of water to a boil. Lower the heat and add small amounts of Rit dye to the water until the desired color is reached. Stir well.

STEP 2. Add light-color plastic buttons to the dye. Some buttons will dye very quickly while others may take up to 20 minutes. Stirring frequently, let the buttons simmer until the desired color is reached. If you need to add more dye, do so while stirring.

STEP 3. Remove the buttons and place them in a strainer. Rinse them thoroughly with cold water. Set them on a paper towel to dry.

Note: Be cautious when using dyed buttons on clothing or quilts because the dye may bleed when the buttons get wet.

Coasters

Finished Size: 4 inches square

(See the coasters in the photo on page 136.)

MATERIALS AND CUTTING

Prewash and press all of your fabrics. Using a rotary cutter, see-through ruler, and cutting mat, prepare the pieces as described below. Measurements for all pieces include ¼-inch seam allowances (to make 4 coasters).

FABRIC	YARDAGE	NO. OF PIECES	DIMENSIONS
Black print for center squares	⅛ yard	4	3½-inch squares
Assorted fabrics for patchwork border	⅛ yard *each* of 4 fabrics	1	1 × 40-inch strip *each*
Backing fabric	⅙ yard	4	4½-inch squares
Flannel for batting	⅙ yard	4	4½-inch squares
Several coordinated fabrics for appliqué stars	Scraps, or ⅛-yard pieces	—	—
Lightweight, sewable fusible web; embroidery floss			

Assembly

STEP 1. For the patchwork border, arrange the four 1 × 40-inch patchwork border strips in a pleasing order. Sew the strips together to make a 2½ × 40-inch strip set. Change sewing direction with each strip sewn, and press the seams in one direction. Cut this strip set in halves, approximately 20 inches each. See **Diagram 5**.

DIAGRAM 5

STEP 2. Resew the halves together to make a 4½ × 20-inch strip set. Using a rotary cutter and ruler, cut sixteen 1 × 4½-inch strips from this strip set. There should be eight squares in each strip. See **Diagram 6**.

DIAGRAM 6

STEP 3. For the top and bottom, use a seam ripper to remove two squares each from eight 1 × 4½-inch patchwork border strips to make eight strips with six squares each. Pin and sew the 1 × 3½-inch patchwork border strips to the tops and bottoms of the four

3½-inch black print center squares. See **Diagram 7**. Press the seams toward the center square.

DIAGRAM 7

STEP 4. Pin and sew the remaining eight 1 × 4½-inch patchwork border strips to the sides, as shown in **Diagram 8**. Press.

DIAGRAM 8

Appliqué

The stars were added to the center squares using the technique described in "Blanket Stitch Appliqué" on page 272. You can machine appliqué with either a satin stitch or blanket stitch if you prefer. Refer to "Machine Appliqué" on pages 271–272. Be sure to use a lightweight, sewable fusible web for all of these techniques.

STEP 1. Refer to "Quick-Fuse Appliqué" on pages 270–271. Trace four stars from the appliqué pattern below.

STEP 2. Position and fuse the stars to the center squares.

STEP 3. Use two strands of embroidery floss to blanket stitch around the edges of the stars.

Finishing

For each coaster, position the top and backing with right sides together. Lay both pieces on top of the flannel and pin all three layers together. Using ¼-inch seams, sew around the edges, leaving a 3-inch opening for turning. Trim the corners, turn the coaster right side out, hand stitch the opening closed, and press.

COASTER LAYOUT

STAR PATTERN

140

SNOWMAN BRIGADE

When it snows, make snowmen! Better yet, make the fun projects shown on the next page before it snows, and you'll be ahead of the game and ready for instant decorating. Hang the Snowfall Friends Banner next to the fireplace, and don't worry about meltdown. The irresistible three-dimensional Snow Buddies (directions on page 145) are made from batting and other scraps that you probably have on hand.

Snowfall Friends Banner

Finished Size: 14 × 30 inches

MATERIALS AND CUTTING			
Prewash and press all of your fabrics. Using a rotary cutter, see-through ruler, and cutting mat, prepare the pieces as described below. Measurements for all pieces include ¼-inch seam allowances.			
FABRIC	**YARDAGE**	**NO. OF PIECES**	**DIMENSIONS**
Black prints for background	¼ yard *each* of 3 fabrics	1	7½-inch square *each*
Assorted fabrics for patchwork lattice	⅛ yard *each* of 8 fabrics	1	1½ × 18-inch strip *each*
Black star print for border	¼ yard	2 2	2½ × 29½-inch strips 2½ × 9½-inch strips

(continued)

MATERIALS AND CUTTING—continued

FABRIC	YARDAGE	NO. OF PIECES	DIMENSIONS
☐ Gold print for binding	¼ yard	2	2¾ × 42-inch strips
		2	2¾ × 21-inch strips
Backing fabric	½ yard	—	—
Lightweight batting	½ yard	—	—
Several coordinated fabrics for appliqué pieces	Scraps, or ⅛-yard pieces	—	—
Fusible web; embroidery floss; permanent fine-point felt pen; assorted buttons; ceramic buttons (optional). (See "Quilting by Mail" on page 280 for information on ordering ceramic buttons.)			

Assembling the Background

Assemble the banner top before adding the appliqué pieces. Be sure to use ¼-inch seams and to press after each sewing step.

STEP 1. For the patchwork lattice, arrange the eight 1½ × 18-inch patchwork lattice strips in a pleasing order. Sew the strips together to make an 8½ × 18-inch strip set. Change sewing direction with each strip sewn, and press the seams in one direction. Using a rotary cutter and ruler, cut ten 1½ × 8½-inch strips from this strip set. There should be 8 squares in each strip. See **Diagram 1**.

8½"

1½"

18"

DIAGRAM 1

STEP 2. For the horizontal lattice strips, use a seam ripper to remove 1 square each from four 1½ × 8½-inch lattice strips to make four 1½ × 7½-inch lattice strips. There should be 7 squares in each strip. Set aside 2 squares for use in Step 3.

STEP 3. For the vertical lattice strips, sew two sets of three 1½ × 8½-inch lattice strips and one 1½-inch square removed in Step 2 to make two 1½ × 25½-inch lattice strips. There should be 25 squares in each strip. See **Diagram 2**.

Scrappy Lattice

If the patchwork lattice looks too orderly or planned and you want to maintain a random appearance, use a seam ripper to separate and rearrange the squares in the horizontal lattice strips. Then resew them together. It is easier to rearrange the horizontal strips than the vertical strips.

1½"

8½"

8½"

8½"

1½"

DIAGRAM 2

STEP 4. Lay out your lattice strips and black print background squares in a pleasing arrangement.

Keep track of your layout while sewing on the lattice strips.

STEP 5. Pin and sew one 1½ × 7½-inch horizontal lattice strip to the top of each 7½-inch black print background square and to the bottom of the bottom square. Press the seams toward the background squares. Join the blocks and press.

STEP 6. Compare the 1½ × 25½-inch vertical lattice strips to the sides. You may need to take in or let out a few seams (⅛ inch or less) to make them fit. Pin and sew the lattice strips to the sides. Press the seams toward the background squares.

STEP 7. Sew the 2½ × 9½-inch border strips to the top and bottom. Press the seams toward the border.

STEP 8. Sew the 2½ × 29½-inch border strips to the sides. Press.

Appliqué

STEP 1. Refer to "Quick-Fuse Appliqué" on pages 270–271. Trace the snowmen and other shapes from the appliqué patterns on pages 146–148.

STEP 2. Position and fuse one design at a time to the center of its corresponding background square. Refer to the photo on page 142 for placement. Note that you have the option of using ceramic buttons for some of the fusible shapes. Buttons should be sewn on after the banner has been quilted.

STEP 3. To embroider the tree trunk, use six strands of embroi-dery floss to stem stitch three rows of stitching very close together. Use two strands of embroidery floss to stem stitch the branches on the tree and the holly vine on the bird-house. See "Decorative Stitches" on page 272.

STEP 4. Use a permanent felt pen to draw design details such as eyes and mouths.

Layering the Banner

Arrange and baste the backing, batting, and top together, following the directions in "Layering the Quilt" on page 275. Trim the batting and backing to ¼ inch from the raw edges of the banner top.

Binding the Banner

Using the two 2¾ × 21-inch binding strips for the top and bottom and the two 2¾ × 42-inch binding strips for the sides, follow the directions for "Binding the Quilt" on pages 275–277.

Finishing Stitches

Machine or hand quilt in the seam lines of the backgrounds, patchwork lattice, and border. Outline the appliqué designs by quilting ⅛ inch from the edges. Quilt a 1¼-inch diagonal grid in the border. Sew assorted buttons to the banner, referring to the appliqué patterns on pages 146–148 for placement.

14"

30"

BANNER LAYOUT

Snow Buddies

Height of Large Snowman: 12 inches
Height of Small Snowman: 10 inches

(See the three-dimensional snowmen in the photo on page 142.)

Materials

To make 1 snowman:

⅓ yard cotton batting
Polyester fiberfill stuffing
1½ cups plastic pellet bean-bag fill
8½-inch square of ribbing
  for hat
Glue gun and glue sticks
5 × 29-inch strip of wool or
  brushed cotton for scarf (for
  small snowman)
Tacky glue
Assorted buttons
⅛ yard wool or flannel for vest (for
  large snowman)
Twigs for arms

Assembly

STEP 1. To make the snowman, use the body pattern on pages 149–150 and the base pattern on page 147. Cut out two bodies and one base from the cotton batting.

STEP 2. With right sides together, pin and sew around the body,

Make a Wreath

Arrange and attach a few pinecones and Snow Buddies to a wreath.

using ¼-inch seam allowances. Leave the armholes open as marked and the bottom edge open between the dots. Clip the curves and turn the body right side out.

STEP 3. Stuff the body with the polyester fiberfill to desired firmness, leaving 1 inch unstuffed for the plastic pellets.

STEP 4. Pin and sew the base to the body with wrong sides together, leaving a 2-inch opening. Add the plastic pellets, and sew the opening closed.

STEP 5. To make the hat, fold the square of ribbing in half, and sew a ¼-inch seam on the edge opposite the fold. Turn the ribbing right side out. Gather one raw edge tightly ¼ inch from the edge, and tie a knot. Turn the remaining raw edge up twice. Use the glue gun to glue the hat to the snowman.

STEP 6. To make the scarf for the small snowman, tie the strip of wool or brushed cotton around the neck, trim the ends to the desired length, and fray them.

STEP 7. Glue face details in place with tacky glue. Glue buttons to the front of the snowman.

STEP 8. To make the vest for the large snowman, use the vest patterns on page 151. Cut out two vest front pieces and one vest back piece from the wool or flannel. Sew the front pieces to the back at the sides, leaving an opening for each twig arm as marked.

STEP 9. To add twig arms, put tacky glue on one end of each twig, and insert the twigs through the holes in the seams on both sides of the body.

Just for Fun

Try using an old sock or sweater cuff instead of ribbing for the hat. Decorate the hat with fused patches, buttons, or small sprigs of greenery. Create a bow tie or neck tie out of fabric, and add it to the snowman, too.

For the face details, make a carrot nose and little chunks of coal, using a colorful modeling compound such as FIMO or Sculpey. Bake the shapes according to the manufacturer's directions, and glue them in place with tacky glue.

APPLIQUÉ PATTERN KEY

——————— Tracing line

- - - - - - Tracing line
(will be hidden behind
other fabric)

Button

Button

Button

Button

Button

Button

Stitching line

SNOWMAN #1 PATTERN

BASE PATTERNS FOR 3-D SNOWMEN

Small snowman

Large snowman

Button

Button

SNOWMAN #2 PATTERN

SNOWMAN #3 PATTERN

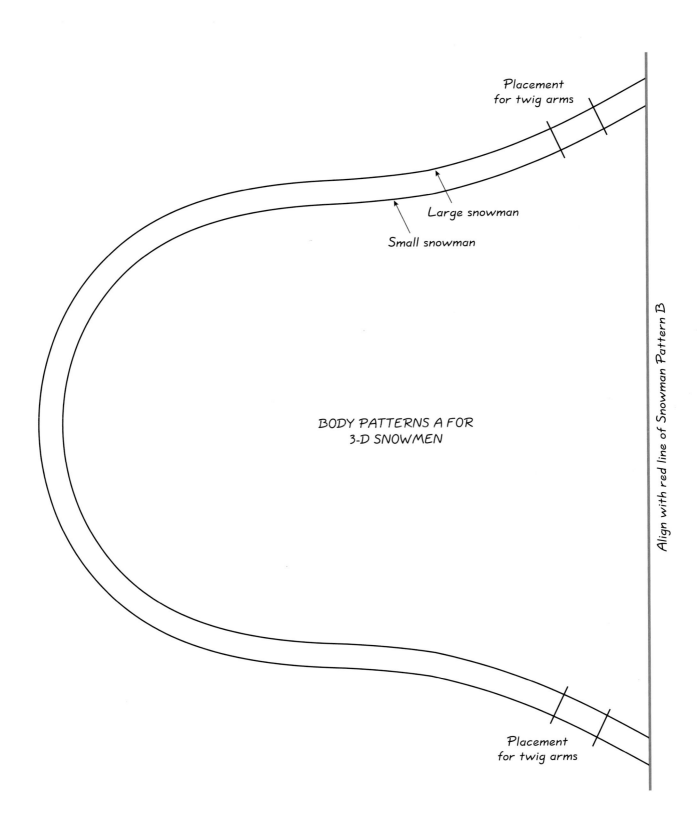

Placement
for twig arms

Large snowman

Small snowman

Align with red line of Snowman Pattern B

BODY PATTERNS A FOR
3-D SNOWMEN

Placement
for twig arms

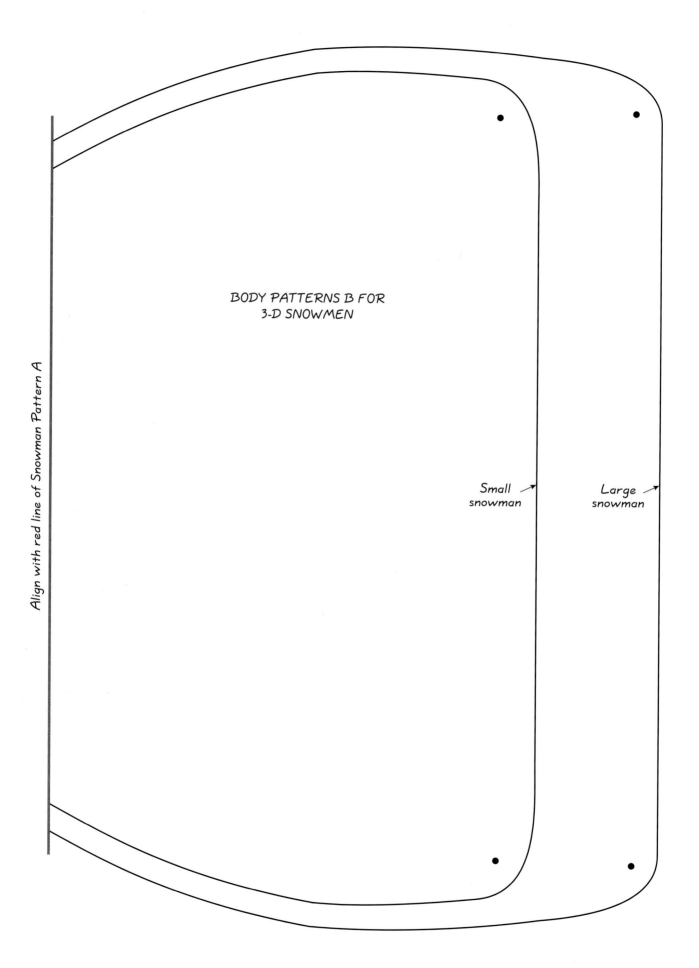

BODY PATTERNS B FOR
3-D SNOWMEN

Small
snowman

Large
snowman

Align with red line of Snowman Pattern A

VEST FRONT PATTERN FOR
LARGE SNOWMAN

Cut 2

Leave open
for twig arms

Arrow indicates straight of grain

VEST BACK PATTERN FOR
LARGE SNOWMAN

Cut 1

Leave open
for twig arms

Place on fold

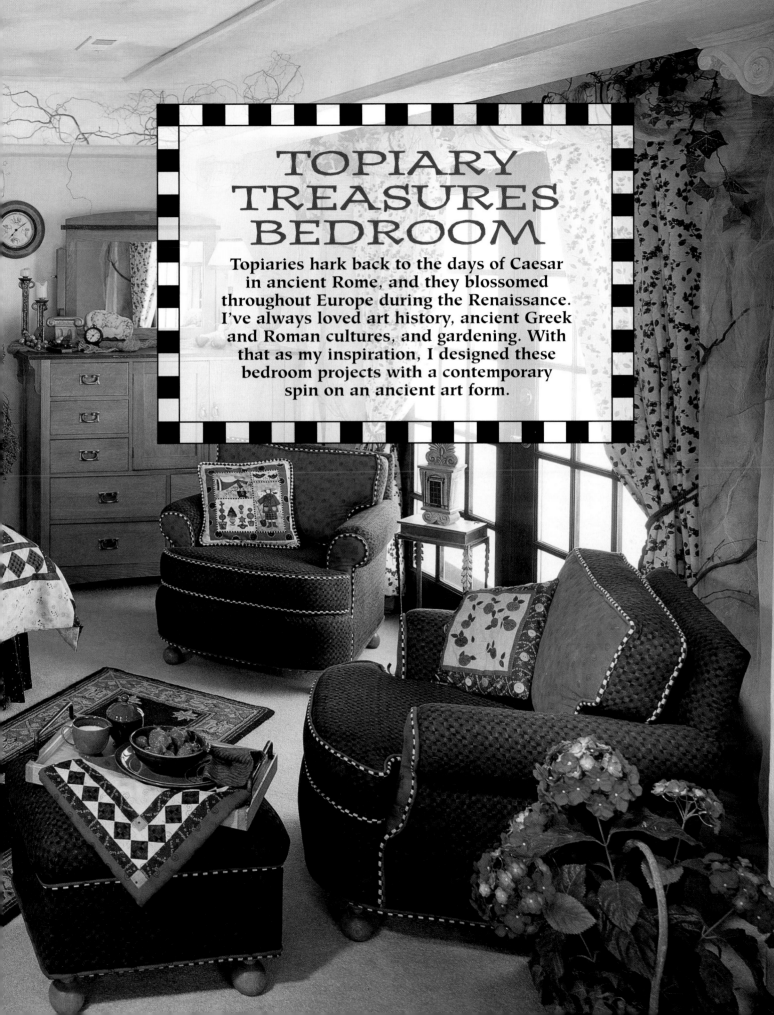

TOPIARY TREASURES BEDROOM

Topiaries hark back to the days of Caesar in ancient Rome, and they blossomed throughout Europe during the Renaissance. I've always loved art history, ancient Greek and Roman cultures, and gardening. With that as my inspiration, I designed these bedroom projects with a contemporary spin on an ancient art form.

TOPIARY TREASURES

With this inviting duvet cover, you'll imagine yourself strolling

through the gardens of a country estate in ancient Rome or an elegant English

manor house of the seventeenth century. Cypress, boxwood, and rosemary were

clipped into various shapes, from smooth balls and cones to spirals, pyramids,

and animals. I've put my topiaries in pots with coordinating vines and bows.

Ruffled pillow shams (directions on page 165) and assorted throw pillows (page

187) will beckon you to kick back and dream your own garden fantasy.

King-Size Duvet Cover

Finished Size: 100 inches square   **Finished Block: 10 × 14 inches**

MATERIALS

The king-size duvet cover is shown in the photo. To make the queen-size version, see page 160. Since there are often size variations in king-size duvets, you may have to adjust the borders of your cover to fit the size of your duvet.

(Obvious directional prints are not recommended.)

6⅛ yards tan print for block and lattice backgrounds

2 yards green print for 1-inch block and outer borders

3 yards red-and-black check for lattice squares

⅝ yard black print for lattice corner squares

2⅛ yards tan floral print for border

¼ yard black print for border corner squares

⅜ yard *each* of 2 green prints for appliqué topiary circles

¼ yard *each* of 2 black prints for appliqué pots

Scraps, or ⅛-yard pieces, of several coordinated fabrics for small appliqué pieces

9½ yards fabric for backing

4½ yards lightweight, sewable fusible web

Thread to match appliqué pieces

3½ yards Tear-Away fabric stabilizer

Ten 1-inch buttons

CUTTING

Prewash and press all of your fabrics. Using a rotary cutter, see-through ruler, and cutting mat, prepare the pieces as described below. Measurements for all pieces include ¼-inch seam allowances.

FABRIC	FIRST CUT		SECOND CUT	
Color	No. of Pieces	Dimensions	No. of Pieces	Dimensions
Tan print	**Block background**			
	7	14½ × 42-inch strips	20	10½ × 14½-inch pieces
	Lattice background			
	43	2½ × 42-inch strips	684	2½-inch squares
Green print	**1-inch block border**			
	34	1½ × 42-inch strips	40	1½ × 10½-inch strips
			40	1½ × 16½-inch strips
	1-inch outer border		Cut 1 strip into the following:	
	9	1½ × 42-inch strips	4	1½ × 10-inch (approximate) strips
Red-and-black check	**Lattice squares**			
	22	4½ × 42-inch strips	171	4½-inch squares
Black print	**Lattice corner squares**			
	4	4½ × 42-inch strips	30	4½-inch squares
Tan floral print	**Border**		Cut 1 strip into the following:	
	9	7½ × 42-inch strips	4	7½ × 10-inch (approximate) strips
Black print	**Border corner squares**			
	1	7½ × 42-inch strip	4	7½-inch squares

Block Borders

STEP 1. Sew the 1½ × 10½-inch green print block border strips to the tops and bottoms of the twenty 10½ × 14½-inch tan print block background pieces. Press the seams toward the border.

STEP 2. Sew the 1½ × 16½-inch green print block border strips to the sides. Press.

Appliqué

The topiaries were added to the background pieces using the technique described in "Machine Appliqué" on pages 271–272. I used a machine blanket stitch, but you can use a machine satin stitch if you prefer. Be sure to use a lightweight, sewable fusible web.

STEP 1. Refer to "Quick-Fuse Appliqué" on pages 270–271. Trace ten topiaries with bows and ten topiaries with vines from the appliqué patterns on pages 162–164.

STEP 2. Position and fuse the topiaries to the background pieces, referring to the **King-Size Duvet Cover Layout** on page 159 for placement.

STEP 3. Stitch around the edges of the topiaries with a machine blanket stitch. Use the Tear-Away fabric stabilizer on the wrong side of the background pieces for an even machine stitch. Remove the stabilizer after stitching.

Piecing the Lattice

You will be making 171 lattice blocks. Refer to "Making Quick Corner Triangles" on page 269 for instructions on making the corner triangle units, and review "Assembly Line Piecing" on page 268. Press the seams toward the triangle just added.

STEP 1. Sew two 2½-inch tan print lattice background squares to each of the 4½-inch red-and-black check lattice squares. See **Diagram 1**. Press.

DIAGRAM 1

STEP 2. Sew two additional 2½-inch tan print lattice background squares to the units from Step 1. See **Diagram 2**. Press.

DIAGRAM 2

STEP 3. Using ¼-inch seams, sew 75 units from Step 2 together, as shown in **Diagram 3**, to make 25 units with three squares each. Press the seams, following the arrows in the diagram. Each of these units will now measure 4½ × 12½ inches. Compare the lattice units to the tops and bottoms of the topiary blocks. You may need to take in or let out a few seams (¹⁄₁₆ inch or less) to make them fit.

Make 25 units for king-size
Make 20 units for queen-size
DIAGRAM 3

Make It Reversible!

Purchase a fabulous fabric that you love for the backing of your Topiary Treasures Duvet Cover, and the cover will be reversible.

STEP 4. Sew the remaining 96 units from Step 2 together, as shown in **Diagram 4**, to make 24 units with four squares each. Press. Each of these units will now measure 4½ × 16½ inches. Compare the lattice units to the sides of the topiary blocks, and adjust as necessary.

Make 24 units for king-size
Make 20 units for queen-size
DIAGRAM 4

Assembling the Top

STEP 1. Referring to the **King-Size Duvet Cover Layout** on page 159 for placement, arrange the topiary blocks and lattice units in their proper positions. Keep track of your layout while sewing the blocks and lattice together.

STEP 2. For Rows #1 and #3, sew 4½ × 16½-inch lattice units and

topiary blocks together in the order shown in **Diagram 5** on the following page. These rows will begin and end with bow blocks. Press the seams toward the blocks.

STEP 3. For Rows #2 and #4, sew 4½ × 16½-inch lattice units and topiary blocks together as in Step 2, but these rows will begin and end with vine blocks. Press the seams toward the blocks.

STEP 4. Sew the 4½-inch black print lattice corner squares and the 4½ × 12½-inch lattice units together, as shown in **Diagram 6** on the following page, to make five rows. Press the seams toward the lattice corner squares.

STEP 5. Sew the lattice rows from Step 4 and the rows of blocks from Steps 2 and 3 together. Press the seams toward the blocks.

Adding Borders

STEP 1. Sew the eight 1½ × 42-inch green print outer border strips together in pairs to make four strips approximately 1½ × 84 inches each. Press the seams to one side. Sew one 1½ × 10-inch green print outer border strip to one end of each 1½ × 84-inch outer border strip, and press.

STEP 2. Pin and sew one outer border strip on to the top and bottom of the duvet cover. Trim the excess length, and press the seams toward the outer border.

STEP 3. Pin and sew the remaining outer border strips to the sides. Trim the excess length and press.

ROWS 1 AND 3

Four-square lattice unit

4¹/₂"

Note: for queen-size omit this block and lattice strip

16¹/₂"

16¹/₂"

DIAGRAM 5

Note: for queen-size omit this lattice strip and lattice corner block

Three-square lattice unit

4¹/₂"

12¹/₂"   4¹/₂"

4¹/₂"

DIAGRAM 6

STEP 4. Sew the eight 7½ × 42-inch tan floral print border strips together in pairs to make four strips approximately 7½ × 84 inches each. Press. Sew one 7½ × 10-inch tan floral print border strip to one end of each 7½ × 84-inch border strip. Press the seams to one side. Measure the outer edges of the duvet cover. Trim the border strips to these measurements.

STEP 5. Pin and sew one border strip to the top and one to the bottom of the duvet cover. Press the seams toward the border.

STEP 6. Sew one 7½-inch black print border corner square to each end of the two remaining border strips. Press the seams toward the border. Pin and sew the border strips to the sides. Press.

Adding the Backing

STEP 1. Cut the backing fabric into three equal lengths, about 110

inches each. Trim the selvage edges off all three pieces.

STEP 2. With right sides together, sew two backing pieces together lengthwise to make one piece approximately 80 × 110 inches. Press. Fold and press ¼ inch to the wrong side along one long edge. Fold again 1 inch to the wrong side. Press. Topstitch along the folded edge to make a hem.

STEP 3. Fold and press ¼ inch to the wrong side along one long edge of the remaining backing piece. Fold again 3 inches to the wrong side. Press. Topstitch along the folded edge to make a hem. Mark placement and make ten vertical buttonholes on the hemmed edge. The first and last buttonholes are spaced 13 inches from the sides, and the remaining eight buttonholes are spaced approximately 9 inches apart.

STEP 4. Position the top and backing piece from Step 3 with right sides together. Center the top

on the backing so that an equal amount of backing extends on each side. The backing will extend beyond the top edge of the duvet cover top by approximately 5 inches. See **Diagram 7.** Pin the two layers together. Using ¼-inch seams, sew around the sides and top edge of the duvet cover where the top is pinned to the backing. Trim the backing to the same size as the top.

Backing piece from Step 3
110"

5"

Duvet cover top
wrong side up

DIAGRAM 7

STEP 5. Position the top and backing piece from Step 2 with right sides together, and pin them in place. The hemmed edge of this

Queen-size does not
include this vertical row
of blocks and lattice units

100"

100"

KING-SIZE DUVET COVER LAYOUT

backing piece will overlap by 3 inches the hemmed edge of the backing piece already sewn to the top. Center the top on the backing so that an equal amount extends on each side. See **Diagram 8**. Pin the two layers together. Using ¼-inch seams, sew around the sides and bottom of the duvet

cover. Trim the backing to the same size as the top. Trim the corners, turn the duvet cover right side out, and press.

STEP 6. Mark placement of the buttons on the bottom backing piece, and sew the buttons in place. Insert your duvet inside the cover.

3"   3"

Duvet cover top
wrong side up

Backing piece from Step 2
DIAGRAM 8

Queen-Size Duvet Cover

Finished Size: 84 × 100 inches

Finished Block: 10 × 14 inches

MATERIALS

(Obvious directional prints are not recommended.)

5¼ yards tan print for block and lattice backgrounds

1¾ yards green print for 1-inch block and outer borders

2½ yards red-and-black check for lattice squares

⅝ yard black print for lattice corner squares

2⅛ yards tan floral print for border

¼ yard black print for border corner squares

⅜ yard *each* of 2 green prints for appliqué topiary circles

¼ yard *each* of 2 black prints for appliqué pots

Scraps, or ⅛-yard pieces, of several coordinated fabrics for small appliqué pieces

8 yards fabric for backing

4 yards lightweight, sewable fusible web

Thread to match appliqué pieces

2½ yards Tear-Away fabric stabilizer

Ten 1-inch buttons

CUTTING

Prewash and press all of your fabrics. Using a rotary cutter, see-through ruler, and cutting mat, prepare the pieces as described below. Measurements for all pieces include ¼-inch seam allowances.

FABRIC	FIRST CUT		SECOND CUT	
Color	No. of Pieces	Dimensions	No. of Pieces	Dimensions
Tan print	**Block background**			
	6	14½ × 42-inch strips	16	10½ × 14½-inch pieces
	Lattice background			
	35	2½ × 42-inch strips	560	2½-inch squares
Green print	**1-inch block border**			
	27	1½ × 42-inch strips	32	1½ × 10½-inch strips
			32	1½ × 16½-inch strips
	1-inch outer border		Cut *1* strip into the following:	
	9	1½ × 42-inch strips	2	1½ × 11-inch strips
Red-and-black check	**Lattice squares**			
	18	4½ × 42-inch strips	140	4½-inch squares

FABRIC	FIRST CUT		SECOND CUT	
Color	No. of Pieces	Dimensions	No. of Pieces	Dimensions
Black print	**Lattice corner squares**			
	4	4½ × 42-inch strips	25	4½-inch squares
Tan floral print	**Border**		Cut *1* strip into the following:	
	9	7½ × 42-inch strips	2	7½ × 11-inch strips
Black print	**Border corner squares**			
	1	7½ × 42-inch strip	4	7½-inch squares

Block Borders

Refer to "Block Borders" on page 156 for instructions. Follow the directions in Steps 1 and 2 to make 16 background blocks with borders.

Appliqué

Refer to "Appliqué" on page 156 for instructions. Follow the directions in Steps 1 through 3 to add topiaries with bows to eight of the background blocks and to add topiaries with vines to the remaining eight background blocks. Use the appliqué patterns on pages 162–164.

Piecing the Lattice

Follow the instructions under "Piecing the Lattice" on page 157. You will be making 140 lattice blocks. The lattice blocks will be sewn together to make 20 lattice units of three squares each and 20 lattice units of four squares each.

Assembling the Top

Refer to Steps 1 through 5 under "Assembling the Top" on page 157. Referring to the **King-Size** Duvet Cover Layout on page 159 for placement, arrange the topiary blocks and lattice units in their proper positions. You will have four rows of four topiary blocks with lattice units between each block. Keep track of your layout while sewing the blocks and lattice together.

Adding Borders

Refer to "Adding Borders" on page 157 for instructions. You will be sewing an additional 11-inch green print outer border strip to just two of the 84-inch strips. The shorter strips will be sewn to the top and bottom of the duvet cover.

For the tan floral print border, the outer measurements will be different for the top and bottom and the sides. Trim the strips to match the dimensions of the pieced top.

Adding the Backing

STEP 1. Cut the backing fabric into three equal lengths, approximately 96 inches each. Trim the selvage edges off all three pieces.

STEP 2. With right sides together, sew two backing pieces together lengthwise to make one piece, approximately 80 × 96 inches. Press. Fold and press ¼ inch to the wrong side along one long edge. Fold again 1 inch to the wrong side. Press. Topstitch along the folded edge to make a hem.

STEP 3. Fold and press ¼ inch to the wrong side along one long edge of the remaining backing piece. Fold again 3 inches to the wrong side. Press. Topstitch along the folded edge to make a hem. Mark placement and make ten buttonholes on the hemmed edge. The first and last buttonholes are spaced 12 inches from the sides, and the remaining eight buttonholes are spaced approximately 7½ inches apart.

STEP 4. Follow Steps 4 through 6 under "Adding the Backing" on page 158 to complete the duvet cover.

APPLIQUÉ PATTERN KEY

———— Tracing line

------ Tracing line
(will be hidden behind
other fabric)

Match
with
Topiary
Circle
Pattern

TOPIARY WITH VINE PATTERN

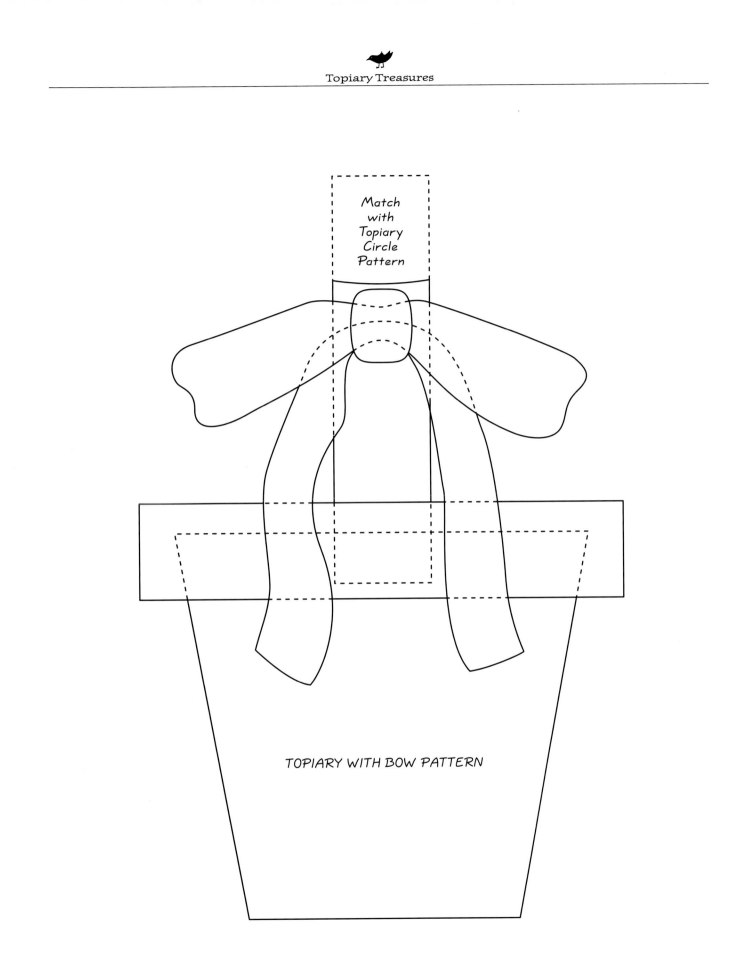

Match
with
Topiary
Circle
Pattern

TOPIARY WITH BOW PATTERN

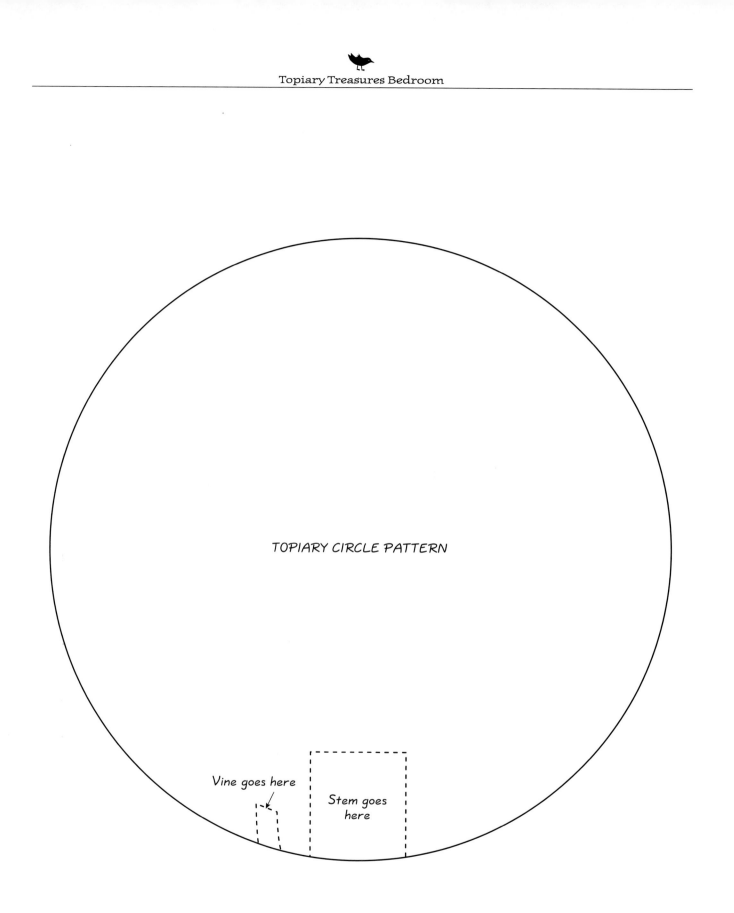

TOPIARY CIRCLE PATTERN

Vine goes here

Stem goes here

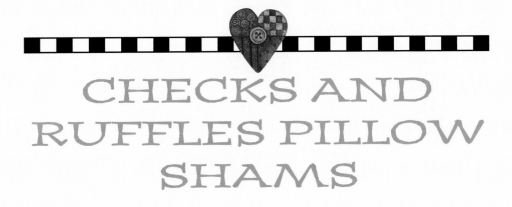

CHECKS AND RUFFLES PILLOW SHAMS

Echoing the square-in-square blocks in the lattice of the

Topiary Treasures duvet cover, the ruffled pillow shams on the following page

are the perfect complement to the coordinated ensemble (directions on page

167). You'll be stylishly ready for quiet bedtime reading or a morning

breakfast in bed. These instructions are written to make three

pillow shams to fit on a king-size bed.

Finished Size: 40 × 32 inches (including ruffle)

MATERIALS

(Obvious directional prints are not recommended.)

To make 3 pillow shams:

 ¼ yard gold print for center

½ yard dark tan print for small triangles

⅞ yard green print for small diamonds and accent border

1 yard tan print for large triangles

⅞ yard red-and-black check for large diamonds

⅛ yard red print for small corner squares

½ yard tan floral print for border

⅓ yard black print for large corner squares

4¾ yards black-and-tan check for ruffle

2¾ yards fabric for backing

Strong crochet thread or #5 pearl cotton

CUTTING

Prewash and press all of your fabrics. Using a rotary cutter, see-through ruler, and cutting mat, prepare the pieces as described below. Measurements for all pieces include ¼-inch seam allowances.

FABRIC	FIRST CUT		SECOND CUT	
Color	No. of Pieces	Dimensions	No. of Pieces	Dimensions
Gold print	**Center**			
	1	4½ × 42-inch strip	3	4½ × 12½-inch pieces
Dark tan print	**Small triangles**			
	8	1½ × 42-inch strips	192	1½-inch squares
Green print	**Small diamonds**			
	3	2½ × 42-inch strips	48	2½-inch squares
	Accent border			
	12	1½ × 42-inch strips	No second cut	
Tan print	**Large triangles**			
	12	2½ × 42-inch strips	192	2½-inch squares
Red-and-black check	**Large diamonds**			
	6	4½ × 42-inch strips	48	4½-inch squares
Red print	**Small corner squares**			
	1	2½ × 42-inch strip	12	2½-inch squares
Tan floral print	**Border**			
	5	2½ × 42-inch strips	6	2½ × 16½-inch strips
			6	2½ × 12½-inch strips
Black print	**Large corner squares**			
	2	4½ × 42-inch strips	12	4½-inch squares
Black-and-tan check	**Ruffle**			
	15	11 × 42-inch strips	No second cut	
Backing fabric	6	15 × 32-inch pieces	No second cut	

Quick Corner Triangles

You will be making three pillow shams. Refer to "Making Quick Corner Triangles" on page 269 and "Assembly Line Piecing" on page 268. Press the seams toward the triangle just added.

STEP 1. Sew two 1½-inch dark tan print squares to each of the forty-eight 2½-inch green print squares. See **Diagram 1**. Press.

DIAGRAM 1

STEP 2. Sew two additional 1½-inch dark tan print squares to the units from Step 1. See **Diagram 2**. Press.

DIAGRAM 2

STEP 3. Sew two 2½-inch tan print squares to each of the forty-eight 4½-inch red-and-black check squares. Refer to **Diagram 3**. Press.

4½"

4½"

DIAGRAM 3

STEP 4. Sew two additional 2½-inch tan print squares to the units from Step 3, as shown in **Diagram 4**. Press.

4½"

4½"

DIAGRAM 4

Assembly

Use ¼-inch seams and press after each sewing step. Follow the arrows in the diagrams for pressing directions.

STEP 1. Sew thirty-six 2½-inch dark tan/green corner triangle units together, as shown in **Diagram 5**, to make six units of six squares each. Press. Each unit will now measure 2½ × 12½ inches.

2½"

2½"

DIAGRAM 5

STEP 2. Compare the units from Step 1 to the tops and bottoms of the 4½ × 12½-inch gold print center pieces. You may need to take in or let out a few seams (¹⁄₁₆ inch or less) to make them fit.

Sew the three 4½ × 12½-inch gold print center pieces between the six units from Step 1. See **Diagram 6**. Press.

12½"

Step 1 Units

4½"

DIAGRAM 6

STEP 3. Sew the remaining twelve 2½-inch dark tan/green corner triangle units together in pairs to make six 2½ × 4½-inch units of two squares each. See **Diagram 7**. Press.

2½"

2½"

Make 6

DIAGRAM 7

STEP 4. Sew the six units from Step 3 between the twelve 2½-inch red print corner squares, as shown in **Diagram 8**. Press.

2½"

2½"

Step 3 Unit

2½"

Make 6

DIAGRAM 8

STEP 5. Sew the three units from Step 2 between the six units from Step 4. See **Diagram 9**. Press.

Step 4 Unit

Step 2 Unit

Step 4 Unit

DIAGRAM 9

STEP 6. Sew the three units from Step 5 between the six 2½ × 16½-inch tan floral border strips. See **Diagram 10**. Press.

16½"

2½"

Step 5 Unit

2½"

DIAGRAM 10

STEP 7. Sew the three units from Step 6 between the six 2½ × 12½-inch tan floral border strips. See **Diagram 11** on the following page. Press.

STEP 8. Sew thirty 4½-inch tan/red-and-black corner triangle units together, as shown in **Diagram 12** on the following page, to make six units of five squares each. Press. Each unit will now measure 4½ × 20½ inches.

STEP 9. Fit, pin, and sew the three units from Step 7 between the six units from Step 8. See **Diagram 13** on the following page. Press.

STEP 10. Sew the remaining eighteen 4½-inch tan/red-and-black corner triangle units together, as shown in **Diagram 14** on the following page, to make six units of three squares each. Press. Each unit will now measure 4½ × 12½ inches.

STEP 11. Sew the six units from Step 10 between the twelve 4½-inch black print corner squares. See **Diagram 15** on the following page. Press.

DIAGRAM 11

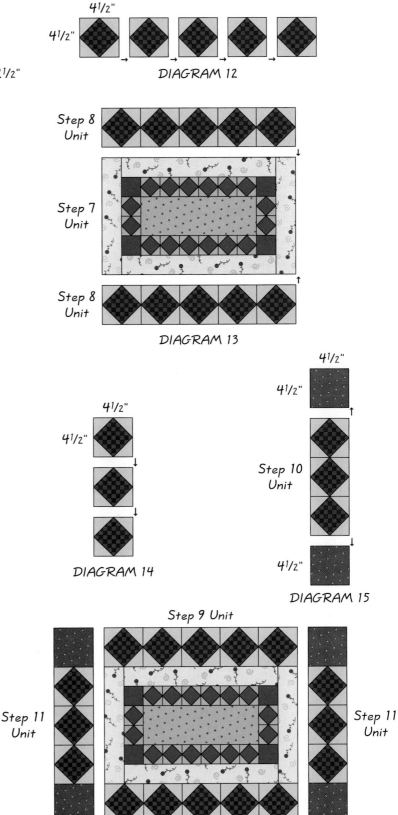

DIAGRAM 12

DIAGRAM 13

DIAGRAM 14

DIAGRAM 15

DIAGRAM 16

STEP 12. Sew the three units from Step 9 between the six units from Step 11. See **Diagram 16.** Press. The pillow tops will now measure 28½ × 20½ inches.

STEP 13. Sew one 1½ × 42-inch accent border strip each to the top and bottom of each unit from Step 12. Trim the excess length of the accent border, and press the seams toward the accent border.

STEP 14. Sew the remaining 1½ × 42-inch accent border strips to the sides of each unit from Step 13. Trim the excess length and press.

Ruffles and Backings

STEP 1. With right sides together, sew the short edges of five 11 × 42-inch black-and-tan check ruffle strips together to make a continuous loop. Press the ruffle in half lengthwise with wrong sides together. Repeat with the remaining ten strips to make two more ruffles.

STEP 2. Sew a gathering stitch along the raw edge of each ruffle by zigzag stitching over the crochet thread or pearl cotton. Divide each ruffle into quarters, and mark.

STEP 3. Measure the pillow sham, and mark the center on the raw edge of each of the four sides.

STEP 4. With right sides together and matching the marks, position and pin a ruffle on each pillow sham top. Gather each ruffle by pulling the gathering cord. Evenly distribute the gathers as you pin the ruffles to the sham tops. Hand baste the ruffles to the sham tops. The ruffles will be sewn in place when the backings are added.

STEP 5. Narrow hem one long edge of each 15 × 32-inch backing piece by folding under ¼ inch to the wrong side. Press. Fold again ¼ inch to the wrong side. Press. Topstitch along the folded edge.

STEP 6. With right sides up, lay one backing piece over the second piece so that the hemmed edges overlap 3 inches. Baste the pieces together at the sides where they overlap. See **Diagram 17.**

Repeat with the remaining four backing pieces to make two more backings.

STEP 7. With the ruffle in the middle, position the pillow sham top and backing with right sides together, and pin them in place. The backing will extend 1 to 1½ inches beyond the edges of the sham top. Using ¼-inch seams, sew around the edges of the pillow sham. Trim the backing to the same size as the sham top. Trim the corners, turn the pillow

Whiten Up!

Try making the pillow shams in white, cream, beige, and ecru for an elegant, more formal look.

sham right side out, and press. Repeat to finish the remaining two pillow shams.

DIAGRAM 17

PILLOW SHAM LAYOUT

TOPIARIES-TO-GO WALL QUILT

Turn the page to see some cute little potted topiaries that look as if they

could have come from a garden show, where small and portable sculpted

plants are a hot trend. Working with fabrics, instead of with branches and

leaves, you have the freedom to shape these garden whimsies and know

they'll stay this way forever—with no more pruning needed!

The three-dimensional cardinal, bow, buttons, and yo-yos

add to the character and charm of this wall quilt.

Finished Size: 32 × 20 inches

MATERIALS AND CUTTING			
Prewash and press all of your fabrics. Using a rotary cutter, see-through ruler, and cutting mat, prepare the pieces as described below. Measurements for all pieces include ¼-inch seam allowances.			
FABRIC	**YARDAGE**	**NO. OF PIECES**	**DIMENSIONS**
Gold print for background and checkerboard	⅝ yard	1	16½ × 24½-inch piece (background)
		2	1½ × 30-inch strips (checkerboard)
		1	1½-inch square (checkerboard)
Black print for accent border, binding, and optional tabs	⅝ yard	2	1 × 24½-inch strips (accent border)
		2	1 × 17½-inch strips (accent border)
		4	2¾ × 42-inch strips (binding)
		1	2½ × 40-inch strip (tabs)
Green print for checkerboard	⅛ yard	2	1½ × 30-inch strips
		1	1½-inch square

(continued)

MATERIALS AND CUTTING —CONTINUED

FABRIC	YARDAGE	NO. OF PIECES	DIMENSIONS
Red print for side border	⅛ yard (cut into one 3½ × 42-inch strip)	2	3½ × 19½-inch strips
Backing fabric	¾ yard	—	—
Lightweight batting	¾ yard	—	—
Green print for large appliqué topiary circle and cone	¼ yard	—	—
Several coordinated fabrics for appliqué pieces and yo-yos	Scraps, or ⅛-yard pieces	—	—

Lightweight, sewable fusible web; green decorative cording (optional); embroidery floss; assorted buttons; Rit dye (optional); organdy ribbon; 6-inch square of red felt for dimensional bird; polyester fiberfill stuffing

Assembling the Background

Assemble the quilt top before adding the appliqué pieces. Be sure to use ¼-inch seams and to press after each sewing step.

STEP 1. Sew the 1 × 24½-inch accent border strips to the top and bottom of the 24½ × 16½-inch gold print background piece. Press the seams toward the accent border.

STEP 2. Sew the 1 × 17½-inch accent border strips to the sides. Press.

STEP 3. Alternating the two colors, sew the four 1½ × 30-inch checkerboard strips together to make a 4½ × 30-inch strip set. Change sewing direction with each strip sewn, and press the seams toward the darker fabric as you go. Cut this strip set into thirds, approximately 10 inches each. See **Diagram 1**.

STEP 4. Resew the thirds together to make a 12½ × 10-inch strip set. Cut this strip set into halves, approximately 5 inches each. See **Diagram 2**.

STEP 5. Resew the halves together to make a 24½ × 5-inch strip set. Using a rotary cutter and ruler, cut two 1½ × 24½-inch strips from this strip set. There should be 24 squares in each strip. See **Diagram 3** on the following page.

STEP 6. Sew the 1½-inch gold print square to the end of one checkerboard strip. Sew the 1½-inch green print square to the end of the second checkerboard strip. See **Diagram 4** on the following page. Press. There should be 25 squares in each strip.

DIAGRAM 1

DIAGRAM 2

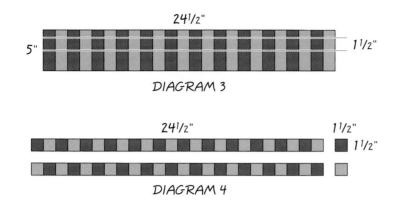

24¹/₂"

5"   1¹/₂"

DIAGRAM 3

24¹/₂"   1¹/₂"

1¹/₂"

DIAGRAM 4

STEP 7. Compare the checkerboard strips to the bottom of the quilt. You may need to take in or let out a few seams (¹/₁₆ inch or less) to make them fit. Make adjustments before you sew the checkerboard strips together. If you do make adjustments, make them in the same place on each strip so that the strips will still match up. Refer to "Fitting Pieced Borders" on page 274 for further instructions. Sew the checkerboard strips together and press. Pin and sew the checkerboard to the bottom of the quilt. Press the seam toward the accent border.

STEP 8. Sew the 3½ × 19½-inch side border strips to the sides. Press the seams toward the side border.

Appliqué

The appliqué pieces were added to the background using the technique described in "Blanket Stitch Appliqué" on page 272. You can machine appliqué with either a satin stitch or blanket stitch if you prefer. Refer to "Machine Appliqué" on pages 271–272 for instructions on either technique. Be sure to use a lightweight, sewable fusible web.

STEP 1. Refer to "Quick-Fuse Appliqué" on pages 270–271. Trace the three potted topiaries from the appliqué patterns on pages 176–181. Choosing one leaf from Topiary #3, trace 20 leaves for the side border.

STEP 2. Position and fuse the appliqué pieces to the background, referring to the **Wall Quilt Layout** for placement. Before fusing Topiary #3 on the right, place the decorative cording under the edges of the circles and the pot. Hand stitch the cording in place. You can also use a machine satin stitch if you prefer. Position and fuse 10 leaves in each side border strip.

STEP 3. Use two strands of embroidery floss to blanket stitch around the edges of the appliqué pieces and stem stitch the curved lines on the rim of the pot. Refer to "Decorative Stitches" on page 272 for instructions. Mark the vines in the side border.

Layering the Quilt

Arrange and baste the backing, batting, and top together, following the directions in "Layering the Quilt" on page 275. Trim the batting and backing to ¼ inch from the raw edges of the quilt top.

Binding the Quilt

Using the four 2¾ × 42-inch binding strips, follow the directions for "Binding the Quilt" on pages 275–276.

Finishing Stitches

STEP 1. Machine or hand quilt in the seam lines of the background and accent border and between

32"

20"

WALL QUILT LAYOUT

the squares of the checkerboard. Outline the appliqué designs by quilting ¹⁄₁₆ inch from the edges. Quilt a 1¼-inch diagonal grid in the background. Use six strands of embroidery floss to quilt the vines in the side border.

STEP 2. Refer to "Making Yo-yos" on pages 272–273. Make five small and nine large yo-yos from the patterns below. Sew the yo-yos to the middle topiary, referring to the **Wall Quilt Layout** for placement.

STEP 3. Sew assorted buttons to the left and right topiaries, Topiary #1 and Topiary #3. You can dye your own buttons with Rit dye. See "How to Dye Buttons" on page 139 for instructions. Tie the organdy ribbon into a bow, and hand sew it to the left topiary.

STEP 4. Make a dimensional bird, following the directions in "How to Make a Dimensional Bird" at right. Hand sew the bird onto the left topiary.

STEP 5. If you want to add hanging tabs, fold the 2½ × 40-inch black print tab strip in half lengthwise with right sides together. Sew a ¼-inch seam along the edge opposite the fold, turn the strip right side out, and press. Topstitch along the edges of both sides. Cut

the strip into five 7½-inch pieces. Fold each piece in half, and stitch a ¼-inch seam along the cut edge. Turn each tab right side out, and press with the seam at the bottom of the tab. Space the tabs evenly across the top of the quilt back. Hand stitch the tabs in place.

How to Make a Dimensional Bird

STEP 1. Make a template for the bird body, including the beak from the pattern on page 177. Cut the 6-inch red felt square in half, and draw around the template on one half. Pin the felt with the traced shape to the second felt piece. Cut out the bird on the drawn line, cutting through both layers.

STEP 2. Trace the bird beak from the pattern on page 177 onto a fusible web. Use a scrap of gold fabric and

quick-fuse the beak to the bird.

STEP 3. Use two strands of embroidery floss to blanket stitch around the edges of the bird. Leave a small opening for stuffing. Lightly stuff the bird with polyester fiberfill, and continue the blanket stitch to close the opening. Use embroidery floss to add a French-knot eye to the bird. See "Decorative Stitches" on page 272.

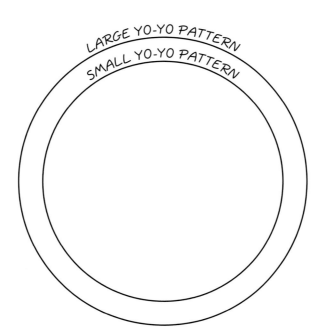

LARGE YO-YO PATTERN
SMALL YO-YO PATTERN

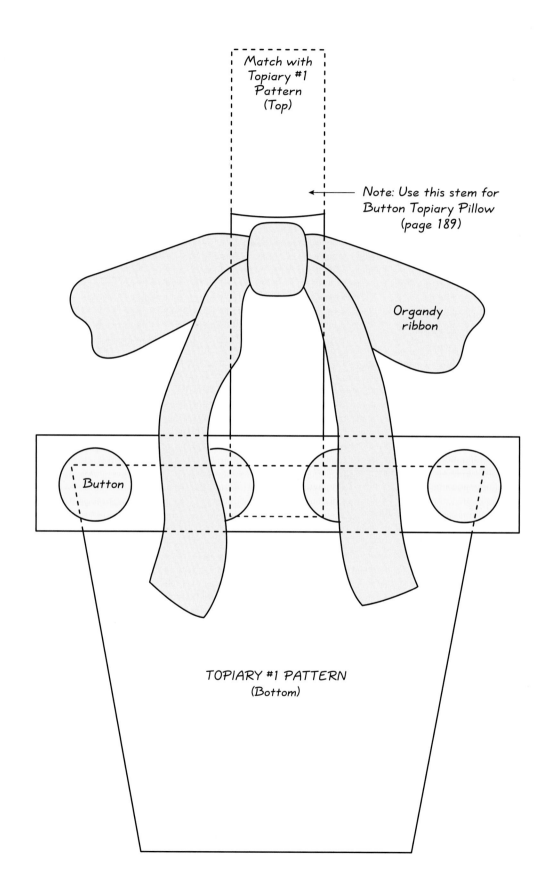

Match with
Topiary #1
Pattern
(Top)

Note: Use this stem for
Button Topiary Pillow
(page 189)

Organdy
ribbon

Button

TOPIARY #1 PATTERN
(Bottom)

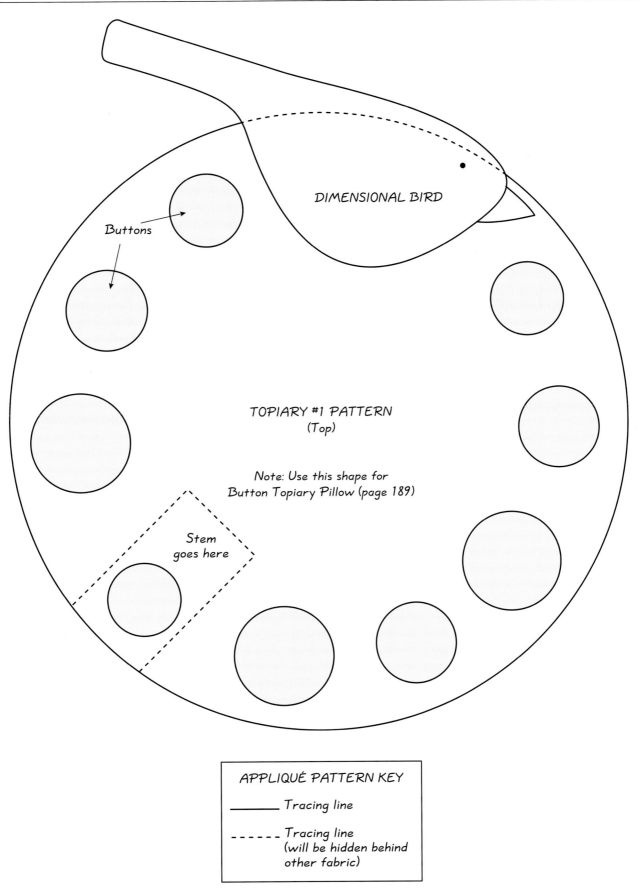

DIMENSIONAL BIRD

Buttons

TOPIARY #1 PATTERN
(Top)

Note: Use this shape for
Button Topiary Pillow (page 189)

Stem
goes here

APPLIQUÉ PATTERN KEY

──────── Tracing line

- - - - - - - Tracing line
(will be hidden behind
other fabric)

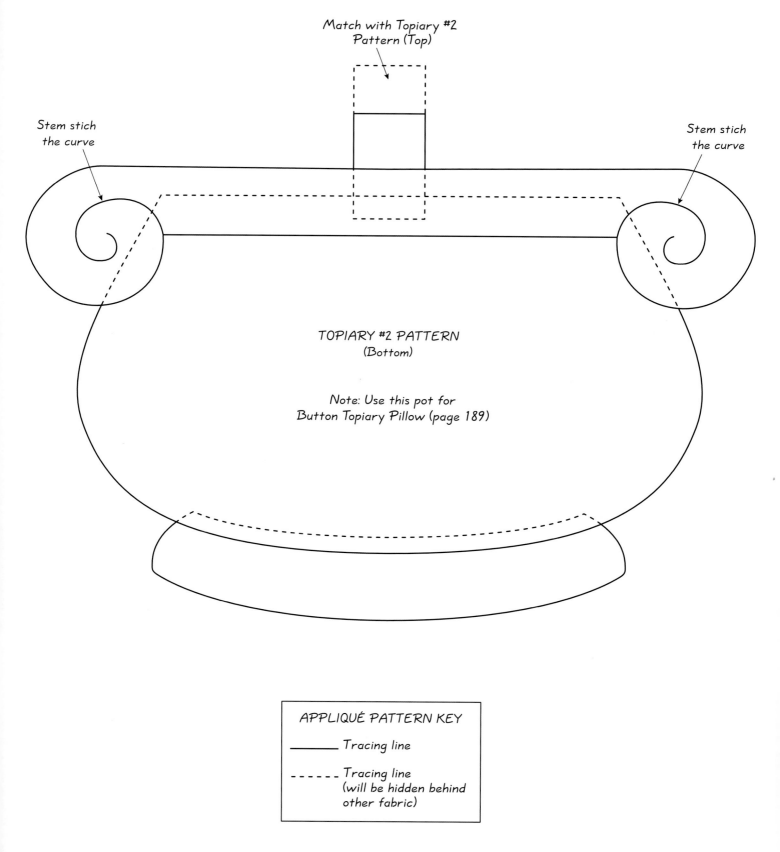

Match with Topiary #2
Pattern (Top)

Stem stich
the curve

Stem stich
the curve

TOPIARY #2 PATTERN
(Bottom)

Note: Use this pot for
Button Topiary Pillow (page 189)

APPLIQUÉ PATTERN KEY

—————— Tracing line

- - - - - - Tracing line
(will be hidden behind
other fabric)

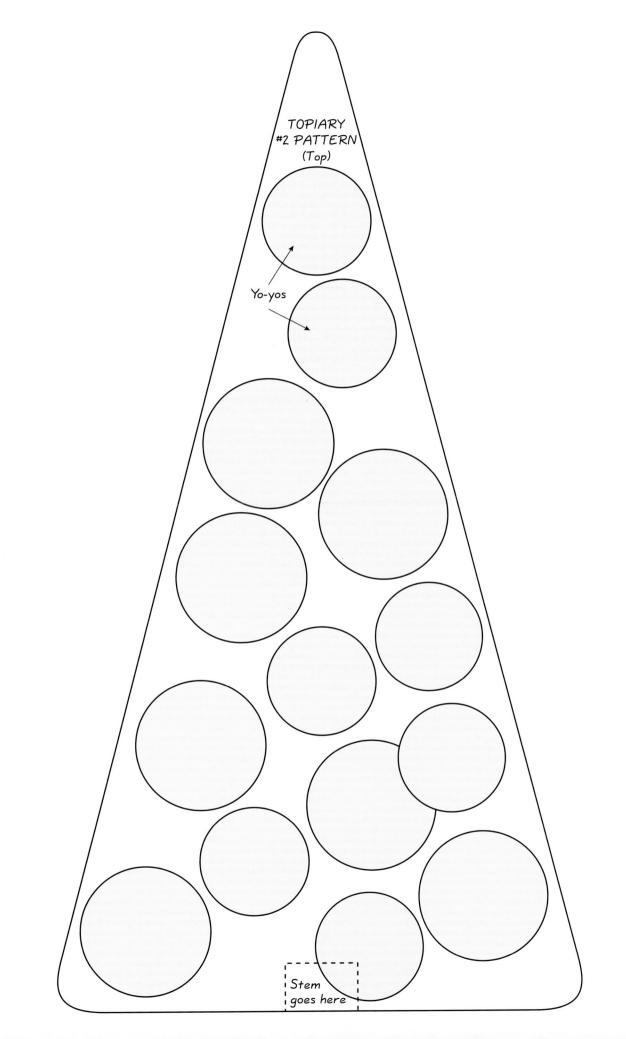

TOPIARY
#2 PATTERN
(Top)

Yo-yos

Stem
goes here

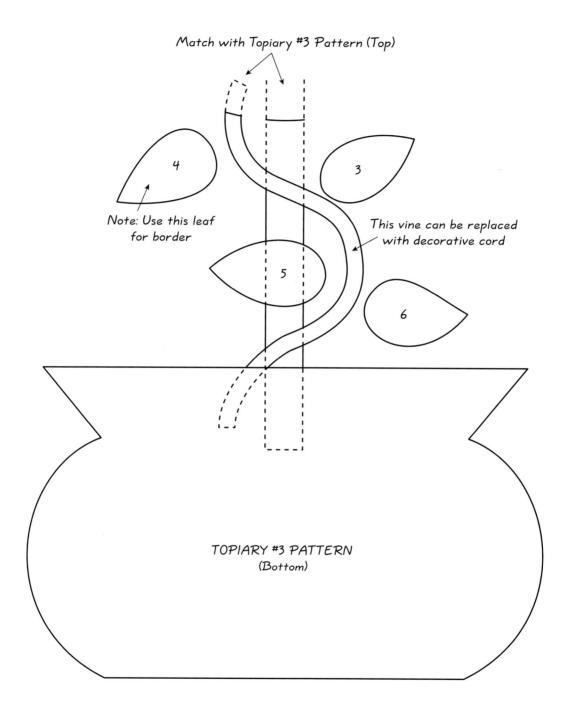

Match with Topiary #3 Pattern (Top)

4

3

Note: Use this leaf
for border

This vine can be replaced
with decorative cord

5

6

TOPIARY #3 PATTERN
(Bottom)

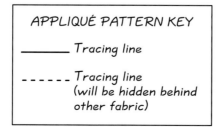

APPLIQUÉ PATTERN KEY

────── Tracing line

- - - - - - Tracing line
(will be hidden behind
other fabric)

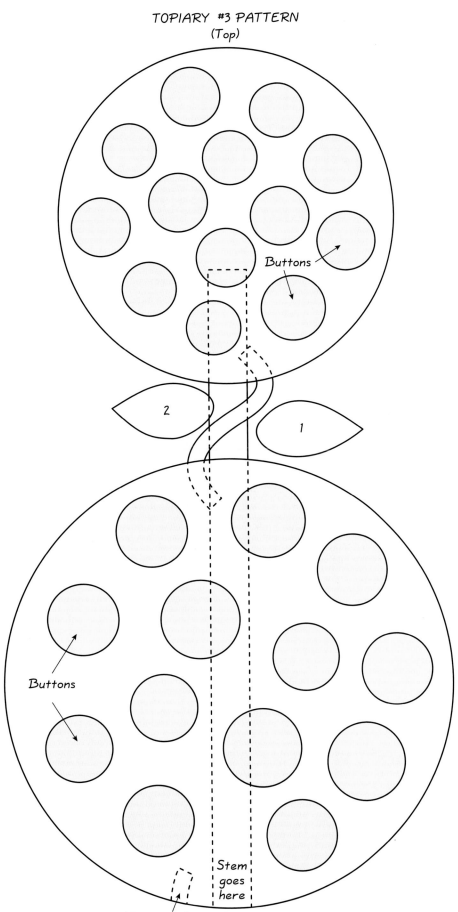

Buttons

Buttons

Stem goes here

Vine goes here

181

TABLE TOPPER

Add a decorator touch to your room with this boldly graphic

Table Topper. The center square carries over the square-in-square theme

set by the lattice of the Topiary Treasures Duvet Cover (directions on page

155). I used home-decorator fabrics in my table topper, left out the batting,

and skipped the quilting. These shortcuts make it especially quick and easy.

Finished Size: 34 inches square

MATERIALS

(Obvious directional prints are not recommended.)

¾ yard green-and-black check for center square and border diamonds

¾ yard red print for triangles and outer border

⅝ yard tan print for small and large triangles

¼ yard black print for 1-inch borders

⅛ yard gold print for corner squares

1⅛ yards fabric for backing

4 decorative tassels

CUTTING

Prewash and press all of your fabrics. Using a rotary cutter, see-through ruler, and cutting mat, prepare the pieces as described below. Measurements for all pieces include ¼-inch seam allowances.

FABRIC	FIRST CUT		SECOND CUT	
Color	No. of Pieces	Dimensions	No. of Pieces	Dimensions
Green-and-black check	**Center square** (Cut this square first.)			
	1	8½-inch square	No second cut	
	Border diamonds			
	4	2½ × 30-inch strips	40	2½-inch squares

(continued)

CUTTING—CONTINUED

FABRIC	FIRST CUT		SECOND CUT	
Color	No. of Pieces	Dimensions	No. of Pieces	Dimensions
Red print	**Triangles** (Cut these squares first.)			
	2	6⅝-inch squares	No second cut	
	Outer border			
	2	5½ × 34½-inch strips	No second cut	
	2	5½ × 24½-inch strips	No second cut	
Tan print	**Small triangles** (Cut these strips first.)			
	7	1½ × 42-inch strips	160	1½-inch squares
	Large triangles			
	2	8⅞-inch squares	No second cut	
Black print	**1-inch borders**			
	4	1½ × 42-inch strips	4	1½ × 22 ½-inch strips
			4	1½ × 16½-inch strips
Gold print	**Corner squares**			
	1	1½ × 42-inch strip	8	1½-inch squares

Quick Corner Triangles

Refer to "Making Quick Corner Triangles" on page 269 for instructions on making the corner triangle units. Press the seams toward the triangle just added.

STEP 1. Sew two 1½-inch tan print squares to each of the forty 2½-inch green-and-black check squares. See **Diagram 1**. Press.

DIAGRAM 1

STEP 2. Sew two additional 1½-inch tan print squares to the units from Step 1. See **Diagram 2**. Press.

2½"

2½"

DIAGRAM 2

Assembly

STEP 1. Using a rotary cutter and ruler, cut the two 6⅝-inch red print squares in half diagonally to make four triangles. See **Diagram 3**.

Cut 6⅝"

6⅝"

Arrow indicates straight of grain

DIAGRAM 3

STEP 2. Using a ¼-inch seam, sew the 8½-inch green-and-black

check square between two red print triangles. Press the seams toward the triangles. Trim the points off the triangles, as shown in **Diagram 4.**

Trim off points after sewing

6⅝"

6⅝"

6⅝"

6⅝"

DIAGRAM 4

STEP 3. Sew the unit from Step 2 between the two remaining red print triangles. Press. Using a rotary cutter and ruler, trim the square to measure 11¾ inches square. See **Diagram 5** on the following page.

11¾ " 11¾ "

DIAGRAM 5

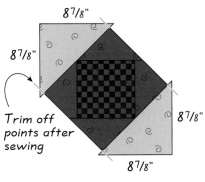

Cut 8⅞"

8⅞"

Arrow indicates straight of grain
DIAGRAM 6

8⅞"

8⅞"

8⅞"

Trim off points after sewing

8⅞"

DIAGRAM 7

16½"

16½"

DIAGRAM 8

STEP 4. Using a rotary cutter and ruler, cut the two 8⅞-inch tan print squares in half diagonally to make four triangles. See **Diagram 6**.

STEP 5. Sew the unit from Step 3 between two tan print triangles. Press the seams toward the triangles. Trim the points off the triangles, as shown in **Diagram 7**.

STEP 6. Sew the unit from Step 5 between the two remaining tan print triangles. See **Diagram 8**. Press. Using a rotary cutter and ruler, trim the square to measure 16½ inches square.

Adding the Borders

STEP 1. Sew one 1½ × 16½-inch black print border strip to the top and one to the bottom of the table topper. Press the seams toward the border.

STEP 2. Sew one 1½-inch gold print corner square to each end of the remaining 1½ × 16½-inch black print border strips. Press the seams toward the border. Pin and sew the border strips to the sides. Press.

STEP 3. Sew eighteen 2½-inch tan/green-and-black corner triangle units together, as shown in **Diagram 9**, to make two pieced border strips with 9 squares each. Press the seams in one direction. Each border strip will now measure 2½ × 18½ inches.

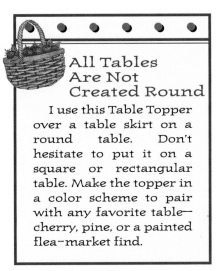

All Tables Are Not Created Round

I use this Table Topper over a table skirt on a round table. Don't hesitate to put it on a square or rectangular table. Make the topper in a color scheme to pair with any favorite table—cherry, pine, or a painted flea-market find.

STEP 4. Compare the pieced border strips to the top and bottom of the table topper. You may need to take in or let out a few seams (1/16 inch or less) to make them fit. Pin and sew the border strips to the top and bottom of the table topper. Press the seams toward the black print border.

STEP 5. Sew the remaining twenty-two 2½-inch tan/green-and-black corner triangle units together, as shown in **Diagram 10**, to make two pieced border strips with 11 squares each. Press. Each border strip will now measure 2½ × 22½ inches.

2½"

2½"

DIAGRAM 10

2½"

2½"

DIAGRAM 9

STEP 6. Fit, pin, and sew the pieced border strips to the sides. Press.

STEP 7. Sew one 1½ × 22½-inch black print border strip to the top and one to the bottom of the table topper. Press the seams toward the black print border.

STEP 8. Sew one 1½-inch gold print corner square to each end of the remaining 1½ × 22½-inch black print border strips. Press the seams toward the border. Pin and sew the border strips to the sides. Press.

STEP 9. Sew the 5½ × 24½-inch red print outer border strips to the top and bottom of the table topper. Press the seams toward the outer border.

STEP 10. Sew the 5½ × 34½-inch red print outer border strips to the sides. Press.

Finishing

Position the top and backing with right sides together, and pin them in place. Using ¼-inch seams, sew around the edges, leaving an 8- to 10-inch opening for turning. Trim the backing to the same size as the top. Trim the corners, turn the table topper right side out, hand stitch the opening closed, and press. Topstitch along the outer edges. Hand sew a decorative tassel to each corner.

34"

34"

TABLE TOPPER LAYOUT

COLOR OPTION

If you've fallen in love with pastels, make the table topper for a special room in pale blue, violet, sea green, and peach.

COZY COUNTRY PILLOWS

Cuddle up with these pillows and a good book for a quiet, relaxing evening. This pillow set can be the final polishing touch to complete a bedroom ensemble or a stylish grouping for a living room or family room. The Yo-yo Topiary Pillow is shown in the drawer in the photo. On the chair are the Button Topiary Pillow, *middle* (directions on page 189), the Yo-yo Vine Pillow, *left* (page 191), and the Sunflower Pillow, *right* (page 192).

YO-YO TOPIARY PILLOW

Finished Size:
20 × 14½ inches

Assembly

See "Materials and Cutting" on page 188. Assemble the pillow top before adding the appliqué pieces. Be sure to use ¼-inch seams and to press after each sewing step.

STEP 1. Sew the three 4½ × 7-inch gold print background pieces together. See **Diagram 1** on page 188. Press the seams, following the arrows in the diagram.

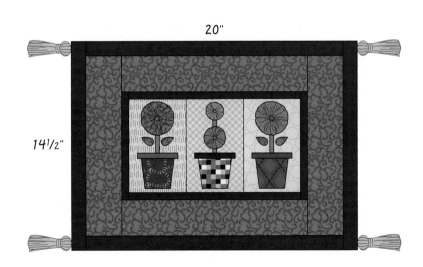

20"

14½"

MATERIALS AND CUTTING *(for Yo-yo Topiary Pillow)*

Prewash and press all of your fabrics. Using a rotary cutter, see-through ruler, and cutting mat, prepare the pieces as described below. Measurements for all pieces include ¼-inch seam allowances.

FABRIC	YARDAGE	NO. OF PIECES	DIMENSIONS
Gold prints for background	⅛ yard *each* of 3 fabrics	1	4½ × 7-inch piece each
Black solid for accent border and binding	¼ yard (cut into two 1× 42-inch strips and two 1½ ×42-inch strips)	2	1 × 12½-inch strips (accent border)
		2	1 × 8-inch strips (accent border)
		2	1½ × 18½-inch strips (binding)
		2	1½ × 15-inch strips (binding)
Green print for wide border	¼ yard (cut into two 3 × 42-inch strips)	2	3 × 13½-inch strips
		2	3 × 13-inch strips
Lining fabric	½ yard	—	—
Lightweight batting	1 yard (includes enough to make a custom-fit pillow form)	2	13 × 18½-inch pieces (custom-fit pillow form)
Backing fabric	½ yard	2	12½ × 15-inch pieces
Several coordinated fabrics for appliqué pieces and yo-yos	Scraps, or ⅛-yard pieces	—	—
Lightweight, sewable fusible web; embroidery floss; 4 decorative tassels; polyester fiberfill stuffing			

4½"   4½"   4½"

7"   7"

DIAGRAM 1

STEP 2. Sew the 1 × 12½-inch accent border strips to the top and bottom of the unit from Step 1. Press the seams toward the accent border.

STEP 3. Sew the 1 × 8-inch accent border strips to the sides. Press.

STEP 4. Sew the 3 × 13½-inch wide border strips to the top and bottom. Press the seams toward the wide border.

STEP 5. Sew the 3 × 13-inch wide border strips to the sides. Press.

STEP 6. Sew the 1½ × 18½-inch binding strips to the top and bottom. Press the seams toward the binding.

STEP 7. Sew the 1½ × 15-inch binding strips to the sides. Press.

Appliqué

The appliqué pieces were added to the background using the technique described in "Blanket Stitch Appliqué" on page 272. You can machine appliqué with either a satin stitch or blanket stitch if you prefer. Refer to "Machine Appliqué" on pages 271–272. Use a lightweight, sewable fusible web.

STEP 1. Refer to "Quick-Fuse Appliqué" on pages 270–271. Trace three topiary pots and stems and two sets of leaves from the appliqué pattern on page 195.

STEP 2. Position and fuse the appliqué pieces to the background, referring to the Yo-yo Topiary Pillow layout on page 187 for placement.

STEP 3. Use two strands of embroidery floss to blanket stitch around the edges of the appliqué pieces. The yo-yos will be added later.

Layering the Pillow Front

Arrange and baste the lining, batting, and top together, following the directions in "Layering the Quilt" on page 275.

Finishing Stitches

STEP 1. Machine or hand quilt in the seam lines of the background pieces and accent border. Outline the appliqué designs by quilting $\frac{1}{16}$ inch from the edges. Quilt a $1\frac{1}{2}$-inch diagonal grid in the wide border. Do not quilt in the seam lines next to the binding.

STEP 2. Trim the batting and lining to the same size as the top.

STEP 3. Refer to "Making Yo-yos" on pages 272–273. Make one small, one medium, and two large yo-yos from the patterns on page 195. Sew the small and medium yo-yos to the center topiary. Sew the large yo-yos to the left and right topiaries.

Making the Pillow Back

STEP 1. Narrow hem one 15-inch edge of each $12\frac{1}{2} \times 15$-inch

backing piece by folding $\frac{1}{4}$ inch to the wrong side. Press. Fold again $\frac{1}{4}$ inch to the wrong side. Press. Topstitch along the folded edge.

STEP 2. With right sides up, lay one backing piece over the second piece so that the hemmed edges overlap $3\frac{1}{2}$ inches. See **Diagram 2.** Baste the pieces together at the top and bottom where they overlap. The pillow back will now measure $20\frac{1}{2} \times 15$ inches.

$20\frac{1}{2}$"

15"

$3\frac{1}{2}$" overlap

DIAGRAM 2

Finishing the Pillow

STEP 1. With right sides together, sew the quilted pillow front to the back, using $\frac{1}{4}$-inch seams. Trim the corners, turn the pillow right side out, and press.

STEP 2. Machine stitch in the seam lines between the binding and the border. Hand sew one tassel to each corner of the pillow.

STEP 3. Refer to "Making Custom-Fit Pillow Forms" on page 194 and follow all directions. Insert the pillow form through the opening in the back of the pillow.

14"

20"

BUTTON TOPIARY PILLOW

Finished Size: 14 × 20 inches
(See the pillow on the chair, middle, in the photo on page 187.)

Assembly

See "Materials and Cutting" on page 190. Assemble the pillow top before adding the appliqué pieces. Be sure to use $\frac{1}{4}$-inch seams and to press after each sewing step.

STEP 1. Sew the $1 \times 8\frac{1}{2}$-inch accent border strips to the top and bottom of the $8\frac{1}{2} \times 14\frac{1}{2}$-inch gold print background piece. Press the seams toward the accent border.

STEP 2. Sew the $1 \times 15\frac{1}{2}$-inch accent border strips to the sides. Press.

STEP 3. Sew the $2 \times 9\frac{1}{2}$-inch wide border strips to the top and bottom. Press the seams toward the wide border.

STEP 4. Sew the $2 \times 18\frac{1}{2}$-inch wide border strips to the sides. Press.

MATERIALS AND CUTTING *(for Button Topiary Pillow)*

Prewash and press all of your fabrics. Using a rotary cutter, see-through ruler, and cutting mat, prepare the pieces as described below. Measurements for all pieces include ¼-inch seam allowances.

FABRIC	YARDAGE	NO. OF PIECES	DIMENSIONS
Gold print for background	⅓ yard	1	8½ × 14½-inch piece
Black solid for accent border and binding	¼ yard (cut into two 1 × 42-inch strips and two 1½ × 42-inch strips)	2	1 × 15½-inch strips (accent border)
		2	1 × 8½-inch strips (accent border)
		2	1½ × 20½-inch strips (binding)
		2	1½ × 12½-inch strips (binding)
Red print for wide border	⅙ yard (cut into two 2 × 42-inch strips)	2	2 × 18½-inch strips
		2	2 × 9½-inch strips
Lining fabric	½ yard	—	—
Lightweight batting	1 yard (includes enough to make a custom-fit pillow form)	2	12½ × 18½-inch pieces (custom-fit pillow form)
Backing fabric	½ yard	2	12½ × 14½-inch pieces
Several coordinated fabrics for appliqué pieces	Scraps, or ⅛- to ¼-yard pieces	—	—

Lightweight, sewable fusible web; embroidery floss; assorted buttons; organdy ribbon; 4 decorative tassels; polyester fiberfill stuffing

STEP 5. Sew the 1½ × 12½-inch binding strips to the top and bottom. Press the seams toward the binding.

STEP 6. Sew the 1½ × 20½-inch binding strips to the sides. Press.

Appliqué

The appliqué pieces were added to the background using the technique described in "Blanket Stitch Appliqué" on page 272. You can machine appliqué with either a satin stitch or blanket stitch if you prefer. Refer to "Machine Appliqué" on pages 271–272. Use a lightweight, sewable fusible web for all of these techniques.

STEP 1. Refer to "Quick-Fuse Appliqué" on pages 270–271. Using the appliqué patterns on pages 177–178 from the Topiaries-to-Go Wall Quilt, trace the circle and stem from Topiary #1 and the pot from Topiary #2.

STEP 2. Position and fuse the appliqué pieces to the background, referring to the Button Topiary Pillow layout on page 189 for placement.

STEP 3. Use two strands of embroidery floss to blanket stitch around the edges of the appliqué pieces. Use two strands of embroidery floss to stem stitch the curved lines on the rim of the pot, referring to "Decorative Stitches" on page 272 for instructions.

Layering the Pillow Front

Arrange and baste the lining, batting, and top together, following the directions in "Layering the Quilt" on page 275.

Finishing Stitches

STEP 1. Machine or hand quilt in the seam lines of the background and accent border. Outline the appliqué design by quilting 1/16 inch from the edges. Quilt a 1-inch diagonal grid in the background and wide border. Do not quilt in the seam lines next to the binding.

STEP 2. Trim the batting and lining to the same size as the top.

STEP 3. Sew assorted buttons to the topiary.

Making the Pillow Back

STEP 1. Narrow hem one 14½-inch edge of each 12½ × 14½-inch backing piece by folding ¼ inch to the wrong side. Press. Fold again ¼ inch to the wrong side. Press. Topstitch along the folded edge.

STEP 2. With right sides up, lay one backing piece over the second piece so that the hemmed edges overlap 3 inches. See **Diagram 3**. Baste the pieces together at the sides where they overlap. The pillow back will now measure 14½ × 20½ inches.

Finishing the Pillow

STEP 1. With right sides together, sew the quilted pillow front to the

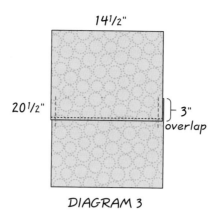

14½"

20½"

3" overlap

DIAGRAM 3

back, using ¼-inch seams. Trim the corners, turn the pillow right side out, and press.

STEP 2. Machine stitch in the seam lines between the binding and the border. Tie the organdy ribbon into a bow, and hand sew it to the topiary. Hand sew one tassel to each corner of the pillow.

STEP 3. Refer to "Making Custom-Fit Pillow Forms" on page 194 and follow all directions. Insert the pillow form through the opening in the back of the pillow.

14"

14"

YO-YO VINE PILLOW

Finished Size: 14 inches square

(See the pillow on the chair, left, in the photo on page 187.)

Assembly

See "Materials and Cutting" on the following page. Be sure to use ¼-inch seams and to press after each sewing step.

STEP 1. Sew the 1 × 9½-inch accent border strips to the top and bottom of the 9½-inch gold print background square. Press the seams toward the accent border.

STEP 2. Sew the 1 × 10½-inch accent border strips to the sides. Press.

STEP 3. Sew the 2½ × 10½-inch wide border strips to the top and bottom. Press the seams toward the wide border.

STEP 4. Sew the 2½ × 14½-inch wide border strips to the sides. Press.

Decorating the Pillow Top

STEP 1. Using the Yo-yo Vine Pillow patterns on pages 196–197, lightly mark vines on the background. Use six strands of embroidery floss and a running stitch to make the vines.

STEP 2. Refer to "Quick-Fuse Appliqué" on pages 270–271 and "Blanket Stitch Appliqué" on page 272. Trace 24 leaves from the appliqué pattern on page 195. Be sure to use a lightweight, sewable fusible web. Position and fuse the leaves to the background, referring to the Yo-yo Vine Pillow patterns on pages 196–197 for placement. Use two strands of embroidery floss to blanket stitch around the edges of the leaves.

MATERIALS AND CUTTING *(for Yo-yo Vine Pillow)*

Prewash and press all of your fabrics. Using a rotary cutter, see-through ruler, and cutting mat, prepare the pieces as described below. Measurements for all pieces include ¼-inch seam allowances.

FABRIC	YARDAGE	NO. OF PIECES	DIMENSIONS
Gold print for background	⅓ yard	1	9½-inch square
Red print for accent border	⅛ yard (cut into two 1 × 42-inch strips)	2 2	1 × 10½-inch strips 1 × 9½-inch strips
Black print for wide border	¼ yard (cut into two 2½ × 42-inch strips)	2 2	2½ × 14½-inch strips 2½ × 10½-inch strips
Backing fabric	⅓ yard	2	14½ × 9½-inch pieces
Several coordinated fabrics for appliqué leaves and yo-yos	Scraps	—	—
Embroidery floss; lightweight, sewable fusible web; assorted buttons (approximately 18); purchased 14-inch pillow form			

STEP 3. Refer to "Making Yo-yos" on pages 272–273. Make four small and five medium yo-yos from the patterns on page 195. Sew the yo-yos to the vines, referring to the Yo-yo Vine Pillow patterns on pages 196–197 for placement.

DIAGRAM 4

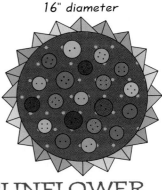

16" diameter

Making the Pillow Back

STEP 1. Narrow hem one 14½-inch edge of each 14½ × 9½-inch backing piece by folding ¼ inch to the wrong side. Press. Fold again ¼ inch to the wrong side. Press. Topstitch along the folded edge.

STEP 2. With right sides up, lay one backing piece over the second piece so that the hemmed edges overlap 3½ inches. See **Diagram 4.** Baste the pieces together at the sides where they overlap. The pillow back will now measure 14½ inches square.

Finishing the Pillow

STEP 1. With right sides together, sew the pillow top to the back, using ¼-inch seams. Trim the corners, turn the pillow right side out, and press.

STEP 2. Hand sew assorted buttons to the border, referring to the Yo-yo Vine Pillow layout on page 191 for placement. Insert the 14-inch pillow form through the opening in the back of the pillow.

SUNFLOWER PILLOW

**Finished Size:
16 inches in diameter**

(See the pillow on the chair, right, in the photo on page 187.)

Assembly

STEP 1. See "Materials and Cutting," on the opposite page. To make the prairie points, fold each 4-inch gold print square in half with wrong sides together. Fold again as shown in **Diagram 5** on the opposite page. Press.

DIAGRAM 5

STEP 2. To divide the black print center circle into fourths, fold it in half, and then fold it in half again as shown in **Diagram 6**. Mark the edges at each fold.

DIAGRAM 6

STEP 3. With right sides together and raw edges even, position and pin one prairie point centered on each mark around the circle. See **Diagram 7**.

DIAGRAM 7

Easy Circles

To draw a circle for the Sunflower Pillow, try one of these easy options:

- Use a pencil tied to a string. Anchor the end of the string with a pin.
- Trace around a plate or bowl that is the right size for the circle.
- Purchase a yardstick compass. These are available in most quilt shops and art supply stores.

STEP 4. Position four additional prairie points in each quarter of the circle, overlapping and spacing them evenly. Pin and baste the prairie points in position.

Making the Pillow Back

STEP 1. Narrow hem one 16-inch edge of each 10 × 16-inch backing piece by folding ¼ inch to the wrong side. Press. Fold again ¼ inch to the wrong side. Press. Topstitch along the folded edge.

STEP 2. With right sides up, lay one backing piece over the second piece so that the hemmed edges overlap 3 inches. See **Diagram 8** on the following page. Baste the pieces together at the sides where they overlap. The pillow back will now measure 16 inches square.

MATERIALS AND CUTTING *(for Sunflower Pillow)*

Prewash and press all of your fabrics. Using a rotary cutter, see-through ruler, and cutting mat, prepare the pieces as described below. Measurements for all pieces include ¼-inch seam allowances.

FABRIC	YARDAGE	NO. OF PIECES	DIMENSIONS
▪ Black print for center	½ yard	1	14½-inch circle
▫ Gold prints for prairie points	⅛ yard *each* of 5 fabrics	4	4-inch squares each
Backing fabric	⅓ yard	2	10 × 16-inch pieces
Batting for custom-fit pillow form	½ yard	2	14½-inch circles
Assorted buttons; polyester fiberfill stuffing			

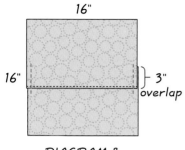

16"

16"

3" overlap

DIAGRAM 8

Finishing the Pillow

STEP 1. With the prairie points in the middle, position the pillow top and back with right sides together and pin them in place. Using ¼-inch seam allowances, sew around the pillow. Trim the back and prairie points to the same size as the top. Clip the seam every ½ inch, and turn the pillow right side out.

STEP 2. Hand sew assorted buttons to the pillow.

STEP 3. Refer to "Making Custom-Fit Pillow Forms," at right, and follow all directions. Use two 14½-inch circles. Insert the pillow form through the opening in the back of the pillow.

Making Custom-Fit Pillow Forms

The secret to an attractive finished pillow is a pillow form that fits perfectly inside the pillow. This cannot always be achieved with standard-size pillow forms, but you can easily make your own. All you need is some batting and polyester fiberfill stuffing.

For Pillows without Binding

STEP 1. Add ½ inch to the finished size of the pillow. Cut two pieces of batting to those dimensions. For example, the Yo-yo Vine Pillow finishes 14 inches square, so you will need to cut two pieces of batting, each 14½ inches square.

STEP 2. Using ¼-inch seams, sew the two pieces of batting together, leaving a 3- to 4-inch opening for turning. Turn the batting so that the seam allowances are on the inside.

STEP 3. Stuff the pillow form with the polyester fiberfill until it reaches the desired firmness. Hand stitch the opening closed.

For Pillows with Binding

Determine the finished size of the binding. Double it and subtract that amount from the finished size of the pillow. Add ½ inch and cut two pieces of batting to those dimensions. For example, the Yo-yo Topiary Pillow finishes 20 × 14½ inches and has a 1-inch finished binding. You will need to cut two pieces of batting, each 18½ × 13 inches. Follow Steps 2 and 3 above to finish the pillow form.

LARGE YO-YO

MEDIUM YO-YO

SMALL YO-YO

YO-YO PATTERNS

LEAF PATTERN FOR
YO-YO VINE PILLOW

APPLIQUÉ PATTERN KEY

———— Tracing line

- - - - - Tracing line
(will be hidden behind
other fabric)

TOPIARY POT PATTERN

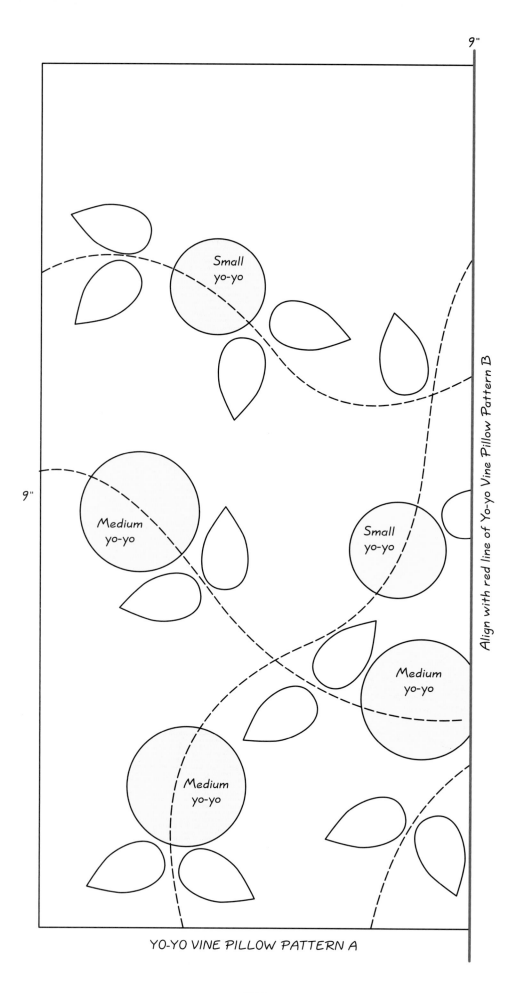

Small
yo-yo

Medium
yo-yo

Small
yo-yo

Medium
yo-yo

Medium
yo-yo

9"

9"

Align with red line of Yo-yo Vine Pillow Pattern B

YO-YO VINE PILLOW PATTERN A

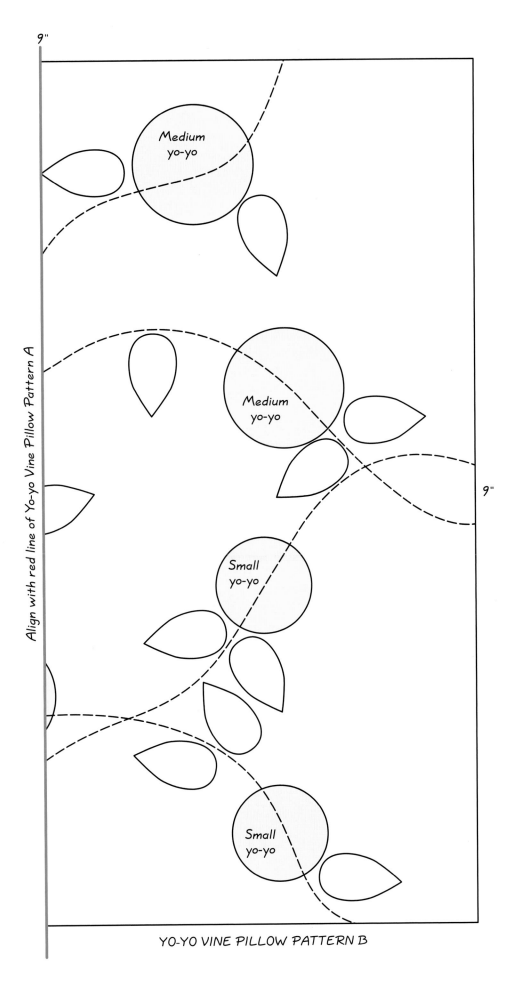

9"

Align with red line of Yo-yo Vine Pillow Pattern A

Medium
yo-yo

Medium
yo-yo

Small
yo-yo

Small
yo-yo

9"

YO-YO VINE PILLOW PATTERN B

SPORTS FEVER KID'S BEDROOM

My nine-year-old son, Murphy, has a serious case of sports fever! He's constantly on the move, playing soccer and baseball, skateboarding, roller blading, or shooting baskets. I had lots of fun playing with the sports theme to design these projects especially for his bedroom. (And I scored lots of points with Murphy in the process!) For a bedroom of hearts and flowers, see page 228.

GO, TEAM!

"Totally awesome" is one way a child might describe this Sports Quilt

and the coordinating Sports Pillowcase (directions on page 205). Just about

every sport is represented in easy machine-appliquéd designs. Pennants,

jerseys, stars, balls, and other sports equipment adorn the quilt, while

skateboards accent the pillowcases. This is the place to be after the game!

Sports Quilt

Finished Size: 75 × 87 inches

MATERIALS

(Obvious directional prints are not recommended.)

■ 4⅛ yards blue solid for background, corner squares, and striped patchwork border. (See Note below.)

■ ⅜ yard red print for inner accent border

⅜ yard *each* of 8 assorted fabrics for patchwork borders

■ 1⅛ yards dark blue print for outer accent border and binding

5½ yards fabric for backing

5½ yards lightweight batting

■ ⅝ yard red print for appliqué background squares

Scraps, or ⅛- to ¼-yard pieces, of several coordinated fabrics for appliqué pieces

4 yards lightweight, sewable fusible web

Permanent fine-point felt pen

Thread to match appliqué pieces

4 yards Tear-Away fabric stabilizer

Note: Sixty-inch-wide lightweight denim was used to avoid piecing the background in the quilt shown in the photo. You will need 3 yards of 60-inch-wide fabric.

CUTTING

Prewash and press all of your fabrics. Using a rotary cutter, see-through ruler, and cutting mat, prepare the pieces as described below. Measurements for all pieces include ¼-inch seam allowances.

FABRIC	FIRST CUT		SECOND CUT	
Color	No. of Pieces	Dimensions	No. of Pieces	Dimensions
Blue solid	**Background** (See Note below.)			
	2	49 × 31-inch pieces	No second cut	
	Large corner squares (Cut these squares from the excess width of the background piece.)			
	4	8½-inch squares	No second cut	
	Small corner squares (Cut these squares from the excess width of the background piece.)			
	4	4½-inch squares	No second cut	
	Striped patchwork border			
	16	2½ × 42-inch strips	No second cut	
Red print	**Inner accent border**		Cut *1* strip into the following:	
	7	1½ × 42-inch strips	2	1½ × 21-inch strips
Assorted fabrics	**Inner patchwork border**—from *each* of the 8 fabrics, cut the following:			
	1	4½ × 42-inch strip	No second cut	
	Striped patchwork border—from *each* of the 8 fabrics, cut the following:			
	2	2½ × 42-inch strips	No second cut	
Dark blue print	**Outer accent border**		Cut *1* strip into the following:	
	7	1½ × 42-inch strips	2	1½ × 21-inch strips
	Binding		Cut *1* strip into the following:	
	9	2¾ × 42-inch strips	2	2¾ × 21-inch strips

Note: If you are using 60-inch-wide fabric for the background, cut one 46½ × 58½-inch piece from the 3 yards of fabric.

Assembling the Background

With right sides together, sew the two 49 × 31-inch blue solid background pieces together with ¼-inch seams to make one piece approximately 49 × 62 inches. Press the seams to one side. Recut this piece into one 46½ × 58½-inch piece. Note: If you are using 60-inch-wide fabric, skip this step.

Appliqué

The appliqué pieces were added to the background using the technique described in "Machine Appliqué" on pages 271–272. Use a small zigzag stitch. Be sure to use a lightweight, sewable fusible web.

STEP 1. Refer to "Quick-Fuse Appliqué" on pages 270–271. Draw five 9-inch squares on the paper side of the fusible web, leaving at least ½ inch between squares. Fuse the drawn squares to the wrong side of the red print appliqué background fabric. Cut out the squares on the drawn lines.

STEP 2. Trace an assortment of 25 sports designs and 15 stars for the background from the appliqué patterns on pages 208–215. Trace 4 soccer balls from the appliqué pattern on page 213 for the large corner squares. See the **Quilt Layout** on page 204 for guidance.

STEP 3. Choose 5 of the appliqué designs from Step 2, and fuse them to the red print appliqué background squares. Refer to "Try an Appliqué Pressing Sheet," at right.

STEP 4. Allowing for ¼-inch seams on the raw edges, position and fuse the appliqué designs to the 46½ × 58½-inch blue solid background piece, referring to the **Quilt Layout** on the following page for placement. Position and fuse the soccer balls to the 8½-inch blue solid corner squares. Use the permanent felt pen to draw stitching lines on the baseballs and seam lines on the basketballs.

STEP 5. Machine appliqué around the edges of the appliqué pieces. Use the Tear-Away fabric stabilizer on the wrong side of the background piece for an even machine stitch. Remove the stabilizer after stitching.

Adding the Borders

STEP 1. Sew one 1½ × 21-inch inner accent border strip to each of two 1½ × 42-inch inner accent border strips to make two strips approximately 1½ × 63 inches each. Press. Sew the border strips to the top and bottom of the background piece. Trim the excess length, and press the seams toward the accent border.

STEP 2. Sew the four remaining 1½ × 42-inch inner accent border strips together in pairs to make two strips approximately 1½ × 84 inches each. Press. Sew the border strips to the sides. Trim the excess length and press.

Try an Appliqué Pressing Sheet

The Appliqué Pressing Sheet by Bear Thread Designs makes positioning appliqué designs a snap. To use the pressing sheet, trace the appliqué designs on a plain sheet of paper, then retrace them onto the back of that paper. Use this reversed image as a guide for positioning and fusing. See "Quilting by Mail" on page 280 for ordering information.

STEP 3. Arrange the eight 4½ × 42-inch inner patchwork border strips in a pleasing order. Sew the strips together to make a 32½ × 42-inch strip set. Change sewing direction with each strip sewn, and press the seams in one direction as you go. Using a rotary cutter and ruler, cut seven 4½ × 32½ strips from this strip set. There should be 8 squares in each strip. See **Diagram 1**.

32½"

42"

4½"

DIAGRAM 1

STEP 4. Sew three 4½ × 32½-inch inner patchwork border strips together to make one 4½ × 96½-inch strip with 24 squares. Use a seam ripper to separate this strip into two 4½ × 48½-inch strips

with 12 squares each. Compare the strips to the top and bottom of the quilt. You may need to take in or let out a few seams (1⁄16 inch or less) to make them fit. Pin and sew the border strips to the top and bottom. Press the seams toward the accent border.

STEP 5. Sew the four remaining 4½ × 32½-inch inner patchwork border strips together in pairs to make two 4½ × 64½-inch strips with 16 squares each. Use a seam ripper to remove 1 square from each strip to make two 4½ × 60½-inch strips with 15 squares each.

STEP 6. Sew one 4½-inch blue solid corner square to each end of the patchwork border strips from Step 5. Press the seams toward the border. Fit, pin, and sew the border strips to the sides. Press.

STEP 7. Sew one 1½ × 21-inch outer accent border strip to each of two 1½ × 42-inch outer accent border strips to make two strips approximately 1½ × 63 inches each. Press. Sew the border strips to the top and bottom. Trim the excess length, and press the seams toward the outer accent border.

STEP 8. Sew the four remaining 1½ × 42-inch outer accent border strips together in pairs to make two strips approximately 1½ × 84 inches each. Press. Sew the border strips to the sides. Trim the excess length and press.

STEP 9. Alternate eight 2½ × 42-inch blue solid patchwork border strips and eight 2½ × 42-inch patchwork border strips of contrasting colors. Sew the strips together to make a 32½ × 42-inch strip set. Change sewing direction with each strip sewn, and press the seams in one direction as you go. Repeat with the remaining patchwork border strips to make a second strip set. Using a rotary cutter and ruler, cut four 8½ × 32½-inch strips from each strip set. There should be 16 pieces in each strip. See **Diagram 2**.

DIAGRAM 2

STEP 10. Sew four 8½ × 32½-inch striped patchwork border strips together in pairs to make two 8½ × 64½-inch strips with 32 pieces each. Use a seam ripper to remove one 3-piece unit from each strip to make two 8½ × 58½-inch strips with 29 pieces each. Set the 3-piece units aside for use in the next step. Fit, pin, and sew the border strips to the top and bottom. Press the seams toward the accent border.

STEP 11. Sew the remaining four 8½ × 32½-inch striped patchwork border strips together in pairs to make two 8½ × 64½-inch strips with 32 pieces each. Sew one 3-piece unit from Step 10 to one end of each strip to make two 8½ × 70½-inch strips with 35 pieces each.

STEP 12. Sew one 8½-inch blue solid corner square to each end of the striped patchwork border

strips from Step 11. Press the seams toward the border. Fit, pin, and sew the border strips to the sides. Press.

Layering the Quilt

STEP 1. Cut the backing fabric in half crosswise, and trim the selvage edges off both pieces. With right sides together, sew the two backing pieces together to make one piece approximately 80 × 99 inches. Press.

STEP 2. Arrange and baste the backing, batting, and top together, following the directions in "Layering the Quilt" on page 275.

Finishing Stitches

Machine or hand quilt as desired. Murphy's quilt was machine quilted around the appliqué designs. A large stipple pattern was quilted in the background, along with freehand stars that were scattered about randomly.

QUILT LAYOUT

Binding the Quilt

STEP 1. Trim the batting and backing to ¼ inch from the raw edges of the quilt top.

STEP 2. Sew the eight 2¾ × 42-inch binding strips together in pairs to make four strips approximately 2¾ × 84 inches each. Sew one 2¾ × 21-inch binding strip to each of two 2¾ × 84-inch binding strips to make two strips approximately 2¾ × 105 inches each.

STEP 3. Using the two 2¾ × 84-inch binding strips for the top and bottom and the two 2¾ × 105-inch binding strips for the sides, follow the directions for "Binding the Quilt" on pages 275–276.

Sports Pillowcase

Finished Size: 30 × 19 inches

(See the pillowcase in the photo on page 200.)

MATERIALS AND CUTTING

Prewash and press all of your fabrics. Using a rotary cutter, see-through ruler, and cutting mat, prepare the pieces as described below. Measurements for all pieces include ¼-inch seams (to make 1 pillowcase).

FABRIC	YARDAGE	NO. OF PIECES	DIMENSIONS
Red plaid for pillowcase	⅞ yard	1	25½ × 39½-inch piece
Blue print for border	⅜ yard	1	10½ × 39½-inch piece
Red print for accent border	⅛ yard	1	1 × 39½-inch strip
Several coordinated fabrics for appliqué pieces	Scraps, or ⅛-yard pieces	—	—
Lightweight, sewable fusible web; Tear-Away fabric stabilizer			

Assembly

STEP 1. Fold the 10½ × 39½-inch border strip in half lengthwise with wrong sides together and press.

STEP 2. Sew the 1 × 39½-inch accent border strip between the 25½ × 39½-inch red plaid pillowcase piece and the 5¼ × 39½-inch folded border strip. See **Diagram 3.** Press the seams toward the accent border. Fold the pillowcase in half crosswise and press.

STEP 3. Refer to "Quick-Fuse Appliqué" on pages 270–271. Be sure to use a lightweight, sewable fusible web. Trace one skateboard from the appliqué pattern on page 215 and two small and two large stars from the appliqué patterns on page 212. Referring to the **Pillowcase Layout** on the following page for placement, position and fuse the appliqué pieces to the border, centering them between the fold and the raw edge.

DIAGRAM 3

STEP 4. Refer to "Machine Appliqué" on pages 271–272. Use a small zigzag stitch to machine appliqué around the edges of the appliqué pieces. Use the Tear-Away fabric stabilizer on the wrong side of the border for an even machine stitch. Remove the stabilizer after stitching.

STEP 5. Fold the pillowcase in half crosswise with right sides together. Using ¼-inch seams, pin and sew the end opposite the border and edge opposite the fold. See **Diagram 4**. Turn the pillowcase right side out and press.

Fold

DIAGRAM 4

19"

30"

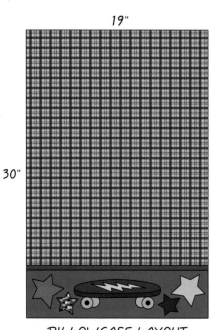

PILLOWCASE LAYOUT

Sports Jacket

Turn a simple denim jacket into something awesome with easy machine-appliquéd designs.

Materials

Child's denim jacket
Scraps, or ⅛- to ¼-yard pieces, of several coordinated fabrics for appliqué pieces
Lightweight, sewable fusible web
Tear-Away fabric stabilizer

Assembly

STEP 1. Refer to "Quick-Fuse Appliqué" on pages 270–271. Be sure to use a lightweight, sewable fusible web. Trace one skateboard and four lightning bolts from the appliqué pattern on page 215, three large stars from page 212, and one set of in-line skates from page 214.

STEP 2. Position and fuse the appliqué pieces to the back of the jacket, referring to the photo below for placement.

STEP 3. Refer to "Machine Appliqué" on pages 271–272. Use a small zigzag stitch to machine appliqué around the edges of the appliqué pieces. Use the Tear-Away fabric stabilizer on the wrong side of the jacket for an even machine stitch. Remove the stabilizer after stitching.

BASKETBALL AND HOOP PATTERNS

Draw lines on basketball
with felt pen

APPLIQUÉ PATTERN KEY

――――― Tracing line

- - - - - Tracing line
(will be hidden behind
other fabric)

BASEBALL MITT PATTERN

FOOTBALL PATTERN

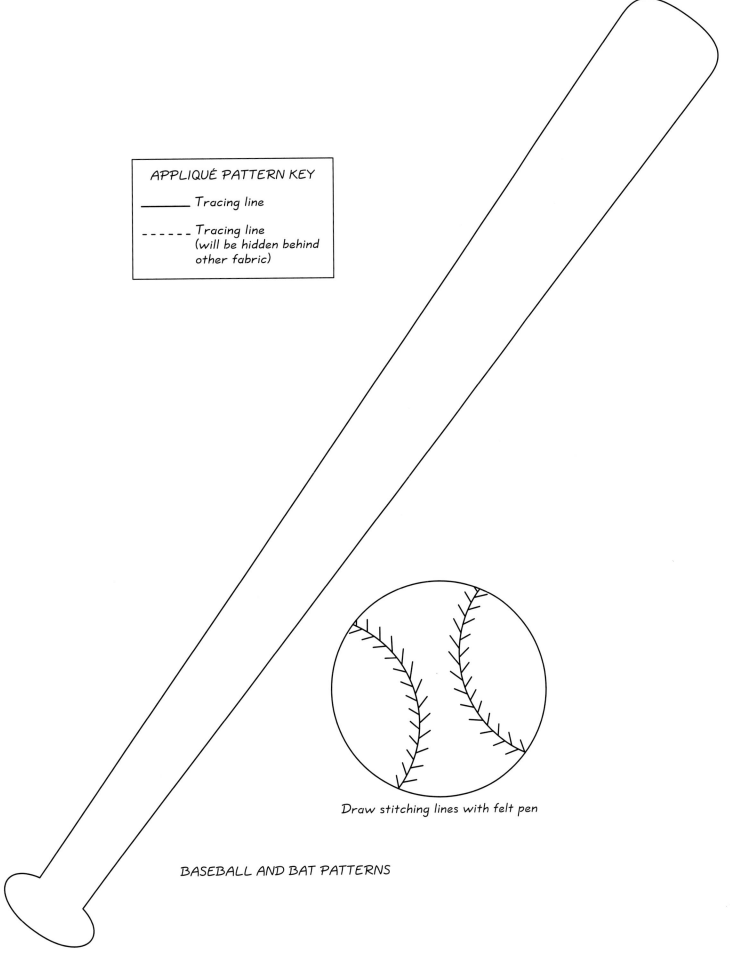

APPLIQUÉ PATTERN KEY

_____ Tracing line

- - - - - - Tracing line
(will be hidden behind
other fabric)

Draw stitching lines with felt pen

BASEBALL AND BAT PATTERNS

HOCKEY PATTERNS

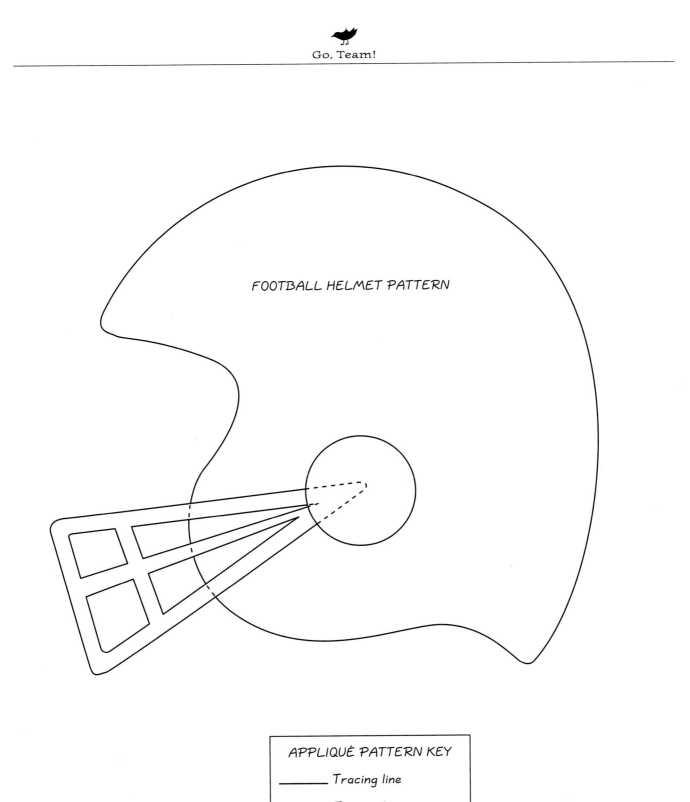

FOOTBALL HELMET PATTERN

APPLIQUÉ PATTERN KEY

——————— Tracing line

– – – – – Tracing line
(will be hidden behind
other fabric)

JERSEY PATTERN

LARGE STAR
PATTERN

SMALL STAR
PATTERN

212

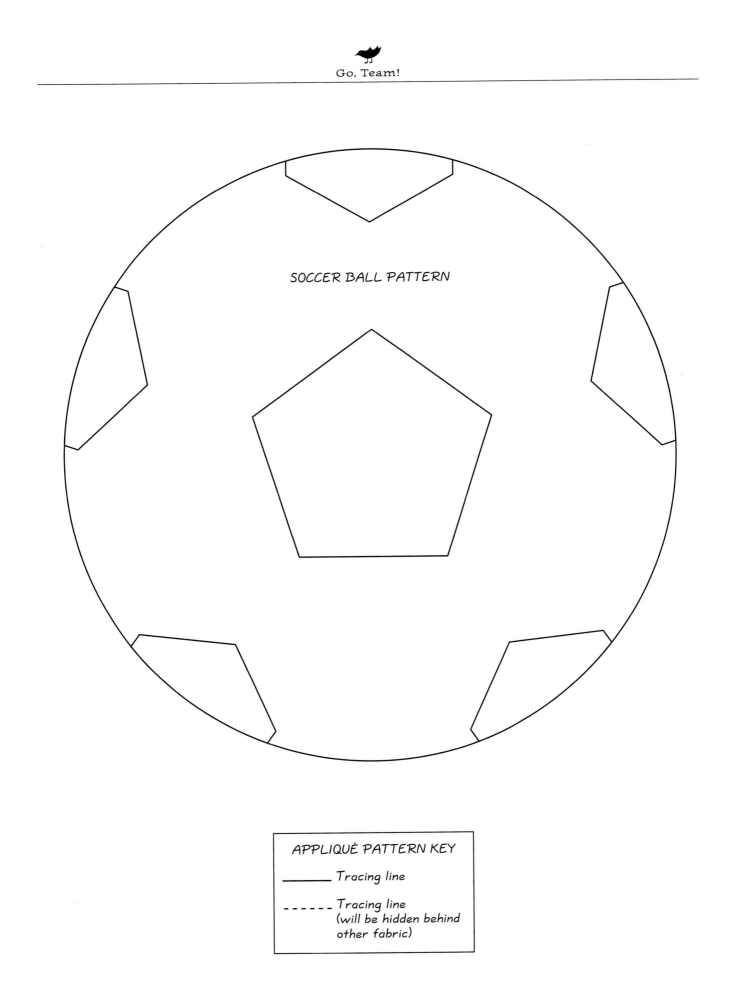

SOCCER BALL PATTERN

APPLIQUÉ PATTERN KEY

——— Tracing line

- - - - - Tracing line
(will be hidden behind
other fabric)

APPLIQUÉ PATTERN KEY

———— Tracing line

- - - - Tracing line
(will be hidden behind
other fabric)

Trace this skate for poster quilt

IN-LINE SKATES PATTERN

SKATEBOARD PATTERN

PENNANT PATTERN

GO!

215

WEEKENDER

POSTER QUILT

Posters are a staple decorating item for kids. Make a fabric version that will thrill any sports-minded youngster. Easy piecing and quick-fuse appliqué guarantee that this project will go together quickly and successfully. In one weekend you'll have a perfect gift for a special young athlete.

Finished Size: 28 × 38 inches

MATERIALS AND CUTTING

Prewash and press all of your fabrics. Using a rotary cutter, see-through ruler, and cutting mat, prepare the pieces as described below. Measurements for all pieces include ¼-inch seam allowances.

FABRIC	YARDAGE	NO. OF PIECES	DIMENSIONS
Blue solid for background and border	⅞ yard	5	9½-inch squares (background)
		2	4½ × 27½-inch strips (border)
Red check for background	⅓ yard	4	9½-inch squares
Black print for accent border	⅛ yard	2	1½ × 27½-inch strips
Black print for binding	⅜ yard	4	2¾ × 42-inch strips
Backing fabric	1 yard	—	—
Flannel for batting	1 yard	—	—
Several coordinated fabrics for appliqué pieces	Scraps, or ⅛- to ¼-yard pieces	—	—
Fusible web; permanent fine-point felt pen			

Assembling the Background

Assemble the quilt top before adding the appliqué pieces. Be sure to use ¼-inch seams and to press the seams after each sewing step.

STEP 1. Sew one 9½-inch red check background square between two 9½-inch blue solid background squares, as shown in **Diagram 1.** Press the seams, following the direction of the arrows in the diagram. Repeat to make a second unit.

DIAGRAM 1

STEP 2. Sew the one remaining 9½-inch blue solid background square between the two remaining 9½-inch red check background squares. Press the seams toward the red check squares.

STEP 3. Sew the unit from Step 2 between the two units from Step 1. See **Diagram 2.** Press.

DIAGRAM 2

STEP 4. Sew the 1½ × 27½-inch accent border strips to the top and bottom. Press the seams toward the accent border.

STEP 5. Sew the 4½ × 27½-inch border strips to the top and bottom. Press the seams toward the accent border.

Appliqué

STEP 1. Refer to "Quick-Fuse Appliqué" on pages 270–271. Referring to the **Quilt Layout,** trace one of each sports design (but just one of the in-line skates) for the background squares and ten additional large stars for the border from the appliqué patterns on pages 207–215.

STEP 2. Quick-fuse each sports design to the center of its corresponding background square.

Soccer Fans

For kids whose favorite sport is soccer, use the soccer ball in all the squares of the Poster Quilt. Or appliqué the child's name, number, and team name in some of the squares. Each background square can be a different fabric, if you want to use up your scraps.

Position and fuse one design at a time, referring to the photo on page 216 for placement. Quick-fuse five large stars to each border strip, allowing for ¼-inch seams.

STEP 3. Use a permanent felt pen to draw stitching lines on the baseball and seam lines on the basketballs.

Layering the Quilt

Arrange and baste the backing, flannel, and top together, following the directions in "Layering the

QUILT LAYOUT

Quilt" on page 275. Trim the flannel and backing to ¼ inch from the raw edges of the quilt top.

Binding the Quilt

Using the four 2¾ × 42-inch binding strips, follow the direc-

tions for "Binding the Quilt" on pages 275–276.

Finishing Stitches

Machine or hand quilt in the seam lines of the background squares, accent border, and

border. Outline the appliqué designs by quilting around the edges. Quilt vertical lines between the stars in the border.

TEAM PILLOWS

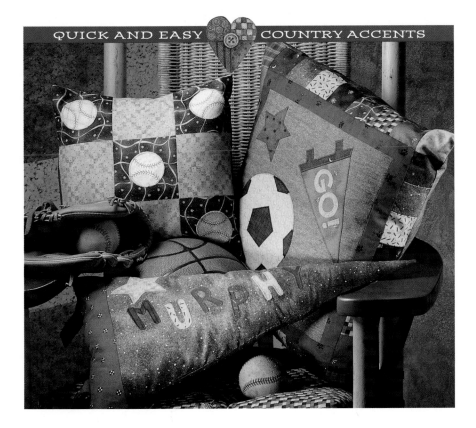

Whether the sport is baseball, soccer, or anything in between, these sportive pillows will be welcome in any team player's bedroom. Soften a chair with them, or add them to a bed for lounging and reading. Shown on the chair are the Personalized Pennant Pillow, *bottom*, the Home Run Nine-Patch Pillow, *top left* (directions on page 221), and the Soccer Ball Pillow, *top right* (page 222).

PERSONALIZED PENNANT PILLOW

Finished Size: 20 × 12 inches

Assembly and Appliqué

STEP 1. See "Materials and Cutting" on the following page. Using a ¼-inch seam, sew the 3 × 14-inch border strip to the 21 × 14-inch green print pennant piece. Press the seam toward the border.

MATERIALS AND CUTTING *(for Personalized Pennant Pillow)*

Prewash and press all of your fabrics. Using a rotary cutter, see-through ruler, and cutting mat, prepare the pieces as described below. Measurements for all pieces include ¼-inch seam allowances.

FABRIC	YARDAGE	NO. OF PIECES	DIMENSIONS
Green print for pennant and backing	¾ yard	1 1	21 × 14-inch piece (pennant) 24 × 14-inch piece (backing)
Red print for border and tabs	⅛ yard	1 1	3 × 14-inch strip (border) 3 × 12-inch strip (tabs)
Several coordinated fabrics for appliqué pieces	Scraps, or ⅛-yard pieces	—	—

Lightweight, sewable fusible web; Tear-Away fabric stabilizer; polyester fiberfill stuffing

STEP 2. Cut the pillow top from the unit from Step 1, as shown in **Diagram 1**. Cut the pillow back to the same size as the front from the 24 × 14-inch green print backing piece.

DIAGRAM 1

STEP 3. Refer to "Quick-Fuse Appliqué" on pages 270–271. Be sure to use a lightweight, sewable fusible web. Trace the large star from the appliqué pattern on page 212. To add a name, draw letters to fit the pennant. The size of the letters will vary depending on the length of the name you are using. Trace the letters in reverse onto the paper side of the fusible web.

STEP 4. Allowing for ¼-inch seams on the raw edges, position and fuse the appliqué pieces to the pennant.

STEP 5. Refer to "Machine Appliqué" on pages 271–272. Use a small zigzag stitch to machine appliqué around the edges of the appliqué pieces. Use the Tear-Away fabric stabilizer on the underside of the pennant for an even machine stitch. Remove the stabilizer after stitching.

A Signature Idea

Have your child print his or her own name to use as a basis for drawing your letters.

Finishing the Pillow

STEP 1. To make the tabs, fold the 3 × 12-inch red print tab strip in half lengthwise with right sides together. Sew a ¼-inch seam along the edge opposite the fold, turn the strip right side out, and press. Topstitch along the edges of both sides. Cut the strip into two 6-inch pieces and fold each piece in half. Position the tabs keeping the raw edges even with the raw edge of the border. Pin and baste the tabs in place. They will be sewn into the seam when the pillow is finished. See **Diagram 2**.

STEP 2. Position the pillow top and backing with right sides together and pin them in place. Using ¼-inch seams, sew around the edges, leaving a 3- to 4-inch opening for turning. Trim the corners and point, turn the pillow right side out, and press. Stuff the pillow with the polyester fiberfill and hand stitch the opening closed.

DIAGRAM 2

12"

12"

HOME RUN NINE-PATCH PILLOW

Finished Size: 12 inches square

(See the pillow on the chair, upper left, in the photo on page 219.)

Assembly and Appliqué

See "Materials and Cutting" below. Assemble the pillow top before adding the appliqué pieces. Be sure to use ¼-inch seams and to press after each sewing step.

STEP 1. Sew the 4½-inch blue print squares and gold print squares together in rows, as shown in **Diagram 3**. Press the

seams toward the blue squares. Sew the rows together and press, following the arrows in the diagram, to complete the pillow top.

12½"

4½"

4½"

4½"

DIAGRAM 3

STEP 2. Refer to "Quick-Fuse Appliqué" on pages 270–271. Be sure to use a lightweight, sewable fusible web. Trace five baseballs from the appliqué pattern on page 209.

STEP 3. Allowing for ¼-inch seams on the raw edges, position and fuse one baseball to the center of each blue print background square.

STEP 4. Refer to "Machine Appliqué" on pages 271–272. Use a small zigzag stitch to machine appliqué around the edges of the baseballs. Use the Tear-Away fabric stabilizer on the underside for an even machine stitch. Remove the stabilizer after stitching. Use the permanent felt pen to draw stitching lines on the baseballs.

Making the Pillow Back

STEP 1. Narrow hem one 12½-inch edge of each 8½ × 12½-inch backing piece by folding ¼ inch to the wrong side. Press. Fold again ¼ inch to the wrong side. Press. Topstitch along the folded edge.

STEP 2. With right sides up, lay one backing piece over the second piece so that the hemmed edges overlap 3½ inches. See **Diagram 4** on the following page. Baste the pieces together at the sides where

MATERIALS AND CUTTING *(for Home Run Nine-Patch Pillow)*

Prewash and press all of your fabrics. Using a rotary cutter, see-through ruler, and cutting mat, prepare the pieces as described below. Measurements for all pieces include ¼-inch seam allowances.

FABRIC	YARDAGE	NO. OF PIECES	DIMENSIONS
■ Blue print for background	⅛ yard	5	4½-inch squares
▦ Gold print for background	⅛ yard	4	4½-inch squares
Backing fabric	⅓ yard	2	8½ × 12½-inch pieces
Several coordinated fabrics for appliqué baseballs	Scraps, or ⅛-yard pieces	—	—
Lightweight, sewable fusible web; Tear-Away fabric stabilizer; permanent, fine-point felt pen; purchased 12-inch pillow form			

they overlap. The pillow back will now measure 12½ inches square.

12½"

12½"

3½" overlap

DIAGRAM 4

Finishing the Pillow

STEP 1. With right sides together, sew the pillow front to the back, using ¼-inch seam allowances. Trim the corners, turn the pillow right side out, and press.

STEP 2. Insert the 12-inch pillow form through the opening in the back of the pillow. To make your own pillow form, refer to "Making Custom-Fit Pillow Forms" on page 194.

18"

18"

SOCCER BALL PILLOW

Finished Size: 18 inches square

(See the pillow on the chair, upper right, in the photo on page 219.)

Assembly and Appliqué

See "Materials and Cutting" on the opposite page. Assemble the pillow top before adding the appliqué pieces. Be sure to use ¼-inch seams and to press after each sewing step.

STEP 1. Sew the 1½ × 12½-inch accent border strips to the top and bottom of the 12½-inch blue solid background square. Press the seams toward the accent border.

STEP 2. Sew the 1½ × 14½-inch accent border strips to the sides. Press.

STEP 3. For the patchwork border, arrange the nine 2½ × 12-inch patchwork border strips in a pleasing order. Sew the strips together to make an 18½ × 12-inch strip set. Using a rotary cutter and ruler, cut four 2½ × 18½-inch strips from this strip set. There should be nine squares in each strip. See **Diagram 5.**

18½"

12"

2½"

DIAGRAM 5

STEP 4. For the top and bottom, use a seam ripper to remove two squares from each of two 2½ × 18½-inch patchwork border strips to make two 2½ × 14½-inch strips with seven squares each. Compare the strips to the top and bottom of the pillow top. You may need to take in or let out a few seams

(⅟₁₆ inch or less) to make them fit. Pin and sew the patchwork border strips to the top and bottom. Press the seams toward the accent border.

STEP 5. Fit, pin, and sew the remaining two 2½ × 18½-inch patchwork border strips to the sides. Press.

STEP 6. Refer to "Quick-Fuse Appliqué" on pages 270–271. Be sure to use a lightweight, sewable fusible web. Trace two large stars from the appliqué pattern on page 212, one soccer ball from page 213, and one pennant from page 210.

STEP 7. Position and fuse the appliqué pieces to the background square, referring to the Soccer Ball Pillow layout for placement.

STEP 8. Refer to "Machine Appliqué" on pages 271–272. Use a small zigzag stitch to machine appliqué around the edges of the appliqué pieces. Use the Tear-Away fabric stabilizer on the underside for an even machine stitch. Remove the stabilizer after stitching.

Making the Pillow Back

STEP 1. Narrow hem one 18½-inch edge of each 11½ × 18½-inch backing piece by folding ¼ inch to the wrong side. Press. Fold again ¼ inch to the wrong side. Press. Topstitch along the folded edge.

MATERIALS AND CUTTING *(for Soccer Ball Pillow)*

Prewash and press all of your fabrics. Using a rotary cutter, see-through ruler, and cutting mat, prepare the pieces as described below. Measurements for all pieces include ¼-inch seam allowances.

FABRIC	YARDAGE	NO. OF PIECES	DIMENSIONS
▪ Blue solid for background	⅜ yard	1	12½-inch square
▪ Red print for accent border	⅛ yard (cut into two 1½ × 42-inch strips)	2 2	1½ × 14½-inch strips 1½ × 12½-inch strips
Assorted fabrics for patchwork border	⅛ yard, or 2½ × 12-inch strip, *each* of 9 fabrics	1	2½ × 12-inch strip *each*
Backing fabric	⅜ yard	2	11½ × 18½-inch pieces
Several coordinated fabrics for appliqué pieces	Scraps, or ⅛- to ¼-yard pieces	—	—
Lightweight, sewable fusible web; Tear-Away fabric stabilizer; purchased 18-inch pillow form			

STEP 2. With right sides up, lay one backing piece over the second piece so that the hemmed edges overlap 3½ inches. See **Diagram 6.** Baste the pieces together at the sides where they overlap. The pillow back will now measure 18½ inches square.

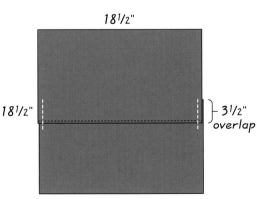

DIAGRAM 6

Finishing the Pillow

STEP 1. With right sides together, sew the pillow front to the back, using ¼-inch seams. Trim the corners, turn the pillow right side out, and press.

STEP 2. Insert the 18-inch pillow form through the opening in the back of the pillow. To make your own pillow form, refer to "Making Custom-Fit Pillow Forms" on page 194.

Debbie's Decorating Diary

I came up with four possible themes for my son, Murphy's, room. I let him choose from Sports, Undersea World, On Safari, or Bugs, Frogs, and Nature. It was a slam dunk choice—Sports!

SPORTING GOODS

QUICK AND EASY ★ COUNTRY ACCENTS

Reward good sportsmanship by making these fun accessories that will add just the right finishing touches to a sports-theme bedroom. Both the Patchwork Sports Valance and the Sports Laundry Bag (directions on page 226) are easy to make with minimal patchwork and machine appliqué.

50"

12"

PATCHWORK SPORTS VALANCE

Finished Size: 50 × 12 inches

These instructions are written for a valance that fits a 33-inch-wide window. You can customize the valance to fit any window. To determine the finished width of the valance, measure your window and multiply the width by 1½. Round up to the nearest even number. Adjust the fabric requirements and cutting dimensions on the following Materials and Cutting list accordingly. Read the first paragraph under each subsequent section for additional directions on customizing your valance.

Appliqué

For a custom valance, cut the background piece 8½ inches long by the width of the valance. It may be necessary to cut two or more pieces. If so, add ¼ inch to each piece for the seam allowance. Choose an appropriate number of sports designs from the appliqué patterns on pages 207–215 to fit the width of the valance. See "Materials and Cutting" on the opposite page.

STEP 1. Using a ¼-inch seam, sew the two 8½ × 25½-inch blue solid background pieces together to make one 8½ × 50½-inch background piece. Press the seam open.

MATERIALS AND CUTTING

Prewash and press all of your fabrics. Using a rotary cutter, see-through ruler, and cutting mat, prepare the pieces as described below. Measurements for all pieces include ¼-inch seam allowances (to make 1 valance).

FABRIC	YARDAGE	NO. OF PIECES	DIMENSIONS
■ Blue solid for background	⅝ yard	2	8½ × 25½-inch pieces
Assorted fabrics for patchwork border	Scrap, or ⅛-yard piece, *each* of 8 fabrics	25	2½-inch squares *total*
■ Red print for border	⅙ yard (cut into three 1½ × 42-inch strips)	2 / 2	1½ × 38½-inch strips / 1½ × 12½-inch strips
Backing fabric	¾ yard	2	12½ × 25½-inch pieces
Several coordinated fabrics for appliqué pieces	Scraps, or ⅛- to ¼-yard pieces	—	—
Lightweight, sewable fusible web; Tear-Away fabric stabilizer			

STEP 2. Refer to "Quick-Fuse Appliqué" on pages 270–271. Be sure to use a lightweight, sewable fusible web. Trace six large stars from the appliqué pattern on page 212, three pennants from page 210, one skateboard from page 215, and one pair of in-line skates from page 214.

STEP 3. Allowing for ¼-inch seams on the raw edges, position and fuse the appliqué pieces to the background, referring to the valance layout on page 224 for placement. It may be helpful to use the Appliqué Pressing Sheet as described on page 203.

STEP 4. Refer to "Machine Appliqué" on pages 271–272. Use a small zigzag stitch to machine appliqué around the edges of the appliqué pieces. Use the Tear-Away fabric stabilizer on the underside of the background. Remove the stabilizer after stitching.

Borders and Backing

For a custom valance, determine how many 2½-inch patchwork border squares you need. Divide the finished width of the valance by 2 and cut that many squares from an assortment of fabrics. Cut each red print border strip 1½ inches by the width of the valance. Cut the backing 12½ inches by the width of the valance. It may be necessary to piece the red border strips and backing. If so, add ¼ inch to each piece for the seam allowance.

STEP 1. Arrange the twenty-five 2½-inch patchwork border squares in a pleasing order. Using ¼-inch seams, sew the squares together to make a 2½ × 50½-inch strip.

STEP 2. Compare the patchwork border strip to the bottom of the blue solid background. You may need to take in or let out a few seams (1⁄16 inch or less) to make it fit. Pin and sew the strip to the bottom of the background. Press the seam toward the background.

STEP 3. Sew one 1½ × 38½-inch red print border strip to each of the 1½ × 12½-inch red border strips to make two 1½ × 50½-inch strips. Press.

STEP 4. Sew the border strips from Step 3 to the top and bottom of the valance front. Press the seams toward the red print border.

STEP 5. Sew the two 12½ × 25½-inch backing pieces together to make one 12½ × 50½-inch backing piece. Press the seam open.

STEP 6. With right sides together, pin the sides of the valance front and backing together. Sew the sides together, beginning at the seam line of the top red print border and the blue solid background. See **Diagram 1**.

Begin stitching

Leave open

DIAGRAM 1

STEP 7. Turn the valance right side out and press the side seams. Press under and topstitch the edges of the unsewn side seams as shown in **Diagram 2**.

DIAGRAM 2

STEP 8. Turn the valance inside out so that right sides are together. Pin and sew the top and bottom of the valance, leaving a 3- to 4-inch opening for turning. Turn the valance right side out, hand stitch the opening closed, and press.

STEP 9. To complete the casing for the rod, pin and stitch in the seam line between the top red print border and blue solid background.

24"

28"

SPORTS LAUNDRY BAG

Finished Size: 24 × 28 inches

(See the laundry bag in the photo on page 224.)

Appliqué

STEP 1. See "Materials and Cutting" on the opposite page. Refer to "Quick-Fuse Appliqué"

on pages 270–271. Be sure to use a lightweight, sewable fusible web. Trace three jerseys and five large stars from the appliqué patterns on page 212.

STEP 2. Fold the 48½ × 23½-inch blue solid background piece in half crosswise with wrong sides together, and press. Allowing for ¼-inch seams on the raw edges, position and fuse the appliqué pieces to the background between the fold and raw edge, referring to the Laundry Bag layout at left for placement.

STEP 3. Refer to "Machine Appliqué" on pages 271–272. Use a small zigzag stitch to machine appliqué around the edges of the appliqué pieces. Use the Tear-

Polarfleece Throw

(See the throw on the top bunk in the photo on page 198.)

Materials

1 purchased Polarfleece throw

Scraps, or ⅛- to ¼-yard pieces, of several coordinated fabrics for appliqué pieces

Lightweight, sewable fusible web

Tear-Away fabric stabilizer

#5 perle cotton

Assembly

STEP 1. See "Quick-Fuse Appliqué" on pages 270–271. Trace an assortment of sports designs from the patterns on pages 207–215.

STEP 2. Position and fuse the designs to the throw.

STEP 3. Refer to "Machine Appliqué" on pages 271–272. Use a small zigzag stitch to machine appliqué around the edges of the appliqué pieces. Use the Tear-Away fabric stabilizer on the underside of the throw for an even machine stitch. Remove the stabilizer after stitching.

STEP 4. If your Polarfleece throw is finished with a large blanket stitch, use two strands of a contrasting color of pearl cotton to hand stitch over every other stitch.

MATERIALS AND CUTTING

Prewash and press all of your fabrics. Using a rotary cutter, see-through ruler, and cutting mat, prepare the pieces as described below. Measurements for all pieces include ¼-inch seam allowances.

FABRIC	YARDAGE	NO. OF PIECES	DIMENSIONS
■ Blue solid for background	1½ yards	1	48½ × 23½-inch piece
■ Red print for accent border	⅛ yard	2	1½ × 42-inch strips
Assorted fabrics for patchwork border	⅙ yard *each* of 6 fabrics	2	4½-inch squares *each*
Lining fabric	1½ yards	1	48½ × 28½-inch piece
Several coordinated fabrics for appliqué pieces	Scraps, or ⅛- to ¼-yard pieces	—	—
Lightweight, sewable fusible web; Tear-Away fabric stabilizer; 1⅔ yards cording for drawstring			

Away fabric stabilizer on the wrong side of the background for an even machine stitch. Remove the stabilizer after stitching.

Assembly

STEP 1. Using ¼-inch seams, sew the twelve 4½-inch patchwork border squares together to make a 4½ × 48½-inch strip.

STEP 2. Sew the two 1½ × 42-inch accent border strips together to make one strip approximately 1½ × 84 inches. Press. Trim the strip to 1½ × 48½ inches.

STEP 3. Sew the lining, patchwork border, accent border, and background together in the order shown in **Diagram 3**. Press the seams, following the arrows in the diagram.

STEP 4. Fold the laundry bag in half with right sides together. Using ¼-inch seams, sew along the ends

and the edge opposite the fold. Leave an opening in the lining for turning and in the accent border for the drawstring. Backstitch on both sides of the accent border to reinforce the drawstring opening. See **Diagram 4**.

STEP 5. Turn the laundry bag right side out, hand stitch the opening closed, and press. Tuck the lining inside and press along the top edge.

STEP 6. To make the drawstring casing, stitch in the seam line on both sides of the accent border. Thread the cording through the casing, and tie a knot in each end.

DIAGRAM 3

DIAGRAM 4

HEARTS AND FLOWERS BEDROOM

Take one girl's bedroom, add these sweet and sentimental projects,

and you'll have an enchanting decorator look. All the projects are based on the

directions for the Sports Fever Kid's Bedroom projects (directions begin on page

201), including the bed quilt, pillowcase, throw pillows, valance, laundry bag,

and jacket. I've changed the motifs and the fabric colors, but the materials,

yardages, cutting, and assembling are basically the same.

Hearts and Flowers Quilt

Finished Size: 75 × 87 inches

Make this sweet girl's quilt following the directions for the Sports Quilt on page 201. Use pinks, yellows, and pale blues and greens rather than bright primary colors. Simply replace the sports designs with the hearts and flowers designs, using the appliqué patterns on page 232. Fuse hearts to the small corner squares and flowers to the large corner squares.

Machine or hand quilt as desired. The quilt in the photo on the opposite page was machine quilted around the appliqué designs. A large stipple and heart pattern was quilted in the background. Make one yo-yo for each flower from the large yo-yo pattern on page 195. Sew a yo-yo to each flower center.

Refer to "Making Yo-yos" on pages 272–273.

Note: The Hearts and Flowers Quilt made from the Sports Quilt directions will be slightly larger than the quilt shown in the photo on the opposite page. There will be more of a drop on the sides of the quilt.

Ruffled Posy Pillow

Finished Size: 18 inches in diameter

(See the pillow on the bed, middle, in the photo on page 228.)

MATERIALS AND CUTTING

Prewash and press all of your fabrics. Using a rotary cutter, see-through ruler, and cutting mat, prepare the pieces as described below. Measurements for all pieces include ¼-inch seam allowances.

FABRIC	YARDAGE	NO. OF PIECES	DIMENSIONS
☐ Green print for pillow top and backing	½ yard	2	12½-inch circles
▦ Blue print for ruffle	⅝ yard	2 1	6½ × 40-inch strips 6½ × 20-inch strip
Several coordinated fabrics for appliqué pieces and yo-yos	Scraps, or ⅛- to ¼-yard pieces	—	—

¼ yard lightweight, sewable fusible web; Tear-Away fabric stabilizer; 1¼ yards strong crochet thread or #5 perle cotton; polyester fiberfill stuffing

Appliqué

STEP 1. Refer to "Quick-Fuse Appliqué" on pages 270–271. Use a lightweight, sewable fusible web. Trace one flower and six leaves from the appliqué patterns on page 232.

STEP 2. Position and fuse the design to the center of the pillow top.

STEP 3. Refer to "Machine Appliqué" on pages 271–272. Use a small zigzag stitch to machine appliqué around the edges of the appliqué pieces. Use the Tear-Away fabric stabilizer on the underside of the pillow top. Remove the stabilizer after stitching.

Finishing the Pillow

STEP 1. Refer to "Making Yo-yos" on pages 272–273. Make one large yo-yo from the pattern on page 232. Sew the yo-yo to the center of the flower.

STEP 2. Using ¼-inch seams, sew the two 6½ × 40-inch and one 6½ × 20-inch ruffle strips together to make a continuous loop. Press the ruffle in half lengthwise with wrong sides together.

STEP 3. Sew a gathering stitch along the raw edge of the ruffle by zigzag stitching over the crochet thread or pearl cotton. Divide the ruffle into quarters and mark.

STEP 4. Divide the pillow top in quarters by gently folding it in half two times. Mark the folds. Matching the marks and keeping the raw edges together, position and pin the ruffle onto the pillow top. Gather the ruffle by pulling the gathering cord. Evenly distribute the gathers as you pin the ruffle to the pillow top. See **Diagram 1**. Baste the ruffle to the pillow top.

DIAGRAM 1

STEP 5. With the ruffle in the middle, position the pillow top and backing with right sides together, and pin them in place. Using ¼-inch seam allowances, sew around the pillow, leaving a 3- to 4-inch opening for turning. Turn the pillow right side out and press. Stuff the pillow with the polyester fiberfill, and hand stitch the opening closed.

HEARTS PILLOW

To create the pillow shown on the bed, left, in the photo on page 228, follow the directions for the Soccer Ball Pillow on page 222. To make the circle of hearts, draw an 8-inch circle on the center of the background square. Using the circle as a positioning guide, fuse nine hearts traced from the appliqué pattern on the following page. Refer to "Making Yo-yos" on pages 272–273. Make five large yo-yos from the pattern on page 195. Sew one yo-yo to each corner of the accent border and one to the center of the pillow.

NINE-PATCH PILLOW

To make the nine-patch pillow shown on the bed, right, in the photo on page 228, choose some pretty pastel fabrics. Follow the directions for the Home Run Nine-Patch Pillow on page 221, replacing the baseballs with five hearts traced from the appliqué pattern on page 232. Refer to "Making Yo-yos" on pages 272–273. Make five small yo-yos from the pattern on page 232. Sew one yo-yo to the center of each heart.

PILLOWCASE

Make a soft and feminine pillowcase by adding hearts and yo-yos to the border. Follow the directions for the Sports Pillowcase on page 205.

Trace four hearts from the appliqué pattern on page 232 and fuse them to the pillowcase border. Refer to "Making Yo-yos" on pages 272–273. Make four small yo-yos from the pattern on page 232. Sew one yo-yo to the center of each heart.

LAUNDRY BAG

Follow the directions for the Sports Laundry Bag on page 226. Replace the jerseys and stars on the bag with hearts and flowers. Trace four hearts, three flowers with round centers, and nine leaves from the appliqué patterns on page 232. Position and fuse the appliqué pieces to the bag, referring to the illustration above for placement.

VALANCE

Follow the directions for the Patchwork Sports Valance on page 224. Replace the sports designs with hearts and flowers, using the appliqué patterns on page 232. Refer to "Making Yo-yos" on pages 272–273. Make one large yo-yo for each flower from the pattern on page 232. Sew a yo-yo to each flower center.

JACKET

Turn a plain denim jacket into a
wardrobe favorite for a young girl.
Follow the directions for the Sports
Jacket on page 206. Trace three
hearts, one flower, and three leaves
from the appliqué patterns below.
Sew assorted buttons to the back
of the jacket.

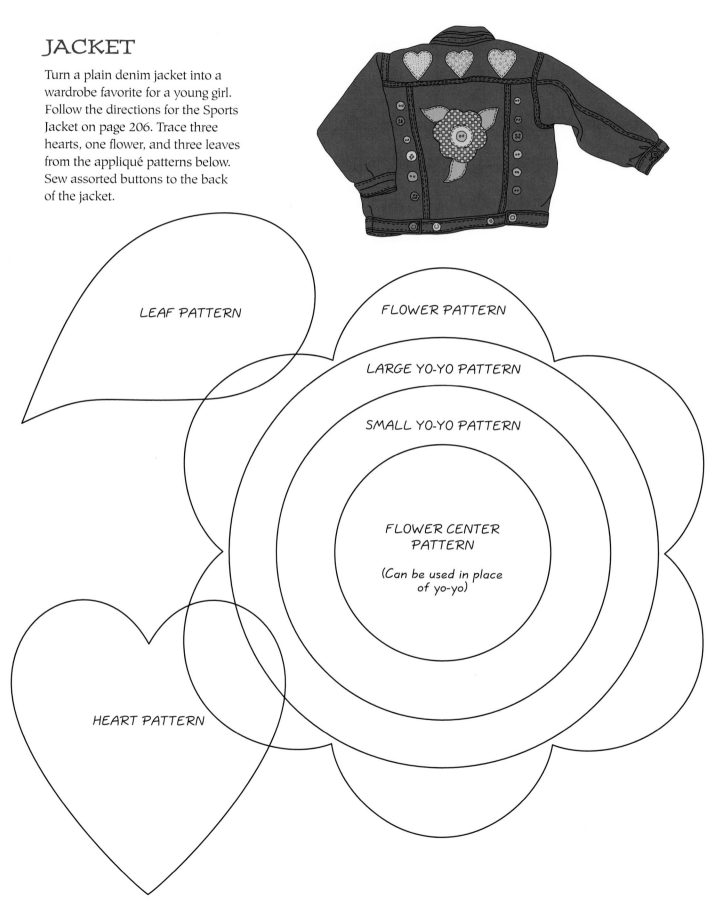

LEAF PATTERN

FLOWER PATTERN

LARGE YO-YO PATTERN

SMALL YO-YO PATTERN

FLOWER CENTER
PATTERN

(Can be used in place
of yo-yo)

HEART PATTERN

CHARMING NOOKS, CRANNIES, AND DOORS

Nearly every house has wonderful little out-of-the-way areas that I like to call nooks and crannies. They are perfect for showcasing different decorating themes. In this section, I've included projects for a Gardening Nook (page 234) and a Christmas Nook (page 243), along with a Holiday Front Door (page 252).

GARDENING NOOK

Whether you're a gardener or not, the sweet Garden Gatherings

Angel hanging on the wall will win you over. The framed Garden Bouquet

(directions on page 237) on the left side of the table is a freshly gathered

bouquet of yo-yos and quick-fused three-dimensional flowers—a great gift

idea! The Tulip Pot (page 238) hanging on the wall is cute

as a button with a button-embellished frame.

Garden Gatherings Angel

Finished Picture Size: 20 ×16 inches　　　　**Finished Framed Size: 24 × 20 inches**

M A T E R I A L S   A N D   C U T T I N G

Prewash and press all of your fabrics. Using a rotary cutter, see-through ruler, and cutting mat, prepare the pieces as described below. Measurements for all pieces include ¼-inch seam allowances.

FABRIC	YARDAGE	NO. OF PIECES	DIMENSIONS
☐ Blue prints for sky background	Scrap, or ⅛-yard piece, *each* of 8 to 12 fabrics	40	2½-inch squares *total*
◼ Green prints for grass background	Scrap, or ⅛-yard piece, *each* of 8 to 12 fabrics	40	2½-inch squares *total*
Muslin for framing strips	⅛ yard (cut into two 1¾ × 42-inch strips)	2 2	1¾ × 20½-inch strips 1¾ × 19-inch strips
Several coordinated fabrics for appliqué pieces, dimensional flowers and leaves, and yo-yos	Scraps, or ⅛- to ¼-yard pieces	—	—
Fusible web; embroidery floss; assorted buttons; 16 × 20-inch piece of cotton batting; 16 × 20-inch frame; tacky glue or masking tape			

Assembly

Assemble the background before adding the appliqué pieces. Be sure to use ¼-inch seams and press seams after each sewing step.

STEP 1. Lay out the 2½-inch blue print background squares in a pleasing arrangement of four rows with ten squares each. Keep track of your layout while sewing the sky background together. Press the seams in Rows #1 and #3 to the left and in Rows #2 and #4 to the right. Join the rows and press.

STEP 2. Repeat Step 1 for the 2½-inch green print squares.

STEP 3. Sew the unit from Step 1 to the unit from Step 2. Press.

STEP 4. Sew the 1¾ × 20½-inch muslin framing strips to the top and bottom. Press the seams toward the framing strips. Sew the 1¾ × 19-inch framing strips to the sides. Press.

Appliqué

STEP 1. Refer to "Quick-Fuse Appliqué" on pages 270–271. Trace the angel from the appliqué patterns on pages 240–241. To make dimensional wings, fuse the wings to the selected wing fabric and cut them out. Instead of fusing the wings to the background, fuse them to the wrong side of a second piece of wing fabric. Trim even with the edges of the fused wings.

STEP 2. Position the wings behind the angel and fuse the angel to the background, referring to the **Angel Layout** for placement. Sew the wings to the background by stitching along the center of each wing. Use two strands of embroidery floss and a running stitch.

STEP 3. Trace a total of 10 to 15 flowers and a total of 35 to 42 leaves from the patterns on page 239. To make dimensional flowers and leaves, fuse the flowers and leaves to the selected fabrics, and cut them out. Instead of fusing the flowers and leaves to the background, fuse each to the wrong side of a second piece of flower or leaf fabric. Trim even with the edges of the fused flowers and leaves. For the bell-shaped flowers, fringe the fluted edge by cutting ½-inch slits approximately ¹⁄₁₆ to ⅛ inch apart.

STEP 4. Refer to "Making Yo-yos" on pages 272–273. Make 25 to 30 yo-yo flowers of assorted sizes from the patterns on page 241.

STEP 5. Position the flowers on the background, referring to the **Garden Gatherings Angel Layout** below for placement. Hand sew the flowers in place with a blind stitch, a button center, or French knots. See "Decorative Stitches" on page 272 for instructions on making French knots.

STEP 6. Mark the bucket handle and flower stems on the background. Use three strands of embroidery floss and a stem stitch to make the handle and stems, referring to "Decorative Stitches" on page 272 for instructions. Hand sew one leaf to each stem. Use two strands of embroidery floss to make a French-knot eye on the angel.

STEP 7. Place the batting on top of the cardboard backing from the picture frame. With the batting in the middle, center and stretch the picture over the cardboard. Secure the edges on the back of the cardboard with the tacky glue or masking tape. Insert the picture in the back of the frame, and secure it.

20½"

16½"

GARDEN GATHERINGS ANGEL LAYOUT

Garden Bouquet

Finished Picture Size: 8 × 10 inches
Finished Framed Size: 10 × 12 inches

(See the bouquet picture on the left side of the table in the photo on page 234.)

MATERIALS AND CUTTING

Prewash and press all of your fabrics. Using a rotary cutter, see-through ruler, and cutting mat, prepare the pieces as described below. Measurements for all pieces include ¼-inch seam allowances.

FABRIC	YARDAGE	NO. OF PIECES	DIMENSIONS
Blue prints for background	Scrap, or ⅛-yard piece, *each* of 5 to 9 fabrics	20	2½-inch squares *total*
Muslin for framing strips	⅛ yard (cut into two 1¾ × 42-inch strips)	2	1¾ × 13-inch strips
		2	1¾ × 8½-inch strips
Several coordinated fabrics for dimensional flowers and leaves and for yo-yos	Scraps, or ⅛-yard pieces	—	—

Fusible web; assorted buttons; embroidery floss; silk ribbon; 8 × 10-inch piece of cotton batting; 8 × 10-inch frame; tacky glue or masking tape

Assembly

Assemble the background before adding the bouquet. Be sure to use ¼-inch seams and to press seams after each sewing step.

STEP 1. Lay out the 2½-inch blue print background squares in a pleasing arrangement of five rows with four squares each. Keep track of your layout while sewing the background together. Press the seams in Rows #1, #3, and #5 to the left and in Rows #2 and #4 to the right. Join the rows and press the seams in one direction.

STEP 2. Sew 1¾ × 8½-inch framing strips to the top and bottom. Press seams toward the framing strips. Sew 1¾ × 13-inch framing strips to the sides. Press.

Appliqué

STEP 1. Refer to "Quick-Fuse Appliqué" on pages 270–271. Trace a total of 4 to 6 flowers and 10 to 12 leaves from the patterns on page 239. To make dimensional flowers and leaves, fuse the flowers and leaves to the selected fabrics, and cut them out. Fuse each to the wrong side of a second piece of flower or leaf fabric. Trim even with the edges of the fused flowers and leaves. For the bell-shaped flowers, fringe the

fluted edge by cutting ½-inch slits approximately 1/16 to ⅛ inch apart. Cut slits in the circular flowers as shown on the pattern.

STEP 2. Refer to "Making Yo-yos" on pages 272–273. Make 8 to 12 yo-yo flowers of assorted sizes from the patterns on page 241.

STEP 3. Referring to the **Garden Bouquet Layout** on the following page, arrange your floral bouquet. Hand sew the flowers in place with a blind stitch, a button center, or French knots. Use two strands of embroidery floss and a backstitch to make the flower stems. See "Decorative Stitches" on page 272 for instructions on backstitching and making French knots. Hand sew the leaves to the stems.

STEP 4. Tie a bow with the silk ribbon and hand sew the bow to the bouquet stems. Drape and tack the ends in place.

STEP 5. Place the batting on top of the cardboard backing from the picture frame. With the batting in the middle, center and stretch the picture over the cardboard. Secure

the edges on the back of the cardboard with the tacky glue or masking tape. Insert the picture in the back of the frame and secure it.

GARDEN BOUQUET LAYOUT

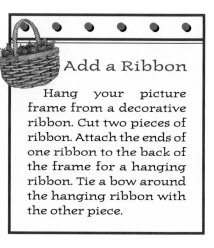

Add a Ribbon

Hang your picture frame from a decorative ribbon. Cut two pieces of ribbon. Attach the ends of one ribbon to the back of the frame for a hanging ribbon. Tie a bow around the hanging ribbon with the other piece.

Tulip Pot

Finished Picture Size: 4 × 6 inches
Finished Framed Size: 7 × 9 inches

(See the tulip picture on the wall in the photo on page 234.)

Materials

7 × 9-inch piece of green print for
　background
Scraps, or ⅛-yard pieces, of several
　coordinated fabrics for appliqué
　pieces
Fusible web
Embroidery floss
Silk ribbon
4 × 6-inch piece of cotton batting
4 × 6-inch frame
Tacky glue or masking tape
Assorted buttons

Assembly

STEP 1. Refer to "Quick-Fuse Appliqué" on pages 270–271. Trace the tulip pot from the

appliqué pattern on the opposite page. Quick-fuse the design to the center of the 7 × 9-inch green print background piece.

STEP 2. Mark the tulip stems on the background. Use two strands of embroidery floss and a stem stitch to make the stems, referring to "Decorative Stitches" on page 272 for instructions.

STEP 3. Tie a bow with the silk ribbon and hand sew the bow to the vase.

STEP 4. Place the batting on top of the cardboard backing from the picture frame. With the batting in the middle, center and stretch the

picture over the cardboard. Secure the edges on the back of the cardboard with the tacky glue or masking tape. Insert the picture in the back of the frame and secure it. Glue assorted buttons to the frame.

4"

6"

TULIP LAYOUT

Painting Tip

Paint your picture frame to coordinate with your pot of tulips. Add a miniature checkerboard around the opening. Instead of gluing buttons to the frame, paint small clusters of tulips!

APPLIQUÉ PATTERN KEY

——— Tracing line

- - - - - Tracing line
(will be hidden behind other fabric)

TULIP POT PATTERN

GARDEN GATHERINGS
ANGEL FLOWER PATTERNS

LEAF PATTERNS

Cut slits

GARDEN BOUQUET FLOWER PATTERNS

ANGEL PATTERN
ASSEMBLY DIAGRAM

Match with
Angel Pattern
B

Match with
Angel Pattern
D

ANGEL PATTERN
A

Match with Angel Pattern C

240

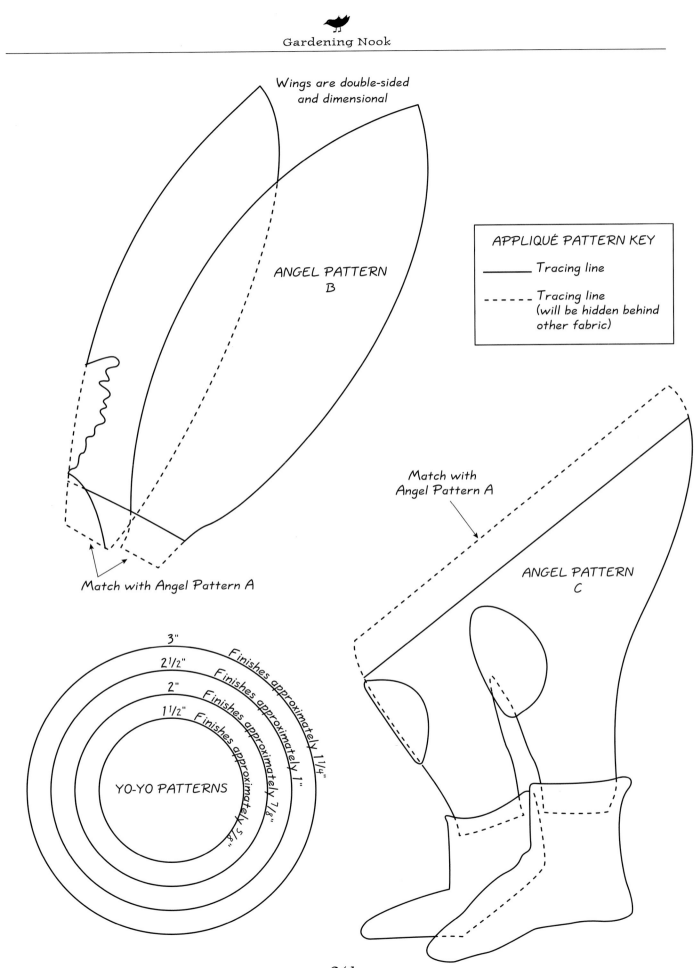

Wings are double-sided
and dimensional

ANGEL PATTERN
B

APPLIQUÉ PATTERN KEY

Tracing line

Tracing line
(will be hidden behind
other fabric)

Match with Angel Pattern A

Match with
Angel Pattern A

ANGEL PATTERN
C

3"
2½"
2"
1½"

Finishes approximately 1¼"
Finishes approximately 1"
Finishes approximately ⅞"
Finishes approximately ⅝"

YO-YO PATTERNS

Match with
Angel Pattern
E

ANGEL PATTERN
E

Match with
Angel Pattern D

APPLIQUÉ PATTERN KEY

—————— Tracing line

------------ Tracing line
(will be hidden behind
other fabric)

Match with
Angel Pattern
A

Stem stitch handle

Every other shape is green

Black

Black rim

Gray

ANGEL PATTERN D

242

CHRISTMAS NOOK

Decorate a nook for Christmas with six quick and easy framed wallhangings, and enjoy it all winter. As seen on the next page, the delightful Merry Snowman and Birdhouse hanging on the wall has a pieced background that adds to its charm. The Embroidered Tree (directions on page 245), resting on the shelf against the wall, is hand stitched—you get a handmade look with minimal effort. The Birdhouse and Candle pictures (page 246) on the wall, along with the Star and Moon fabric pieces (page 247) on the shelves, are great fun to make from your scraps. They make wonderful gifts, as well!

Merry Snowman and Birdhouse

Finished Picture Size: 12 × 14 inches   **Finished Framed Size: 15 × 18 inches**

MATERIALS AND CUTTING

Prewash and press all of your fabrics. Using a rotary cutter, see-through ruler, and cutting mat, prepare the pieces as described below. Measurements for all pieces include ¼-inch seam allowances.

FABRIC	YARDAGE	NO. OF PIECES	DIMENSIONS
Gray prints for sky background	Scrap, or ⅛-yard piece, *each* of 6 to 8 fabrics	30	2½-inch squares *total*
Tan prints for snow background	Scrap, or ⅛-yard piece, *each* of 6 to 8 fabrics	12	2½-inch squares *total*
Muslin for framing strips	⅛ yard (cut into two 1¾ × 42-inch strips)	2 2	1¾ × 12½-inch strips 1¾ × 17-inch strips
Several coordinated fabrics for appliqué pieces	Scraps, or ⅛- to ¼-yard pieces	—	—
Fusible web; embroidery floss; assorted buttons; 11 × 14-inch piece of cotton batting; 11 × 14-inch frame; tacky glue or masking tape			

Assembly

Assemble the background before adding the appliqué pieces. Be sure to use ¼-inch seams and to press after each sewing step.

STEP 1. Lay out the 2½-inch gray print background squares in a pleasing arrangement of five rows with six squares each. Keep track of your layout while sewing the sky background together. Press the seams in Rows #1, #3, and #5 to the left and in Rows #2 and #4 to the right. Join the rows and press.

STEP 2. Lay out the 2½-inch tan print background squares in a pleasing arrangement of two rows with six squares each. Keep track of your layout while sewing the snow background together. Press the seams in Row #1 to the right and in Row #2 to the left. Join the rows and press.

STEP 3. Sew the unit from Step 1 to the unit from Step 2. Press.

STEP 4. Sew the 1¾ × 12½-inch framing strips to the top and bottom. Press the seams toward the framing strips. Sew the 1¾ × 17-inch framing strips to the sides. Press.

Appliqué

STEP 1. Refer to "Quick-Fuse Appliqué" on pages 270–271. Trace the snowman and birdhouse from the appliqué patterns on pages 249–250. Quick-fuse the design to the background, referring to the photo on the opposite page for placement.

STEP 2. Mark the holly stem and bird legs on the background. Use two strands of embroidery floss and a backstitch to make the stem and legs. Use three strands of embroidery floss to make French knots for the snowman face and bird eyes. See "Decorative Stitches" on page 272 for instructions on backstitching and making French knots. If desired, sew assorted buttons to the birdhouse and holly stem.

STEP 3. Place the batting on top of the cardboard backing from the picture frame. With the batting in the middle, center and stretch the picture over the cardboard. Secure the edges on the back of the cardboard with the tacky glue or masking tape. Insert the picture in the back of the frame and secure it.

MERRY SNOWMAN AND BIRDHOUSE LAYOUT

Embroidered Tree

Finished Picture Size: 11 × 14 inches
Finished Framed Size: 13 × 16 inches

(See the tree picture on the wall in the photo on the opposite page.)

Materials

15 × 18-inch piece of brown solid wool for background
Scraps of several coordinated fabrics for appliqué stars
Fusible web
Embroidery floss
Assorted ceramic buttons
11 × 14-inch piece of cotton batting
11 × 14-inch frame
Tacky glue or masking tape
11 × 14-inch mat with 8 × 11-inch opening

Assembly

STEP 1. Transfer the embroidery design from the pattern on page 251 to the center of the 15 × 18-inch brown solid background piece.

Ceramic Buttons

The charming ceramic buttons featured in the Embroidered Tree are by Debbie Mumm designs for Mill Hill. Look for these and many other delightful designs in your local quilt shop. If you are unable to find them, see "Quilting by Mail" on page 280.

STEP 2. Refer to "Quick-Fuse Appliqué" on pages 270–271. Trace the stars from the appliqué pattern on page 251. Quick-fuse the stars to the background,

referring to the pattern on page 251 for placement.

STEP 3. Use three strands of embroidery floss and a backstitch to make the tree and snow. Use two strands of embroidery floss to make French knots for the falling snow. See "Decorative Stitches" on page 272 for instructions.

STEP 4. Sew assorted ceramic buttons to the background, referring to the pattern on page 251 for placement.

STEP 5. Place the batting on top of the cardboard backing from the picture frame. With the batting in the middle, center and stretch the picture over the cardboard. Secure

the edges on the back of the cardboard with the tacky glue or masking tape. Insert the mat and picture in the back of the frame and secure them.

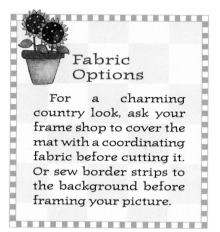

Fabric Options

For a charming country look, ask your frame shop to cover the mat with a coordinating fabric before cutting it. Or sew border strips to the background before framing your picture.

Birdhouse or Candle

Finished Picture Size: 5 × 7 inches
Finished Framed Size: 8 × 10 inches

(See the birdhouse and candle pictures on the wall in the photo on page 244.)

Materials
To make 1 picture:

5 × 7-inch piece of tan print for background
Scraps of several coordinated fabrics for appliqué pieces
Fusible web
Embroidery floss
Assorted buttons
5 × 7-inch piece of cotton batting
5 × 7-inch frame
Tacky glue

Assembly

STEP 1. Refer to "Quick-Fuse Appliqué" on pages 270–271. Trace the birdhouse from the appliqué pattern on page 250 or the candle from page 248. Quick-fuse the design to the center of the 5 × 7-inch tan print background piece, referring to the photo on page 244 for placement.

STEP 2. For the birdhouse picture, use two strands of embroidery floss to make a French-knot

eye on the bird, referring to "Decorative Stitches" on page 272 for instructions. Sew buttons to the birdhouse to make the "holes." For the candle picture, mark the lines for the "glow" on the background.

Take Brush in Hand
Paint your frame with coordinating colors to complement your design.

Use two strands of embroidery floss and a running stitch to outline the glow. Sew buttons to the holly leaves to make berries.

STEP 3. Place the batting on top of the cardboard backing from the picture frame. With the batting in the middle, center the picture on the cardboard. Secure the edges of the batting and background with tacky glue. Insert the picture in the back of the frame and secure it.

5½"

5½"

Star or Moon

Finished Picture Size: 3 inches square
Finished Framed Size: 5½ inches square

(See the star and moon pictures on the shelves in the photo on page 244.)

Materials

To make 1 picture:

3-inch square of red wool or felt for background
Scraps of coordinated fabrics for star or moon appliqués
⅛ yard, or 4-inch piece, fusible web
Embroidery floss
Button
3-inch square of cotton batting
3 × 3-inch frame
Tacky glue

Assembly

STEP 1. Refer to "Quick-Fuse Appliqué" on pages 270–271. Trace the star or moon from the appliqué patterns on page 250. Quick-fuse the design to the center of the red background square, referring to the photo on page 244 for placement.

STEP 2. Use two strands of embroidery floss to sew a running stitch around the star. Sew a button to the center of the star. For the moon picture, use two strands of embroidery floss and a backstitch to make the eyebrow. Use two strands of embroidery floss to sew a running stitch around the moon and to make a French-knot eye. See "Decorative Stitches" on page 272 for instructions on backstitching and making French knots.

STEP 3. Place the batting on top of the cardboard backing from the picture frame. With the batting in the middle, center the picture on the cardboard. Secure the edges of the batting and background with the tacky glue. Insert the picture in the back of the frame and secure it.

Add a Checkerboard

Paint a miniature checkerboard around the opening of the frame.

APPLIQUÉ PATTERN KEY

———— Tracing line

- - - - - Tracing line
(will be hidden behind
other fabric)

CANDLE PATTERN

Align bird legs here

BIRD PATTERN

MERRY SNOWMAN PATTERN

APPLIQUÉ PATTERN KEY

——— Tracing line

- - - - - Tracing line
(will be hidden behind
other fabric)

STAR PATTERN

BIRDHOUSE PATTERN

MOON
PATTERN

← Cut off branch
here for
framed birdhouse

250

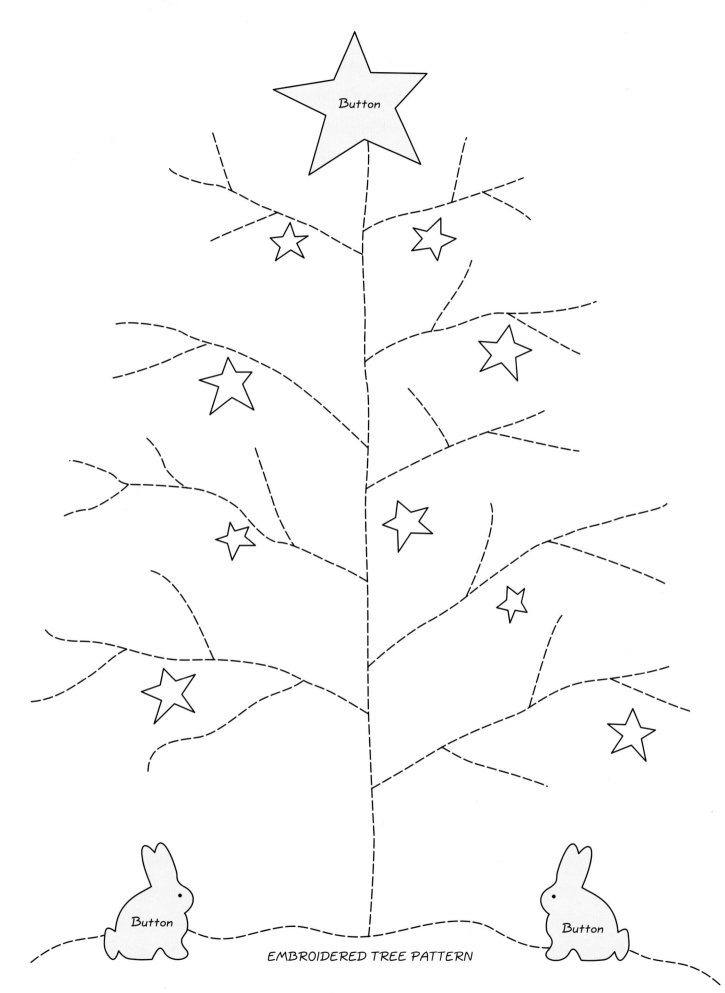

Button

Button

Button

EMBROIDERED TREE PATTERN

251

HOLIDAY FRONT DOOR

Welcome guests to your home with this personalized Christmas Stocking Door Banner. Add a tree decorated with handmade Felt Ornaments (directions on page 257), a Christmas Garland (page 257), and a Rustic Holiday Swag (page 258) above the door, and you'll have an entryway dressed for the warmest of entrances. It may be just enough to tempt Santa to climb down from the roof and use the front door.

Christmas Stocking Door Banner

Finished Size: 21 × 25 inches

MATERIALS AND CUTTING

Prewash and press all of your fabrics. Using a rotary cutter, see-through ruler, and cutting mat, prepare the pieces as described below. Measurements for all pieces include ¼-inch seam allowances.

FABRIC	YARDAGE	NO. OF PIECES	DIMENSIONS
Tan print for background	½ yard	1	13½ × 17½-inch piece
Black solid for accent border and binding	½ yard	2	1 × 18½-inch strips (accent border)
		2	1 × 13½-inch strips (accent border)
		4	2¾ × 42-inch strips (binding)
Red print for checkerboard	⅛ yard	2	1½ × 42-inch strips
Green print for checkerboard	⅛ yard	2	1½ × 42-inch strips

(continued)

MATERIALS AND CUTTING — CONTINUED

FABRIC	YARDAGE	NO. OF PIECES	DIMENSIONS
Gold print for patchwork points border	¼ yard (cut into three 2½ × 42-inch strips)	40	2½-inch squares
Black print for patchwork points border	¼ yard (cut into three 2½ × 42-inch strips)	18 / 4	2½ × 4½-inch pieces / 2½-inch squares
Gold print for tabs	⅛ yard	1	2½ × 32-inch strip
Backing fabric	¾ yard		
Lightweight batting	¾ yard		
Red solid wool for stocking top	⅙ yard	1	4 × 7¾-inch piece
Red plaid wool for stocking bottom	⅜ yard	—	—
Lining fabric for stocking	⅜ yard	—	—
Several coordinated felt or overdyed wool fabrics for holly leaves, appliqué pieces, and yo-yos	Scraps, or ⅛-yard pieces	—	—

Marking pencil; embroidery floss; lightweight, sewable fusible web; #3 pearl cotton; polyester fiberfill stuffing; ½-inch dowel, 24 inches long, stained; tacky glue

Assembly

STEP 1. Using ¼-inch seams, sew the 1 × 13½-inch accent border strips to the top and bottom of the tan print background. Press the seams toward the accent border.

STEP 2. Sew the 1 × 18½-inch accent border strips to the sides. Press.

STEP 3. To make the checkerboard, alternate the two colors and sew the four 1½ × 42-inch checkerboard strips together to make a 4½ × 42-inch strip set. Change sewing direction with

each strip sewn, and press the seams toward the darker fabric as you go. Cut this strip set into fourths, approximately 10 inches each. See **Diagram 1.**

DIAGRAM 1

STEP 4. Resew the fourths together to make a 16½ × 10-inch strip set. Using a rotary cutter and ruler, cut five 1½ × 16½-inch strips from this strip set. There should be 16 squares in each strip. See **Diagram 2.**

DIAGRAM 2

STEP 5. For the top and bottom, use a seam ripper to remove 2 squares from each of two

1½ × 16½-inch strips to make two 1½ × 14½-inch strips with 14 squares each. Compare the strips to the top and bottom. You may need to take in or let out a few seams (⅟₁₆ inch or less) to make them fit. Referring to the **Door Banner Layout** on the following page for placement of the red and green squares, pin and sew the checkerboard strips to the top and bottom.

STEP 6. For the sides, use a seam ripper to remove two units of 4 squares each from one 1½ × 16½-inch strip. Sew one unit to each of the two remaining 1½ × 16½-inch strips to make two 1½ × 20½-inch strips with 20 squares each. Fit, pin, and sew the checkerboard strips to the sides.

Quick Corner Triangles

Refer to "Making Quick Corner Triangles" on page 269. Press the seams toward the triangle just added.

STEP 1. Sew eighteen 2½-inch gold print squares to the eighteen 4½ × 2½-inch black print pieces, as shown in **Diagram 3**. Press.

DIAGRAM 3

STEP 2. Sew eighteen additional 2½-inch gold print squares to the 18 units from Step 1. See **Diagram 4**. Press.

DIAGRAM 4

STEP 3. Sew the four remaining 2½-inch gold print squares to the four 2½-inch black print squares. See **Diagram 5**. Press.

DIAGRAM 5

Patchwork Points Border

STEP 1. For the top and bottom, sew eight 4½ × 2½-inch corner triangle units together to make two strips with four triangle units each. See **Diagram 6**. Press.

STEP 2. Referring to the photo on page 252 for placement of the gold and black triangles, fit, pin, and sew the patchwork points border strips to the top and bottom. Press the seams toward the patchwork points border.

STEP 3. For the sides, sew the remaining ten 4½ × 2½-inch corner triangle units together to make two strips with five triangle units each. See **Diagram 7**. Press.

STEP 4. Referring to the photo on page 252 for placement of the gold and black triangles, sew a 2½-inch corner triangle unit to each end of the two patchwork points border strips from Step 3. See **Diagram 8**. Press.

STEP 5. Fit, pin, and sew the patchwork points border strips to the sides. Press.

Layering the Banner

Arrange and baste the backing, batting, and top together, following the directions in "Layering the Quilt" on page 275. Trim the batting and backing to ¼ inch from the raw edges of the banner top.

Binding the Banner

Using the four 2¾ × 42-inch binding strips, follow the directions for "Binding the Quilt" on page 275–276.

Finishing Stitches

Machine or hand quilt in the seam lines of the accent border, checkerboard squares, and patchwork points. Quilt a 1-inch diagonal grid in the background.

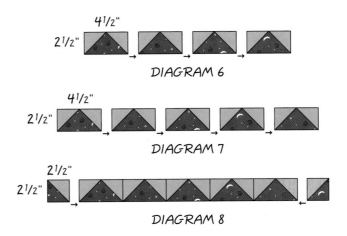

DIAGRAM 6

DIAGRAM 7

DIAGRAM 8

Making the Stocking

STEP 1. Allowing for ¼-inch seams on the raw edges, use the marking pencil to write a name on the 7¾ × 4-inch stocking top. Use two strands of embroidery floss and a running stitch to sew the name.

STEP 2. Cut out the stocking bottom and lining, using the pattern on pages 263–265. Using a ¼-inch seam, sew the stocking top to the stocking bottom. Press the seam toward the stocking top.

STEP 3. Position the stocking front and lining with right sides together, and pin them in place. Sew around the edges, leaving a 4-inch opening for turning. Trim the corners, clip the curves, turn the stocking right side out, hand stitch the opening closed, and press.

STEP 4. Refer to "Quick-Fuse Appliqué" on page 270–271. Trace the heel and toe from the appliqué patterns on page 261 and fuse them to the stocking. Be sure to use a lightweight, sewable fusible web.

STEP 5. Use two strands of embroidery floss and a running stitch to sew the center lines on the heel and toe. Use two strands of embroidery floss to blanket stitch the straight edges of the heel and toe. Leaving the top edge unstitched, use the pearl cotton to blanket stitch around the outside edges of the stocking.

STEP 6. Trace four small holly leaves (two fronts and two backs) from the pattern on page 258. For each holly leaf, position the front and back with wrong sides together. Use two strands of embroidery floss and a running stitch to sew around the edges of each leaf, leaving a small opening for stuffing. Lightly stuff each leaf with the polyester fiberfill, and continue stitching. Sew a running stitch in the center of the leaf.

STEP 7. Refer to "Making Yo-yos" on pages 272–273. Make three yo-yo berries from the pattern on page 258. When making yo-yos out of felt or wool, do not turn under the seam allowance as you gather.

STEP 8. Position and sew the two holly leaves and three yo-yo berries to the stocking, referring to the **Door Banner Layout** below for placement.

STEP 9. Position, pin, and hand sew the stocking to the banner, leaving the top edge open.

Hanging the Banner

STEP 1. To make hanging tabs, fold the 2½ × 32-inch gold print strip in half lengthwise with right sides together. Sew a ¼-inch seam on the edge opposite the fold, turn the strip right side out, and press. Topstitch along the edge of both sides. Cut the strip into four 8-inch pieces. Fold each piece in half, and stitch a ¼-inch seam along the cut edges. Turn each tab, and press it with the seam at the bottom, inside the tab. Space the tabs evenly across the top of the banner back. Hand stitch the tabs in place.

STEP 2. Make 8 holly leaves and 12 yo-yo berries, following the directions in Steps 6 and 7 under "Making the Stocking," above. Sew the holly leaves and berries to the tabs.

STEP 3. Refer to the directions for Felt Ornaments on the opposite page to make one left-facing cardinal and one right-facing cardinal. Insert the dowel through the banner tabs. Glue one cardinal to each end of the dowel.

DOOR BANNER LAYOUT

Felt Ornaments

(See the ornaments on the tree in the photo on page 252.)

Materials

Scraps of several coordinated
  fabrics
Felt for backing
Fusible web
Pinking shears
#3 pearl cotton
Glue gun and glue sticks
Raffia
Assorted buttons

Assembly

STEP 1. Refer to "Quick-Fuse Appliqué" on pages 270–271. Trace assorted holly leaves, stars, and cardinals from the appliqué patterns on pages 258–262. Fuse each design to the wrong side of the selected fabric and cut it out. Fuse this shape to the felt background, and cut it out approximately ¼ inch from the edges with pinking shears.

STEP 2. For the holly leaf, use the pearl cotton and a running stitch to sew a vein in the center of the leaf. For the stars, glue a raffia bow and button to the front.

STEP 3. To make a hanger, cut an 8- to 10-inch length of pearl cotton. Fold it in half and knot the ends together. Glue the knotted end to the back of the ornament.

Christmas Garland

(See the garland on the tree in the photo on page 252.)

Materials

Scraps of several coordinated
  fabrics
Felt for backing
Fusible web
Pinking shears
#3 pearl cotton
Glue gun and glue sticks
Heavyweight jute
Assorted buttons

Assembly

STEP 1. Make as many holly leaves and cardinals as desired for your garland, following the directions for Felt Ornaments, above.

STEP 2. Cut the jute to the desired garland length. Position the holly leaves and cardinals on the jute, and glue them in place. Glue a button to the top of each set of holly leaves.

Rustic Holiday Swag

(See the swag above the door in the photo on page 252.)

Materials

Scraps of several coordinated
    fabrics
Felt for backing
Fusible web
Pinking shears
#3 pearl cotton
Glue gun and glue sticks
Purchased twig and vine swag
Assorted buttons

Assembly

STEP 1. Make the large star, cardinals, and small holly leaves, following the directions for Felt Ornaments on page 257.

STEP 2. Position the star, cardinals, and holly leaves on the swag, referring to the photo on page 252. Glue them in place. Glue a button to the top of the holly leaves.

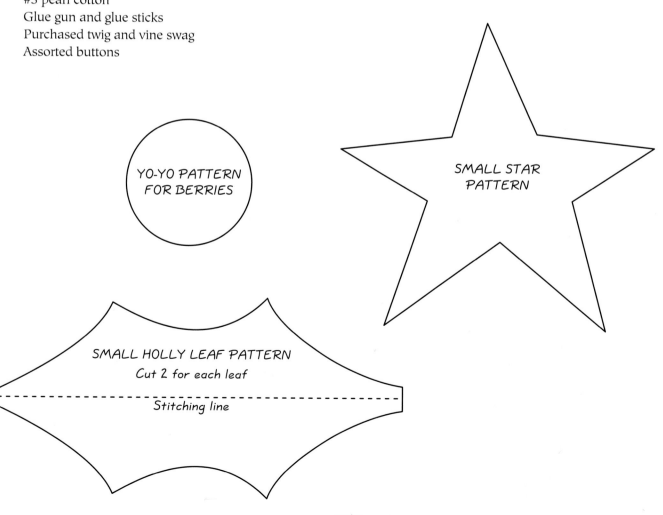

YO-YO PATTERN
FOR BERRIES

SMALL STAR
PATTERN

SMALL HOLLY LEAF PATTERN
Cut 2 for each leaf

Stitching line

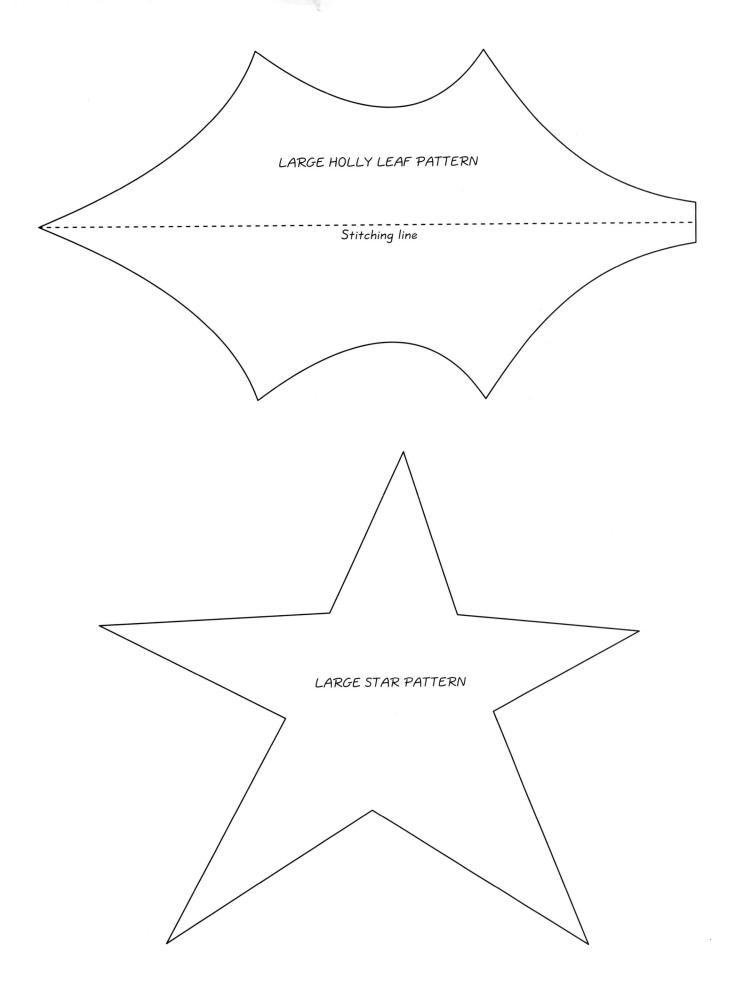

LARGE HOLLY LEAF PATTERN

Stitching line

LARGE STAR PATTERN

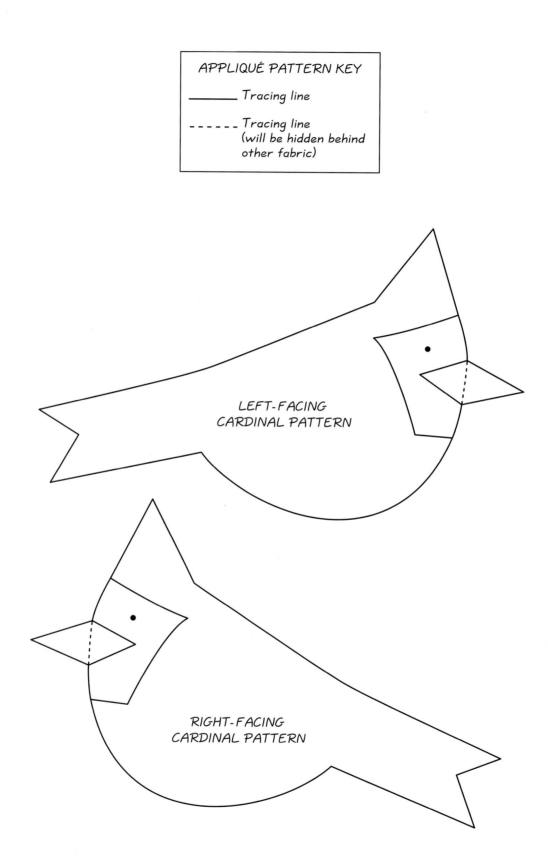

APPLIQUÉ PATTERN KEY

———— Tracing line

- - - - - Tracing line
(will be hidden behind
other fabric)

LEFT-FACING
CARDINAL PATTERN

RIGHT-FACING
CARDINAL PATTERN

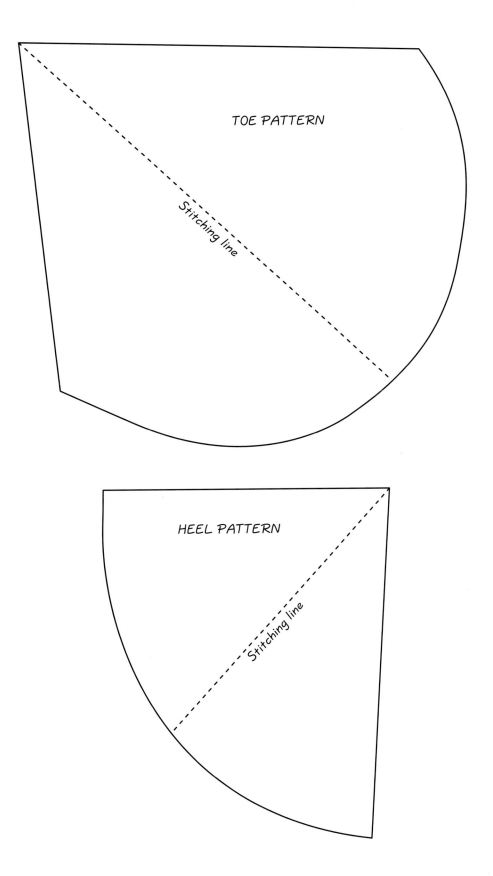

TOE PATTERN

Stitching line

HEEL PATTERN

Stitching line

TREETOP STAR PATTERN

STOCKING TOP

LINING AND STOCKING BOTTOM

Cut one lining, wrong side of fabric up
Cut one stocking bottom, right side of fabric up

Cut off here for stocking bottom

Align with red line of Stocking Pattern B and C

STOCKING PATTERN
A

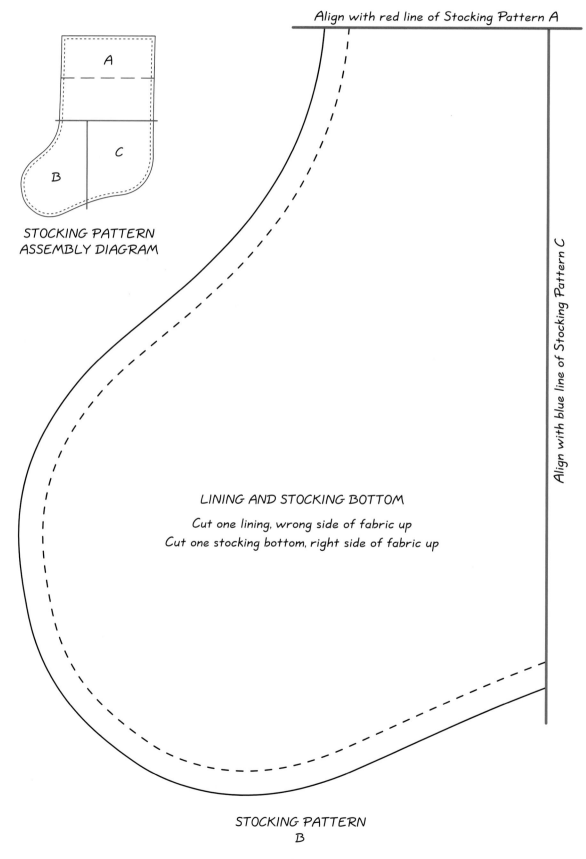

Align with red line of Stocking Pattern A

Align with blue line of Stocking Pattern C

STOCKING PATTERN
ASSEMBLY DIAGRAM

A

B

C

LINING AND STOCKING BOTTOM

Cut one lining, wrong side of fabric up
Cut one stocking bottom, right side of fabric up

STOCKING PATTERN
B

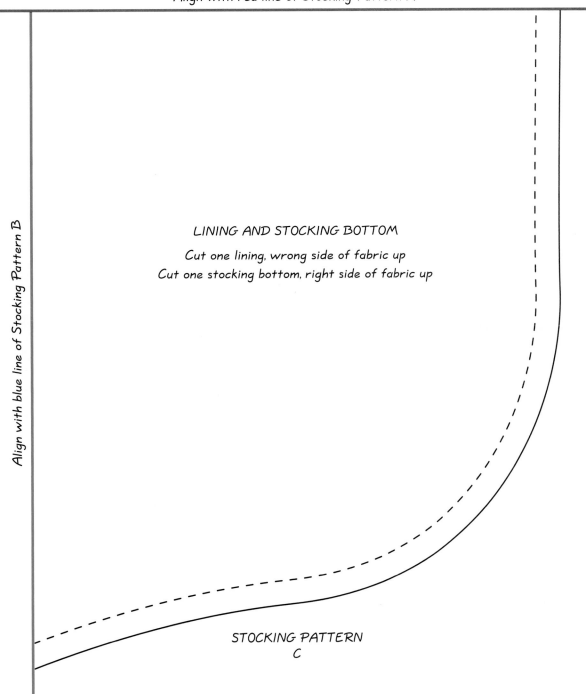

Align with red line of Stocking Pattern A

Align with blue line of Stocking Pattern B

LINING AND STOCKING BOTTOM

Cut one lining, wrong side of fabric up
Cut one stocking bottom, right side of fabric up

STOCKING PATTERN
C

QUICK COUNTRY QUILTING BASICS

Investing in the appropriate tools and learning the correct techniques will ensure that your projects go together quickly and accurately. Be sure to read and understand the techniques before you start any of the projects in this book. Refer to these pages whenever you need a refresher on any details.

CUTTING AND PIECING

In this section, I list all the tools and supplies you need to get started quilting. I also explain rotary cutting and simple sewing techniques that will help you piece your quilt together in no time at all!

What You Need for Cutting and Piecing

Sewing Machine: You need a sewing machine that has a good, reliable straight stitch for piecing. For machine appliqué, it should do a nice, even zigzag stitch.

Rotary Cutter and Cutting Mat: Rotary cutters are available in quilt shops, in fabric stores, and through mail-order catalogs. I prefer the 45 mm blade. A bigger blade gives you more control and lasts longer.

You should never use a rotary cutter without a cutting mat. The cutting mat is the surface on which you lay your fabric before cutting. The mat protects the tabletop as well as the blade of your cutter. Get the largest size mat you have room for. The 24 × 36-inch mat is an all-around good size.

See-Through Ruler: There are many shapes and sizes of these rigid plastic rulers on the market. To start out, I recommend a 6 × 24-inch ruler with a 45 degree angle line marked on it.

Sewing Thread: Select good-quality thread for piecing. Use beige or gray when piecing light fabrics, and dark gray when piecing dark fabrics.

Iron, Ironing Board, and Towel: Use your iron on the Cotton setting and keep the soleplate clean. (See "Pressing Advice" on page 269 for more details on pressing seams.)

Seam Ripper: When fitting pieced borders, a seam ripper is the perfect tool to remove extra pieces.

Scissors: Although most fabric cutting for my projects is done with a rotary cutter, you will also need a good, sharp pair of scissors.

Rotary Cutting

If this is the first time you will be using a rotary cutter, read through these directions carefully, and practice on scrap fabrics. Precise cutting is the first step in precision sewing. Take time to measure and cut your strips and pieces accurately. Begin by prewashing and pressing your fabrics. Be certain that you line your ruler up precisely with the edges of your fabric.

In the project directions, the length for a strip cut across the width is 42 inches. Variation in fabric widths has been considered in the yardage and cutting dimensions. If your fabric is less than 40 inches wide, you may need to purchase extra yardage and cut an extra strip.

STEP 1. After washing and pressing your fabric, refold selvage to selvage. Make sure the fabric is straight. Position the folded fabric so that the selvage edges are facing away from you and the folded edge is facing toward you. See **Diagram 1**.

Selvage edges

Fold

DIAGRAM 1

STEP 2. Use your see-through ruler as a cutting guide. Align one of the horizontal lines of the ruler with the folded edge of the fabric so that the ruler is square with the fabric. See **Diagram 2**. Using some pressure, hold the ruler in position, and use the rotary cutter to trim off the uneven edges on the right end of the fabric. Stop about halfway through the cut to move your hand up on the ruler. This will help to keep the ruler from slipping. You should now have a perfectly straight edge of fabric.

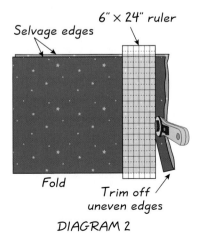

Selvage edges

6" × 24" ruler

Fold

Trim off uneven edges

DIAGRAM 2

STEP 3. Rotate your fabric so that the cut edges are on your left. To move your fabric, simply rotate your cutting mat. If you pick up the fabric, you risk disturbing the layers.

STEP 4. Determine the width of the first strip you want to cut. Align that line on the ruler with the cut edges of the fabric. For example, if the strip is 3 inches wide by 42 inches long, align the 3-inch line on the ruler directly over the cut edge of the fabric. A horizontal line of the ruler should also line up with the folded edge. See **Diagram 3**. When the ruler is lined up perfectly with the cut edge and the fold, hold the ruler in position, and cut.

Fold

Selvage edges

DIAGRAM 3

STEP 5. After cutting the strips, many projects require you to make a second cut from those strips. You can leave your strip folded in half so that you can cut more than one piece at a time. Lay the ruler on top of the strip. Line up one of the horizontal lines on your ruler with the long edge of your strip. Trim off the selvage end of the strip to square and straighten the edge of the fabric. See **Diagram 4**. Rotate the fabric so that this cut end is on the left. Cut the pieces as specified in the project. See **Diagram 5**.

Notes for Lefties

If you're left-handed, as I am, it may be more comfortable to measure and make your cuts from the right end of the folded fabric. Simply reverse the directions in Steps 2 and 3. Trim off the uneven edges on the left end of the fabric in Step 2. Rotate the fabric so that the trimmed edges are on your right in Step 3. Keep in mind that the diagrams are drawn for right-handers.

Fold

Trim off selvages

DIAGRAM 4

DIAGRAM 5

Assembly Line Piecing

For the quickest piecing, apply the principles of an assembly line to your sewing. By repeating the same step over and over, you will make your piecing quick and efficient.

Let's say you are working on a quilt that has 12 blocks. The first step directs you to sew together two squares. You repeat this step of sewing the squares together 12 times (once for each block). As you proceed through the rest of the assembly steps, all of your blocks will take shape at the same time and will be completed all at once.

Continuous-Seam Technique

Any time you are using the assembly line method to piece your blocks, you can use the continuous-seam method of sewing them together.

Line up all the same pieces for the first step for each block next to your sewing machine. With right sides together, stitch the first two pieces together. Leave them where they are. Place the next set of pieces directly behind the set you have just sewn, and continue sewing. Add each set without breaking your seam until you have joined all the sets together.

You will end up with a long chain of pieces joined together by thread. See **Diagram 6**. Clip the threads between the pieces, and press.

DIAGRAM 6

Precise Piecing

To achieve precise piecing, take your time, be patient, and make sure you are sewing with an exact ¼-inch seam allowance.

Mark the throat plate on your sewing machine with masking tape exactly ¼ inch from the center of the needle. Be sure to make a test after your tape is positioned. If you adhere a few layers of tape, the tape will create a ridge to guide your fabric as you sew. Press as you sew to make sure your seams lie flat.

You may want to look for a specialty ¼-inch foot. Check with your sewing machine manufacturer to see if such a foot is made for your model. If not, there is a universal foot called the Little Foot that can be used with most machines.

In each project, block measurements are indicated after the piecing instructions. It is important that your blocks match these measurements.

Making Quick Corner Triangles

I use an easy technique to simplify the construction of pieces with triangles in one or more corners. Quick corner triangles are formed by simply sewing fabric squares to other squares and rectangles.

STEP 1. With a pencil and ruler, lightly draw a diagonal line from corner to corner on the wrong side of the fabric square that will form the triangle. This will be your sewing line. See **Diagram 7**.

Sewing line

DIAGRAM 7

STEP 2. With right sides together, place the square on the corresponding piece. Matching raw edges, pin the pieces in place, and sew on the drawn diagonal line.

STEP 3. Trim off the excess fabric, leaving a ¼-inch seam allowance. See **Diagram 8**. Press all seams toward the triangles, except when otherwise indicated. Measure each piece after adding the corner triangle. The dimensions should be the same size as the piece you started with before adding the square.

Trim ¼" away from sewing line   *Finished corner triangle unit*

DIAGRAM 8

Speedy Strips

With this very easy technique, you will be able to assemble checkerboards and multicolor patchwork or scrap borders in no time flat. The directions for each project will tell you the number of strips to cut and which fabrics to use to create the required strip sets.

Sew the strips together along the long edges, alternating the fabrics as directed. As you add

Pressing Advice

To prepare your ironing board for pressing, lay a terry cloth towel on the ironing board. It will provide a cushion to absorb the indentations that your seam allowances make on the front of your quilt block or top. The nap of the towel also helps prevent distortion of your fabrics when pressing.

Always press after each sewing step. First, iron the unit in the closed position (right sides together) to set the stitches. Next, open the unit and carefully finger press the seam. Then, use an iron to set the seam. With the unit right side up, bring the iron straight down on the seam. Be careful not to stretch the unit out of shape by moving the iron with too much force across your fabrics. I prefer to use a steam iron on the Cotton setting.

The arrows in the project diagrams indicate pressing direction for each step. By following these arrows, you will ensure that your seams lie flat.

269

each strip, always pause to press the seam. Press the seams toward the darker fabric or all in the same direction. Change sewing direction with each strip sewn. It will help avoid the warping that can occur when sewing several long strips together.

Once you have joined all the strips, you will have a large strip set. The project directions will then tell you how to cut and resew the strip set. (See "Pieced Borders" on pages 273–274 for more details on making checkerboard, patchwork, and scrap borders.)

APPLIQUÉ

Most of the appliqué projects that I've included in this book are designed for the quick-fuse technique using fusible web. A simple stroke of the iron fuses designs in place on a background. As a general guide, designs with very small pieces use the quick-fuse appliqué technique with no stitching. Designs with larger pieces can be done with machine appliqué or a hand blanket stitch.

What You Need for Appliqué

Sewing Thread: For machine appliqué, use a thread that is specifically meant for machine embroidery or a good-quality, all-purpose thread. For blanket stitch embroidery, use a good-quality embroidery floss.

Needles: Use an embroidery needle for blanket stitch embroidery.

Scissors: Use good-quality, sharp scissors for cutting designs out of fused fabric. It is nice to have two sizes of scissors, large ones for bigger pieces and smaller embroidery scissors for little pieces.

Iron: I recommend an iron without an automatic shut-off when working with quick-fuse appliqué.

Fusible Web: This paper-backed fusible adhesive is sold in precut packets or on bolts at most fabric and quilting stores. There are lightweight and heavyweight types. If you plan to do machine appliqué or a blanket stitch, use a lighter weight, *sewable fusible web*. For quick-fuse appliqué projects with edges that will not be sewn, use a heavier weight, *nonsewable fusible web*.

Tear-Away Fabric Stabilizer: Use tear-away stabilizer (sold with interfacings, under names like Stitch-N-Tear) behind the background fabric when doing machine appliqué. This keeps your fabrics from puckering and helps you achieve an even stitch.

Permanent Fine-Point Felt Pen: Use this type of pen to draw details such as eyes, noses, and mouths on various appliqué designs.

Embroidery Floss: Embroidery floss is used for the blanket stitch appliqué. Use black for an old-fashioned look, or coordinate floss color with your appliqué fabrics.

Quick-Fuse Appliqué

This is the quickest and easiest way to do appliqué. If you plan to machine stitch or do a blanket stitch, be sure to use a lightweight, sewable fusible web. For appliqué projects that will not be sewn, use a heavyweight, nonsewable fusible web.

STEP 1. Trace each of the parts of the selected appliqué design individually onto the paper side of the fusible web. Since you can see through the fusible web, you can lay it directly over the design in the book and trace the parts. The patterns are always the reverse of the finished design.

STEP 2. Using sharp paper scissors, cut loosely around the traced shapes on the fusible web, as shown in **Diagram 1**. Do not cut along the lines at this point.

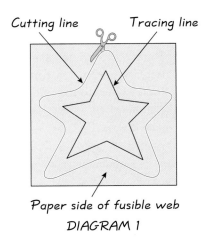

Cutting line   Tracing line

Paper side of fusible web
DIAGRAM 1

STEP 3. Check the manufacturer's instructions for the proper iron setting to use with that brand of fusible web. Fuse each piece of fusible web to the *wrong* side of your selected fabrics. Place the fusible web with the paper side up and the webbing side against your fabric.

STEP 4. When all the pieces are fused, cut out the appliqué shapes

following the tracing lines. See **Diagram 2.** Remove the paper backing from the fusible web. A thin fusing film will remain on the wrong side of the fabric.

Wrong side   Cut on
of fabric   tracing line

DIAGRAM 2

STEP 5. Arrange and center all the pieces of the appliqué design on the background fabric. Allow ¼ inch for the seam allowances on the edges of the background fabric if you are appliquéing before piecing. Refer to the appliqué

pattern as you position the pieces; the dotted lines indicate where certain pieces should be placed underneath others. When everything is arranged, fuse the pieces in position with your iron. If you used a heavyweight, nonsewable fusible web, you're done. See "Machine Appliqué" below or "Blanket Stitch Appliqué" on page 272 if you plan to stitch the edges of your appliqué pieces.

Machine Appliqué

This technique may be your best choice for projects you would like to launder. You can use a small, narrow zigzag stitch, a satin stitch, blanket stitch, or another decorative stitch. Use an appliqué foot if your machine has one. Always practice first to adjust your machine settings.

STEP 1. Fuse all the appliqué pieces in place on the background fabric, as directed in "Quick-Fuse Appliqué" on the opposite page.

STEP 2. To use tear-away stabilizer, cut a piece large enough to cover the area you'll be stitching. Pin the stabilizer to the wrong side of the background fabric in the stitching area. This keeps your fabrics from puckering and helps you do an even appliqué stitch.

STEP 3. Coordinate several thread colors to match the various appliqué fabric colors. Use these for the top threads, changing them as needed. If you can loosen your bobbin thread tension, you may be able to use a neutral-color bobbin thread for all of the appliqué.

Special Tips for Quick-Fuse Appliqué

• Laundering is NOT recommended for quick-fused wallhangings, ornaments, and other projects.

• When working with very small pieces, use a straight pin to move all your pieces into place.

• The Appliqué Pressing Sheet by Bear Thread Designs is helpful in positioning appliqué designs. To use the pressing sheet, trace the appliqué design onto a plain sheet of

paper; then retrace it onto the back of that paper. Use this reversed image as a guide for positioning and fusing on the pressing sheet. See "Quilting by Mail" on page 280 for ordering information.

• After fusing, check your iron for residue, and use iron cleaner as needed. Keep a towel on your ironing board to protect both the ironing surface and any clothing that may be ironed later!

STEP 2. Thread a needle and make a double knot at one end. Turning in a ⅛- to ¼-inch seam allowance as you go, sew running stitches close to the folded edge. Your stitches should be ⅛ to ³⁄₁₆ inch long.

Making Yo-yos

STEP 1. Make a template for the desired size yo-yo. Trace around the template on the wrong side of the fabric, and cut out along the line.

STEP 4. Stitch along the edges of each appliqué piece. When you're finished, pull away the stabilizer from the back of the fabric.

Blanket Stitch Appliqué

This hand-stitching technique is simple and gives a very traditional, old-fashioned look to your quilt. Blanket stitch is best suited to appliqué projects with relatively large, simple pieces.

After you have fused the appliqué design to the background fabric with a lightweight, sewable fusible web, use embroidery floss to outline the edges of the appliqué pieces with the blanket stitch. Use two to three strands of embroidery floss, and refer to **Diagram 3** for guidance on how to do the stitch.

DIAGRAM 3

Decorative Stitches

Backstitch

Thread the needle and knot one end. Bring the needle up at point A, one stitch length away from the beginning of the line you are stitching. Insert the needle down at point B and bring it up at point C. Repeat, inserting the needle at the end of the stitch just completed.

Backstitch

French Knot

Thread the needle and knot one end. Bring the needle up through the fabric at the point where you want the knot. Wrap the thread around the needle two times and hold the thread taut with your finger. Insert the needle back into the fabric close to where it came up. Pull the needle through to the back. The knot will remain on top.

French knot

Stem Stitch

Thread the needle and knot one end. Pull the needle up at point A, insert it down at point B, and then pull it up at point C, a point approximately halfway between points A and B.

Stem stitch

STEP 3. When you reach your beginning point, gather the stitches tightly to close the circle. Smooth and flatten the yo-yo so that the hole is in the center. Knot and cut off the gathering thread.

Hint: If the center hole of the yo-yo is too big, try making larger stitches.

PUTTING IT ALL TOGETHER

Once your blocks are pieced or appliquéd, you are ready to join them together to make the quilt. Lattice strips are the "glue" that holds the individual quilt blocks together, defining and enhancing the overall quilt design. For a smooth, flat quilt top, press all the seams toward the lattice as you sew.

Borders

In many of the projects in this book, the first border is an accent border that sets off the quilt top. The second border is usually wider and picks up one of the main colors or fabrics of the quilt. I often combine several of the quilt fabrics into pieced borders to tie it all together.

Pieced Borders

Pieced borders may look difficult and time-consuming, but looks can be deceiving! Using your rotary cutter and the technique described in "Speedy Strips" on pages 269–270, they go together in no time at all.

A checkerboard border consists of two colors, a light and a dark, and can be one or more rows. Checkerboards add a delightful touch to many quilts. Patchwork borders add a unifying look. They consist of many of the fabrics in the quilt, and each piece is the same size. A scrap border is made from many fabrics in the quilt, but the pieces are of varying widths.

The pieced borders in this book always start with a strip set. Below are some helpful guidelines for making checkerboard, patchwork, and scrap borders. In each project, you will find the necessary yardages and specific cutting and sewing instructions.

STEP 1. Arrange all the strips in a pleasing order, and sew them together side by side along the long edges to create a strip set. As you sew, press all the seams toward the darker fabric or in the same direction. The project directions may have you cut this strip set into halves, thirds, or other increments. See **Diagram 1** for an example of a strip set cut in half. **Diagram 2** shows the halves sewn together and cut again. In this example, the strip set is cut and resewn twice before the border strips are finally cut, as shown in **Diagram 3**.

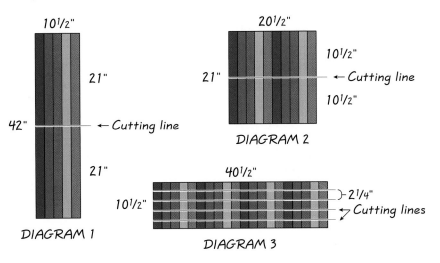

DIAGRAM 1

DIAGRAM 2

DIAGRAM 3

STEP 2. Use a seam ripper to remove excess pieces as directed in the project. Fit, pin, and sew border strips to the quilt top and bottom, raw edge to raw edge. Press seams away from the pieced border. Fit, pin, and sew border strips to the sides of the quilt. Press.

Choosing a Batting

Batting is made of cotton, polyester, a blend of cotton and polyester, or wool. Cotton batting gives a very flat, traditional look. Some people find that cotton batts are harder to hand quilt but easier to machine quilt than polyester batts.

Since most of my quilts are used for wallhangings, I prefer a thin, lightweight, polyester batting. Thin batting enhances the country look of my quilts—something that thicker, puffier batting won't do.

Polyester batting is easy to hand quilt, and there is no minimum amount of quilting necessary.

Fitting Pieced Borders

Count the pieces in the border strips. With the exception of scrap borders, there should be the same number of pieces in both the top and bottom border strips. The same should be true of the side border strips.

A pieced border strip will have a fair amount of give. Depending on the length, it can be stretched to fit an extra ⅛ to ¼ inch if necessary. You can stretch your strip by gently tugging on it as you sew. Be careful not to overstretch.

If your pieced border strip needs to be adjusted more than ⅛ to ¼ inch, I suggest making your adjustments by taking in or letting out a few of the seams. For example, let's say a 16-piece patchwork border strip is ½ inch too long. Take in eight seams by ¹⁄₁₆ inch. This will not disrupt the overall look of the border.

Because pieced borders will stretch, always pin them in position before sewing them to the quilt top. Press all the seams away from the pieced border.

Marking the Quilt Top

It's easiest to mark the quilting design onto the quilt top before you layer and baste it. I prefer Quilter's Rule or Clover chalk pencils for marking.

Keep your pencil sharp to ensure neat quilting lines. Always mark lightly and do a test on scrap fabric first to make sure that you can clean away any lines that remain after quilting.

Marking a Grid

Your see-through ruler can make this marking quite easy. Using a 45 degree angle line as your reference, mark your first line at a 45 degree angle to the horizontal seam lines of the quilt. See the middle illustration in **Diagram 4** on the opposite page. Then continue to mark lines across your quilt in regular increments. Next, align the 45 degree angle on your ruler with one of the vertical seam lines of the quilt, and mark your grid lines in the other direction. These intersecting lines will form a grid that you can use to quilt nice, straight lines. See the bottom illustration in **Diagram 4** on the opposite page.

Outline Quilting

There are two options for outline quilting pieced blocks, lattice, and borders. You can quilt "in the ditch," which means you add a line of stitches directly next to a seam line. This requires no marking. Quilt along the seam line on the side that does not have the seam allowance. The other option

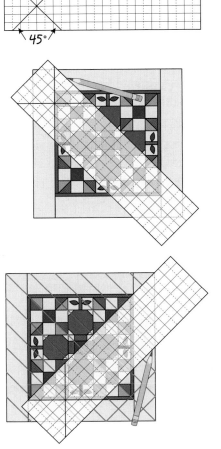

DIAGRAM 4

Layering the Quilt

Your next task is to layer the quilt top, batting, and backing, and baste them all together. Refer to **Diagram 5** for all of the layering steps.

DIAGRAM 5

is to quilt ¼ inch from the seam line. If you do this, I recommend using quilter's ¼-inch masking tape rather than marking. Position the tape and use the edge as your quilting guide. Lift up the tape and reuse it until the stickiness is gone. Do not leave the tape on your quilt for long periods of time, because some sticky residue may remain on the fabric.

To outline appliqué designs, quilt ¹⁄₁₆ to ⅛ inch away from the edges of the designs.

STEP 1. Cut the batting and backing pieces 4 to 6 inches larger than the quilt top.

STEP 2. Press the quilt top and backing. Find a large work area, such as the dining room table. Lay the backing piece down first with the right side facing down. Lay the batting on top of the backing, and smooth it out. Then place the quilt top (face up) on top. Make sure everything is centered and that the backing, batting, and quilt top are flat and smooth.

STEP 3. The backing and batting should extend 2 to 3 inches beyond the quilt top on all four sides, since some shifting may take place during basting and quilting.

STEP 4. To keep the layers in place as you baste, pin them together. Place a pin every 6 inches in vertical and horizontal rows. Begin basting in the center, and work out to the outer edges of the quilt. Baste vertically and horizontally, forming a 3- to 4-inch grid. Don't skimp on this basting. It is critical to keep the layers flat while you are quilting. Last, baste or pin completely around the outer edges of the quilt top.

Basting Hints

Here are some tips for making basting easier.

- Use longer needles than you normally use for hand stitching.
- Thread several needles with extra-long lengths of thread before you begin.
- Take long stitches, 1 to 3 inches in length.
- Divide your quilt into quarters for basting. Work in one quarter at a time, basting from the center to the outer edges.

Binding the Quilt

For the wall-size and other small projects in this book that you will be hand quilting, it's okay to add the binding to the quilt before doing the actual quilting. For larger projects and those that you will be machine quilting, quilt *before* binding.

STEP 1. Cut the binding strips as indicated in the directions for each project. Press the strips in half with wrong sides together.

STEP 2. Trim the batting and backing to ¼ inch from the raw edges of the quilt top.

STEP 3. With the raw edges even, lay the binding strips on the top and bottom edges of the quilt top. Pin the binding strips in place. Sew ¼ inch from the quilt edge. Trim the excess length of the binding, and press the seams toward the binding.

STEP 4. Align the raw edges of the binding strips with the edges of the quilt sides. Repeat the sewing and pressing directions given in Step 3. Your quilt should now look like the one shown in **Diagram 6.**

Raw edge   *Raw edge*

Quilt front

Backing and batting edge

Raw edge

Fold

Seam line

Quilt back

DIAGRAM 6

STEP 5. Fold the top and bottom bindings around to the back, so that the folded edge of the binding meets the seam line, as shown in **Diagram 7.** Press and pin in position.

Top

Quilt back

DIAGRAM 7

STEP 6. Fold the side bindings around to the back so that the folded edges meet the seam lines. Press and pin in position. Hand stitch all the way around the binding. Stitch closed the little opening at all four corners, as shown in **Diagram 8.**

Top

Side

Quilt back

DIAGRAM 8

Helpful Hints for Attaching Binding

When sewing through several layers, the top layer is pushed forward, and that can stretch and warp your binding. To prevent this from happening, follow these tips.

- Don't skimp on pins when pinning the binding to the quilt.
- Increase the stitch length on your sewing machine.
- Sew at a slow pace.
- Use a walking foot or an even feed attachment if you have one for your machine. It feeds all the layers through at the same rate.

Finishing Small Appliqué Projects

Some of the small appliqué projects direct you to use a self-binding method. You layer the top and

Tools for Hand Quilting

These are the items that you'll need in your sewing basket if you plan to do hand quilting.

Quilting Needles: These are also called betweens. If you are a beginning quilter, I suggest starting with a package of needles with an assortment of sizes. Size 10 is a commonly used size and is the needle I prefer.

Quilting Thread: Be sure to use extrastrong thread made especially for quilting. Choose a quilting thread color that coordinates with the background fabric. If you want your quilting

stitches to show up more, use a contrasting thread color.

Thimble: Choosing a comfortable thimble may require some trial and error before you settle on one you like. I prefer a leather thimble. Look for one with elastic (it stays on your finger better), a slit for your fingernail, and extra reinforcement at the fingertip.

Quilting Hoop or Frame: Hoops or frames hold the three layers taut and smooth while you are quilting, making it less likely that the fabric will pucker or wrinkle under the stitching.

backing with right sides together on top of the batting, stitch around the edges (leaving an opening for turning), turn right side out, and hand stitch the opening closed. For these projects, consider using the same fabric for the backing that you use for the binding. That way, the backing fabric won't stand out if it sneaks around to the front.

Quilting by Hand

The quilting stitch is a series of running stitches made along the lines of the quilting design you have marked. At first, you should concentrate on even stitches; as you gain experience, your stitches will naturally become smaller. Good quilting stitches are small and even.

STEP 1. Cut a length of quilting thread (approximately 18 inches), thread the needle, and knot one end.

STEP 2. About ½ inch from the point where you want to begin stitching, insert the needle through the top layer of fabric. See **Diagram 9**. Bring it up right where you want to take the first stitch. Pull on the thread until the knot rests against the surface of the fabric. With a gentle tug, pull the thread to pop the knot through the fabric, as shown in the diagram. The knot will stay securely anchored in the batting, hidden out of sight. Whenever you need to start a new thread, repeat this procedure to bury the knot.

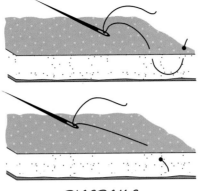

DIAGRAM 9

STEP 3. Push just the tip of the needle down through the three layers, using the finger with the thimble on your top hand, as shown in **Diagram 10**. As soon as your finger on the underside feels the needle come through, rock it up again toward the surface. (Simultaneously press down on the head of the needle with the thimble finger and push up against the needle tip with a finger on the underside.) See **Diagram 11**.

DIAGRAM 10

DIAGRAM 11

STEP 4. Pull the needle through the fabric using the thumb and forefinger of your top hand. Pull the thread taut, but don't pull it too tight, or the fabric will pucker.

STEP 5. To end a line of stitching, bring the needle up where you want to stop. Wrap the thread around the end of the needle two times. Pull the needle through these circles of thread to form a knot. Push the needle back down through the top of the quilt and pull it up about ½ inch away. Tug on the thread to pop the knot through the top of the fabric and bury it in the batting layer. See **Diagram 12**. Pull on the thread and clip it close to the surface of the quilt. The end should disappear back beneath the quilt top.

DIAGRAM 12

Quilting by Machine

Just like hand quilting, machine quilting takes some practice. I highly recommend using a walking foot or an even feed attachment. It can help avoid the problem of having the three layers bunch up.

Machine quilting works best on smaller projects, like the appliqué wallhangings, where you quilt in the ditch along the borders. If you are trying machine quilting for the first time, keep in mind that the smaller the project, the easier it will be to quilt.

The layering process is the same as for hand quilting. Instead of hand basting, however, use safety pins to hold the layers together while you quilt. Position them so that they won't get in the way of where you plan to quilt. Do all the quilting before you add the binding (unless it is a self-binding).

STEP 1. Coordinate the thread color with the quilt top and coordinate the bobbin thread with the backing fabric.

STEP 2. Set your machine for normal straight stitching. You may want to increase the stitch length for stitching through the three layers. Starting in the center of the quilt and working out toward the edges, machine stitch in the ditch to outline the blocks and borders.

Hanging Sleeves

To make a hanging sleeve, cut a strip approximately 5 inches wide by the width of the quilt. Hem the 5-inch edges by folding under ½ inch and stitching. With right sides together, fold the strip in half lengthwise, and sew the length of the strip. Turn the sleeve right side out and press. Hand stitch the sleeve to the back of your quilt, and run a wooden dowel through it.

Quilt Labels

Be sure to add a label to the back of your quilt. Include your name, the name of the quilt, the year you made it, and where you made it. Use a permanent fine-point felt pen. Attach the label to the back of the quilt with your preferred appliqué method.

ACKNOWLEDGMENTS

This book was created with the combined talents of many people. I would like to thank and acknowledge all the dedicated and creative people who had a hand in making this book a reality. This book was my most ambitious undertaking yet, but it was worth the effort. I am very proud of it and of all those who worked diligently to make the projects and the rooms works of art.

Special thanks go to Kelly Fisher, Senior Editor, who coordinated the efforts of the Mumm's the Word editorial and sewing team. This includes Jodi Gosse and Geri Zimmer, Creative and Editorial Assistants, and Candy Huddleston, Seamstress. Not only did they sew all the beautiful projects in the book, but they also spent many a tedious hour poring over every word and number to ensure that the instructions were clear, complete, and accurate. Thanks also for sharing ideas and creativity.

I would also like to thank Nancy Kirkland, our freelance Seamstress and Quilter, and Mairi Fischer, our freelance Hand Quilter, for their dedication and fine stitching.

Jackie Saling, Art Studio Assistant (also known as my right-hand assistant), is a tremendously hard worker and has never uttered the words, "I can't do it." She never knows what I'm going to ask her to do, but she's always willing. Even the not-so-glamorous assignments, such as coordinating and hauling props to photo locations and back again, are met with a positive attitude. Jackie is a very accomplished painter. She prepared many photo props and consulted on all the room-decorating projects.

Marcia Smith, Art Director, styled and directed many of the photos. The two-page spreads for the part openers were the most complex, and she made sure that they all worked and looked beautiful. She coordinated many of the shoots and attended to all the details. Thanks to Marcia for all her planning and vision.

A very special thank-you goes to Bob Barros of Barros & Barros for creating the beautiful photographs throughout the book. He always went the extra mile on every shoot and took the time to perfect the lighting to make the projects and rooms glow.

Lois Hansen, Mark Meyer, and Barb Chase, Photo Assistants, packed up and hauled endless supplies of lights, cords, power packs, and other equipment to all our photo locations. They helped to coordinate props and find the right locations to capture the right look. Thanks to all of them for their tireless efforts and for bringing snacks to the shoots!

Lynn Guier and Bill Mound, freelance Interior Designers, designed and remodeled the master bedroom, Murphy's bedroom, and the birdhouse bathroom in my home for this book. They are extremely inspired, resourceful, and wonderful to collaborate with. They spent many days and nights in my home! I thank them for sharing their enormous talents.

Thanks go to Nancy Eubanks, freelance Painter, for sharing her skills and artistic flair in custom painting the kitchen chairs and the sofa table in the dining room. Thanks to Retta Warehime, friend and fellow quilter, who sewed the dust ruffle and draperies for the master bedroom. Melcina Siebert deserves praise for her stellar work in reupholstering the chairs for the master bedroom. She used my home decor fabrics and added the crowning touch with double piping.

Lou McKee, Artist, and Sandy Ayers, freelance Artist, lent gifted hands in helping me paint the pages for "Country Decorating with Debbie Mumm," as well as some pen-and-ink illustrations.

I want to add a thank-you to all my other friends, family, and staff whose support and enthusiasm make it possible and fun for me to create.

Lastly, a very special thank-you to the talented Suzanne Nelson and Ellen Pahl, Editors, and Carol Angstadt, Book Designer, of Rodale Press, who lent their skills, creativity, and dedication to the book. I very much appreciate the opportunity to work with you. I thank them for supporting and encouraging me and having faith in me to create this book.

QUILTING BY MAIL

Sources for Products and Supplies Mentioned in the Book

Angel Hair
The Quilting B
224 Second Street SE
Cedar Rapids, IA 52401
(319) 363-1643

Note: Yarns #05 and #23 were used for the angel hair in the Angel Quilt on page 33. In the Angel Table Runner on page 38, yarn #26 was used for the angel hair.

Appliqué Pressing Sheet
Product #206
Bear Thread Designs
Route 1, Box 1640
Belgrade, MO 63622
(573) 766-5695

Debbie Mumm's Ceramic Buttons
Gay Bowles Sales, Inc.
Mill Hill
P.O. Box 1060
Janesville, WI 53547-1060
(800) 447-1332
Fax (608) 754-0665

Narrow Loop Turner or Bow Whip
Nancy's Notions
333 Beichl Avenue
P.O. Box 683
Beaver Dam, WI 53916-0683
(800) 833-0690

Sources for General Quilting Supplies

Keepsake Quilting
Route 25B, P.O. Box 1618
Centre Harbor, NH 03226-1618
(800) 865-9458

The Quilt Farm
P.O. Box 7877
Saint Paul, MN 55107
(800) 435-6201

Quilts and Other Comforts
P.O. Box 2500
Louisiana, MO 63353
(800) 881-6624

PHOTOGRAPHY LOCATIONS

Thank you to all the folks who generously allowed us in their homes with vanfuls of photo props and equipment.

The lovely dining room was in the home of Judy and George Orr in Spokane, Washington.

The family room was photographed in a cabin on Hayden Lake, Idaho.

The kitchen in the interior and on the cover was shot in Triber's Barn antique shop, owned by Helen and Darrell Triber, in Otis Orchards, Washington.

The bathroom, bedroom, and boy's room were in the home of Debbie Mumm in Spokane, Washington.

The girl's room was in the home of Lois Hansen in Spokane, Washington.

The nooks and crannies were in the home of Candy and Mark Weaver in Spokane, Washington.

The front door was the entryway to the home of my neighbors Lori and Joe Orr in Spokane, Washington.

Quick Country

Christmas
Quilts

Contents

Acknowledgments

I want to extend a giant thank you to Kelly Fisher, my talented and hardworking assistant. Kelly contributed her considerable sewing talents and did a marvelous job of writing and editing many of the project directions. Thank you for creative input, your commitment to quality, and your keen eye for detail.

Jodi Gosse, who also assists me, deserves an equally big thank you for her numerous contributions, which include sewing many of the projects and writing creative introductions and project directions. Thank you for sharing your delightful talents and for your dedication.

I am also very grateful to Kathy Grabowski, my office manager, for her unwavering support and dedication. And thanks for keeping things fun and laughing with me.

Special appreciation also goes to Mairi Fischer, who hand quilted most of the projects in the book. Her work is gorgeous and she's delightful to work with. Best wishes to you in your new home in Texas. We miss you here in Spokane!

Because we kept Mairi's fingers so busy, Nancy Kirkland helped us out tremendously by hand quilting the Pine Tree Lodge Mantel Tree Quilt. Your work is beautiful.

Thank you to Angela Poole, who made several duplicates of the Pine Tree Lodge Ornaments so that we could fill a large tree with them.

I also want to applaud my loyal, dedicated, and hard-working office and production staff at Mumm's the Word: Barbara Carlson, Betty Hastings, Carol Jesperson, Darlene Linahan, Emma Paulsen, Theresa Stone, Terri Thompson, Janie Umphrey, Pat Walter, and Sharon Wynne. Thank you for your continual support.

It is such a pleasure to work with the very talented and creative staff at Rodale Press. Not only are they dedicated to creating quality products, but they're just plain nice people! Thank you for the opportunities you've provided for me. Very special thanks to the two editors I worked with to create this book, Suzanne Nelson and Ellen Pahl. I appreciate your sharing creativity, ideas, and tremendous editorial skills to create such a fun and beautiful book! Carol Angstadt, Marianne Laubach, and Mitch Mandel were also responsible for helping to make this a visually appealing and wonderful book—thanks for the fun we had photographing the cover!

I also want to thank the Spokane Chapter of the Washington State Quilters, whose members shared special Christmas traditions for use in the Introduction and in the Holiday Planner.

To my father, Richard Kvare, my mother, Ardis Kvare, and my sister, Julie Lind, thank you for the memories and traditions of a lifetime of happy Christmases together. I appreciate all the support and encouragement you've given me over the years.

Introduction

One of my fondest memories of Christmas as a child was making decorations for our home. Even though the decorations were not very sophisticated and often involved Styrofoam and sequins, I was very proud of them. I still remember the anticipation and excitement I felt every year when I unpacked those decorations and set them out in their usual spot. Having these rituals was an important part of Christmas for me. I know that's one of the reasons why designing quilts and decorations for Christmas is one of my favorite things.

To a child, Christmas is pure magic. As we get older, the traditions and rituals we knew as children become even more important to us. To create a warm, magical feeling of Christmas in our homes, it's important to keep traditions and rituals alive as well as to create new ones. I asked some quilting friends here in Spokane about their traditions, and many were very gracious in sharing them with me.

Robin Rash's mother made or bought her an ornament every year for Christmas from the time she was born. When she married at 26, she had 26 ornaments to put on her first tree. She is now continuing this tradition with her children by making them each an ornament for every Christmas. What a lovely and special collection of ornaments they'll have!

Another quilting friend, Chris Mewhinney, has a variety of Christmas quilts, wallhangings, and pillows that she has made over the years. (The pillows were made from quilt blocks from an annual Christmas block exchange, which is a ritual with her quilt group.) Each year on the day after Thanksgiving, she decorates her farmhouse with these. She also brings out her set of Christmas dishes at this time and uses them every evening throughout the rest of the holiday season.

Mary Jane Thompson, of Veradale, Washington, is in the process of making a Christmas quilt for each of her grandchildren. On December 1, the quilts go on the beds and are used as a coverlet over their bedspreads. Children feel special because they have their very own quilt, and it decorates their bedroom for the holidays. On January 1, the quilts are put away until the next December.

In my family, we have a small artificial tree that my son puts in his room every year. This gives him a special place to display all the ornaments he's made in school and also the ones he has received from his Aunt Julie, who makes him one every year. Another quilting friend, Gayle Gregory, does the same thing, but she takes a picture of each child next to the tree. This way, she can track their growth from year to year.

In this spirit of sharing traditions, it is my hope that with this book you'll begin some new holiday traditions and create wonderful Christmas heirlooms for you and your family. The book is brimming with ideas for Christmas gifts, decorations, ornaments, table settings, invitations, and packaging suggestions (in the "Festive Flourishes" boxes). There are literally hundreds of inspiring ideas, and I bet you'll want to try them all!

To help you figure out what you want to make and do (and have fun while you're at it), I've included a special section called the "Country Quilter's Holiday Planner." You can organize yourself well in advance so you won't overlook anyone or anything you'd like to do for Christmas. Some of the quilters' holiday traditions submitted by my quilting friends here in Spokane were incorporated into this Holiday Planner.

Use the projects and photographs for inspiration and the planner to help you get organized. For an unhurried countdown to Christmas, it's best to get started making things in October. Better yet, if you can get motivated, start in July! Lots of people I've talked with work on Christmas projects and gifts year-round. That's a great way to keep on top of things and keep the giving spirit of Christmas with you always.

I find making lists keeps me on track when I'm going in eight different directions. Set goals for each month. Make it more fun by setting up a Santa's Workshop party. Get together with friends to sew, create, and decorate. Be sure to treat yourselves with a break of hot cocoa and cookies.

Getting your family together to work on projects can lead to the most satisfying and fun occasions. One quilting friend said that she planned on making the Trim-a-Tree quilt and having everyone in the family make one of the ornaments on Thanksgiving Day. That really makes it a family heirloom and a fun family activity!

Quilters are creative people who are involved in making beautiful handmade quilts and crafts. Sometimes we put an unfair burden on ourselves with the expectation that we need to create perfect, decorated-to-the-hilt homes—just to keep up with our own reputation! Remember to keep it enjoyable, and don't try to outdo yourself!

Most important, when you're up to your elbows in Christmas projects, take a few minutes to relish the joy and contentment you feel when you're creating a quilt. Anticipate how good you'll feel when you present a handmade gift. Imagine how your home will look with stockings that you've made hanging from the mantel, the table runner on your holiday table, or the handmade ornaments on the tree. And then really enjoy the warm, festive feeling that you create for your home. Your handmade quilts and crafts will become a tradition that will bring joy to you and your family year after year.

Happy Quilting, and have a very Merry Christmas!

Debbie Mumm

Country Quilter's Holiday Planner

Sew your way to Christmas with dozens of fun and festive ideas for gifts, decorations, and parties. Follow Santa's example and plan ahead for this favorite time of the year. Use this helpful October-through-December guide for inspiration.

October

WEEK ONE

Make Your Christmas Gift List and Check It Twice

Put on the Christmas music, and list everyone you need gifts for. Decide what you're going to make for each person, and include a deadline of when you'd like the project to be finished. Remember to add extra time into your schedule for gifts that need to be shipped. Also, be realistic! Don't take on more than you can actually handle. Remember, this should be fun, and no one wants you staying up all night to make his or her gift!

Don't Forget...

Christmas is a wonderful time of year to say thank you or acknowledge how much you appreciate the people whose kindnesses make a difference to you all year long—a special teacher, the baby-sitter, coworkers, longtime friends, and neighbors. Make sure to include these people on your gift list.

Take an Inventory

Once you've decided on the projects you'll be making, look over all your patterns for supplies you'll need. Go through your fabric collection and make a list of the materials and supplies to buy. Be sure to have extra rotary blades on hand.

Hold a Scrap Swap

Rejuvenate your fabric collection by hosting a scrap exchange with quilting and sewing friends. Bring what you don't want; take what you like.

GIFT IDEAS

DAD - Field and Stream Fish Wallhanging

MOM - Yuletide Place Mats and Napkins

SIS - Santa Sampler Wallhanging

UNCLE - Tooltime Banner

AUNT - Hearts and Buttons Tie, Button Pin, and Earrings

TEACHER - Teacher's Pet Lunchbag

WEEK TWO

Tune Up Your Sewing Machine

Clean and oil it, or take it in for service if necessary. You'll want to make sure it's in perfect working order for all your holiday sewing.

Shop for Supplies

Head out to the fabric store or quilt shop with your list of supplies, and buy what you'll need for your projects. (With any luck, you'll hit a pre-holiday sale!)

WEEK THREE

Plan a Weekly Party

Get together once a week with two or three friends to work on Christmas projects. It's amazing what you'll accomplish, and you'll have lots of fun doing it!

Keep a Well-Stocked Ornament Grab Basket

Make a myriad of quick and easy ornaments to keep on hand for hostess gifts, gifts for visitors, and Christmas carolers. The ornaments in Cookie Cutter Christmas (page 106) and the Rustic Twig Ornaments (page 150) are especially fast and fun to put together.

WEEK FOUR

Cultivate a Caring Spirit

Find at least one way to make a contribution to benefit your community or those in need. Organize or rally your quilt group to make quilts for a homeless shelter or other charity.

In Spokane, my hometown, the Valley Quilters combine forces with a local woodworker every year to make cradles and doll quilts for needy children in our area. In addition to the doll quilts, the women make mattress pads, sheets, and little pillows. One year when I visited this group, they gave away 125 cradles and quilts.

Decide on a Christmas Theme

Pick a theme for your Christmas decorating, and make projects to fit within that theme. Get the children involved, too. Last year, the first year in our new house, we decorated the family room with a lodge look—the inspiration for the projects in Pine Tree Lodge (page 140).

GIFT IDEAS

Give a set of basic quilting supplies with a gift certificate for a beginning quilting class.

★

You be the teacher. Take a friend along with you to your favorite quilt shop and help pick out a project and fabrics. Then offer to spend an hour or so each week giving your friend "private" quiltmaking lessons.

★

Give a tape or compact disc of "music to sew by" or a videotape to watch while basting or quilting.

★

Fill a basket with an assortment of neutral-color sewing and quilting thread, straight pins, and quilting needles, and decorate it with a torn fabric ribbon.

★

Present a gift subscription for a quilting magazine.

November

WEEK ONE

Ready, Set, Sew
Use this week to really concentrate on your projects and make progress stitching them together.

Make Your Christmas Wish List
Make a "Quilter's Wish List" of everything you would like to receive and where to get it.

A QUILTER'S WISH LIST

Six more hours a day to quilt

An extra-large flannel design board

A stocking full of fat quarters

A gift certificate from a fabric store

An all-expenses-paid trip to a quilt show

A light box

A bobbin that never runs out

A house that cleans itself

A bolt of Heat n Bond

A gift certificate for a quilting class

WEEK TWO

Make Your Own Christmas Cards

Visit a stationery store or quick-print shop to pick up card-weight paper and envelopes. Fuse an appliqué design from any of the projects in the book to the cards, and add special holiday greetings. If you'll be hand-delivering the cards, you can fuse a star or tree to the outside envelope.

Make a Keepsake Ornament

Make a special ornament for each child in your life. Do this each year, and they'll have their own collection to take with them when they leave home. Be sure to sign and date each one. See the ornaments in Cookie Cutter Christmas (page 106) and Pine Tree Lodge (page 140) for inspiration.

Catalog-Shop

Place your orders for mail-order gifts. You can even shop for quilter friends this way, using one of the many well-stocked mail-order quilt catalogs.

WEEK THREE

Address and Sign Christmas Cards

Get a head start by signing and addressing your cards now. Seal and put stamps on those that don't need any letters. Write your special notes as you have time.

Untangle the Christmas Lights

Organize the holiday decorations, replace burned-out lights, and make sure you have plenty of extension cords.

WEEK FOUR

Put Up the Outdoor Lights

Or add this to someone else's "To Do" list and use this time to sew!

Make a Wreath

Use any of the ornament designs in the book to dress up a wreath. Add a bow to make it special. The Cookie Cutter Wreath (page 113) is a fun project that could add Christmas spirit to your kitchen.

MAKING THE MOST OF YOUR TIME AND ENERGY

When you're doing quick-fuse Penstitch appliqué on a wallhanging, do some gift bags and boxes at the same time.

★

Make two of everything. It's more efficient, and you'll either end up with two gifts or have one to give and one to keep for yourself.

★

Set up a gift-wrapping station in an out-of-the-way place so you don't have to put everything away after each wrapping session.

★

Schedule 15 minutes each day for hand quilting. Put on Christmas music, make a mug of hot chocolate, and relax.

★

Take advantage of mail-order catalogs for gifts that you'll be buying. You'll save time and energy that you can devote to the pleasurable process of making gifts and decorations.

Measure the Mantel

Determine the length of garland you'll need and the number of ornaments you might want for accenting the garland. The Fireplace Garland of stars (page 97) is a fun way to brighten up the mantel.

Get Out All the Christmas Quilts

Display and enjoy all your Christmas quilts and wallhangings and add a festive look after Thanksgiving.

Wrap It Up

Review the "Festive Flourishes" for each project. Make any special wrapping paper now.

December

DAILY COUNTDOWN

1 Get Your Advent Calendar Out
Or add extra buttons and ornaments to Trim-a-Tree (page 81), and make that your family's Advent calendar.

2 Have an Ornament Swap
Each person makes 12 of the same ornament and exchanges them.

3 Plan Your Holiday Get-Together
Decide on the guest list, menu, invitations, and table decorations. See Yuletide Tables (page 66) for ideas.

4 Get the Kids Involved
Make no-sew ornaments, fused gift bags, sweatshirts, or pajamas by adapting any of the appliqué designs in the book.

5 Ship Out-of-Town Packages
Make sure long-distance friends and relatives receive their gifts on time. Wrap and ship early.

6 Pop Corn for the Garland
Pop the corn. Let it sit out in a paper bag for a day. This makes it easier to string.

7 Get the Christmas Tree
Save any extra greens to decorate the mantel and fill baskets and vases. Drape the Fireplace Garland (page 97) among the greens for a homespun touch.

8 Bake Cookies
Fill quick-fused gift boxes with homemade cookies.

9 Make No-Calorie Cookies
Give a gift of assorted Cookie Cutter Christmas Ornaments (page 110) in a small basket or tin instead of the usual sugar- and fat-laden varieties.

PARTY IDEAS

Progressive Craft Party
Make a wreath at one house; move on to another house to make ornaments. At a third house, do quick-fuse Penstitch appliqué. Collapse in front of a fireplace with a mug of warm spiced cider at the last house!

Holiday Stitch Fest
Invite your quilting friends in for an afternoon of Christmas music and refreshments. Have them bring their works in progress to stitch in the company of friends. You could also combine this with a cookie exchange.

Finishing Party
This will be the last get-together before Christmas to finish up your projects. It can be a "Quilt Till You Wilt" party that lasts until midnight or until everyone's projects are done!

Crafty Kids
Have a kids' craft afternoon to make simple gifts and ornaments such as the Rustic Twig Ornaments (page 150) or the Country Cotton Ornaments (page 146). Make an ornament garland, following the directions for the Fireplace Garland (page 97).

10 Wrap It Tonight

Get a helper and wrap all the presents you have so far in one evening. Temporarily identify the packages with sticky notes.

11 Tie It Up Tomorrow

Spend this evening adding bows and tags to the packages you wrapped last night. Do one package with a special festive flourish for each recipient. Use the helpful hints that appear throughout the projects in this book for inspiration on unique packaging ideas.

12 Spend the Day Sewing

It's the best stress buster around!

13 Adopt a Family

Get together with a group of friends, family, or coworkers and adopt a less-fortunate family for the holidays. Include some handmade ornaments and bake extra treats to go in a gift basket for them.

14 Work on Your Projects

15 Take a Break

Pamper yourself today and take time out from your hectic schedule. Have lunch with friends. Get a massage and a manicure. (Fingernails that spend a lot of time under thimbles still need attention!)

16 Go Shopping

Try to finish up all your shopping today, and buy the groceries you'll need for entertaining.

17 Date of the Big Holiday Party

Lots to do, but try to stay calm. Listen to music and take short breaks throughout the day to relax.

18 Try Assembly-Line Wrapping

If you still have presents to wrap, try this fun and fast-moving way to finish up. Dad heads the assembly line with the wrapping. Mom adds the bows. Big sister writes and attaches the tags, and little brother places them under the tree.

19 Make a Christmas Gift for Yourself

Each year, make a special decoration for your own home to add to your collection of holiday heirlooms. If you're a Santa collector, you'll find a whole range of sure-to-please fellows that follow in this book, from Sew Many Santas (page 34) to Christmas Spirits (page 45).

20 Go Christmas Caroling

Gather friends and neighbors together for hot mulled cider and hot chocolate afterward. Keep it simple and remember the spirit of Christmas. Let them all take home a handmade and dated ornament from the batch you made back in October.

21 Keep in Touch

Sit down and make a phone call to chat with a friend or relative you haven't seen for a while.

22 Have a Holiday Film Fest

Pick out your favorites from old standbys like *Miracle on 34th Street, White Christmas, It's a Wonderful Life,* and *How the Grinch Stole Christmas.* Pop a big bowlful of popcorn, build a fire, gather the family, and snuggle together under quilts you've made to enjoy some time together.

23 Go Stargazing

Count your blessings. Step outside, and take a moment to gaze up at the sky. Use these night minutes of solitude to reconnect with the spirit of the season—the joy, wonder, and magic—that too often get lost in our rush to get everything done.

24 Give a Special Gift

Celebrate the true spirit of Christmas. Give a handmade gift to someone special who isn't on your gift list. Encourage that person to do the same for someone else next year.

25 *It's Christmas!!*

Enjoy and make merry!

DECORATING IDEAS

Trim a tabletop tree with a quilting theme: Make button ornaments, hang small spools of thread from the branches, use a piece of fabric for a skirt, or use batting for snow underneath.

Make bows from leftover strips of red and green plaids, homespuns, and Christmas prints to tie on baskets and greenery throughout the house.

Debbie
Mumm

Jolly Old Saint Nicholas

**Welcome to a celebration of Santa Claus! Choose your favorite,
from the stately Old Saint Nick to a soaring Santa Claus in Christmas Spirits.
Or make the Santa Sampler to capture the many looks of Santa. You can
even make a lovely Sew Many Santas Christmas card holder
featuring the jolly old elf himself.**

Before you begin, take a minute to read through this checklist. These are important pointers you should keep in mind to make sure that each of your quilts is a success.

★ Be sure to read "Techniques for Quick Country Quilting," beginning on page 226. This will familiarize you with the tools you'll need; the techniques for time-saving cutting, piecing, and appliqué; and finishing instructions.

★ Check the "Festive Flourishes" box for each project to get clever and unique ideas for packaging and wrapping your gift.

★ Take advantage of the helpful hints in the "Sew Smart" boxes. There you'll find tips for making a technique quicker or easier.

★ Prewash and press all of your fabrics. Washing will remove any sizing from the fabrics, and pressing ensures accuracy when cutting.

★ Read the step-by-step directions from start to finish, and look at all the diagrams before you cut and sew any fabric.

★ Always use a ¼-inch seam allowance, unless there is a special note that tells you a different seam allowance is required.

★ Refer to the **Fabric Key** for each project as a help in following the diagrams.

★ Pay attention to the pressing directions given in the step-by-step text and to the pressing arrows shown in the diagrams.

Old Saint Nick

31"

22"

THREE-SANTA QUILT LAYOUT

'Tis the season to sew and be of good cheer . . . and here's just the fellow to fill your sewing room with glad tidings. Old Saint Nick stars in these simple-to-stitch quilts. Choose a trio of stately Santas or a single Santa with his sack to give as a gift or add to your collection of Christmas decorations. Then stir up a mug of steaming hot cocoa and have fun looking through your fabrics to pick out just the right ones to get started.

Three-Santa Quilt

Finished Quilt: 31 × 22 inches
Finished Block: 7 × 15 inches

Materials

Obvious directional prints are not recommended.

FABRIC A
Use three fabrics.
Santa Suit, Hat, and
    Patchwork Border ⅛ yard
        each of *three* fabrics

FABRIC B
Block Background ¼ yard
Lattice and Borders ½ yard
    TOTAL ¾ yard

FABRIC C
Use three fabrics.
Beard and Tassel ⅛ yard
        each of *three* fabrics

FABRIC D
Boots, Gloves, and
    Patchwork Border ⅛ yard

FABRIC E
Use three fabrics.
Accent Fur and
    Patchwork Border ⅛ yard
        each of *three* fabrics

FABRIC F
Use three fabrics.
Face ⅛ yard
    (or 1½ × 2½-inch piece)
        each of *three* fabrics

BINDING ⅓ yard

BACKING ¾ yard

LIGHTWEIGHT BATTING ¾ yard

NOTIONS AND SUPPLIES
Black embroidery floss for French
    knot eyes (optional)

Cutting Directions

Prewash and press all of your fabrics. Using a rotary cutter, see-through ruler, and cutting mat, prepare the strips as described in the first column in the chart below. Then from those strips, cut the pieces listed in the second column. Some portions of the quilt need to be cut only once, so no additional cutting information will appear in the second column.

To help you stay organized, the cutting requirements for each fabric are subdivided into sections that correspond to the sections of the block. Put all the fabrics for each section in one group. You will have three groups of fabrics for each block.

	FIRST CUT		SECOND CUT	
	NO. OF STRIPS	DIMENSIONS	NO. OF PIECES	DIMENSIONS
FABRIC A	**Before You Cut:** Cut the 3½ × 5½-inch Section Three piece first, followed by the 1½ × 30-inch Patchwork Border strip.			
	Santa Suit and Hat: from *each* of the *three* fabrics, cut the following			
	1	3½ × 5½-inch piece (Section Three)		
	1	2½ × 4½-inch piece (Section Two)		
	2	2½-inch squares (Section Two)		
	1	2½ × 1-inch piece (Section One)		
	2	1½ × 5-inch pieces (Section Two)		
	1	1½ × 4½-inch piece (Section One)		
	Patchwork Border			
	1	1½ × 30-inch strip		
FABRIC B	**Block Background**			
	1	2½ × 44-inch strip	3	2½ × 3½-inch pieces (Section Three)
			3	2½-inch squares (Section Three)
			3	2½-inch squares (Section One)
			3	2 × 4½-inch pieces (Section Three)
	3	1½ × 44-inch strips	3	1½ × 6½-inch pieces (Section Two)
			3	1½ × 3½-inch pieces (Section One)
			6	1½ × 2½-inch pieces (Section One)
			9	1½-inch squares (Section One)
			6	1½-inch squares (Section Two)
			3	1 × 4½-inch pieces (Section Three)

	FIRST CUT		SECOND CUT	
	NO. OF STRIPS	DIMENSIONS	NO. OF PIECES	DIMENSIONS
FABRIC B	**Lattice**			
	4	1½ × 44-inch strips	2	1½ × 24½-inch strips
			2	1½ × 17½-inch strips
			3	1½ × 15½-inch strips
	Patchwork Border			
	1	1½ × 44-inch strip	1	1½ × 30-inch strip
	Outer Border			
	4	1½ × 44-inch strips	2	1½ × 28½-inch strips
			2	1½ × 21½-inch strips
FABRIC C	**Beard and Tassel:** from *each* of the *three* fabrics, cut the following			
	2	2½ × 4½-inch pieces (Section Two)		
	3	1½-inch squares (Section One)		
FABRIC D	**Boots and Gloves**			
	1	1½ × 44-inch strip	6	1½ × 2½-inch pieces (Section Three)
			6	1½-inch squares (Section Two)
			6	1½-inch squares (Section Three)
	Patchwork Border			
	1	1½ × 44-inch strip	1	1½ × 30-inch strip
FABRIC E	**Before You Cut:** Cut the 1½ × 30-inch strip for the Patchwork Border first, followed by the Accent Fur pieces.			
	Patchwork Border: from *each* of the *three* fabrics, cut the following			
	1	1½ × 44-inch strip	1	1½ × 30-inch strip
	Accent Fur: from *each* of the *three* fabrics, cut the following			
	1	1½ × 5½-inch piece (Section Three)		
	2	1½ × 1-inch pieces (Section Two)		
	1	1 × 2½-inch piece (Section One)		
FABRIC F	**Face:** from *each* of the *three* fabrics, cut the following			
	1	1½ × 2½-inch piece (Section One)		
BINDING	4	2¾ × 44-inch strips		
BACKING & BATTING	From *each* of the backing and batting, cut the following			
	1	35 × 26-inch piece		

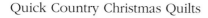

Quick Corner Triangles

Refer to "Making Quick Corner Triangles" on page 234. You will be making three Santa blocks, each of a different fabric combination. Before sewing, coordinate the fabrics for each of the three combinations. Keep track of the combinations as you sew. Refer to the **Fabric Key** for fabric identification, and press in the direction of the triangle just added.

Steps for quick corner triangle units are subdivided into the three block sections. For easier block assembly, return the completed corner triangle units to the groups of cut pieces for each section and refer to the **Block Diagram** as you sew.

Fabric Key	
⊡	FABRIC A (Suit)
◩	FABRIC B (Background)
◙	FABRIC C (Beard)
▨	FABRIC D (Boots/Gloves)
⊞	FABRIC E (Fur)
☐	FABRIC F (Face)

SECTION ONE

SECTION TWO

SECTION THREE

BLOCK DIAGRAM

Section One (Face and Hat)

Step 1. Sew three 1½-inch Fabric B squares to three 1½ × 4½-inch Fabric A pieces, as shown in **Diagram 1.** Press.

DIAGRAM 1

Step 2. Sew three additional 1½-inch Fabric B squares to the opposite end of the three Step 1 units. Press. See **Diagram 2.**

DIAGRAM 2

Step 3. Sew three 1½-inch Fabric C squares to three 1½ × 3½-inch Fabric B pieces, as shown in **Diagram 3.** Press.

DIAGRAM 3

Step 4. Sew three 1½-inch Fabric C squares to three 1½ × 2½-inch Fabric B pieces. Press. See **Diagram 4.**

DIAGRAM 4

Section Two (Beard and Arms)

Step 1. Sew three 2½-inch Fabric A squares to three 2½ × 4½-inch Fabric C pieces. See **Diagram 5.** Press.

DIAGRAM 5

Step 2. Sew three additional 2½-inch Fabric A squares to the opposite end of the Step 1 units. See **Diagram 6.** Press.

DIAGRAM 6

Step 3. Sew three 1½-inch Fabric B squares to three 1½ × 5-inch Fabric A pieces. Press. See **Diagram 7.**

DIAGRAM 7

Step 4. Sew three 1½-inch Fabric B squares to three 1½ × 5-inch Fabric A pieces, as shown in **Diagram 8.** Press. These corner triangles are sewn in the opposite direction from those in Step 3.

DIAGRAM 8

Section Three (Lower Body and Feet)

Step 1. Sew three 1½-inch Fabric D squares to three 2½ × 3½-inch Fabric B pieces, as shown in **Diagram 9.** Press.

3½"

2½"

DIAGRAM 9

Step 2. Sew three 1½-inch Fabric D squares to three 2½-inch Fabric B squares. See **Diagram 10.** Press.

2½"

2½"

DIAGRAM 10

Making the Blocks

Throughout this section, refer to the **Fabric Key** to identify the fabric placements in the diagrams. Also, it's a good idea to reveiw "Assembly-Line Piecing" on page 234 before you get started. It's more efficient to do the same step for each block at the same time than to piece an entire block together at one time. Pay close attention that corner triangles are positioned the same as shown in the diagrams. Be sure to use ¼-inch seam allowances and press as you go. Follow the arrows in each diagram for pressing direction.

SEW SMART

If you find it difficult to keep track of all the different fabrics for these blocks, it may be easier to assemble these sections one block at a time.

Section One (Face and Hat)
Step 1. Sew three 1½-inch Fabric B squares to three 1½-inch Fabric C squares. See **Diagram 11.**

(Remember to sew one each of the three fabric combinations.) Position them with right sides together and line them up next to your sewing machine. Follow the directions in "Continuous-Seam Technique" on page 235 to join all three sets together. Press seams and cut joining threads. Remember, you will be making three blocks at a time. Be sure to maintain your fabric combinations for the three different Santa blocks.

1½"

1½"

1½"

DIAGRAM 11

Step 2. Sew three 1 × 2½-inch Fabric E pieces to three 1 × 2½-inch Fabric A pieces. See **Diagram 12.** Press.

2½"

1"

1"

DIAGRAM 12

Step 3. Sew three 1½ × 2½-inch Fabric B pieces to three Step 2 units, as shown in **Diagram 13.** Press.

2½"

1½"

STEP 2 UNIT

DIAGRAM 13

Step 4. Sew three 1½ × 4½-inch Fabric A/B corner triangle units to three Step 3 units. See **Diagram 14.** Press.

4½"

1½"

STEP 3 UNIT

DIAGRAM 14

Step 5. Sew three Step 1 units to three Step 4 units. See **Diagram 15.** Press.

STEP 1 UNIT   STEP 4 UNIT

DIAGRAM 15

Step 6. Sew three Step 5 units to three 2½-inch Fabric B squares, as shown in **Diagram 16.** Press.

STEP 5 UNIT

2½"

2½"

DIAGRAM 16

Step 7. Sew three 1½ × 3½-inch Fabric B/C corner triangle units to the left end of three 1½ × 2½-inch Fabric F pieces. Sew three 1½ × 2½-inch Fabric B/C corner triangle units to the right end of these same three units. See **Diagram 17.** Press.

3½"   2½" 2½"

1½"   1½"

DIAGRAM 17

Step 8. Sew three Step 6 units to three Step 7 units, as shown in **Diagram 18.** Press.

STEP 6 UNIT

STEP 7 UNIT

DIAGRAM 18

Section Two (Beard and Arms)

Step 1. Sew six 1 × 1½-inch Fabric E pieces to six 1½-inch Fabric D squares for the gloves. You will be making two of each Fabric D/E combination. See **Diagram 19.** Press.

Make 2 sets per block.
1½"
1"
1½"

DIAGRAM 19

Step 2. Sew three 1½ × 5-inch Fabric A/B corner triangle units to three of the six Step 1 units for the left arm. See **Diagram 20.** Press.

1½"
5"
STEP 1 UNIT

DIAGRAM 20

Step 3. Sew three 1½ × 5-inch Fabric A/B corner triangle units to the remaining three Step 1 units for the right arm. See **Diagram 21.** Press.

1½"
5"
STEP 1 UNIT

DIAGRAM 21

Step 4. Sew three 2½ × 4½-inch Fabric C pieces to three 2½ × 4½-inch Fabric A/C corner triangle units, as shown in **Diagram 22.** Press.

4½"
2½"
2½"

DIAGRAM 22

Step 5. Sew three Step 4 units to three 2½ × 4½-inch Fabric A pieces. See **Diagram 23.** Press.

STEP 4 UNIT
2½"
4½"

DIAGRAM 23

Step 6. Sew three Step 2 units to the left side of three Step 5 units. Sew three Step 3 units to the right side of these same units. See **Diagram 24.** Press.

STEP 5 UNIT
STEP 2 UNIT
STEP 3 UNIT

DIAGRAM 24

Step 7. Sew three 1½ × 6½-inch Fabric B pieces to the left side of three Step 6 units. See **Diagram 25.** Press.

1½"
6½"
STEP 6 UNIT

DIAGRAM 25

Section Three
(Lower Body and Feet)

Step 1. Sew three 3½ × 5½-inch Fabric A pieces to three 1½ × 5½-inch Fabric E pieces, as shown in **Diagram 26.** Press.

5½"
3½"
1½"

DIAGRAM 26

Step 2. Sew three 2 × 4½-inch Fabric B pieces to three Step 1 units. See **Diagram 27.** Press.

2"
4½"
STEP 1 UNIT

DIAGRAM 27

Step 3. Sew three Step 2 units to three 1 × 4½-inch Fabric B pieces. See **Diagram 28.** Press.

STEP 2 UNIT
1"
4½"

DIAGRAM 28

Step 4. Sew three 2½ × 3½-inch Fabric B/D corner triangle units to the left side of three 1½ × 2½-inch Fabric D pieces. See **Diagram 29.** Press.

3½" 1½"
2½"
2½"

DIAGRAM 29

Step 5. Sew three 2½ × 2½-inch Fabric B/D corner triangle units to the right side of three 1½ × 2½-inch Fabric D pieces. See **Diagram 30.** Press.

1¹⁄₂" 2¹⁄₂"

DIAGRAM 30

Step 6. Sew three Step 4 units to three Step 5 units, as shown in **Diagram 31.** Press.

DIAGRAM 31

Step 7. Sew three Step 3 units to three Step 6 units. See **Diagram 32.** Press.

DIAGRAM 32

Assembling the Blocks

Step 1. Sew Section One to Section Two. Press toward Section Two. See **Diagram 33.**

DIAGRAM 33

Step 2. Sew Section One/Two to Section Three. Press toward Section Three. See **Diagram 34.** Your blocks should now measure 7½ × 15½ inches.

DIAGRAM 34

Step 3. Add twinkling eyes to your Santas with French knots, if you like. See "French Knots" on page 23.

Lattice

Step 1. Lay out your blocks in a pleasing arrangement. Keep track of your layout while sewing on the lattice.

Step 2. Sew 1½ × 15½-inch Fabric B lattice strips to the right side of *each* block. Press all seams toward the lattice.

Step 3. Sew the blocks into one row of three Santas. Press.

Step 4. Sew 1½ × 24½-inch Fabric B strips to the top and bottom. Press. Sew 1½ × 17½-inch Fabric B strips to the sides. Press.

Patchwork Border

Step 1. Take the eight 1½ × 30-inch patchwork border strips (one each of three Fabric As, one each of three Fabric Es, one Fabric B, and one Fabric D) and arrange them in a pleasing order.

Step 2. Sew the strips together to make an 8½ × 30-inch strip set, as shown in **Diagram 35.** Change sewing direction with each strip

sewn to help keep the strip set straight. Press all the seams in one direction as you go. Cut this strip set in thirds (approximately 10 inches each).

DIAGRAM 35

Step 3. Resew the thirds together to make a 24½ × 10-inch strip set. See **Diagram 36.**

DIAGRAM 36

Step 4. Using a rotary cutter and ruler, cut this strip set into five 1½ × 24½-inch strips.

Step 5. For the top and bottom borders, use a seam ripper to remove two sets of two squares from one 1½ × 24½-inch strip. Sew two squares to each of two patchwork border strips to make two strips with 26 squares each. Fit, pin in position, and sew the patchwork border strips to the top and bottom of the quilt. If the border doesn't fit the quilt top, see "Hints on Fitting Pieced Borders" on page 244. Press all seams toward the lattice.

Step 6. For the side borders, use a seam ripper to remove 5 squares from each of the two remaining patchwork border strips to make two strips with 19 squares each. Fit, pin in position, and sew the patchwork border strips to the quilt sides. Press.

Outer Border

Step 1. Sew the 1½ × 28½-inch Fabric B outer border strips to the quilt top and bottom. Press all seams toward the outer border.

Step 2. Sew the 1½ × 21½-inch Fabric B outer border strips to the quilt sides. Press.

Layering the Quilt

Arrange and baste the backing, batting, and top together, following the directions in "Layering the Quilt" on page 245. Trim the batting and backing to ¼ inch from the raw edge of the quilt top.

Binding the Quilt

Using the four 2¾ × 44-inch binding strips, follow the directions in "Binding the Quilt" on page 246.

Finishing Stitches

Machine or hand quilt in the seam line around each Santa. Quilt in the seam line around the coat, hat, face, beard, gloves, boots, and fur trim. Quilt a 1½-inch diagonal grid in the background. Quilt in the seam line around the patchwork border and between the squares of the border.

Festive Flourishes

Along with your gift, add a plate of cookies for Saint Nick's best helper on a cute Santa plate, or wrap up a Christmas mug with an assortment of gourmet cocoa or coffee. If the recipient is a quilter, you could give a Christmas mug filled with fabric.

Single Santa

Finished Wallhanging: 18 × 22 inches
Finished Block: 11 × 15 inches

SINGLE SANTA LAYOUT

Materials

Obvious directional prints are not recommended.

FABRIC A
Santa Suit, Hat, and
   Patchwork Border   ⅛ yard

FABRIC B
Block Background   ¼ yard
Borders   ¼ yard
   TOTAL   ½ yard

FABRIC C
Beard and Tassel   ⅛ yard

FABRIC D
Boots, Gloves, and
   Patchwork Border   ⅛ yard

FABRIC E
Accent Fur and
   Patchwork Border   ⅛ yard

FABRIC F
Face   1½ × 2½-inch piece

FABRIC G
Bag and Patchwork Border   ¼ yard

BINDING   ⅛ yard

BACKING   ⅔ yard

LIGHTWEIGHT BATTING   ⅔ yard

APPLIQUÉ STAR
Coordinated fabric scrap

NOTIONS AND SUPPLIES
Black embroidery floss for French knot eyes (optional)

Cutting Directions

Prewash and press all of your fabrics. Using a rotary cutter, see-through ruler, and cutting mat, prepare the strips as described in the first column in the chart below.

Then from those strips, cut the pieces listed in the second column. Some portions of the quilt need to be cut only once, so no additional cutting information will appear in the second column. The cutting

requirements for each fabric are subdivided into sections that correspond to sections of the block. Put all the fabric pieces for each section in one group. You will have four groups of fabrics.

	FIRST CUT		SECOND CUT	
	NO. OF STRIPS	**DIMENSIONS**	**NO. OF PIECES**	**DIMENSIONS**
FABRIC A	**Before You Cut:** Cut the 3½ × 5½-inch Section 3 piece first, followed by the 1½ × 30-inch Patchwork Border strip.			
	Santa Suit and Hat			
	1	3½ × 5½-inch piece (Section Three)		
	1	2½ × 4½-inch piece (Section Two)		
	2	2½-inch squares (Section Two)		
	1	2½ × 1-inch piece (Section One)		
	2	1½ × 5-inch pieces (Section Two)		
	1	1½ × 4½-inch piece (Section One)		
	Patchwork Border			
	1	1½ × 30-inch strip		
FABRIC B	**Block Background**			
	1	4½ × 44-inch strip	1	4½ × 8½-inch piece (Section Four)
			1	4½ × 2-inch piece (Section Three)
			1	4½ × 1-inch piece (Section Three)
			1	2½ × 3½-inch piece (Section Three)
			1	2½-inch square (Section One)
			1	2½-inch square (Section Three)
			2	2½-inch squares (Section Four)
	1	1½ × 44-inch strip	1	1½ × 6½-inch piece (Section Two)
			1	1½ × 3½-inch piece (Section One)
			1	1½ × 3-inch piece (Section Four)
			2	1½ × 2½-inch pieces (Section One)
			3	1½-inch squares (Section One)
			2	1½-inch squares (Section Two)
			2	1½-inch squares (Section Four)

(continued)

Single Santa Cutting Chart—Continued	FIRST CUT		SECOND CUT	
	NO. OF STRIPS	DIMENSIONS	NO. OF PIECES	DIMENSIONS
FABRIC B *(continued)*	**Inner Border**			
	2	1½ × 44-inch strips	2	1½ × 17½-inch strips
			2	1½ × 11½-inch strips
	Patchwork Border			
	1	1½ × 44-inch strip	1	1½ × 30-inch strip
	Outer Border			
	2	1½ × 44-inch strips	2	1½ × 21½-inch strips
			2	1½ × 15½-inch strips
FABRIC C	**Beard and Tassel**			
	2	2½ × 4½-inch pieces (Section Two)		
	3	1½-inch squares (Section One)		
FABRIC D	**Before You Cut:** Cut the strip for the Patchwork Border first. Use the remainder of the 1½ × 44-inch strip to cut the pieces for the boots and gloves.			
	Patchwork Border			
	1	1½ × 44-inch strip	1	1½ × 30-inch strip
	Boots and Gloves			
	2	1½ × 2½-inch pieces (Section Three)		
	2	1½-inch squares (Section Two)		
	2	1½-inch squares (Section Three)		
FABRIC E	**Before You Cut:** Cut the strip for the Patchwork Border first. Use the remainder of the 1½ × 44-inch strip to cut the pieces for the accent fur.			
	Patchwork Border			
	1	1½ × 44-inch strip	1	1½ × 30-inch strip
	Accent Fur			
	1	1½ × 5½-inch piece (Section Three)		
	2	1½ × 1-inch pieces (Section Two)		
	1	1 × 2½-inch piece (Section One)		
FABRIC F	**Face**			
	1	1½ × 2½-inch piece (Section One)		

FIRST CUT			SECOND CUT	
NO. OF STRIPS	**DIMENSIONS**	**NO. OF PIECES**	**DIMENSIONS**	
FABRIC G	**Before You Cut:** Cut the strip for the Patchwork Border first.			
	Patchwork Border			
1	1½ × 44-inch strip	1	1½ × 30-inch strip	
	Bag			
1	3½ × 44-inch strip	1	3½ × 4½-inch piece (Section Four)	
		1	3½-inch square (Section Four)	
	Before You Cut: Use the remainder of the 1½ × 44-inch strip cut for the Patchwork Border to cut the following pieces.			
1	1½ × 4½-inch piece (Section Four)			
1	1½ × 1-inch piece (Section Four)			
BINDING	2	1 × 44-inch strips	2	1 × 22½-inch strips
			2	1 × 17½-inch strips
BACKING	1	22 × 26-inch piece		
BATTING	1	22 × 26-inch piece		

Quick Corner Triangles

Refer to "Quick Corner Triangles" for the Three-Santa Quilt, beginning on page 14. Follow all the steps in that section. Since you will be making only one Santa block, the numbers will change from three to one and from six to two.

Fabric Key

- **FABRIC A** (Suit)
- **FABRIC B** (Background)
- **FABRIC C** (Beard)
- **FABRIC D** (Boots/Gloves)
- **FABRIC E** (Fur)
- **FABRIC F** (Face)
- **FABRIC G** (Bag)

Section Four (Bag)

Step 1. Sew one 2½-inch Fabric B square to one 3½-inch Fabric G square, as shown in **Diagram 37.** Press.

3½"

3½"

DIAGRAM 37

Step 2. Sew one 2½-inch Fabric B square to one 3½ × 4½-inch Fabric G piece. See **Diagram 38.** Press.

3½"

4½"

DIAGRAM 38

Step 3. Sew one 1½-inch Fabric B square to one 1½ × 4½-inch Fabric G piece. See **Diagram 39.** Press.

1½"

4½"

DIAGRAM 39

Step 4. Sew one additional 1½-inch Fabric B square to the opposite end of the Step 3 unit. See **Diagram 40.** Press.

1½"

4½"

DIAGRAM 40

Making the Block

Your cut pieces and quick corner triangles should be grouped by section for easier piecing. For Sections One, Two, and Three, follow all the steps in "Making the Blocks" for the Three-Santa Quilt, beginning on page 15. Since you will be making only one block, the numbers will change from three to one and from six to two.

Section Four (Bag)

Step 1. Sew one 1½ × 1-inch Fabric G piece to one 1½ × 3-inch Fabric B piece. See **Diagram 41.** Press.

DIAGRAM 41

Step 2. Sew the Step 1 unit to one 3½ × 3½-inch Fabric B/G corner triangle unit. See **Diagram 42.** Press.

DIAGRAM 42

Step 3. Sew one 1½ × 4½-inch Fabric B/G corner triangle unit to one 3½ × 4½-inch Fabric B/G corner triangle unit. See **Diagram 43.** Press.

DIAGRAM 43

Step 4. Sew the Step 2 unit to the Step 3 unit. See **Diagram 44.** Press.

STEP 2 UNIT

STEP 3 UNIT

DIAGRAM 44

Step 5. Sew one 4½ × 8½-inch Fabric B piece to the Step 4 unit, as shown in **Diagram 45.** Press.

4½"

8½"

STEP 4 UNIT

DIAGRAM 45

Assembling the Block

Step 1. Follow Steps 1 and 2 under "Assembling the Blocks" for the Three-Santa Quilt on page 17.

Step 2. Sew the block made in Step 1 to Section Four, the bag. Press toward Section Four. See **Diagram 46.** Your block should now measure 11½ × 15½ inches.

SECTION FOUR

DIAGRAM 46

Step 3. Make French knots for Santa's twinkling eyes, if you like. (See "French Knots" on the opposite page.)

Inner Border

Step 1. Sew 1½ × 11½-inch Fabric B strips to the block top and bottom. Press toward the Fabric B strips.

Step 2. Sew 1½ × 17½-inch Fabric B strips to the sides. Press.

Patchwork Border

Step 1. Take the five 1½ × 30-inch patchwork border strips (one each of Fabrics A, B, D, E, and G) and arrange them in a pleasing order.

Step 2. Sew the strips together to make a 5½ × 30-inch strip set, as shown in **Diagram 47.** Change sewing direction with each strip sewn. Press all the seams in one direction as you go.

5½"

10"

CUTTING LINES

30"

10"

10"

DIAGRAM 47

Step 3. Cut this strip set in thirds (approximately 10 inches each), referring to the cutting lines in **Diagram 47.** Resew together into one 15½ × 10-inch strip set.

Step 4. Using a rotary cutter and ruler, cut this strip set into five 1½ × 15½-inch strips. See **Diagram 48.**

15½"

1½"

10"

CUTTING LINES

DIAGRAM 48

Step 5. For the top and bottom borders, remove 2 squares each from two 1½ × 15½-inch strips with a seam ripper, to make two strips with 13 squares each. Fit, pin in position, and sew the patchwork border strips to the top and bottom of the block. If the border doesn't fit, see "Hints on Fitting Pieced Borders" on page 244. Press all seams away from the patchwork border.

Step 6. For the side borders, remove two sets of 4 squares from a 1½ × 15½-inch patchwork border strip. Sew a set of 4 squares onto each of the two remaining 1½ × 15½-inch patchwork border strips, to make two strips with 19 squares each. Fit, pin in position, and sew the border strips to the sides. Press.

Outer Border

Step 1. Sew 1½ × 15½-inch Fabric B outer border strips to the wallhanging top and bottom. Press all seams toward the outer border.

Step 2. Sew 1½ × 21½-inch Fabric B outer border strips to the wallhanging sides. Press.

Binding

Step 1. Sew 1 × 17½-inch binding strips to the wallhanging top and bottom. Press all seams toward the binding.

Step 2. Sew 1 × 22½-inch binding strips to the wallhanging sides. Press.

FRENCH KNOTS

These knots make wonderful eyes! Add these extra details before layering and quilting.

Thread the needle with four to six strands of floss. Knot one end. Bring the needle up through the fabric at the point where you want the knot. Wrap the thread around the needle three times and hold the thread taut with your finger. Insert the needle back into the fabric close to where it came up. Pull the needle through to the back. The knot will remain on top.

FRENCH KNOT

Star Appliqué

Machine or hand appliqué a star to the Single Santa block using the **Star Appliqué Pattern** on this page. (Refer to "Machine Appliqué" on page 239 or "Hand Appliqué" on page 240.) See the **Single Santa Quilt Layout** on page 18 for placement.

Finishing

Step 1. Position the top and backing with right sides together. Lay both pieces on top of the batting and pin all three layers together. Sew together, leaving a 3- to 4-inch opening for turning. Trim the batting and backing to the same size as the top.

Step 2. Trim the corners, turn right side out, press, and hand stitch the opening. Press.

Step 3. Machine or hand quilt in the seam line around the Santa (including coat, hat, fur trim, face, beard, gloves, and boots), bag, and star. Quilt a 1½-inch diagonal grid in the background. Quilt in the seam line around the patchwork border and binding.

STAR APPLIQUÉ PATTERN

Santa Sampler

Finished Quilt: 31 × 26 inches

31"

26"

SANTA SAMPLER QUILT LAYOUT

Here's Santa Claus in all his glory . . . carrying his pack, blowing his trumpet, up on the rooftop. This sampler is cause for good cheer—quick appliqué makes it extra easy. Everyone loves Santa, so you can whip one up for just about anyone on your gift list. Embellish these seven merry fellows with buttonhole embroidery, and then for added charm, trim with tiny buttons, bright beads, and miniature jingle bells. Happy holidays and ho, ho, ho!

Festive Flourishes

Create a fabric Santa sack to wrap up your sampler. Use Santa Claus fabric, or fuse Santa to background fabric. Use ½ yard of fabric, sew up the sides, and tie the top of the bag with a strip of fabric or cording. Just for fun, hang a no-sew Santa ornament from the tie. After the gift has been given, the bag can be filled with stuffing and placed under the tree or next to the fireplace. It will look like part of the holiday decor. Or, the bag can be passed on within your extended family so it will be used year after year for oversized, hard-to-wrap gifts. It will become a tradition to see this bag show up under the tree.

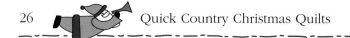

Materials and Cutting

Using a rotary cutter, see-through ruler, and cutting mat, prepare the pieces as described in the chart below. Measurements for all pieces include ¼-inch seam allowances.

	YARDAGE	NO. OF PIECES	DIMENSIONS
			CUTTING
Background	⅛- to ¼-yard pieces of seven different fabrics	1	5½ × 8½-inch piece (Block #1)
		1	5½ × 10-inch piece (Block #2)
		1	5½ × 10½-inch piece (Block #3)
		1	3½ × 13-inch piece (Block #4)
		1	7 × 13-inch piece (Block #5)
		1	7½ × 11½-inch piece (Block #6)
		1	7½ × 7-inch piece (Block #7)
Lattice	⅙ yard (6 inches; cut into five 1 × 44-inch strips)	2	1 × 23½-inch strips
		2	1 × 19½-inch strips
		2	1 × 18½-inch strips
		1	1 × 13-inch strip
		1	1 × 10½-inch strip
		1	1 × 7½-inch strip
		1	1 × 5½-inch strip
Half-Inch Accent Border	⅛ yard	4	1 × 44-inch strips
Wide Border	⅜ yard	4	3 × 44-inch strips
Binding	⅓ yard	4	2¾ × 44-inch strips
Backing	⅞ yard		
Lightweight Batting	⅞ yard		
Appliqué Pieces	⅛-yard pieces or several coordinated scraps		

Appliqué film, sewable
  (See "Buttonhole Embroidery Appliqué" on page 240.)
Embroidery floss, black, and colors to match appliqué fabrics

Five ³/₁₆-inch black buttons for eyes and coat
Small gold bell for hat
Black, extra-fine point, permanent felt-tip pen

Buttonhole Appliqué

The appliqués in Santa Sampler were designed especially for using the Buttonhole Embroidery technique described on page 240. However, you may use quick-fuse Penstitch (page 239) or machine appliqué (page 239) if you prefer. Be sure to use a *sewable* appliqué film for the buttonhole embroidery or machine appliqué technique. Use a heavier weight *non-sewable* appliqué film for quick-fuse Penstitch appliqué.

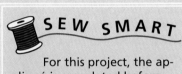

SEW SMART

For this project, the appliqué is completed before the blocks are assembled into the wallhanging top. This makes it easier to complete the buttonhole embroidery; you can do your stitching on one block at a time. This way, you can keep your blocks with you and work on them whenever you find time.

Step 1. Trace one of each of the seven Santa designs onto appliqué film using the **Santa Sampler Appliqué Patterns** on pages 29–33. Fuse the film onto the assorted pieces of fabric and cut the shapes out of the fabric.

Step 2. Arrange the appliqué designs in the center of each of the corresponding background pieces and fuse in position.

Step 3. Use the buttonhole embroidery stitch to outline the pieces.

Step 4. Sew two ³⁄₁₆-inch black buttons onto the Santa in Block #7 for eyes.

Step 5. Use two strands of embroidery floss to make French knots for eyes on the other Santas. (See "French Knots" on page 23.) Sew three small black buttons to Santa's coat in Block #2. Sew a small gold bell to the end of Santa's hat in Block #6.

Background Assembly

Use ¼-inch seam allowances and press all seams toward the lattice after each sewing step. Refer to the diagrams for each step.

Step 1. Sew a 1 × 5½-inch lattice strip between Block #1 and Block #2. See **Diagram 1**. Press.

DIAGRAM 1

Step 2. Sew a 1 × 13-inch lattice strip between Block #4 and Block #5, as shown in **Diagram 2**. Press.

Step 3. Sew a 1 × 10½-inch lattice strip to the top of the Step 2 unit. Press. Sew Block #3 to the top of this unit. Press. See **Diagram 3**.

DIAGRAM 2

DIAGRAM 3

Step 4. Sew a 1 × 7½-inch lattice strip between Block #6 and Block #7. See **Diagram 4**. Press.

DIAGRAM 4

Step 5. Sew 1 × 18½-inch lattice strips to the sides of the Step 3 unit. See **Diagram 5**. Press.

DIAGRAM 5

Step 6. Sew the Step 1 unit to the left side of the Step 5 unit. Press. Sew the Step 4 unit to the right side of the same unit. Press. See **Diagram 6.**

Step 7. Sew 1 × 23½-inch lattice strips to the wallhanging top and bottom. Press.

Step 8. Sew 1 × 19½-inch lattice strips to the wallhanging sides. Press.

SANTA'S GARLAND OF STARS

The garland of stars in Santa Block #5 can be fused in place or strung on a piece of embroidery floss. If you fuse the stars in place, draw the line between the stars with your permanent felt-tip pen. To string the stars, fuse the stars to the wrong side of a scrap of fabric. This fabric will be the back side of the stars. Cut out the stars, using the cut edge as a guide. Thread a 10-inch piece of embroidery floss through a needle. Tie a knot at one end. From the back of the wallhanging top, bring the needle up through the fabric at the edge of Santa's right mitten. Thread the four stars onto the thread, referring to the appliqué design on page 30. Insert the needle back into the fabric at the edge of Santa's left mitten, and tie a knot on the back. Trim the ends of the thread.

Half-Inch Accent Border

Sew 1 × 44-inch accent border strips to the wallhanging top and bottom. Trim the excess and press all seams toward the half-inch border. Sew 1 × 44-inch accent border strips to the wallhanging sides. Trim the excess and press.

Wide Border

Sew 3 × 44-inch wide border strips to the wallhanging top and bottom. Trim the excess and press all seams toward the wide border. Sew 3 × 44-inch wide border strips to the wallhanging sides. Trim the excess and press.

Finishing Stitches

Step 1. Using the finished top as a guide, cut the backing and batting pieces 4 inches larger than the quilt top.

Step 2. Arrange and baste the backing, batting, and top together following the directions in "Layering the Quilt" on page 245. Trim the batting and backing to ¼ inch from the raw edge of the quilt top.

Step 3. Using four 2¾ × 44-inch binding strips, follow the directions in "Binding the Quilt" on page 246.

Step 4. Machine or hand quilt in the seam line around the background pieces and the borders. Outline the appliqué designs by quilting 1⁄16 inch away from the edge of the designs. Quilt a 1½-inch diagonal grid in the wide border.

DIAGRAM 6

Appliqué Pattern Key

———————— TRACING LINE

- - - - - - - - TRACING LINE
(will be hidden behind
other fabric)

Place hat on
Santa's head here.

SANTA SAMPLER
APPLIQUÉ
PATTERNS

SANTA BLOCK #4

SANTA BLOCK #1

SANTA SAMPLER
APPLIQUÉ PATTERNS

PATTERN PIECE B

Match dots with Pattern Piece A.

SANTA
BLOCK #5

PATTERN PIECE A

Match dots with Pattern Piece B.

Appliqué Pattern Key

———— TRACING LINE

– – – – TRACING LINE
(will be hidden behind other fabric)

SANTA BLOCK #3

SANTA BLOCK #2

SANTA BLOCK #6

SANTA SAMPLER APPLIQUÉ PATTERNS

SANTA BLOCK #7

Appliqué Pattern Key

_____ TRACING LINE

- - - - - - - TRACING LINE
(will be hidden behind
other fabric)

Sew Many Santas

27"

27"

NINE-BLOCK QUILT LAYOUT

You can never have too many Santas! Make nine patchwork Santas in plaids and shades of red for a nine-block quilt, or put three of the jolly guys to work holding Christmas cards and letters. No matter what, these Santas are "sew" easy to make. Wishing you happy sewing and all the joys of ho, ho, ho-ing!

Nine-Block Santa Quilt

Finished Quilt: 27 inches square
Finished Block: 6 inches square

Materials

Obvious directional prints are not recommended.

FABRIC A

Use three fabrics.
Santa Suit and Hat   ⅛ yard
each of *three* fabrics

FABRIC B

Use three fabrics.
Block Background   ⅛ yard
each of *three* fabrics
Note: If you prefer to use only one background fabric for all the blocks, a total of ¼ yard is needed.

FABRIC C

Use three fabrics.
Face   ⅛ yard
each of *three* fabrics

FABRIC D

Use three fabrics.
Beard   ⅛ yard
each of *three* fabrics

(continued)

Materials—Continued

FABRIC E

Use three fabrics.
Hat Trim   ⅛ yard
        each of *three* fabrics

FABRIC F

Lattice   ¼ yard
Outer Border   ¼ yard
    TOTAL   ½ yard

FABRIC G

Half-Inch Accent Border   ⅙ yard
                      (6 inches)

FABRIC H

Use two fabrics.
Pieced Border   ⅛ yard
        each of *two* fabrics

BINDING   ⅓ yard

BACKING   ⅞ yard

LIGHTWEIGHT BATTING   ⅞ yard

NOTIONS AND SUPPLIES

Eighteen ⅛-inch black buttons
    for eyes
Nine assorted ½- to ⅝-inch buttons
    and/or bells for hats

Cutting Directions

Prewash and press all of your fabrics. Using a rotary cutter, see-through ruler, and cutting mat, prepare the strips as described in the first column in the chart below. Then from those strips, cut the pieces listed in the second column. Some portions of the quilt need to be cut only once, so no additional cutting information will appear in the second column. Measurements for all pieces include ¼-inch seam allowances.

	FIRST CUT		SECOND CUT	
	NO. OF STRIPS	**DIMENSIONS**	**NO. OF PIECES**	**DIMENSIONS**
FABRIC A	**Santa Suit and Hat:** from *each* of the *three* fabrics, cut the following			
	1	3½ × 44-inch strip	3	3½ × 2½-inch pieces
			6	3 × 2-inch pieces
			9	1½-inch squares
FABRIC B	**Block Background:** from *each* of the *three* fabrics, cut the following			
	1	2 × 44-inch strip	3	2 × 2½-inch pieces
			12	2 × 1½-inch pieces
	1	1½ × 44-inch strip	9	1½-inch squares
			6	1 × 1¾-inch pieces
	Note: If you choose to use only one background fabric, cut two 2 × 44-inch strips and two 1½ × 44-inch strips. Cut three times as many pieces as directed in the second column.			
FABRIC C	**Face:** from *each* of the *three* fabrics, cut the following			
	3	1½ × 2½-inch pieces		
FABRIC D	**Beard:** from *each* of the *three* fabrics, cut the following			
	3	3½ × 3-inch pieces		
	6	1 × 1½-inch pieces		
FABRIC E	**Hat Trim:** from *each* of the *three* fabrics, cut the following			
	3	1 × 4-inch pieces		

	FIRST CUT		SECOND CUT	
	NO. OF STRIPS	**DIMENSIONS**	**NO. OF PIECES**	**DIMENSIONS**
FABRIC F	Lattice			
	5	1½ × 44-inch strips	2	1½ × 22½-inch strips
			4	1½ × 20½-inch strips
			6	1½ × 6½-inch strips
	Outer Border			
	4	1½ × 44-inch strips		
FABRIC G	Half-Inch Accent Border			
	4	1 × 44-inch strips		
FABRIC H	Pieced Border: from *each* of the *two* fabrics, cut the following			
	2	1½ × 33-inch strips		
BINDING	4	2¾ × 44-inch strips		

Quick Corner Triangles

Refer to "Making Quick Corner Triangles" on page 234 for how to make corner triangle units. You will be making nine Santa blocks, three each of three different fabric combinations. Before you start sewing, coordinate the fabrics for each of the three combinations. Keep track of the combinations as you sew the quick corner triangle units. Use the assembly-line method (see page 234) to make enough of the same corner triangle pieces for all nine blocks. Refer to the **Fabric Key** for

fabric identification, and press in the direction indicated by the arrow in each diagram.

Step 1. Sew nine 1½-inch Fabric B squares to nine 2½ × 3½-inch Fabric A pieces. See **Diagram 1.** Press. Remember to make three each of your three different fabric combinations.

DIAGRAM 1

Step 2. Sew nine 1½-inch Fabric A squares to nine 1½ × 2-inch Fabric B pieces, as shown in **Diagram 2.** Press.

DIAGRAM 2

Step 3. Sew nine 1½-inch Fabric B squares to nine 2 × 3-inch Fabric A pieces. See **Diagram 3.** Press.

DIAGRAM 3

Step 4. Sew nine 1½-inch Fabric B squares to nine 2 × 3-inch Fabric A pieces. See **Diagram 4.** Press. These corner triangle pieces are sewn in the opposite direction from those in Step 3. Refer to the diagram for proper placement.

DIAGRAM 4

Fabric Key

FABRIC A (Santa Suit & Hat)
FABRIC B (Background)
FABRIC C (Face)
FABRIC D (Beard)
FABRIC E (Hat Trim)

Step 5. Sew nine 1½-inch Fabric A squares to nine 3 × 3½-inch Fabric D pieces. See **Diagram 5.** Press.

DIAGRAM 5

Step 6. Sew nine additional 1½-inch Fabric A squares to the nine Step 5 units, as shown in **Diagram 6.** Press.

DIAGRAM 6

Making the Blocks

Throughout this section, refer to the **Fabric Key** on page 37 as needed. Also, it's a good idea to review "Assembly-Line Piecing" on page 234 before you get started. It's more efficient to do the same step for each block at the same time than to piece an entire block together at one time. Pay close attention that the corner triangles are positioned the same as shown in the diagrams. Be sure to use ¼-inch seam allowances and press as you go. Follow the arrows in each diagram for pressing direction.

Step 1. Sew nine 2 × 2½-inch Fabric B pieces to nine 2½ × 3½-inch Fabric A/B corner triangle units. See **Diagram 7.** Press.

Step 2. Sew nine 1½ × 2-inch Fabric A/B corner triangle units to nine 1½ × 2-inch Fabric B pieces. See **Diagram 8.** Press.

DIAGRAM 7

DIAGRAM 8

Step 3. Sew nine Step 1 units to nine Step 2 units, as shown in **Diagram 9.** Press.

DIAGRAM 9

Step 4. Sew nine 1 × 1¾-inch Fabric B pieces to each end of nine 1 × 4-inch Fabric E pieces. See **Diagram 10.** Press.

DIAGRAM 10

Step 5. Sew nine 1 × 1½-inch Fabric D pieces to each end of nine 1½ × 2½-inch Fabric C pieces. See **Diagram 11.** Press.

DIAGRAM 11

Step 6. Sew nine 1½ × 2-inch Fabric B pieces to each end of

nine Step 5 units, as shown in **Diagram 12.** Press.

DIAGRAM 12

Step 7. Sew nine 2 × 3-inch Fabric A/B corner triangle units to each side of nine 3 × 3½-inch Fabric A/D corner triangle units. Refer to **Diagram 13** for proper corner triangle placement. Press.

DIAGRAM 13

Step 8. Sew nine Step 3 units to nine Step 4 units. See **Diagram 14.** Press.

DIAGRAM 14

Step 9. Sew nine Step 6 units to nine Step 7 units. See **Diagram 15.** Press.

DIAGRAM 15

Step 10. Sew nine Step 8 units to nine Step 9 units as shown in

Diagram 16. Press. Your blocks should measure 6½ × 6½ inches.

DIAGRAM 16

The Lattice

Step 1. Lay out your blocks in a pleasing arrangement. Keep track of your layout while sewing on the lattice.

Step 2. Sew 1½ × 6½-inch lattice strips to each side of the three center blocks (one from each of the three rows). See **Diagram 17.** Press all seams toward the lattice.

DIAGRAM 17

Step 3. Sew a block to each side of the lattice strips to make three rows of three blocks. See **Diagram 18.** Press.

DIAGRAM 18

Step 4. Sew 1½ × 20½-inch lattice strips to the bottom of all three rows and to the top of the top

row. Press. Stitch the three rows together. Press.

Step 5. Sew 1½ × 22½-inch lattice strips to the sides. Press.

Half-Inch Accent Border

Step 1. Sew 1 × 44-inch Fabric G accent border strips to the quilt top and bottom. Trim the excess and press all seams toward the accent border.

Step 2. Sew 1 × 44-inch Fabric G strips to the quilt sides. Trim the excess and press.

Pieced Border

Step 1. Sew the four 1½ × 33-inch Fabric H strips together, alternating the two colors. Change sewing direction with each strip sewn. Press seams toward the darker fabric as you go. See **Diagram 19.**

DIAGRAM 19

Step 2. Cut this strip set in thirds (approximately 11 inches each),

referring to the cutting lines in **Diagram 19.** Resew the thirds together to make an 11 × 12½-inch strip set. See **Diagram 20.**

DIAGRAM 20

Step 3. Cut this strip set into eight 1 × 12½-inch strips using a rotary cutter and ruler. Refer to the cutting lines in **Diagram 20.** Sew the strips together into pairs to make four 1 × 24½-inch strips.

Step 4. For the top and bottom pieced border strips, use a seam ripper to remove 1 piece from each of two strips, making two strips with 23 pieces each. Remove a different color fabric from each of the two strips. This will ensure that when adding side borders, the alternating fabric pattern will be continuous.

Step 5. Using the photograph on page 34 and the **Nine-Block Quilt Layout** on page 35 as guides for color placement, fit, pin in position, and sew the borders to the quilt top and bottom. If the border doesn't fit, see "Hints on Fitting Pieced Borders" on page 244 to make adjustments. Press all seams toward the half-inch border.

Step 6. Fit, pin in position, and sew the remaining two 1 × 24½-inch pieced border strips to the quilt sides. Press.

Outer Border

Step 1. Sew 1½ × 44-inch Fabric F outer border strips to the top and bottom of the quilt. Trim the excess and press the seams toward the outer border.

Step 2. Sew 1½ × 44-inch Fabric F strips to the sides. Trim the excess and press.

Layering the Quilt

Arrange and baste the backing, batting, and top together, following the directions in "Layering the Quilt" on page 245. Trim the batting and backing to ¼ inch from the raw edge of the quilt top.

Binding the Quilt

Using the 2¾ × 44-inch binding strips, follow the directions in "Binding the Quilt" on page 246.

Finishing Stitches

Machine or hand quilt in the seam line around each Santa block. Outline the hat, hat trim, face, beard, and suit. Quilt swirls in each beard and ½-inch vertical lines in the background behind each Santa.

Festive Flourishes

If you make the Nine-Block Santa Quilt as a gift, use scraps of the leftover fabric to make a ribbon. First, wrap the box in plain brown kraft paper, then rip a piece of red plaid fabric along the grain to make enough length to tie around the box into a bow. Buy a length of red or green grosgrain ribbon and small jingle bells. Thread the bells along the length of ribbon and hold in place every 2 inches or so with knots; add these bell-laden ribbons to the fabric bow. The box will jingle with a faint echo of Santa when the lucky person opens it on Christmas morning.

If you don't have enough time to complete the project but you know the recipient loves to sew, put together a kit with everything needed to make the project—fabrics, buttons, thread, pattern book, sewing notions, etc. Wrap your package in one of the fabrics, and tie it up with a fabric bow. Make an identical kit for yourself, and make plans to get together several times over the year to work on your projects together. You'll share the joy of making it together and have a whole year to get it done!

Outline the half-inch accent and pieced borders. Quilt a 1¼-inch diagonal grid in the lattice and outer border.

Bring Santa to life by sewing ⅛-inch black buttons on him for eyes. Dig through your button collection, and sew assorted sizes and colors of buttons to the tip of each hat, or add a merry jingle bell to each.

Christmas Card Keeper

Finished Size: 29 × 14 inches
Finished Block: 6 inches square

29"

14"

CARD KEEPER LAYOUT

Materials

Obvious directional prints are not recommended.

FABRIC A
Use three fabrics.
Santa Suit and Hat   ⅛ yard
each of *three* fabrics

FABRIC B
Use three fabrics.
Block Background   ⅛ yard
each of *three* fabrics

FABRIC C
Use three fabrics.
Face   ⅛ yard
(or one 1½ × 3-inch piece)
each of *three* fabrics

FABRIC D
Use three fabrics.
Beard   ⅛ yard
        (or one 3½ × 6½-inch piece)
                each of *three* fabrics

FABRIC E
Use three fabrics.
Hat Trim   ⅛ yard
        (or one 1 × 4-inch piece)
                each of *three* fabrics

FABRIC F
Half-Inch Block Border   ⅛ yard
Outer Border   ⅛ yard
    TOTAL   ¼ yard

FABRIC G
Pocket Lattice and Lining   ¼ yard
Background Panel   ⅜ yard
    TOTAL   ⅝ yard

FABRIC H
Half-Inch Accent Border   ⅛ yard

FABRIC I
Use two fabrics.
Pieced Border   ⅛ yard
                each of *two* fabrics

FABRIC J
Binding   ⅛ yard
Hanging Tabs   ⅛ yard
        (or one 3⅞ × 27-inch strip)
    TOTAL   ¼ yard

COTTON FLANNEL
    (for inside pocket)   ¼ yard

BACKING   ½ yard

LIGHTWEIGHT BATTING   ½ yard

NOTIONS AND SUPPLIES
Six ⅛-inch black buttons for eyes
Three assorted ½- to ⅝-inch buttons and/or bells for hats
⅜-inch wooden dowel and wooden bead dowel ends

Cutting Directions

Prewash and press all of your fabrics. Using a rotary cutter, see-through ruler, and cutting mat, prepare the strips as described in the first column in the chart below. Then from those strips, cut the pieces listed in the second column. Some portions of the quilt need to be cut only once, so no additional cutting information will appear in the second column.

	FIRST CUT		SECOND CUT	
	NO. OF STRIPS	**DIMENSIONS**	**NO. OF PIECES**	**DIMENSIONS**
FABRIC A	**Santa Suit and Hat:** from *each* of the *three* fabrics, cut the following			
	1	3½ × 2½-inch piece		
	2	3 × 2-inch pieces		
	3	1½-inch squares		
FABRIC B	**Block Background:** from *each* of the *three* fabrics, cut the following			
	1	2 × 2½-inch piece		
	4	2 × 1½-inch pieces		
	3	1½-inch squares		
	2	1 × 1¾-inch pieces		
FABRIC C	**Face:** from *each* of the *three* fabrics, cut the following			
	1	1½ × 2½-inch piece		
FABRIC D	**Beard:** from *each* of the *three* fabrics, cut the following			
	1	3½ × 3-inch piece		
	2	1 × 1½-inch pieces		

(continued)

Christmas Card Keeper Cutting Chart—Continued	FIRST CUT		SECOND CUT	
	NO. OF STRIPS	DIMENSIONS	NO. OF PIECES	DIMENSIONS
FABRIC E	**Hat Trim:** from *each* of the *three* fabrics, cut the following			
	1	1 × 4-inch piece		
FABRIC F	**Half-Inch Block Border**			
	3	1 × 44-inch strips	6	1 × 6½-inch strips
			6	1 × 7½-inch strips
	Outer Border			
	2	1½ × 44-inch strips	2	1½ × 27½-inch strips
			2	1 × 13½-inch strips
FABRIC G	**Pocket Lattice and Lining**			
	1	8½ × 24½-inch piece		
	2	1½ × 7½-inch strips		
	Background Panel			
	1	9½ × 25½-inch piece		
FABRIC H	**Half-Inch Accent Border**			
	2	1 × 44-inch strips	2	1 × 25½-inch strips
			2	1 × 10½-inch strips
FABRIC I	**Pieced Border:** from *each* of the *two* fabrics, cut the following			
	2	1½ × 27-inch strips		
FABRIC J	**Binding**			
	3	1 × 44-inch strips	2	1 × 28½-inch strips
			2	1 × 14½-inch strips
	Hanging Tabs			
	1	3⅞ × 27-inch strip		
FLANNEL	1	8½ × 24½-inch piece		
BACKING	1	18 × 33-inch piece		
BATTING	1	18 × 33-inch piece		

Before You Begin

The assembly techniques for the blocks in the Christmas Card Keeper are the same as those given for the Nine-Block Santa Quilt. Throughout these directions, you will be referred back to the Nine-Block Santa Quilt for steps that are identical.

The card keeper is assembled in two sections—the Pocket and the Background Panel. After both sections are complete, the pocket section will be attached to the background panel section.

Quick Corner Triangles

Follow all the steps for "Quick Corner Triangles" for the Nine-Block Santa Quilt, beginning on page 37, to make the corner triangle units. You will be making three blocks, each of a different fabric combination, rather than nine blocks. Before you start sewing, coordinate the fabrics for each of the three combinations.

Making the Blocks

Follow all the steps for "Making the Blocks" for the Nine-Block Santa Quilt on page 38. You will be making a total of three Santa blocks, rather than nine. Remember to keep track of your three fabric combinations as you sew.

Assembling the Pocket Section

Step 1. Sew the 1 × 6½-inch Fabric F block border strips to the top and bottom of each of the three blocks. Press seams toward the border.

Step 2. Sew the 1 × 7½-inch Fabric F strips to both sides of each of the three blocks. Press.

Step 3. Sew the 1½ × 7½-inch Fabric G pocket lattice strips to the sides of the center block. Press seams toward the lattice.

Step 4. Sew a block to each side of the lattice strips. See **Diagram 21.** Press.

DIAGRAM 21

Finishing the Pocket

Step 1. Position the pocket top and the Fabric G pocket lining piece with right sides together. Lay both pieces on top of the flannel, and pin all three layers together. Using a ¼-inch seam allowance, sew together, leaving an opening for turning. Trim the corners, turn right side out, handstitch the opening, and press.

Step 2. Machine or hand quilt in the seam line around each Santa block. Outline the hat, hat trim, face, beard, and suit. Quilt swirls in each beard and ½-inch vertical lines in the background behind each Santa.

Step 3. Bring Santa to life by sewing ⅛-inch black buttons on him for eyes. Dig through your button collection and sew assorted sizes and colors of buttons to the tip of each hat, or add jingle bells instead.

Making the Background Panel

Half-Inch Accent Border

Step 1. Sew the 1 × 25½-inch Fabric H accent border strips to

the top and bottom of the 9½ × 25½-inch Fabric G piece. Press all seams toward the accent border.

Step 2. Sew the 1 × 10½-inch Fabric H strips to the sides. Press.

Pieced Border

Step 1. Sew the four 1½ × 27-inch Fabric I border strips together, alternating colors. Change sewing direction with each strip sewn. Press seams toward the darker fabric as you go. See **Diagram 22.**

DIAGRAM 22

Step 2. Cut this 4½ × 27-inch strip set in thirds (approximately 9 inches). Resew the thirds together to make a 9 × 12½-inch strip set. See **Diagram 23.**

DIAGRAM 23

Step 3. Using a rotary cutter and ruler, cut this strip set into seven 1 × 12½-inch strips.

Step 4. Sew four of these strips into pairs to make two 1 × 24½-inch strips.

Step 5. Using a seam ripper, remove two sets of 2 pieces from one 1 × 12½-inch strip. Add one set to each of the 1 × 24½-inch strips (made in Step 4) to make two strips with 26 pieces each. Fit, pin in position, and sew the borders to the quilt top and bottom. If the border doesn't fit the quilt top, see "Hints on Fitting Pieced Borders" on page 244 to make the necessary adjustments. Press seams toward the accent border.

Step 6. Using a seam ripper, remove 1 piece from each of the two remaining 1 × 12½-inch strips to make two strips with 11 pieces each. To ensure a continuous alternating fabric pattern, remove a different color fabric from each of the two strips. Fit, pin in position, and sew to the quilt sides. Press.

Outer Border

Step 1. Sew the 1½ × 27½-inch Fabric F outer border strips to the top and bottom of the quilt. Press seams toward the outer border strips.

Step 2. Sew the 1 × 13½-inch Fabric F strips to the sides. Press.

Binding

Step 1. Sew the 1 × 28½-inch Fabric J binding strips to the quilt top and bottom. Press seams toward the binding.

Step 2. Sew the 1 × 14½-inch Fabric J strips to the quilt sides. Press. See **Diagram 24.**

CARD KEEPER
BACKGROUND PANEL

DIAGRAM 24

Finishing

Step 1. To make hanging tabs, fold the 3⅞ × 27-inch Fabric J strip in half lengthwise, wrong sides together, and press. Reopen, then fold each long edge into the center fold and press again. Topstitch along the edge of both sides of the fabric strip.

Step 2. Using a ruler and rotary cutter, cut five 4-inch pieces from the strip. Fold each piece in half so the cut ends meet, and press.

Step 3. On the right side of the card keeper background panel, space the tabs evenly across the top and pin them in position. Place the raw edges of the tabs even with the raw edge of the binding. Baste the tabs into place. They will be sewn into the seam when the card keeper is finished.

Step 4. Position the top and backing with right sides together. Lay both pieces on top of the batting, and pin all three layers together. Using a ¼-inch seam allowance, sew together, leaving an opening for turning. Trim the backing and batting to the same size as the top. Trim the corners, turn right side out, handstitch the opening, and press.

Step 5. Machine or hand quilt in the seam line around all borders and the binding. Quilt vertical lines spaced about ½ to ¾ inch apart on the main background fabric. (The card keeper in the photograph was quilted along the stripe pattern in the background fabric.)

Step 6. Position and pin the pocket on top of the background panel approximately 1 inch from the half-inch accent border seam.

Step 7. Topstitch in the seam line on each side of the pocket lattice strips.

Step 8. Handstitch or machine topstitch along the pocket sides and bottom edge. Be sure to leave the pocket tops open so you can insert all your Christmas cards and letters.

Step 9. Cut a ⅜-inch dowel the width of the Christmas Card Keeper, plus 2 inches. Stain or paint the dowel and the wooden dowel ends to coordinate with your card keeper. Run the dowel through the hanging tabs, and glue the dowel ends on.

Festive Flourishes

Before the cards and letters start rolling in, use the pockets of the card keeper to stash fun little pre-holiday gifts for your favorite Christmas elves.

Christmas Spirits

Christmas Spirits

Soaring Santas and graceful angels will bring glad tidings and good cheer to anyone on your gift list! Adorn a holiday sweatshirt or create a charming Christmas wallhanging using speedy no-sew appliqué or machine appliqué.

Soaring Santas Wallhanging

Finished Size: 29 × 19 inches

Materials and Cutting

Using a rotary cutter, see-through ruler, and cutting mat, prepare the pieces as described in the chart below.

Measurements for all pieces include ¼-inch seam allowances. Directional fabrics are not recommended for borders. Before cutting, you may choose to tea dye some of your fabrics to get that warm, country look. (Or use a commercial fabric dye in a tan color.)

| | YARDAGE | NO. OF PIECES | CUTTING |
			DIMENSIONS
Background	¼ yard *each* of *four* fabrics	1	**Before You Cut:** From *each* of the *four* fabrics, cut the following. 6½ × 11½-inch piece
Appliqué Pieces	⅛-yard pieces or several coordinated scraps		
Scrap Lattice	Several coordinated 16-inch strips in widths ranging from 1 to 2 inches		
Wide Border	¼ yard (cut into three 2 × 44-inch strips)	2 2	2 × 18½-inch strips 2 × 25½-inch strips
Binding	¼ yard (cut into three 2¾ × 44-inch strips)	2	**Before You Cut:** From *one* of the 44-inch strips, cut the following. 2¾ × 22-inch strips
Backing	¾ yard	1	25 × 35-inch piece
Lightweight Batting	¾ yard	1	25 × 35-inch piece
Appliqué film Black, extra-fine point, permanent felt-tip pen			

29"

19"

SANTA WALLHANGING LAYOUT

Scrap Lattice

Step 1. The scrap lattice strips should be 16 inches long and vary in width from 1 to 2 inches. Piece the strips together to make a 15½ × 16-inch strip set. See **Diagram 1.** Change sewing direction with each strip sewn, and press seams in one direction.

15½"

1½"

16"

CUTTING LINES

DIAGRAM 1

Step 2. Using a rotary cutter and ruler, cut nine 1½ × 15½-inch strips, as shown in **Diagram 1.**

Step 3. Take one of the 1½ × 15½-inch strips and cut it into two 1½ × 6½-inch strips.

Step 4. Sew together three sets of two 1½ × 15½-inch strips to make three 1½ × 30½-inch strips. Trim these strips down to three 1½ × 23½-inch strips.

Step 5. Lay out your background blocks in a pleasing arrangement. Sew one 1½ × 6½-inch scrap lattice strip between the two background blocks in the top row.

Press all seams toward the background. See **Diagram 2** below. Repeat for the bottom row.

Step 6. Fit, pin in position, and sew a 1½ × 23½-inch scrap lattice strip to the top of both rows and to the bottom of the bottom row. Press all seams toward the background blocks.

Step 7. Fit, pin in position, and sew the two rows together. Press.

Step 8. Fit, pin in position, and sew 1½ × 15½-inch scrap lattice strips to the sides of the wallhanging. Press.

Borders

Sew the 2 × 25½-inch border strips to the top and bottom of the wallhanging. Press all seams toward the border. Sew the 2 × 18½-inch border strips to the sides. Press.

Appliqué

The appliqués in these projects were designed especially to use the quick-fuse technique described in "Quick-Fuse Appliqué" on page 238. However, you may use buttonhole embroidery or machine appliqué if you prefer. (See "Buttonhole Embroidery Appliqué" on page 240 and "Machine Appliqué" on page 239.)

Step 1. Trace four Santas for the wallhanging, using the **Christmas Spirits Appliqué Patterns** on page 50.

SEW SMART

It is easier to center the appliqués on each block if the quilt top is already assembled.

Step 2. Quick-fuse the designs to the center of each background piece. Position and fuse one design at a time. Use the photograph on page 45 as a placement guide.

Step 3. Use the permanent felt-tip pen to draw eyes and Penstitch details as desired.

Layering the Quilt

Arrange and baste the backing, batting, and top together following the directions in "Layering the Quilt" on page 245. Trim the batting and backing to ¼ inch from the raw edge of the quilt top.

Binding the Quilt

Using the two 44-inch binding strips for the top and bottom and the two 22-inch strips for the sides, follow the directions in "Binding the Quilt" on page 246.

Finishing Stitches

Machine or hand quilt in the seam line around the background pieces and the borders. Outline the appliqué designs by quilting ¹⁄₁₆ inch away from the edge of the designs. Quilt a 1-inch diagonal grid in the background pieces and the borders.

LATTICE STRIP

11½"

11½"

6½"

BACKGROUND BLOCK

BACKGROUND BLOCK

6½"

DIAGRAM 2

Angel Wallhanging

Finished Size: 30 × 20 inches

Materials and Cutting

Using a rotary cutter, see-through ruler, and cutting mat, prepare the pieces as described in the chart below. Measurements for all pieces include ¼-inch seam allowances. Obvious directional prints are not recommended for borders.

	YARDAGE	CUTTING	
		NO. OF PIECES	DIMENSIONS
Background	¼ yard *each* of *four* fabrics	1	**Before You Cut:** From *each* of the *four* fabrics, cut the following. 6½ × 11½-inch piece
Appliqué Pieces	⅛-yard pieces or several coordinated scraps		
Scrap Lattice	Several coordinated 16-inch strips in widths ranging from 1 to 2 inches		
Half-Inch Accent Border	⅛ yard (cut into two 1 × 44-inch strips)	2 2	1 × 16½-inch strips 1 × 25½-inch strips
Wide Border	¼ yard (cut into four 2 × 44-inch strips)	2 2	2 × 19½-inch strips 2 × 26½-inch strips
Binding	¼ yard (cut into three 2¾ × 44-inch strips)	2	**Before You Cut:** From *one* of the 44-inch strips, cut the following. 2¾ × 22-inch strips
Backing	¾ yard	1	26 × 36-inch piece
Lightweight Batting	¾ yard	1	26 × 36-inch piece
Appliqué film Black, extra-fine point, permanent felt-tip pen			

Before You Begin

The assembly techniques for the Angel Wallhanging are the same as those given for the Soaring Santas Wallhanging. The only difference is that the Angel Wallhanging has a half-inch accent border. Throughout these directions, you will be referred back to the Soaring Santas Wallhanging for steps that are identical.

Scrap Lattice

Follow Steps 1 through 8 in "Scrap Lattice" for the Soaring Santas Wallhanging on page 47.

Half-Inch Accent Border

Step 1. Sew 1 × 25½-inch accent border strips to the wallhanging top and bottom. Press all seams toward the accent border.

Step 2. Sew 1 × 16½-inch accent border strips to the wallhanging sides. Press.

💗 SEW CREATIVE 💗

You can mix and match your Santas and angels for these wallhangings. Use two Santas and two angels on one wall quilt, if you like.

Wide Border

Step 1. Sew the 2 × 26½-inch border strips to the top and bottom of the wallhanging. Press all seams toward the wide border.

Step 2. Sew the 2 × 19½-inch border strips to the sides. Press.

Appliqué

The appliqués in the Angel Wallhanging were designed especially to use the quick-fuse technique described in "Quick-Fuse Appliqué" on page 238. However, you may use buttonhole embroidery or machine appliqué if you prefer. (See "Buttonhole Embroidery Appliqué" on page 240 and "Machine Appliqué" on page 239.)

Step 1. Trace four angels using the **Christmas Spirits Appliqué Patterns** on page 51.

Step 2. Quick-fuse the designs in the center of each background piece. Position and fuse one design at a time. Use the photograph on page 45 as a placement guide.

Step 3. Use the permanent felt-tip pen to draw eyes and Penstitch details if desired.

Completing the Quilt

Follow the directions in "Layering the Quilt" through "Finishing Stitches" for the Soaring Santas Wallhanging on page 47.

Christmas Spirits Sweatshirts

These sweatshirts make great gifts. The fusible appliqué is so quick and easy, you can make one or even two of these in an evening! For a more stylish, finished look, add a purchased knit collar to the neckline of your sweatshirt.

Materials

PREWASHED SWEATSHIRT

APPLIQUÉ PIECES
Several coordinated scraps or ⅛-yard pieces of fabric
Black, extra-fine point, permanent felt-tip pen
Appliqué film

Appliqué

The appliqués for the Christmas Spirits Sweatshirt were designed especially to use the quick-fuse technique described in "Quick-Fuse Appliqué" on page 238, with a heavier weight nonsewable appliqué film. However, you may substitute buttonhole embroidery or machine appliqué if you prefer. Machine appliqué would be the preferred method if you would like to be able to machine launder your finished sweatshirt. Before you begin, refer to "Timesaving Methods for Appliqué" on page 237 for basic guidelines and "Laundering Tips for Sweatshirts" on page 51.

> **SEW SMART**
>
> If you're using the quick-fuse appliqué technique, choose a heavier weight non-sewable appliqué film product that does not need the edges sewn to remain intact and that is laundry-safe.
>
> If you are finishing your sweatshirt with buttonhole embroidery or machine appliqué, use a sewable appliqué film, and use a stabilizer behind the machine appliqué. We recommend using tear-away paper (available at fabric and quilt stores) behind the design as you are machine appliquéing the designs to the sweatshirt.

Step 1. Trace the appliqué designs onto appliqué film using the **Christmas Spirits Appliqué Patterns** on pages 50–51. Trace one Santa or angel, one moon, and four stars. Fuse to assorted scraps of fabric, then cut the appliqué shapes out of the fabric.

Step 2. Center the Santa or angel design on the sweatshirt front, approximately 2 to 3 inches below the neckline. Add the moon and four stars to the sweatshirt using the photograph on page 49 as a placement guide. Press in position and quick-fuse appliqué.

Step 3. Use the permanent felt-tip pen to draw eyes and Penstitch details if desired.

Festive Flourishes

For the angel quilt or sweatshirt, wrap the box in gold or silver paper onto which you've fused some red fabric stars. Encircle it with gold star garland. Or, wrap either project in a box covered with plain kraft paper, tied with 1-inch ribbon. On the ends of the ribbon, fuse star-shaped appliqués from the project, back to back, to create an interesting ribbon accessory.

CHRISTMAS SPIRITS APPLIQUÉ PATTERNS

LAUNDERING TIPS FOR SWEATSHIRTS

Special precautions must be taken for quick-fuse appliqué projects that may need laundering.

• Prewash both the sweatshirt and the fabrics to prevent color bleeding and shrinkage of fabrics when laundering the finished project. Also, the appliqué film will adhere better if your fabrics are prewashed.

• If you choose to simply fuse your design to the sweatshirt, use appliqué film that allows laundering. Be sure to read the manufacturer's instructions and follow them carefully. We recommend washing your fused sweatshirt inside out in cold water on a delicate cycle or hand washing. Line dry. If your sweatshirt will get repeated washings, you can expect it to last about one season—which isn't a problem for growing children.

• If any of your appliqué pieces start to lift, re-press them down. If there is not enough fusing film remaining, you may need to replace that piece.

Appliqué Pattern Key

———————— TRACING LINE

- - - - - - - - TRACING LINE
(will be hidden behind other fabric)

CHRISTMAS SPIRITS APPLIQUÉ PATTERN

Deck the Halls

From walls to tables, you'll have no trouble bedecking your home
for the holidays with these charming wallhangings and the country table
ensemble. Easy-to-make nutcrackers, toy soldiers, Scandinavian Christmas
tree, table runner, place mats, tablecloth, and napkins will make
choosing what to make first the only difficult task.

Before you begin, take a minute to read through this checklist. These are important pointers you should keep in mind to make sure that each of your quilts is a success.

★ Be sure to read "Techniques for Quick Country Quilting," beginning on page 226. This will familiarize you with the tools you'll need; the techniques for time-saving cutting, piecing, and appliqué; and finishing instructions.

★ Check the "Festive Flourishes" box for each project to get clever and unique ideas for packaging and wrapping your gift.

★ Take advantage of the helpful hints in the "Sew Smart" boxes. There you'll find tips for making a technique quicker or easier.

★ Prewash and press all of your fabrics. Washing will remove any sizing from the fabrics, and pressing ensures accuracy when cutting.

★ Read the step-by-step directions from start to finish, and look at all the diagrams before you cut and sew any fabric.

★ Always use a ¼-inch seam allowance, unless there is a special note that tells you a different seam allowance is required.

★ Refer to the **Fabric Key** for each project as a help in following the diagrams.

★ Pay attention to the pressing directions given in the step-by-step text and to the pressing arrows shown in the diagrams.

March of the Toy Soldiers

22"

26½"

QUILT LAYOUT

These toy soldiers are poised and ready with their drums to welcome the holidays or to stand guard all year long! Put on some Christmas music, and you'll have these blocks sewn up in no time with the easy strip set construction. This quilt would be perfect for just about anyone—fans of *The Nutcracker Suite,* kids, musicians, and toy lovers of all ages.

Finished Quilt: 22 × 26½ inches
Finished Block: 3 × 15 inches

Materials

Obvious directional prints are not recommended.

FABRIC A
Pants, Sleeves, and
   Patchwork Border   ¼ yard

FABRIC B
Block Background   ¼ yard
Lattice   ¼ yard
   TOTAL   ½ yard

FABRIC C
Shirt and Patchwork Border   ¼ yard

FABRIC D
Hat, Gloves, Boots, Drum Rims,
   and Patchwork Border   ¼ yard

FABRIC E
Face   ⅛ yard

FABRIC F
Drum and Patchwork Border ⅙ yard
                        (6 inches)

FABRIC G
Half-Inch Border   ⅛ yard
Binding   ⅓ yard
   TOTAL   ⅜ yard

BACKING   ¾ yard

LIGHTWEIGHT BATTING   ¾ yard

NOTIONS AND SUPPLIES
Ten ⅛-inch black buttons for eyes

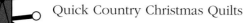

Cutting Directions

Prewash and press all of your fabrics. Using a rotary cutter, see-through ruler, and cutting mat, prepare the strips as described in the first column in the chart below. Then from those strips, cut the pieces listed in the second column. Some portions of the quilt need to be cut only once, so no additional cutting information will appear in the second column. Measurements for all pieces include ¼-inch seam allowances.

	FIRST CUT		SECOND CUT	
	NO. OF STRIPS	**DIMENSIONS**	**NO. OF PIECES**	**DIMENSIONS**
FABRIC A	Pants and Sleeves			
	1	5½ × 44-inch strip	1	5½ × 15-inch strip
			1	5 × 12-inch strip
	Patchwork Border			
	1	1½ × 44-inch strip	2	1½ × 21-inch strips
FABRIC B	Block Background			
	1	5½ × 44-inch strip	2	5½ × 12-inch strips
	1	¾ × 44-inch strip	2	¾ × 12-inch strips
	Lattice			
	5	1½ × 44-inch strips	2	1½ × 21-inch strips
			3	1½ × 19½-inch strips
			4	1½ × 15½-inch strips
			4	1½ × 3-inch strips
FABRIC C	Shirt			
	1	4½ × 44-inch strip	1	4½ × 15-inch strip
	Patchwork Border			
	1	1½ × 44-inch strip	2	1½ × 21-inch strips
FABRIC D	Hat, Gloves, Boots, and Drum Rims			
	1	3½ × 44-inch strip	1	3½ × 15-inch strip
			1	1½ × 15-inch strip
			1	1 × 12-inch strip
	1	1 × 44-inch strip	10	1 × 3½-inch strips
	Patchwork Border			
	1	1½ × 44-inch strip	2	1½ × 21-inch strips

	FIRST CUT		SECOND CUT	
	NO. OF STRIPS	DIMENSIONS	NO. OF PIECES	DIMENSIONS
FABRIC E	Face			
	1	2½ × 44-inch strip	1	2½ × 15-inch strip
FABRIC F	Drum			
	1	3 × 44-inch strip	1	3 × 12-inch strip
	Patchwork Border			
	1	1½ × 44-inch strip	2	1½ × 21-inch strips
FABRIC G	Half-Inch Border			
	2	1 × 44-inch strips	2	1 × 21½-inch strips
	Binding			
	4	2¾ × 44-inch strips		

Sewing and Cutting the Strip Sets

Sew the strips together following **Diagrams 1 through 6.** Use accurate ¼-inch seam allowances. Be sure to press seams as you go, following the arrows shown in the diagrams. Refer to the **Fabric Key** for fabric identification. You will be making three different strip sets.

Fabric Key

FABRIC A (Pants, Sleeves)
FABRIC B (Background)
FABRIC C (Shirt)
FABRIC D (Hat, Gloves, Boots, Drum Rims)
FABRIC E (Face)
FABRIC F (Drum)

Strip Set 1. Use one 3½ × 15-inch Fabric D strip, one 2½ × 15-inch Fabric E strip, one 4½ × 15-inch Fabric C strip, one 5½ × 15-inch

Fabric A strip, and one 1½ × 15-inch Fabric D strip. See **Diagram 1.** Use a rotary cutter and ruler to cut this strip set into five 2½ × 15½-inch strips. See **Diagram 2.**

DIAGRAM 1

DIAGRAM 2

Strip Set 2. Use two 5½ × 12-inch Fabric B strips, one 5 × 12-inch Fabric A strip, and one 1 × 12-inch Fabric D strip. See **Diagram 3.** Cut this strip set into ten 1 × 15½-inch strips. See **Diagram 4.**

DIAGRAM 3

DIAGRAM 4

Strip Set 3. Use two ¾ × 12-inch Fabric B strips and one 3 × 12-inch Fabric F strip. See **Diagram 5.** Cut this strip set into five 2 × 3½-inch pieces. See **Diagram 6.**

DIAGRAM 5

DIAGRAM 6

Making the Toy Soldier Blocks

You will be making five Toy Soldier blocks. For *each* block sew one 1 × 15½-inch strip set (from Strip Set 2) to each side of one 2½ × 15½-inch strip set (from Strip Set 1). See **Diagram 7.** Press seams toward the center.

DIAGRAM 7

Stars

Use the **Star Appliqué Pattern** on the opposite page, and quick-fuse or hand appliqué a star on each soldier's shirt. Refer to the photograph on page 54 for placement. (Refer to "Timesaving Methods for Appliqué" on page 237.)

Making the Drum Blocks

You will be making five Drum blocks. For *each* block sew one 1 × 3½-inch Fabric D strips to the top and bottom of one 2 × 3½-inch strip set (from Strip Set 3). See **Diagram 8.** Press seams toward Fabric D.

DIAGRAM 8

Lattice

Step 1. Sew 1½ × 15½-inch Fabric B lattice strips to the right side of four Toy Soldier blocks. See **Diagram 9.** Press all seams toward the lattice.

DIAGRAM 9

Step 2. Sew together the four Toy Soldier blocks with lattice. Add the Toy Soldier block without lattice to the right end of the row. See **Diagram 10.** Press.

DIAGRAM 10

Step 3. Sew 1½ × 3-inch Fabric B lattice strips to the right side of four Drum blocks. Press all seams toward the lattice. See **Diagram 11.**

DIAGRAM 11

Step 4. Sew together the four Drum blocks with lattice. Add the Drum block without lattice to the right end of the row. See **Diagram 12.** Press.

DIAGRAM 12

Step 5. Sew 1½ × 19½-inch Fabric B lattice strips to the top and bottom of the strip of Toy Soldier blocks. Press.

Step 6. Sew a 1½ × 19½-inch Fabric B strip to the bottom of the strip of Drum blocks. Press.

Step 7. Sew the row of Toy Soldier blocks to the top of the row of Drum blocks. Press.

Step 8. Sew 1½ × 21-inch Fabric B strips to the quilt sides. Press.

Borders

Step 1. Sew 1 × 21½-inch Fabric G border strips to the top and bottom of the quilt. Press all seams toward the border.

Step 2. Arrange the eight 1½ × 21-inch patchwork border strips (two each of Fabrics A, C, D, and F) in a pleasing order. Sew together, alternating sewing direction with each strip sewn. Press all seams in one direction as you go. Make an 8½ × 21-inch strip set. Cut into thirds (7 inches each), referring to the cutting lines in **Diagram 13.**

DIAGRAM 13

Step 3. Resew the thirds together to make a 7 × 24½-inch strip set. Using a rotary cutter and ruler, cut two 2½ × 24½-inch strips. See **Diagram 14.**

DIAGRAM 14

Step 4. With a seam ripper, remove three pieces from each of the two strips to make two strips with 21 pieces each. Fit, pin in position, and sew the borders to the top and bottom of the quilt. If the border doesn't fit, see "Hints on Fitting Pieced Borders" on page 244. Press all seams toward the half-inch border.

Faces

Using the **Toy Soldier Face Guide** on this page and a pencil, lightly draw two circles on each face as guides for quilting the cheeks. Mark the position of the eyes, and sew two ⅛-inch black buttons on each face.

Layering the Quilt

Arrange and baste together the backing, batting, and top, following the directions in "Layering the Quilt" on page 245. Trim the batting and backing to ¼ inch from the raw edge of the quilt top.

Binding the Quilt

Using the four 2¾ × 44-inch binding strips, follow the directions in "Binding the Quilt" on page 246.

Finishing Stitches

Machine or hand quilt in the seam line around each soldier, drum, hat, face, star, glove, boot, and drum rim. Quilt around each appliquéd star, between the pieces in the top and bottom patchwork border, and on both sides of the half-inch border strip. Quilt a 1½-inch diagonal grid in the background. Using

black thread, quilt a vertical line in the center of the pants and boots to give the appearance of two legs. Quilt diagonal lines on the drums (for the strings) with black thread, referring to the **Drum Quilting Guide** on this page. Quilt circles on each face with coordinating thread, and add a touch of color to cheeks using a red pencil.

DRUM QUILTING GUIDE

STAR APPLIQUÉ PATTERN

TOY SOLDIER FACE GUIDE

Festive Flourishes

Look for a toy soldier or drum ornament to adorn your package. Or make the drum ornament from Trim-a-Tree on page 81. If your recipient is a drummer, tie a new pair of drumsticks in ribbon on the outside of the package.

$\mathcal{N}$utcracker Suite

24"

29"

QUILT LAYOUT

Finished Quilt: 24 × 29 inches
Finished Block: 3½ × 10½ inches

Materials

Obvious directional prints
are not recommended.

FABRIC A
Use four fabrics.
Jacket, Hat, Base, and
  Patchwork Border   ⅙ yard
     (6 inches) *each* of *four* fabrics

FABRIC B
Block Background   ¼ yard
Lattice   ¼ yard
Outer Border   ¼ yard
   TOTAL   ¾ yard

FABRIC C
Use four fabrics.
Pants, Gloves, Belt, and
  Patchwork Border   ⅙ yard
                    each of *four* fabrics

FABRIC D
Shoulder Decor and
  Patchwork Border   ⅛ yard

FABRIC E
Use four fabrics.
Hair and Beard   ⅛ yard
                    each of *four* fabrics

FABRIC F
Face   ⅛ yard

BINDING   ⅓ yard

BACKING   ⅞ yard

LIGHTWEIGHT BATTING ⅞ yard

NOTIONS AND SUPPLIES
Black embroidery floss for eyes

$\mathcal{W}$hat would Christmas be without the familiar music from the ballet that shares its name with this wall quilt? Spend some soothing time in your sewing room listening to strains of Tchaikovsky while stitching these handsome nutcrackers. If you have a collection of nutcrackers, just think what a lovely addition this quilt will make to your holiday display!

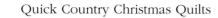

Cutting Directions

Prewash and press all of your fabrics. Using a rotary cutter, see-through ruler, and cutting mat, prepare the strips as described in the first column in the chart below. Then from those strips, cut the pieces listed in the second column. Some portions of the quilt need to be cut only once, so no additional cutting information will appear in the second column. Measurements for all pieces include ¼-inch seam allowances.

	FIRST CUT		SECOND CUT	
	NO. OF STRIPS	DIMENSIONS	NO. OF PIECES	DIMENSIONS
FABRIC A	**Jacket, Hat, and Base:** from *each* of the *four* fabrics, cut the following			
	1	2½ × 44-inch strip	2	2½ × 3-inch pieces
			2	2½ × 1-inch pieces
			2	2-inch squares
			4	1¼ × 3-inch pieces
			2	1 × 3-inch pieces
	Patchwork Border: from *each* of the *four* fabrics, cut the following			
	1	1½ × 44-inch strip	1	1½ × 24-inch strip
FABRIC B	**Block Background**			
	1	3 × 44-inch strip	16	3 × 1½-inch pieces
	2	1¼ × 44-inch strips	16	1¼ × 4½-inch pieces
	1	1 × 44-inch strip	16	1-inch squares
	Lattice			
	5	1½ × 44-inch strips	2	1½ × 24½-inch strips
			3	1½ × 17½-inch strips
			6	1½ × 11-inch strips
	Outer Border			
	4	1½ × 44-inch strips	2	1½ × 28½-inch strips
			2	1½ × 21½-inch strips
FABRIC C	**Pants, Gloves, and Belt:** from *each* of the *four* fabrics, cut the following			
	1	2½ × 44-inch strip	2	2½ × 4½-inch pieces
			2	2½ × 1-inch pieces
			4	1¼ × 1-inch pieces
	Patchwork Border: from *each* of the *four* fabrics, cut the following			
	1	1½ × 44-inch strip	1	1½ × 24-inch strip

FIRST CUT			SECOND CUT	
	NO. OF STRIPS	DIMENSIONS	NO. OF PIECES	DIMENSIONS
FABRIC D	**Shoulder Decor**			
	1	1 × 44-inch strip	16	1 × 1¼-inch pieces
	Patchwork Border			
	1	1½ × 44-inch strip	1	1½ × 24-inch strip
FABRIC E	**Hair:** from *each* of the *four* fabrics, cut the following			
	4	1½-inch squares		
	Beard: from *each* of the *four* fabrics, cut the following			
	1	3 × 6-inch piece		
FABRIC F	**Face**			
	1	1½ × 44-inch strip	8	1½ × 2-inch pieces
BINDING	4	2¾ × 44-inch strips		

Quick Corner Triangles

Refer to "Making Quick Corner Triangles" on page 234. You will be making eight Nutcracker blocks, two each of four different fabric combinations. Coordinate the fabrics for each of the four combinations, and keep track of them as you sew. Refer to the **Fabric Key** for fabric identification, and press all seams in the direction of the triangle just added.

Fabric Key

FABRIC A (Jacket, Hat, Base)
FABRIC B (Background)
FABRIC C (Pants, Gloves, Belt)
FABRIC D (Shoulder Decor)
FABRIC E (Hair, Beard)
FABRIC F (Face)

Step 1. Sew eight 1½-inch Fabric E squares to eight 1½ × 3-inch Fabric B pieces. See **Diagram 1.** Press.

DIAGRAM 1

Step 2. Sew eight 1½-inch Fabric E squares to eight 1½ × 3-inch Fabric B pieces. Press. These are sewn in the opposite direction from Step 1. See **Diagram 2.**

DIAGRAM 2

Assembling the Sections

Before you get started, review "Assembly-Line Piecing" on page 234. Pay close attention that corner triangles are positioned as shown in the diagrams. Be sure to use ¼-inch seams and press as you go, in the direction indicated by the arrow in each diagram.

Section One (Head)

Step 1. Sew eight 2-inch Fabric A squares to eight 1½ × 2-inch Fabric F pieces. (Sew two each of the four fabric combinations.) See **Diagram 3.** Press.

DIAGRAM 3

Step 2. Sew eight 1½ × 3-inch Fabric B/E corner triangle units to the left side of the eight Step 1 units. See **Diagram 4.** Press.

DIAGRAM 4

Step 3. Sew eight 1½ × 3-inch Fabric B/E corner triangle units to the right side of the eight Step 2 units. See **Diagram 5.** Press.

DIAGRAM 5

Section Two (Body)

Step 1. Sew sixteen 1 × 1¼-inch Fabric D pieces to sixteen 1¼ × 3-inch Fabric A pieces. See **Diagram 6.** Press. (Sew four each of the four fabric combinations.)

DIAGRAM 6

Step 2. Sew sixteen 1 × 1¼-inch Fabric C pieces to sixteen Step 1 units. See **Diagram 7.** Press.

DIAGRAM 7

Step 3. Sew eight 2½ × 3-inch Fabric A pieces to eight 1 × 2½-inch Fabric C pieces. See **Diagram 8.** Press.

DIAGRAM 8

Step 4. Sew eight 1 × 2½-inch Fabric A pieces to eight Step 3 units. See **Diagram 9.** Press.

DIAGRAM 9

Step 5. Sew sixteen Step 2 units to both sides of eight Step 4 units. See **Diagram 10.** Press.

DIAGRAM 10

Section Three (Legs)

Step 1. Sew sixteen 1¼ × 4½-inch Fabric B pieces to both sides of eight 2½ × 4½-inch Fabric C pieces. See **Diagram 11.** Press.

DIAGRAM 11

Step 2. Sew sixteen 1-inch Fabric B squares to both sides of eight 1 × 3-inch Fabric A pieces. See **Diagram 12.** Press.

DIAGRAM 12

Step 3. Sew eight Step 1 units to eight Step 2 units, as shown in **Diagram 13.** Press.

DIAGRAM 13

Assembling the Blocks

Step 1. Referring to **Diagram 14,** sew all three sections together in order. Press all seams toward Section Two. Your blocks should now measure 4 × 11 inches.

DIAGRAM 14

Step 2. Hand appliqué a beard to each nutcracker. Use the **Beard Appliqué Pattern** on the opposite page. (Refer to "Hand Appliqué" on page 240.)

Step 3. Using two strands of embroidery floss, make two French knots on each face for eyes. (See "French Knots" on page 23.)

Lattice

Step 1. Lay out the Nutcracker blocks in a pleasing arrangement, with two rows of four blocks each. Keep track of your layout while sewing on the lattice.

Step 2. Sew 1½ × 11-inch Fabric B lattice strips to the right side of all the Nutcracker blocks except the last block in each row. Press all seams toward the lattice.

Step 3. Sew together three blocks with lattice. To the right end of the row, add one block without lattice. Repeat to make two rows of four blocks. Press.

Step 4. Sew 1½ × 17½-inch Fabric B strips to the bottom of both rows and to the top of the top row. Press. Stitch the two rows together. Press.

Step 5. Sew 1½ × 24½-inch Fabric B strips to the sides. Press.

Patchwork Border

Step 1. Take the nine 1½ × 24-inch patchwork border strips (one of Fabric D and one each of the four Fabric As and Fabric Cs) and arrange them in a pleasing order.

Step 2. Sew the strips together to make a 9½ × 24-inch strip set, as shown in **Diagram 15.** Press all the seams in one direction as you go.

Step 3. Cut this strip set in thirds (approximately 8 inches each), referring to the cutting lines in **Diagram 15.** Resew the thirds together to make an 8 × 27½-inch strip set. See **Diagram 16.**

DIAGRAM 15

DIAGRAM 16

Step 4. From this strip set, cut four 1½ × 27½-inch strips, using a rotary cutter and ruler. Refer to the cutting lines in **Diagram 16.**

Step 5. For the top and bottom borders, use a seam ripper to remove 8 squares from each of two strips to make two strips with 19 squares each. Fit, pin in position, and sew these patchwork border strips to the top and bottom of the quilt. If the border doesn't fit, see "Hints on Fitting Pieced Borders" on page 244. Press all seams toward the lattice.

Step 6. For the side borders, use a seam ripper to remove 1 square from each of the two remaining strips to make two strips with 26 squares each. Fit, pin in position, and sew the patchwork border strips to the sides. Press.

Outer Border

Step 1. Sew 1½ × 21½-inch Fabric B outer border strips to the quilt top and bottom. Press all seams toward the outer border.

Step 2. Sew 1½ × 28½-inch Fabric B strips to the quilt sides. Press.

Layering the Quilt

Arrange and baste the backing, batting, and quilt top together, following the directions in "Layering the Quilt" on page 245. Trim the batting and backing to ¼ inch from the raw edge of the quilt top.

Binding the Quilt

Using the four 2¾ × 44-inch binding strips, follow the directions in "Binding the Quilt" on page 246.

Finishing Stitches

Machine or hand quilt in the seam line around each nutcracker. Quilt in the seam line around the face, hair, beard, shoulder decor, arms, belt, gloves, and base. Quilt a vertical line in the center of the pants to resemble two legs. Quilt in the seam line on both sides of the patchwork border. Quilt a 1½-inch diagonal grid in the background, extending it out through the outer border.

Festive Flourishes

Tie a color-coordinated fabric bow to a basket, fill it with nuts, and give it with the Nutcracker Suite quilt for a fun theme gift! Or, if you're making the quilt for a ballet lover, add a pair of tickets to The Nutcracker Suite.

BEARD APPLIQUÉ PATTERN

Yuletide Tables

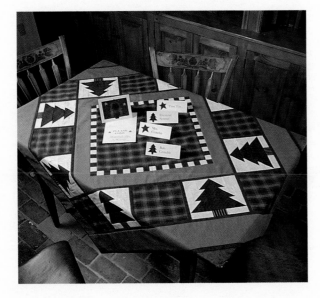

Deck your tables with a warm and homey assortment of trees, plaids, and checkerboards in this coordinated set, which includes a tablecloth, table runner, place mats, and napkins. Warm tans, deep reds, and rich greens are combined to make cheerful holiday accents for entertaining family and friends. You can also send handmade invitations and make a place card for each guest. Fill your favorite candlesticks with cream-color or beeswax candles to complete the festive holiday mood.

Tablecloth

Finished Size: 49 inches square
Finished Block: 8 × 7 inches

Materials

Obvious directional prints are not recommended.

FABRIC A

Tree	⅓ yard

FABRIC B

Block Background	½ yard
Checkerboard Border	⅛ yard
TOTAL	⅝ yard

FABRIC C

Trunk	⅛ yard

FABRIC D

Checkerboard Border	⅛ yard
Accent Border	⅜ yard
TOTAL	½ yard

FABRIC E

Center Square	⅝ yard
Border Squares	½ yard
TOTAL	1⅛ yards

FABRIC F

Inner Border	⅓ yard
Outer Border	⅔ yard
TOTAL	1 yard

BINDING ¼ yard

BACKING 3 yards

Cutting Directions

Prewash and press all of your fabrics. Using a rotary cutter, see-through ruler, and cutting mat, prepare the strips as described in the first column in the chart below. Then from those strips, cut the pieces listed in the second column. Some strips need to be cut only once, so no additional cutting information will appear in the second column. Measurements for all pieces include ¼-inch seam allowances.

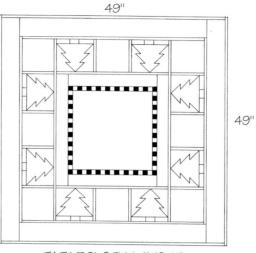

49"

49"

TABLECLOTH LAYOUT

	FIRST CUT		SECOND CUT	
	NO. OF STRIPS	DIMENSIONS	NO. OF PIECES	DIMENSIONS
FABRIC A	Tree			
	4	2½ × 44-inch strips	8	2½ × 8½-inch pieces
			8	2½ × 6½-inch pieces
			8	2½ × 4½-inch pieces
FABRIC B	Block Background			
	4	2½ × 44-inch strips	64	2½-inch squares
	3	1½ × 44-inch strips	16	1½ × 3½-inch pieces
			16	1½ × 2½-inch pieces
	Checkerboard Border			
	2	1½ × 44-inch strips		
FABRIC C	Trunk			
	1	1½ × 44-inch strip	8	1½ × 2½-inch pieces
FABRIC D	Checkerboard Border			
	2	1½ × 44-inch strips		
	Accent Border			
	10	1 × 44-inch strips	2	1 × 40½-inch strips
			4	1 × 39½-inch strips
			2	1 × 24½-inch strips
			12	1 × 7½-inch strips

	FIRST CUT		SECOND CUT	
	NO. OF STRIPS	DIMENSIONS	NO. OF PIECES	DIMENSIONS
FABRIC E	**Center Square**			
	1	17½-inch square		
	Border Squares			
	2	7½ × 44-inch strips	8	7½-inch squares
FABRIC F	**Inner Border**			
	3	3 × 44-inch strips	2	3 × 24½-inch strips
			2	3 × 19½-inch strips
	Outer Border			
	5	4½ × 44-inch strips		
BINDING	5	1 × 44-inch strips		

Quick Corner Triangles

Refer to "Making Quick Corner Triangles" on page 234 for how to make corner triangle units. You will be making eight Tree blocks. Use the assembly-line method (see page 234) to make the same corner triangle pieces for all eight blocks. Refer to the **Fabric Key,** and press in the direction of the triangle just added. For clarity, seam allowances are shown in the diagrams.

Fabric Key

FABRIC A (Tree)
FABRIC B (Background)
FABRIC C (Trunk)

Step 1. Sew eight 2½-inch Fabric B squares to eight 2½ × 4½-inch Fabric A pieces. See **Diagram 1.** Press.

DIAGRAM 1

Step 2. Sew eight additional 2½-inch Fabric B squares to eight Step 1 units. See **Diagram 2** for proper placement. Press.

STEP 1 UNIT

DIAGRAM 2

Step 3. Sew eight 2½-inch Fabric B squares to eight 2½ × 6½-inch Fabric A pieces. See **Diagram 3.** Press.

DIAGRAM 3

Step 4. Sew eight additional 2½-inch Fabric B squares to the eight Step 3 units. See **Diagram 4.** Press.

STEP 3 UNIT

DIAGRAM 4

Step 5. Sew eight 2½-inch Fabric B squares to eight 2½ × 8½-inch Fabric A pieces, as shown in **Diagram 5.** Press.

DIAGRAM 5

Step 6. Sew eight additional 2½-inch Fabric B squares to eight Step 5 units. See **Diagram 6.** Press.

STEP 5 UNIT

DIAGRAM 6

Making the Blocks

Review "Assembly-Line Piecing" on page 234 before you get started. It's more efficient to do the same step for each block at the same time than to piece an entire block together at one time. Pay close attention that the corner triangles

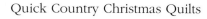

are positioned as shown in the diagrams. Be sure to use ¼-inch seam allowances and press as you go. Follow the arrows in the diagrams for pressing direction. You will be making a total of eight Tree blocks.

Step 1. Sew eight 2½-inch Fabric B squares to each side of eight 2½ × 4½-inch Fabric A/B corner triangle units, as shown in **Diagram 7.** Press.

DIAGRAM 7

Step 2. Sew eight 1½ × 2½-inch Fabric B pieces to each side of eight 2½ × 6½-inch Fabric A/B corner triangle units. See **Diagram 8.** Press.

DIAGRAM 8

Step 3. Sew eight 1½ × 3½-inch Fabric B pieces to each side of eight 1½ × 2½-inch Fabric C pieces. See **Diagram 9.** Press.

DIAGRAM 9

Step 4. Sew eight Step 1 units to the top of eight Step 2 units. See **Diagram 10.** Press.

DIAGRAM 10

Step 5. Sew eight Step 4 units to the top of eight 2½ × 8½-inch Fabric A/B corner triangle units. See **Diagram 11.** Press.

DIAGRAM 11

Step 6. Sew eight Step 5 units to the top of eight Step 3 units, as shown in **Diagram 12.** Press. Your blocks should now measure 8½ × 7½ inches.

DIAGRAM 12

Checkerboard Border

Step 1. Alternating the two Fabric B strips with the two Fabric D strips, sew the four 1½ × 44-inch strips together. Change sewing direction with each strip sewn. Press seams toward the darker fabric as you go. See **Diagram 13.**

DIAGRAM 13

Step 2. Cut the 4½ × 44-inch strip set in thirds (approximately 14 inches each), referring to the cutting lines in **Diagram 13.** Resew the thirds together to make a 12½ × 14-inch strip set. See **Diagram 14.**

DIAGRAM 14

Step 3. Cut the 12½ × 14-inch strip set in half, referring to the cutting line in **Diagram 14.** Resew the halves together to make a 7 × 24½-inch strip set. See **Diagram 15.**

DIAGRAM 15

Step 4. Using a rotary cutter and ruler, cut four 1½ × 24½-inch strips, referring to the cutting lines in **Diagram 15.** There should be 24 squares in each strip.

Step 5. For the top and bottom borders, use a seam ripper to remove 7 squares from each of two strips to make two strips with 17 squares each. These two strips need to start and end with a light square. Fit, pin in position, and sew the border strips to the top and bottom of the 17½-inch center square. If the border doesn't fit the center square, see "Hints on Fitting Pieced Borders" on page 244. Press all seams toward the center square.

Step 6. For the side borders, use a seam ripper to remove 5 squares from each of the two remaining strips to make two strips with 19 squares each. These two strips need to start and end with a dark square. Fit, pin in position, and sew the border strips to the sides. Press.

Inner Border

Sew 3 × 19½-inch Fabric F inner border strips to the tablecloth top and bottom. Press all seams toward the inner border. Sew one 3 × 24½-inch Fabric F inner border strip to each side of the tablecloth. Press.

Tree Block and Accent Borders

When assembling the Tree block border, refer to the diagram for each step. Press in the direction indicated by the arrows in each diagram.

Assembling the Top and Bottom Borders

Step 1. Sew one 1 × 7½-inch Fabric D accent border strip to each side of two 7½-inch Fabric E border squares. Press all seams toward the accent borders. See **Diagram 16.**

DIAGRAM 16

Step 2. Sew one Tree block to each side of the two Step 1 units. See **Diagram 17.** Press.

STEP 1
UNIT

DIAGRAM 17

Step 3. Sew one 1 × 24½-inch Fabric D strip to the top of each Step 2 unit. See **Diagram 18.** Press.

STEP 2 UNIT

DIAGRAM 18

Assembling the Side Borders

Step 1. Sew one 1 × 7½-inch Fabric D strip to each side of four Tree blocks. See **Diagram 19.** Press.

1"   8½"   1"

7½"   7½"

DIAGRAM 19

Step 2. Sew one Step 1 unit to each side of two 7½-inch Fabric E border squares. See **Diagram 20.** Press.

STEP 1
UNIT   7½"   STEP 1
UNIT

7½"

DIAGRAM 20

Step 3. Sew one 7½-inch Fabric E border square to each side of the two Step 2 units. See **Diagram 21.** Press.

Step 4. Sew one 1 × 39½-inch accent border strip to the top of the two Step 3 units. See **Diagram 22.** Press.

Adding the Borders to the Tablecloth

Step 1. Sew the top and bottom Tree block borders to the top and bottom of the tablecloth. Refer to the **Tablecloth Layout** on page 68 for placement. Press all seams toward the accent border.

7½"   STEP 2 UNIT   7½"

7½"   7½"

DIAGRAM 21

39½"   1"

STEP 3 UNIT

DIAGRAM 22

Step 2. Sew the side Tree block borders to the tablecloth sides. Press.

Step 3. Sew 1 × 39½-inch Fabric D accent border strips to the table-cloth top and bottom. Press.

Step 4. Sew 1 × 40½-inch Fabric D accent border strips to the table-cloth sides. Press.

Outer Border

Step 1. Sew two 4½ × 44-inch Fabric F outer border strips to the tablecloth top and bottom. Trim the excess and press all seams toward the outer border.

Step 2. For the side borders, cut one 4½ × 44-inch Fabric F outer border strip in half to make two 4½ × 22-inch strips. Sew one 4½ × 22-inch strip to each of the two remaining 4½ × 44-inch Fabric F strips to make two strips approximately 4½ × 66 inches each. Press.

Step 3. Sew these two outer border strips to the sides of the table-cloth. Trim the excess and press.

Binding

Step 1. Cut one 1 × 44-inch bind-ing strip into four strips approxi-

mately 1 × 10 inches each. Sew one of these strips to each of four 1 × 44-inch binding strips to make four binding strips approximately 1 × 54 inches each. Press.

Step 2. Sew 1 × 54-inch binding strips to the tablecloth top and bottom. Trim the excess and press all seams toward the binding.

Step 3. Sew one 1 × 54-inch bind-ing strip to each side of the table-cloth. Trim the excess and press.

SEW SMART

Since turning a project this large can be awkward, you may prefer to put on a tradi-tional quilt binding. Refer to "Binding the Quilt" on page 246. With this method you can machine quilt your tablecloth before adding the binding. This will prevent any bunching up of excess fabric near the binding. You will need ½ yard of fabric to bind the tablecloth using this technique.

Finishing

Step 1. Cut the 3-yard piece of backing fabric into two 1½-yard

SEW SMART

Purchase clear vinyl to use over the top of your table-cloth to protect it from spills. Clear vinyl is available at fabric stores by the yard. Another option is to have a piece of glass custom-cut to cover the top of the table and tablecloth.

lengths. Trim the selvage edges off both backing pieces. With right sides together, sew the halves together to make one piece approximately 88 × 54 inches. Press.

Step 2. Position the top and back-ing with right sides together, and pin in position. Trim the backing so that it extends 2 inches beyond the top all around. Using a ¼-inch seam allowance, sew together, leaving an opening for turning. Trim the back-ing to the same size as the top.

Step 3. Trim corners, turn right side out, and hand stitch the opening. Press.

Step 4. Machine stitch in the seam around the center square, the two-and-a-half-inch inner border, and the four-inch outer border.

Table Runner

58"

TABLE RUNNER LAYOUT

Finished Size: 58 × 13 inches
Finished Block: 8 × 7 inches

Materials

Obvious directional prints are not recommended.

FABRIC A

Tree	⅙ yard (6 inches)
Binding	⅓ yard
TOTAL	½ yard

FABRIC B
Block Background	⅓ yard
Checkerboard Border	⅙ yard
TOTAL	½ yard

FABRIC C
Trunk	⅛ yard

FABRIC D
Checkerboard Border	⅙ yard
Block Border	⅙ yard
TOTAL	⅓ yard

FABRIC E
Border	⅜ yard

BACKING   1¾ yards

COTTON FLANNEL   1¾ yards

Note: There is enough excess backing fabric and flannel to make the four place mats on page 75.

Cutting Directions

Prewash and press all your fabrics. Using a rotary cutter, see-through ruler, and cutting mat, prepare the strips as described in the first column in the chart below. Then from those strips, cut the pieces listed in the second column. Some strips need to be cut only once, so no additional cutting information will appear in the second column.

	FIRST CUT		SECOND CUT	
	NO. OF STRIPS	**DIMENSIONS**	**NO. OF PIECES**	**DIMENSIONS**
FABRIC A	**Tree**			
	2	2½ × 44-inch strips	4	2½ × 8½-inch pieces
			4	2½ × 6½-inch pieces
			4	2½ × 4½-inch pieces
	Binding			
	4	2¾ × 44-inch strips		
FABRIC B	**Block Background**			
	3	2½ × 44-inch strips	32	2½-inch squares
			8	2½ × 1½-inch pieces
	1	1½ × 44-inch strip	8	1½ × 3½-inch pieces
	Checkerboard Border			
	3	1½ × 44-inch strips	5	1½ × 20-inch strips
FABRIC C	**Trunk**			
	1	1½ × 44-inch strip	4	1½ × 2½-inch pieces
FABRIC D	**Checkerboard Border**			
	3	1½ × 44-inch strips	5	1½ × 20-inch strips
	Block Border			
	4	1 × 44-inch strips	16	1 × 8½-inch strips
FABRIC E	**Border**			
	Before You Cut: From *three* of the 44-inch strips, cut the pieces as directed in the second column. The remaining three strips require no further cutting.			
	6	2 × 44-inch strips	10	2 × 9½-inch strips

Making the Blocks

Step 1. Refer to "Quick Corner Triangles" and "Making the Blocks" for the Tablecloth, beginning on page 69. Follow all the directions in those sections. Since you will be making four Tree blocks, make only four units of each step instead of eight.

Step 2. Sew one 1 × 8½-inch Fabric D block border strip to the top and bottom of each of the four Tree blocks. Press all seams toward the block border.

Step 3. Sew one 1 × 8½-inch Fabric D strip to each side of the four Step 2 blocks. Press.

Making the Checkerboard Border

Step 1. Alternating the five Fabric B strips with the five Fabric D strips, sew the 1½ × 20-inch strips together. Change sewing direction with each strip sewn. Press seams toward the darker fabric as you go. See **Diagram 23.**

Step 2. Using a rotary cutter and ruler, cut this strip set into ten 1½ × 10½-inch strips, referring to the cutting lines in **Diagram 23.** There should be ten squares in each strip.

DIAGRAM 23

Step 3. Use a seam ripper to remove a light square from the end of five strips and a dark square from the end of the other five strips. The checkerboard strips should now measure 1½ × 9½ inches. If adjustments are necessary, see "Hints on Fitting Pieced Borders" on page 244.

Step 4. Sew these strips together in pairs to make five checkerboard sets. Press.

Assembling the Table Runner

Step 1. Sew one 2 × 9½-inch Fabric E border strip to the top and bottom of each of the five checkerboards. See **Diagram 24.** Press all seams toward the border.

DIAGRAM 24

Step 2. Sew four of the Step 1 checkerboard units to the bottom of four Tree blocks. See **Diagram 25.** Press. You will have one remaining checkerboard unit.

DIAGRAM 25

Step 3. Sew the Step 2 units together to make two pairs. See **Diagram 26.** Press.

DIAGRAM 26

SEW SMART

Position the tree blocks so the treetops all point to the center checkerboard unit.

Step 4. Sew the remaining Step 1 checkerboard unit between the two Step 3 units. See **Diagram 27** for proper placement. Press.

Step 5. Cut one 2 × 44-inch Fabric E border strip in half to make two 2 × 22-inch strips. Sew one 2 × 22-inch strip to each of the two remaining 2 × 44-inch Fabric E strips to make two strips approximately 2 × 66 inches each. Press.

Step 6. Sew the Step 5 strips to the long sides of the table runner. Trim the excess and press.

Layering

Arrange and baste the backing, flannel, and top together, following directions in "Layering the

DIAGRAM 27

Quilt" on page 245. Trim the flannel and backing to ¼ inch from the raw edge of the quilt top.

Binding

Cut one 2¾ × 44-inch Fabric A binding strip in half to make two 2¾ × 22-inch strips. Sew one of these strips to each of two other 2¾ × 44-inch Fabric A binding strips to make two strips approximately 2¾ × 66 inches each. Cut the remaining 2¾ × 44-inch Fabric A strip in half to make two 2¾ × 22-inch strips. Use these strips and follow the directions in "Binding the Quilt" on page 246.

Finishing Stitches

Machine or hand quilt in the seam line around each tree, each Tree block, each block border, and each checkerboard square. Quilt a 1½-inch diagonal grid in the border strips.

 # Place Mats

Finished Size: 15 × 12 inches
Finished Block: 8 × 7 inches

15"

12"

PLACE MAT LAYOUT

Materials (for four place mats)

Obvious directional prints are not recommended.

FABRIC A
Tree   ⅙ yard (6 inches)

Binding   ¼ yard
    TOTAL   ⅜ yard

FABRIC B
Block Background   ⅓ yard
Checkerboard Border   ⅛ yard
    TOTAL   ⅜ yard

FABRIC C
Trunk   ⅛ yard

FABRIC D
Checkerboard Border   ⅛ yard
Block Border   ⅙ yard
    TOTAL   ¼ yard

FABRIC E
Wide border   ⅓ yard

BACKING   ⅞ yard

COTTON FLANNEL   ⅞ yard

Cutting Directions

Prewash and press all of your fabrics. Using a rotary cutter, see-through ruler, and cutting mat, prepare the strips as described in the first column in the chart below. Then from those strips, cut the pieces listed in the second column. Some strips need to be cut only once, so no additional cutting information will appear in the second column. Measurements for all pieces include ¼-inch seam allowances.

	FIRST CUT		SECOND CUT	
	NO. OF STRIPS	DIMENSIONS	NO. OF PIECES	DIMENSIONS
FABRIC A	**Tree**			
	2	2½ × 44-inch strips	4	2½ × 8½-inch pieces
			4	2½ × 6½-inch pieces
			4	2½ × 4½-inch pieces
	Binding			
	7	1 × 44-inch strips	8	1 × 14½-inch strips
			8	1 × 12½-inch strips

(continued)

Place Mats Cutting Chart—Continued	FIRST CUT		SECOND CUT	
	NO. OF STRIPS	DIMENSIONS	NO. OF PIECES	DIMENSIONS
FABRIC B	**Block Background**			
	3	2½ × 44-inch strips	32	2½-inch squares
			8	2½ × 1½-inch pieces
	1	1½ × 44-inch strip	8	1½ × 3½-inch pieces
	Checkerboard Border			
	2	1½ × 44-inch strips		
FABRIC C	**Trunk**			
	1	1½ × 44-inch strip	4	1½ × 2½-inch pieces
FABRIC D	**Checkerboard Border**			
	2	1½ × 44-inch strips		
	Block Border			
	4	1 × 44-inch strips	16	1 × 8½-inch strips
FABRIC E	**Wide Border**			
	5	2 × 44-inch strips	8	2 × 11½-inch strips
			8	2 × 9½-inch strips
BACKING	4	14 × 17-inch pieces		
FLANNEL	4	14 × 17-inch pieces		

Making the Blocks

Refer to "Quick Corner Triangles" and "Making the Blocks" for the Tablecloth, beginning on page 69. Follow all the directions in those sections. Since you will be making four Tree blocks, make only four units of each step instead of eight.

Block Border

Sew 1 × 8½-inch Fabric D block border strips to the top and bottom of each of the four Tree blocks. Press all seams toward the block border. Sew 1 × 8½-inch Fabric D block border strips to each side of the four Tree blocks. Press.

Wide Border

Sew 2 × 9½-inch Fabric E wide border strips to the top and bottom of each of the four blocks. Press all seams toward the wide border. Sew 2 × 11½-inch Fabric E strips to each side of the four blocks. Press.

Checkerboard Border

Step 1. Alternating the two Fabric B strips with the two Fabric D strips, sew the four 1½ × 44-inch strips together. Change sewing direction with each strip sewn. Press seams toward the darker fabric as you go. See **Diagram 28.**

DIAGRAM 28

Step 2. Cut this 4½ × 44-inch strip set in thirds (approximately 14 inches each), referring to the cutting lines in **Diagram 28.** Resew the thirds together to make a 12½ × 14-inch strip set. See **Diagram 29.**

DIAGRAM 29

Step 3. From this strip set, cut eight 1½ × 12½-inch strips, referring to the cutting lines in **Diagram 29.** There should be 12 squares in each strip.

Step 4. Use a seam ripper to remove 1 light square from each strip to make eight identical strips with 11 squares each. Fit, pin in position, and sew the checkerboard border strips to each side

of the four placemats. If the border doesn't fit, see "Hints on Fitting Pieced Borders" on page 244 to make the necessary adjustments. Press all seams toward the wide border.

Binding

Sew 1 × 14½-inch Fabric A binding strips to the top and bottom of each placemat. Press all seams toward the binding. Sew 1 × 12½-inch Fabric A strips to each side of each place mat. Press.

Finishing

Step 1. For each place mat, position the top and backing with right sides together. Lay both pieces on top of the flannel, and pin all three layers together. Sew together, leaving a 3- to 4-inch opening for turning. Trim the flannel and backing to the same size as the top.

Step 2. Trim the corners, turn right side out, hand stitch the opening, and press.

Step 3. Machine or hand quilt in the seam line around the trees, borders, checkerboard squares, and binding. Quilt a 1½-inch diagonal grid in the wide border.

Festive Flourishes

Add to your gift a book on holiday entertaining, a recipe file, or a napkin-folding booklet. Tie up a couple of wooden spoons in your package bow, or wrap up a package of holiday note cards.

Lined Napkins
Finished Size: 18 inches square

Materials and Cutting
(for four napkins)

Using a rotary cutter, see-through ruler, and cutting mat, prepare the pieces as described in the chart below. Measurements for all pieces include ¼-inch seam allowances. Obvious directional prints are not recommended.

	YARDAGE	NO. OF PIECES	CUTTING — DIMENSIONS
Center Square	1 yard	4	15½-inch squares
Checkerboard Fabric A	⅓ yard	6	1½ × 44-inch strips
Checkerboard Fabric B	⅓ yard	6	1½ × 44-inch strips
Binding	¼ yard (cut into eight 1 × 44-inch strips)	8 / 8	1 × 18½-inch strips / 1 × 17½-inch strips
Backing	1⅛ yards	4	18½-inch squares

18"

18"

NAPKIN LAYOUT

12½"

14"

44"   ← CUTTING LINES

14"

14"

DIAGRAM 30

CUTTING LINES   36½"

14"   31½"

DIAGRAM 31

Making the Checkerboard Border

Step 1. Sew together the twelve 1½ × 44-inch checkerboard strips (six each of Checkerboard Fabric A and Checkerboard Fabric B), alternating the two colors. Change sewing direction with each strip sewn. Press seams toward the darker fabric as you go. See **Diagram 30**.

Step 2. Cut this 12½ × 44-inch strip set in thirds (approximately 14 inches each), referring to the cutting lines in **Diagram 30**. Resew the thirds together to make a 36½ × 14-inch strip set. See **Diagram 31**.

Step 3. From this strip set, cut eight 1½ × 36½-inch strips, referring to the cutting lines in **Diagram 31**. There should be 36 squares in each strip.

Step 4. Use a seam ripper to divide each of the eight strips into three strips, one strip with 15 squares, one with 17 squares, and one with 4 squares. The 15-square strip sets should all begin and end with the light color. The 17-square strip sets should all begin and end with the dark color. You will not use the strips with 4 squares.

Step 5. For the top and bottom borders, use the 15-square strips. Fit, pin in position, and sew one border strip to the top and bottom of each 15½-inch center square. If the border doesn't fit the center

square, see "Hints on Fitting Pieced Borders" on page 244 to make the necessary adjustments. Press all seams toward the center.

Step 6. For the side borders, use the 17-square strips. Fit, pin, and sew border strips to the sides of each center square. Press.

Binding

Sew 1 × 17½-inch binding strips to the top and bottom of each napkin. Press all seams toward binding. Sew 1 × 18½-inch binding strips to each side of each napkin. Press.

Finishing Stitches

Step 1. For each napkin, position the top and backing with right sides together. Sew together, leaving a 3- to 4-inch opening for turning.

Step 2. Trim the corners, turn right side out, hand stitch the opening, and press.

> ❤ **SEW CREATIVE** ❤
>
> Make a simple country-style napkin ring by cutting a pinked fabric strip approximately 1 × 36 inches. Cut the ends at a 45 degree angle. Tie in a bow around the napkin.

Party Invitations

Finished Size: 5½ × 4¼ inches

Materials (for two invitations)

CARD STOCK
8½ × 11-inch card-weight paper

APPLIQUÉ PIECES
Several coordinated scraps or ⅛-yard pieces of fabric

NOTIONS AND SUPPLIES
Appliqué film, nonsewable
Transfer lettering: Chartpak, Caslon 36 point *or*
Black, extra-fine point, permanent felt-tip pen
Note: Most stationery stores and quick-print shops carry a variety of paper and envelopes for you to create your own invitations.

> **SEW SMART**
>
> To get a clean, crisp fold, lightly score your fold line on the right side of the card stock. Be careful not to cut through the card.

Making the Invitations

Using a cork-backed ruler and a razor blade, cut the card stock in half to make two 5½ × 8½-inch pieces. (Or you could use your rotary cutter and a rotary blade that's too dull for fabric.) Fold the pieces in half to make 5½ × 4¼-inch cards with top folds.

Appliqué

Refer to "Quick-Fuse Appliqué" on page 238.

Step 1. Trace one large tree and background, and four small star designs for each invitation, using the **Tree and Star Appliqué Patterns** on page 80.

Step 2. Cut two 5 × 4-inch pieces of appliqué film, and fuse each to the back of the background fabric. Trim both to 4½ × 3¼ inches. Remove the paper backing.

Step 3. Quick-fuse the background piece, tree, and stars in the center of each card front. Position and fuse the entire design all at one time.

Step 4. Use an extra-fine point, permanent felt-tip pen to write your personal invitation on the inside of the card, or use transfer lettering for a more formal look. Quick-fuse a small star on each side of your message.

SEW SMART

For my invitations, I used transfer lettering to write PLEASE COME. I thought this gave a more polished look to my invitation. Transfer lettering is available at art supply stores and comes in various sizes and styles. Use a ruler to draw a faint pencil line where you want to position the words. Use a soft-lead pencil to rub each letter in place. Be sure to rub the entire letter off before lifting the transfer paper. If a letter cracks or you make a mistake, you can remove it with a piece of Scotch tape.

Place Cards

Finished Size: 5½ × 2⅛ inches

Materials (for four place cards)

CARD STOCK

8½ × 11-inch card-weight paper

APPLIQUÉ PIECES

Several coordinated scraps or ⅛-yard pieces of fabric

NOTIONS AND SUPPLIES

Appliqué film, nonsewable
Transfer lettering: Chartpak, Caslon 36 point *or*
Black, extra-fine point, permanent felt-tip pen

Note: Most stationery stores and quick-print shops carry a variety of paper for you to create your own place cards.

Making the Place Cards

Using a cork-backed ruler and a razor blade, cut the card stock in half to make two 5½ × 8½-inch pieces and then in half again to make four 5½ × 4¼-inch pieces. Fold each piece in half to make a 5½ × 2⅛-inch place card with a top fold. To get a clean, crisp fold, lightly score your fold line on the right side of the card stock. Be careful not to cut through the card.

Appliqué

Refer to "Quick-Fuse Appliqué" on page 238.

Step 1. Trace a large star or a small tree design for each place card, using the **Tree and Star Appliqué Patterns** on page 80. Quick-fuse to the left side of the place card.

Step 2. Use transfer lettering to add your guest's name to the place card. (See "Sew Smart" on this page.) Or, you may choose to write the name on the place card with an extra-fine point, permanent felt-tip pen.

Appliqué Pattern Key

―――――― TRACING LINE

- - - - - - TRACING LINE
(will be hidden behind
other fabric)

TREE AND STAR APPLIQUÉ PATTERNS

Trim-a-Tree

Finished Quilt: 23 × 28 inches

Materials
Obvious directional prints are not recommended.

FABRIC A
Tree   ⅛ yard

FABRIC B
Background   ½ yard

FABRIC C
Tree Base   ⅛ yard

FABRIC D
Half-Inch Accent Border   ⅛ yard

FABRIC E
Wide Border   ¼ yard
Binding   ⅜ yard
    TOTAL   ⅝ yard

BACKING   ¾ yard

LIGHTWEIGHT BATTING   ¾ yard

APPLIQUÉ AND ORNAMENT FABRICS
Stars and Ornaments
    Several coordinated scraps or ⅛-yard pieces

NOTIONS AND SUPPLIES
Fifteen ½- to ¾-inch buttons
Appliqué film
Black, extra-fine point, permanent felt-tip pen
Black pearl cotton or crochet thread for hangers
Buttons, beads, and bells for ornaments

23"

28"

QUILT LAYOUT

O h, Christmas tree! This Scandinavian-style folk-art tree with its charming array of ornaments lets you bring a touch of Christmas to any room in your home. Simple piecing makes sewing the tree a snap, and quick-fuse Penstitch appliqué makes the ornaments superquick. Buttons on the branches serve as decorative hangers for the ornaments. This is the perfect tree for children to trim, and who knows—this could become a family tradition they look forward to every year!

Cutting Directions

Prewash and press the quilt fabrics. Using a rotary cutter, see-through ruler, and cutting mat, prepare the strips as described in the first column in the chart below. From those strips, cut the pieces listed in the second column. (Parts of the quilt have only one cut.) Measurements for all pieces include ¼-inch seam allowances.

	FIRST CUT		SECOND CUT	
	NO. OF STRIPS	DIMENSIONS	NO. OF PIECES	DIMENSIONS
FABRIC A	Tree			
	2	1 × 44-inch strips	1	1 × 18½-inch strip
			1	1 × 15½-inch strip
			1	1 × 12½-inch strip
			1	1 × 9½-inch strip
			1	1 × 7½-inch strip
FABRIC B	Background			
	Before You Cut: Cut the pieces in the order listed.			
	2	4½ × 44-inch strips	1	4½ × 17½-inch piece
			2	4½ × 5½-inch pieces
			2	4½-inch squares
			2	4½ × 3-inch pieces
			2	4½ × 1½-inch pieces
			1	4 × 7½-inch piece
			2	2½ × 7-inch pieces
	1	4 × 44-inch strip	1	4 × 15½-inch piece
			1	4 × 12½-inch piece
			1	4 × 9½-inch piece
			1	1 × 2½-inch piece
FABRIC C	Tree Base			
	1	2½ × 4½-inch piece		
FABRIC D	Half-Inch Accent Border			
	Before You Cut: From *one* of the 44-inch strips, cut the pieces as directed in the second column. The remaining two 44-inch strips require no further cutting.			
	3	1 × 44-inch strips	2	1 × 22-inch strips
FABRIC E	Wide Border			
	Before You Cut: From *one* of the 44-inch strips, cut the pieces as directed in the second column. The remaining two 44-inch strips require no further cutting.			
	3	2½ × 44-inch strips	2	2½ × 22-inch strips
	Binding			
	4	2¾ × 44-inch strips		

Making the Tree Sections

Be sure to use accurate ¼-inch seam allowances and press as you go. Follow the arrows in each diagram for pressing direction.

Fabric Key

▥ FABRIC A
(Tree)

☐ FABRIC B
(Background)

⊠ FABRIC C
(Base)

Section One

Section One is the 4½ × 17½-inch Fabric B piece and is complete as is.

Section Two

Step 1. Sew one 1 × 7½-inch Fabric A piece to one 4 × 7½-inch Fabric B piece. See **Diagram 1.** Press.

DIAGRAM 1

Step 2. Sew one 4½ × 5½-inch Fabric B piece to each end of the Step 1 unit. See **Diagram 2.** Press.

DIAGRAM 2

Section Three

Step 1. Sew one 1 × 9½-inch Fabric A piece to one 4 × 9½-inch Fabric B piece. See **Diagram 3.** Press.

DIAGRAM 3

Step 2. Sew one 4½-inch Fabric B square to each end of the Step 1 unit. See **Diagram 4.** Press.

DIAGRAM 4

Section Four

Step 1. Sew one 1 × 12½-inch Fabric A piece to one 4 × 12½-inch Fabric B piece. See **Diagram 5.** Press.

DIAGRAM 5

Step 2. Sew one 3 × 4½-inch Fabric B piece to each end of the Step 1 unit. See **Diagram 6.** Press.

DIAGRAM 6

Section Five

Step 1. Sew one 1 × 15½-inch Fabric A piece to one 4 × 15½-inch Fabric B piece. See **Diagram 7.** Press.

DIAGRAM 7

Step 2. Sew one 1½ × 4½-inch Fabric B piece to each end of the Step 1 unit. See **Diagram 8.** Press.

DIAGRAM 8

Joining the Sections

Referring to **Diagram 9,** sew all the sections together in order. Press all seams toward Section Five. The tree block should now measure 17½ × 20½ inches.

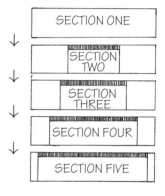

DIAGRAM 9

Assembling the Tree

Step 1. Using your rotary cutter and ruler, cut the tree block exactly in half, as shown in **Diagram 10.** Each half will measure 8¾ × 20½ inches.

DIAGRAM 10

Step 2. Sew one 1 × 2½-inch Fabric B piece to one 1 × 18½-inch Fabric A piece. See **Diagram 11.** Press.

1"

2½"

↓

18½"

DIAGRAM 11

Step 3. Sew the Step 2 unit between the two Step 1 halves, as shown in **Diagram 12.** Press.

→ ←

DIAGRAM 12

Step 4. Sew one 2½ × 7-inch Fabric B piece to each side of one 2½ × 4½-inch Fabric C piece. See **Diagram 13.** Press.

7"   4½"   7"

2½"   2½"

→   ←

DIAGRAM 13

Step 5. Sew the Step 4 unit to the bottom of the Step 3 unit. See **Diagram 14.** Press.

STEP 3
UNIT

↓

STEP 4
UNIT

DIAGRAM 14

Borders

Step 1. Sew 1 × 22-inch Fabric D accent border strips to the quilt top and bottom. Trim the excess and press seams toward the accent border. Sew 1 × 44-inch Fabric D strips to the quilt sides. Trim the excess and press.

Step 2. Sew 2½ × 22-inch Fabric E wide border strips to the quilt top and bottom. Trim the excess and press seams toward the wide border. Sew 2½ × 44-inch Fabric E strips to the quilt sides. Trim the excess and press.

Fused Stars

The stars on my quilt were simply fused to the background. Refer to "Timesaving Methods for Appliqué" on page 237 to decide which technique you will use. Trace eight small stars and one large star using the **Appliqué Ornament Patterns** on pages 88–89. Using the **Quilt Layout** on page 82 as a placement guide, position small stars on the quilt background at the ends of each tree branch and the large star at the tree's top.

Layering the Quilt

Arrange and baste the backing, batting, and top together, following the directions in "Layering the

Quilt" on page 245. Trim the batting and backing to ¼ inch from the raw edge of the quilt top.

Binding the Quilt

Using the 2¾ × 44-inch binding strips, follow the directions in "Binding the Quilt" on page 246.

Finishing Stitches

Machine or hand quilt in the seam line around the tree, base, accent border, and wide border. Outline the fused stars by quilting ¹⁄₁₆ inch away from the star edges in the background. Quilt a 1½-inch diagonal grid in the background. Using the Small Star appliqué pattern on page 89 as a template, randomly quilt stars in the wide border, spacing the stars approximately 4 to 5 inches apart.

Making the Ornaments

Step 1. Follow the instructions in "Two-Sided, No-Sew Ornaments" on page 86.

Step 2. Trace the design details such as doors, windows, and hearts for each ornament onto the paper side of the appliqué film.

Step 3. Cut the appliqué film loosely around the design details traced in Step 2. Fuse the traced patterns to the wrong side of selected fabrics. Cut out the design details, remove the paper backing, and fuse to the ornament fronts. Trim any fabrics that hang over the edges of the ornaments.

Step 4. Add the Penstitch details with an extra-fine point, permanent felt-tip pen. Draw about ¹⁄₁₆-inch-long lines on the appliqué fabric to look like a running stitch about ¹⁄₁₆ inch from the fabric edge.

TWO-SIDED, NO-SEW ORNAMENTS

Choose a heavier appliqué film for the ornaments, such as nonsewable Heat n Bond. (Laundering of the finished ornaments is not recommended.) Consult with the staff at your quilt or fabric store to learn the best product available. Appliqué films vary. Always read manufacturer's directions regarding product usage.

Step 1. On the paper side of the appliqué film, trace around the entire outside edge (heavier line) of the ornament designs. Trace one pattern for each ornament. See **Diagram 1.**

APPLIQUÉ FILM

CUTTING LINE

TRACING LINE

DIAGRAM 1

Step 2. For each ornament, cut the appliqué film loosely around each traced ornament design, as shown in **Diagram 1.** Cut a second piece of appliqué film slightly larger than the ornament. This second piece of appliqué film will remain unmarked.

    Note: Since the paper will remain on the second piece, avoid red or dark lines on the appliqué film when using a light-color fabric. The line may show through the fabric.

Step 3. Fuse the traced pattern to the wrong side of the main ornament fabric. Cut the traced pattern out along the drawn line. See **Diagram 2.** Remove the paper

backing from these pieces. A thin fusing film will remain on the fabric.

FABRIC—WRONG SIDE

CUT

DIAGRAM 2

Step 4. Fuse the second piece of appliqué film (with no tracing) to the wrong side of the fabric that will be the back side of the ornament. See **Diagram 3.** Do not remove the paper backing.

APPLIQUÉ FILM PAPER SIDE UP

WRONG SIDE OF FABRIC

DIAGRAM 3

Step 5. Take the cut piece and fuse it to the paper side of the unmarked piece. It is important to leave the paper on this second piece to give the ornament stability. See **Diagram 4.** Using the cut piece as a guide, trim the second piece to match the cut piece. Now your ornament has a matching front and back!

Trim around ornament front.

WRONG SIDE OF FABRIC

APPLIQUÉ FILM (PAPER SIDE UP)

DIAGRAM 4

Design Details

Some design details were added by gluing beads and buttons to the ornaments as described below. You may substitute fabric pieces for the buttons if you prefer. Draw in eyes and mouths with an extra-fine point, permanent felt-tip pen.

• **Candy Cane:** Use light fabric as the main ornament fabric, and add red pieces for stripes.

• **Cat:** Fuse the black nose, and draw a line below it. Glue on two black seed beads for eyes. Cut a piece of fabric ¾ × 3 inches, and tie a knot in the center for the cat's bow. Trim the ends and glue the bow to the cat's neck. Attach a small gold bell to the bow with needle and thread or with glue.

• **Christmas Tree:** Glue 12 red seed beads to the tree.

• **Church:** Use the church fabric as the main ornament fabric. Add the roof section, windows, door, and heart to this piece.

• **Drum:** Cut four 1-inch pieces of black pearl cotton or crochet thread. Glue the four pieces to the drum, making a zigzag pattern, as shown on page 88. Glue five gold seed beads at the ends of the strings.

• **Gift Box:** Cut a strip of fabric ⅜ × 14 inches. Wrap the fabric strip around the square in both directions, and tie a bow on the top. Trim the ends of the bow.

• **Gingerbread Boy:** Glue on two black seed beads for eyes. Add cheeks with red pencil. Cut a piece of fabric ¾ × 3 inches, and tie a knot in the center for the bow tie. Trim the ends and glue the bow to the gingerbread boy's neck. Add two ¼-inch round buttons to the body.

• **Goose:** Make the goose and wreath as two separate pieces. To cut out the inner circle on the wreath, cut a slit in the narrow side of the wreath. Slip the wreath over the goose's neck. Glue on a black seed bead for an eye, and add the cheek with red pencil.

• **Heart:** Trim the rectangular piece with pinking shears before fusing it to the center of the heart. Glue a small button to the center.

• **House:** Use the house fabric as the main ornament fabric. Add the roof section, door, and windows to this piece.

• **Mitten:** Use the mitten fabric as the main ornament fabric. Add the zigzag trim to this piece.

• **Mouse:** Glue on two black seed beads for eyes. Outline the nose and the edges of the head and arms with an extra-fine point, permanent felt-tip pen to make them stand out from the mouse body.

• **Snowman:** For eyes, glue on two black seed beads. Use black seed beads or an extra-fine point, permanent felt-tip pen for the mouth. Add cheeks with red pencil. Cut a strip of fabric ⅜ × 4 inches, and tie it around the snowman's neck for a scarf.

• **Stocking:** Use the stocking fabric as the main ornament fabric.

Add the trim, toe, and heel to this piece.

• **Train:** With black pearl cotton or crochet thread, sew through the four holes in each of two ⁷⁄₁₆-inch buttons to make an "X" on the top of the button. Tie the thread in a knot on the back of each button, and then glue a button to the center of each wheel. The window is positioned on top of the train.

Attaching Buttons to the Quilt Top

Lay your ornaments on the quilt top to get an idea of how the ornaments need to be spaced across the branches. Mark on the branches where each button is to be placed. Hand sew the 15 buttons in place. One ornament will hang from each button.

The Hangers

Step 1. Cut a 6-inch length of black pearl cotton or crochet thread for each ornament. Fold

SEW SMART

Add the hangers to each ornament after the quilt top is put together and the buttons are sewn on. This way the hanger can be made exactly the length necessary for each ornament.

the thread in half and position the ends of the thread on the back side of the ornament.

Step 2. Temporarily hold the hanger in place with a piece of Scotch tape. Hang the ornament on the appropriate button, and adjust the length of the hanger if necessary. Put a drop of glue on the ornament back to hold the hanger in place, and remove the tape. Trim the ends of the thread. See **Diagram 15.**

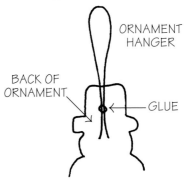

ORNAMENT HANGER

BACK OF ORNAMENT

GLUE

DIAGRAM 15

Festive Flourishes

Personalize the ornaments for the person receiving this as a gift. Add the person's name to one of the ornaments, like the stocking. Or make the house ornament in a light fabric and write, "Murphy's House" to personalize it that way.

APPLIQUÉ ORNAMENT PATTERNS

CROCHET THREAD

GOLD SEED BEADS

Wreath slides over neck.

SLIT

GIFT BOX

BUTTONS

APPLIQUÉ ORNAMENT PATTERNS

BUTTON

Trim edges of
rectangle with
pinking shears.

RED
RED
RED
RED
RED
RED

BUTTONS

SMALL STAR

LARGE STAR

Appliqué Pattern Key

—————— TRACING LINE
(Heavier line is
outside ornament
tracing line.)

Debbie Mumm

'Tis the Season

Everything's here to make you jolly, from stocking quilts and stockings to fill to gingerbread boys and snowmen. These would make wonderful gifts for children or grown-ups. They'll add a light-hearted Christmas touch to any corner of your home.

Before you begin, take a minute to read through this checklist. These are important pointers you should keep in mind to make sure that each of your quilts is a success.

★ Be sure to read "Techniques for Quick Country Quilting," beginning on page 226. This will familiarize you with the tools you'll need; the techniques for time-saving cutting, piecing, and appliqué; and finishing instructions.

★ Check the "Festive Flourishes" box for each project to get clever and unique ideas for packaging and wrapping your gift.

★ Take advantage of the helpful hints in the "Sew Smart" boxes. Here you'll find tips for making a technique quicker or easier.

★ Prewash and press all of your fabrics. Washing will remove any sizing from the fabrics, and pressing ensures accuracy when cutting.

★ Read the step-by-step directions from start to finish, and look at all the diagrams before you cut and sew any fabric.

★ Always use a ¼-inch seam allowance, unless there is a special note that tells you a different seam allowance is required.

★ Refer to the **Fabric Key** for each project as a help in following the diagrams.

★ Pay attention to the pressing directions given in the step-by-step text and to the pressing arrows shown in the diagrams.

Christmas Sampler Stockings

STOCKING LAYOUT

Stockings

Finished Size: 12 × 22 inches

Making these Christmas stockings is just half the fun—imagine what a thrill Santa will get filling these sweet sampler stockings to the brim with toys and treasures! Quick-fuse Penstitch appliqué lets you include lots of holiday details on each stocking, from trumpets and trains to stars and angels. For an added touch of holiday spirit, decorate your mantel with a festive folk-art garland that's wonderfully quick and easy.

Festive Flourishes

Use the stocking as packaging for an extra-special gift. Fill it with small toys for a child, sewing supplies for a quilter, herbs and spices for someone who loves to cook, a bottle of wine, or an assortment of teas.

Materials and Cutting
(for one stocking)

Prewash and press all of your fabrics. Using a rotary cutter, see-through ruler, and cutting mat, prepare the pieces as described in the chart below. Measurements for all pieces include ¼-inch seam allowances.

	YARDAGE	NO. OF PIECES	DIMENSIONS
			CUTTING
Lower Stocking Background	Assorted scraps of seven fabrics	1	5½ × 4½-inch piece (Block #1)
		1	8½ × 4½-inch piece (Block #2)
		1	7½ × 4½-inch piece (Block #3)
		1	6½ × 4½-inch piece (Block #4)
		1	6½ × 3½-inch piece (Block #5)
		1	7½ × 3½-inch piece (Block #6)
		1	4½ × 7½-inch piece (Block #8)
Stocking Top Background	⅛ yard	1	8½ × 3½-inch piece
Backing	⅜ yard		**Before You Cut:** Cut the backing piece first.
		1	13 × 24-inch piece
Heel		1	4½ × 7½-inch piece (Block #7)
Toe		1	5½ × 7½-inch piece (Block #9)
Half-Inch Accent Border	⅛ yard	2	1 × 8½-inch strips
Checkerboard Fabric A	⅛ yard	2	1 × 16-inch strips
Checkerboard Fabric B	⅛ yard	2	1 × 16-inch strips
Lining	¾ yard		
Muslin	⅜ yard	1	13½ × 24-inch piece
Cotton Flannel	⅜ yard	1	13½ × 24-inch piece
Bias Binding* and Hanging Tab	½ yard		
Appliqué Pieces	⅛-yard pieces or several coordinated scraps		

Appliqué film, heavyweight, nonsewable
Black, extra-fine point, permanent felt-tip pen
Buttons and beads as listed with each appliqué design

*If you prefer, you can purchase bias binding. You will need 2 yards of double-fold tape. You will then need only a 2 × 5-inch piece of fabric for the hanging tab.

Background Section Assembly

You will assemble the stocking first and then fuse the appliqué designs in place. Use accurate ¼-inch seam allowances and press seams after each sewing step, following the direction of the arrows in the diagrams. See the **Background Section Layout** for placement of background pieces.

BACKGROUND SECTION LAYOUT

Step 1. Sew one 5½ × 4½-inch piece (Block #1) to one 8½ × 4½-inch piece (Block #2). See **Diagram 1.** Press.

DIAGRAM 1

Step 2. Sew one 7½ × 4½-inch piece (Block #3) to one 6½ × 4½-inch piece (Block #4). See **Diagram 2.** Press.

DIAGRAM 2

Step 3. Sew one 6½ × 3½-inch piece (Block #5) to one 7½ × 3½-inch piece (Block #6). See **Diagram 3.** Press.

DIAGRAM 3

Step 4. Sew one 4½ × 7½-inch heel piece (Block #7) to one 4½ × 7½-inch piece (Block #8). See **Diagram 4.** Press.

DIAGRAM 4

Step 5. Sew the Step 4 unit to one 5½ × 7½-inch toe piece (Block #9), as shown in **Diagram 5.** Press.

DIAGRAM 5

Step 6. Referring to **Diagram 6,** sew together all units from Steps 1 through 5 in order. Press seams toward the bottom of the stocking. The background section should now measure 13½ × 18½ inches.

DIAGRAM 6

Step 7. Make a pattern using the **Stocking Pattern** on pages 102–105, and cut the lower stocking from the background section. Place the pattern piece on the right side of the background section with the top edge of the pattern even with the raw edge of the background, as shown in **Diagram 7.** Position the pattern piece 2 inches from the left edge and 3 inches from the right edge of the background section.

DIAGRAM 7

Checkerboard Border

Step 1. Sew the four 1 × 16-inch checkerboard strips together, alternating the two strips of each color. Change the sewing direction with each strip sewn. Press seams toward the darker fabric as you go. Cut this 2½ × 16-inch strip set into halves (approximately 8 inches each), referring to the cutting line in **Diagram 8.**

DIAGRAM 8

Step 2. Resew the halves together to make a 4½ × 8-inch strip set. See **Diagram 9.** Cut this strip set in half again.

DIAGRAM 9

Step 3. Resew the halves together to make an 8½ × 4-inch strip set. See **Diagram 10.** From this strip set, cut two 1 × 8½-inch strips.

DIAGRAM 10

Completing the Stocking Front

Step 1. Sew checkerboard strips to the top and bottom of the 8½ × 3½-inch stocking top background piece. Press seams toward the background piece. See **Diagram 11.** If the checkerboard border doesn't fit, see "Hints on Fitting Pieced Borders" on page 244 to make the necessary adjustments.

DIAGRAM 11

Step 2. Sew 1 × 8½-inch accent border strips to the top and bottom of the Step 1 unit. Press seams toward the accent border. See **Diagram 12.**

DIAGRAM 12

Step 3. Sew the Step 2 unit to the top of the lower stocking piece. Press. See **Diagram 13.**

DIAGRAM 13

Appliqué

The appliqués for these stockings were designed especially for the technique described in "Quick-Fuse Appliqué" on page 238. There are three sets of appliqué designs for three different stocking fronts. The appliqué designs are numbered to correspond with the numbered background pieces.

> ### ♥ SEW CREATIVE ♥
> You may choose to combine the designs shown in the photograph or mix and match different designs to create your own combination.

Step 1. See the **Stocking Top Appliqué Patterns** on page 98. Choose one design, and trace three of that one. Select your designs from the **Stocking Sampler Appliqué Patterns** found on pages 99–105. Position and fuse one design at a time in the center of each corresponding background piece. Use the photograph on page 92 as a placement guide.

Step 2. Use a permanent felt-tip pen to mark Penstitch details and to draw design details such as eyes and mouths.

> ### ♥ SEW CREATIVE ♥
> Some details on the appliqué designs are added by gluing beads, buttons, and bows to the stockings. Specifics are listed with each appliqué design pattern. You may substitute fabric pieces for buttons if you prefer.

Layering and Quilting the Stocking Front

Step 1. Press the 13½ × 24-inch pieces of muslin and flannel, and layer them with the muslin on the bottom (right side down), the flannel in the middle, and the stocking on top, right side up. Make sure that everything is centered and that the muslin and flannel are flat. The muslin and flannel should extend ¾ to 1 inch beyond the stocking front. To secure the layers together, hand baste completely around the edge of the stocking front. See **Diagram 14.**

DIAGRAM 14

Step 2. Machine or hand quilt in the seam line on each side of the half-inch accent border and the background piece. Quilt in all the seam lines between the background pieces. Outline the appliqué designs by quilting ¹⁄₁₆ inch away from the edge of the designs.

Step 3. Trim the muslin and flannel to ¼ inch from the raw edge of the stocking front. Then trim the muslin and flannel even with the *top edge only* of the stocking front.

Assembling the Stocking

Step 1. Cut one stocking back, using the completed stocking front as a pattern. Place the muslin side of the stocking front on the *wrong side* of the backing fabric before cutting.

Step 2. Fold the lining fabric in half with right sides together. Again using the stocking front as a pattern, cut two lining pieces.

Step 3. Position the stocking front and one lining piece with right sides together. (Match the shape of the heel and toe together.) Sew together with a ¼-inch seam allowance at the top edge. Fold wrong sides together, and press across the top edge.

Step 4. To make the hanging tab, cut a piece of fabric 2 × 5 inches. Fold in half lengthwise with wrong sides together, and press. Fold each long edge into the center fold and press again. Topstitch along the edge of both sides of the fabric strip. Fold the hanging tab in half.

Step 5. Position the hanging tab ½ inch from the raw edge on the heel side of the stocking, and baste it to the right side of the stocking back. See **Diagram 15**. Position the stocking back with the remaining lining piece with right sides together, and sew them together with a ¼-inch seam allowance at the top edge. Fold wrong sides together, and press across the top edge.

1/2"

STOCKING BACK (RIGHT SIDE OF FABRIC)

DIAGRAM 15

Step 6. Lay the stocking back made in Step 5 on a table with the lining

facing up. Position the stocking front made in Step 3 on top of the stocking back, lining up top edges and outside edges. Pin the outside edges, and baste the stocking together ¹⁄₁₆ inch from all the raw edges.

Bias Binding

Follow the steps below to make your own bias binding. (If you prefer, you may substitute ready-made double-fold bias tape.)

Step 1. Cut an 18-inch square of fabric. Cut the square in half diagonally from corner to corner. From each half, cut two 2¾-inch-wide strips. See **Diagram 16.**

18"

CUT
CUT
CUT
CUT
CUT

2³/4"

18"

DIAGRAM 16

Step 2. Sew the four binding strips together on the diagonal to make one continuous strip. With right sides together, lay one end of one strip at a 90 degree angle to the end of a second strip, and sew diagonally from one edge to the other, as shown in **Diagram 17.** Trim the seam allowance to ¼ inch and press.

Trim ¹/4" away from sewing line.

SEWING LINE

DIAGRAM 17

Step 3. Press the bias strip in half lengthwise with the wrong sides together.

Binding the Stocking

Step 1. Position the bias binding at the top right side of the stocking front with ½ inch extended beyond the top of the stocking. Align raw edges of the binding with the raw edge of the stocking front. (The flannel, lining, and stocking back will extend another ¼ inch from the edge of the binding and the stocking front.) Sew ¼ inch from the stocking front edge, going through all layers of the stocking; ease the bias binding around the toe and heel as you continue around the stocking. Be careful not to catch the hanging tab in the seam as you sew on the binding. Trim excess binding to leave ½ inch extended beyond the top of the stocking. Press the binding toward the raw edge of the stocking.

Step 2. Bring the binding around to the back of the stocking, folding in the top edges. Press, pin in position, and hand stitch in place.

 # Fireplace Garland

This garland is designed to decorate your mantel, but could be equally wonderful on a tree or wreath. The garland is approximately 8 feet long; the decorated portion is 75 inches long, with 10 inches of jute at each end for hanging.

GARLAND LAYOUT

Materials

The fabric and batting listed here will make 1 star. You will need to make 15 stars for an 8-foot garland.

NOTIONS AND SUPPLIES

Two 3½ × 4½-inch pieces of fabric
Matching thread
One 3½ × 4½-inch piece of cotton batting
Coordinated fabric scraps for fused hearts
95 inches of heavyweight jute
Sixteen ½-inch red wooden beads
Appliqué film
Assorted buttons, ⅜- to ¾-inch (one for each star)
Coordinated fabric scraps for fabric ties

Making the Stars

Step 1. Using plastic or cardboard, make a template of the large star from Block #4 of the **Stocking Sampler Appliqué Patterns** on page 103.

Step 2. For each star, use a pencil to trace around the star template onto the right side of one 3½ × 4½-inch piece of selected fabric, allowing at least ¼ inch of space around the edges of the star. The tracing line is your sewing line.

Step 3. Put the marked fabric piece on top of a 3½ × 4½-inch cotton batting piece. Put a 3½ × 4½-inch fabric piece on the bottom, right side down, to make a "sandwich."

Step 4. Using a small straight stitch and thread that matches the star fabric, sew all the way around the star on the drawn line.

Step 5. Trim ¼ inch away from the sewn line all the way around the star.

Step 6. Trace the heart from the star appliqué design on page 103 onto appliqué film. Referring to "Quick-Fuse Appliqué" on page 238, fuse a heart to the center of the star. Hand sew or glue a button to the center of the heart.

Stringing the Garland

Step 1. String 16 wooden beads onto a 95-inch piece of heavyweight jute. You can purchase colored beads, or tint plain wooden ones with a commercial dye such as Rit.

Step 2. Cut thirty-two ½ × 3½-inch pieces of assorted light-color fabrics. Tie one fabric piece onto the jute on each side of each bead.

Step 3. Slide the beads and fabric ties on the jute string, spacing the beads 5 inches apart. Center and hand sew a star to the jute between the ties. (Use a large stitch on the back of the star that will allow the star to slide on the jute.) Leave about 10 inches of jute at each end of the garland.

Festive Flourishes

Use the garland as ribbon to decorate a package for an extra bonus gift. You could also decorate the outside of a basket with the garland and fill it with pinecones and potpourri.

STOCKING TOP APPLIQUÉ PATTERNS

BUTTON

BUTTONS

BUTTON

STOCKING SAMPLER APPLIQUÉ PATTERNS

Appliqué Pattern Key

———————— TRACING LINE

– – – – – – – TRACING LINE
(will be hidden behind other fabric)

STOCKING BLOCK #5

Put buttons in the center of the wheels.

STOCKING BLOCK #1

BLACK SEED BEAD

BLACK SEED BEAD EYE

Draw line with pen.

STOCKING BLOCK #6

RED SEED BEADS

STOCKING BLOCK #2

STOCKING SAMPLER APPLIQUÉ PATTERNS

Appliqué Pattern Key

────────── TRACING LINE

---------- TRACING LINE
(will be hidden behind other fabric)

Add a ribbon bow.

Add red and white seed beads for candy sprinkles.

RED

RED

RED

RED

RED

RED

STOCKING BLOCK #8

Draw wire with pen.

STOCKING BLOCK #5

WHITE SEED BEADS

BUTTON EYE

STOCKING BLOCK #2

STOCKING BLOCK #8

STOCKING
BLOCK #6

OR BELL →

BLACK SEED
BEAD EYES →

STOCKING
BLOCK #8

Draw lines
with pen.

RED SEED
BEADS →

STOCKING
BLOCK #3

← BUTTON

STOCKING
BLOCK #1

STOCKING
BLOCK #3

BUTTONS

Appliqué Pattern Key

——————— TRACING LINE

– – – – – – – TRACING LINE
(will be hidden behind other fabric)

STOCKING BLOCK #2

BLACK SEED BEAD EYES

OR BUTTON

STOCKING BLOCK #1

Attach to Stocking Pattern Section B at the dots.

STOCKING PATTERN SECTION A

BUTTON

STOCKING
BLOCK #4

STOCKING
BLOCK #6

Use this star for garland.

STOCKING
BLOCK #3

STOCKING
BLOCK #5

BLACK SEED
BEAD EYES

Attach to Stocking Pattern Section A at the dots.

Attach to Stocking Pattern Sections C and D at the dots.

STOCKING PATTERN SECTION B

Attach to Stocking Pattern Section B at the dots.

STOCKING
BLOCK #8

Attach to Stocking Pattern Section D at the dots.

STOCKING PATTERN SECTION C

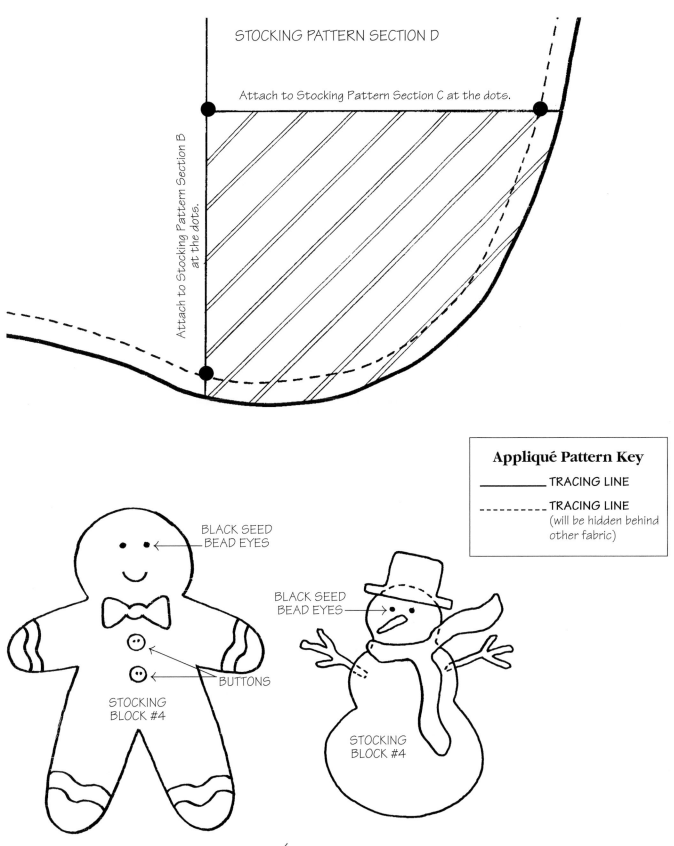

STOCKING PATTERN SECTION D

Attach to Stocking Pattern Section C at the dots.

Attach to Stocking Pattern Section B at the dots.

Appliqué Pattern Key

——————— TRACING LINE

- - - - - - - - TRACING LINE
(will be hidden behind other fabric)

BLACK SEED BEAD EYES

BUTTONS

STOCKING BLOCK #4

BLACK SEED BEAD EYES

STOCKING BLOCK #4

STOCKING SAMPLER APPLIQUÉ PATTERNS

Cookie Cutter Christmas

19"

16½"

WALLHANGING LAYOUT

Deck the halls, walls, packages, baskets, and gift bags with dozens of delicious "cookie cutter" wallhangings, ornaments, and gift tags. The wallhangings feature either gingerbread boys or Santas and snowmen. Make ornaments or gift tags using these charmers plus an assortment of other equally sweet designs—angel, Mr. Moon, apple, kitty cat, reindeer, stars, tree, stocking, heart-in-hand, or mitten. Add your own festive touches with beads and buttons. It's so easy to "bake" up a batch for your friends and relatives today. They'll "eat them up!"

Santas and Snowmen or Gingerbread Boys Wallhanging

Finished Size: 19 × 16½ inches

Materials

FABRIC A
Background   ⅙ yard (6 inches)

FABRIC B
Checkerboard Lattice, Half-Inch
   Border, and Binding   ¼ yard

FABRIC C
Checkerboard Lattice   ⅛ yard

FABRIC D
Wide Border   ⅙ yard

BACKING   ⅝ yard

LIGHTWEIGHT BATTING   ⅝ yard

APPLIQUÉ PIECES
Several coordinated scraps or
   ⅛-yard pieces

NOTIONS AND SUPPLIES
Appliqué film, nonsewable
Black, extra-fine point, permanent
   felt-tip pen
Assorted buttons and beads
   (Look for black half-round beads
   at your favorite craft store, or
   see "Quilting by Mail" on page
   250 for mail-order sources.)

Cutting Directions

Prewash and press all of your fabrics. Using a rotary cutter, see-through ruler, and cutting mat, prepare the strips as described in the first column in the chart below. Then from those strips, cut the pieces listed in the second column. Some portions of the quilt need to be cut only once, so no additional cutting information will appear in the second column. Measurements for all pieces include ¼-inch seam allowances.

| | FIRST CUT | | SECOND CUT | |
	NO. OF STRIPS	DIMENSIONS	NO. OF PIECES	DIMENSIONS
FABRIC A	**Background**			
	1	4½ × 44-inch strip	6	4½ × 5½-inch pieces
FABRIC B	**Checkerboard Lattice**			
	3	1 × 44-inch strips		
	Half-Inch Accent Border			
	2	1 × 44-inch strips	2	1 × 14½-inch strips
			2	1 × 13-inch strips
	Binding			
	2	1 × 44-inch strips	2	1 × 18½-inch strips
			2	1 × 17-inch strips
FABRIC C	**Checkerboard Lattice**			
	3	1 × 44-inch strips		
FABRIC D	**Wide Border**			
	2	2 × 44-inch strips	2	2 × 15½-inch strips
			2	2 × 16-inch strips

Background Assembly

Assemble the wallhanging top before doing the quick-fuse Penstitch appliqué. Use accurate ¼-inch seam allowances, and press seams after each sewing step, following the direction of the arrows in the diagrams. Refer to the diagrams for each step. For the borders and the binding, refer to the **Wallhanging Layout** on page 107.

Checkerboard Lattice

Step 1. Sew the six 1 × 44-inch Fabric B and Fabric C strips together, alternating the three strips of each color. Change sewing direction with each strip sewn. Press seams toward the darker fabric as you go. See **Diagram 1.**

Step 2. Cut this 3½ × 44-inch strip set into halves (approximately 22 inches each), referring to the cutting line in **Diagram 1.** Resew the halves together to make a 6½ × 22-inch strip set. See **Diagram 2.**

Step 3. Cut this 6½ × 22-inch strip set in half again, referring to the cutting line in **Diagram 2.** Resew the halves together to make a 12½ × 11-inch strip set. See **Diagram 3.**

Step 4. From this strip set, cut eight 1 × 12½-inch strips, referring to the cutting lines in **Diagram 3.** There should be 24 squares in each strip.

3½"

22"

44"

CUTTING LINE

22"

DIAGRAM 1

6½"

22"

11"

CUTTING LINE

11"

DIAGRAM 2

12½"

11"

1"

CUTTING LINES

DIAGRAM 3

Step 5. For the checkerboard lattice between the background pieces, use two 1 × 12½-inch strips. Using a seam ripper, separate each of the two strips into two 1 × 5½-inch strips. These four strips will have ten squares each. Using the **Wallhanging Layout** on page 107 and **Diagram 4** as guides for placement of dark and light colors, sew one strip to each side of two 4½ × 5½-inch background pieces. (These should be the center block from each row.) Press all seams toward the background pieces. Note that the placement of the checkerboard is different for the top and bottom rows. If the checkerboard lattice doesn't fit, see "Hints on Fitting Pieced Borders" on page 244 to make the necessary adjustments.

TOP ROW

1"   4½"   1"

BOTTOM ROW

1"   4½"   1"

5½"

DIAGRAM 4

Step 6. Sew one 4½ × 5½-inch background piece to each side of the Step 5 units to make two rows of three blocks each. See **Diagram 5.** Press.

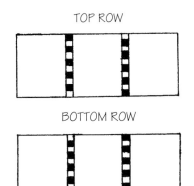

TOP ROW

BOTTOM ROW

DIAGRAM 5

Step 7. For the top, center, and bottom checkerboard, remove three sets of 2 squares from one of the 1 × 12½-inch strips. Sew one set of two squares to one end of three 1 × 12½-inch strips to make three strips with 26 squares each.

Step 8. Sew a checkerboard lattice strip from Step 7 to the top of each row and one to the bottom of the bottom row. Press. See the **Wallhanging Layout** for placement of dark and light colors. Sew the rows together. Press.

Step 9. With a seam ripper, remove 1 square from each of the two remaining 1 × 12½-inch strips, to make two strips with 23 squares each. Refer to the **Wallhanging Layout** for color placement, and sew the checkerboard lattice strips to the wallhanging sides. Press.

Half-Inch Accent Border

Sew 1 × 14½-inch Fabric B accent border strips to the wallhanging top and bottom. Press all seams toward the accent border. Sew 1 × 13-inch Fabric B strips to the wallhanging sides. Press.

Wide Border

Sew 2 × 15½-inch Fabric D strips to the wallhanging top and bottom. Press all seams toward the accent border. Sew 2 × 16-inch Fabric D strips to the wallhanging sides. Press.

Binding

Sew 1 × 18½-inch binding strips to the wallhanging top and bottom. Press all seams toward the binding. Sew 1 × 17-inch binding strips to the wallhanging sides. Press.

Appliqué

Step 1. Refer to "Penstitch Appliqué" on page 239. Trace four hearts, and three snowmen and three Santas for the Santas and Snowman Wallhanging, or six gingerbread shapes for the Gingerbread Boys Wallhanging, using the **Cookie Cutter Appliqué Patterns** on pages 114–116.

Step 2. Position and fuse one appliqué design at a time to the center of each background piece. Use the photograph on page 106 as a placement guide. Add Penstitch and details such as eyes and mouths. See "Design Details" on the opposite page for more ideas.

Step 3. Position and fuse a heart from page 116 to the borders in each corner of the wallhanging.

Finishing

Step 1. Position the top and the backing with right sides together. Lay both pieces on top of the batting and pin all three layers together. Sew them together, leaving a 3- to 4-inch opening for turning. Trim the batting and backing to the same size as the quilt top.

Step 2. Trim corners, turn right side out, and press. Hand stitch the opening. Press.

Step 3. Machine or hand quilt in the seam line around the lattice, both borders, and the binding. Quilt a grid or diagonal lines in the wide border, as shown in the **Walhanging Layout** on page 107. You could also quilt 1/16 inch from the edge of the appliqué pieces.

Festive Flourishes

Attach a tin cookie cutter to the outside of your package. Or make a batch of cutout cookies, put them in a tin, wrap with a fabric bow, and attach a gingerbread boy ornament to the top of the tin. You could also put cookies in a fabric-lined basket with a handle. Tie a bow to the top of the handle, and let a cookie cutter gingerbread boy ornament hang from the bow.

Cookie Cutter Ornaments

Materials

ORNAMENT FABRICS
Several coordinated scraps or 1/8-yard pieces

APPLIQUÉ PIECES
Several coordinated scraps or 1/8-yard pieces

NOTIONS AND SUPPLIES
Appliqué film, nonsewable
Black pearl cotton or crochet thread for hangers
Black, extra-fine point, permanent felt-tip pen
Buttons, beads, acrylic paint, or glue as specified for each design
Red pencil

Making the Ornaments

Step 1. Refer to "Two-Sided, No-Sew Ornaments" on page 86 for more detailed instructions.

Step 2. Using the **Cookie Cutter Appliqué Patterns** on pages 114–116, trace one main pattern and two sets of the design details such as faces, stars, and hands for each ornament. Trace one set as drawn, and trace one set in reverse. To trace in reverse, have the designs photocopied and then trace to the wrong side of the photocopy, *or* trace to the right side of a piece of paper and then trace again on the wrong side of that paper.

Step 3. Cut appliqué film loosely around the pattern and design details traced in Step 2. Fuse the pattern to the wrong side of the main ornament fabric.

Step 4. Cut a second piece of appliqué film that is slightly larger than the ornament. This second piece of appliqué film will remain unmarked, and you will leave the paper on the unmarked piece of appliqué film. Fuse this second piece of appliqué film (with no tracing) to the wrong side of the fabric that will be the back side of the ornament.

Step 5. Take the cut ornament and fuse it to the paper side of the unmarked piece. Using the cut piece as a guide, trim the second piece to match the cut ornament.

Step 6. Fuse the traced details to the wrong side of selected fabrics. Cut out the design details, remove the paper backing, and fuse to the ornament fronts and backs. Trim any fabrics that hang over the edges of the ornaments.

Design Details

Add interesting details by gluing beads and buttons to the designs, or you can fuse fabric in the shape of buttons and stars. Draw in eyes and mouths with a permanent felt-tip pen. Draw Penstitches along the edges of the ornaments, and remember to add the "stitches" to both sides of the ornaments.

• **Angel:** Fuse the hands, hair, dress, face, and heart. Mark the eyes with a felt-tip pen, and put blush on the cheeks with a red pencil.

• **Apple:** Attach a hanger to the top of the apple, following the directions in "Hangers" on page 112. Tie a knot in the thread approximately ½ inch from the top of the apple. Sew through the ends of each leaf, as indicated on the apple appliqué pattern on page 115. Put one leaf on each of the two threads.

• **Cat:** Add eyes with black half-round beads.

• **Gingerbread Boy:** Glue on half-round beads for the eyes. Glue on two small, round stoneware buttons.

• **Mittens:** For a hanger, cut thread approximately 8 inches long. Thread a sharp needle, and tie a knot in one end. Run the thread through the top of one mitten and then through the top of the second mitten. Tie a knot in the end. One mitten will be at each end of the thread.

• **Moon and Stars:** Add mouth and cheek outlines with a felt-tip pen. Color in the cheek with a red pencil. The stars are attached to the moon with separate pieces of thread. For the eye on the moon, glue on a black half-round bead.

• **Reindeer:** Glue on black half-round beads to give your reindeer eyes. Add a glow to his cheeks with a red pencil. Don't forget to cut black fabric for his nose, or red fabric if it's Rudolph!

• **Santa and Bag:** Glue two small star stoneware buttons to Santa's suit, and attach the bag to Santa's hand with a separate piece of thread. Add Santa's eyes with a felt-tip pen, and give his cheeks a rosy glow with a red pencil.

• **Snowman:** Glue on black antique glass seed beads for the eyes and mouth. Add cheeks with a red pencil. Glue three small star stoneware buttons to the snowman's body.

• **Tree:** The "popcorn and berry" garland is made and attached to the tree before it is fused together. To make the garland, cut a piece of thread approximately 18 inches long, and thread it through a small needle (small enough to go through the seed bead hole). Put one bead on the thread, and tie a knot around that bead approximately 1 to 2 inches from the end of the thread. That bead and knot will keep the other beads on the thread. Continue to string beads, alternating red and white antique glass seed beads in a random order.

Festive Flourishes

Fill a fabric-lined basket with holiday baking supplies such as nuts, brown sugar, chocolate chips, nutmeg, cookie cutters, a wooden spoon, and a new set of measuring spoons. Be sure to include a couple of your favorite holiday cookie recipes. Tie a fabric bow on the basket handle, and hang a gingerbread boy ornament on it.

When you have approximately 12 inches of beads strung, tie another knot around the last bead. Peel the paper backing from the front of the ornament, place one of the ends of the thread in between the ornament front and back, and fuse the two pieces together. Cut out the ornament, following the edge of the front. Be careful not to cut the thread that is holding the bead garland in place. Wrap the bead garland around the ornament from one side of the tree to the other. Use a drop of white craft glue to hold the garland in place on the edges of the ornament.

Continue to wrap the garland from side to side until you reach the top of the tree. You may need to untie the top knot and remove some of the beads so the garland will end at the edge of the ornament. To end the garland, simply glue the last bead on the garland to the edge of the tree. Use red acrylic paint to paint small white stoneware star buttons. Glue two red buttons and one white star button to each side of the tree.

Hangers

Cut a 6- to 8-inch length of black pearl cotton or crochet thread for each ornament. (Depending on your tree, you may wish to use a longer or shorter hanger.) Thread each through a sharp needle and pull through the top of each ornament. Tie the loose ends in a secure knot.

SEW SMART

You may need to use pliers to help work the needle through the ornament. If the layers at the top of the ornament separate when adding the hanger, just re-press the top of the ornament after the hanger is attached.

Gift Tags

Materials

GIFT TAG FABRICS

Several coordinated scraps or ⅛-yard pieces
Scraps of light-color fabrics for writing on back of tags

APPLIQUÉ PIECES

Several coordinated scraps or ⅛-yard pieces

NOTIONS AND SUPPLIES

Appliqué film, nonsewable
Black pearl cotton or crochet thread for hangers
Black, extra-fine point, permanent felt-tip pen
Buttons and beads as specified for each design

Making the Gift Tags

Gift tags can be used on packages, bags, and to decorate gift baskets. (See the photograph on page 110.) Follow the instructions for "Two-Sided, No-Sew Ornaments" on page 86, but cut only one set of design details. Leave the back side of the ornament plain for the gift tag.

Step 1. Cut a piece of appliqué film approximately 1½ × 2½ inches. Fuse the film to the wrong side of a scrap of light-color fabric. Trim the fabric to the edges of the paper.

Step 2. Remove the paper backing from the film, and trim the edges of the tag with pinking shears. (You may have to adjust the size of the tag to fit the ornament design that you have selected.)

Festive Flourishes

For a gift bag, fold the top of a lunch-size brown paper bag to the back by approximately 2 inches. Using a paper punch, make two holes in the paper bag, approximately 1 inch from the top folded edge of the bag and approximately ¾ inch from each side of the bag center. Put an 18-inch length of jute through the holes, add the gift tag, and tie the jute in a bow. If you like, add a small piece of greenery to the bow. Tie a knot in each end of the jute.

Step 3. Position the tag on the back side of the ornament, and fuse in position.

Step 4. Use an extra-fine point, permanent felt-tip pen to write the words *To:* and *From:* on the tag, as shown in **Diagram 6.** To add a hanger, refer to "Hangers" on the opposite page.

Write letters in pencil first, then in extra-fine point, permanent marker. If you like, add dots to the ends of the letters as in **Diagram 6.** It can help disguise unevenness in your printing.

To:
From:

DIAGRAM 6

COOKIE CUTTER WREATH

This cookie cutter wreath is a fun way to add some Christmas cheer to your kitchen! You could use any of the ornament designs in the book—add them, along with a bow, to a wreath to make a special gift for a friend or to adorn your own front door.

Materials

PURCHASED 14-INCH GRAPEVINE WREATH

FABRIC STRIP ⅛ yard

ORNAMENT FABRICS
Several coordinated scraps or ⅛-yard pieces

APPLIQUÉ PIECES
Several coordinated scraps or ⅛-yard pieces

NOTIONS AND SUPPLIES
Appliqué film, nonsewable
Twelve 1/16-inch half-round black beads
Twelve ⅜-inch round stoneware buttons
Tacky glue
Raffia
6 long cinnamon sticks
Hot glue and hot-glue gun

Making the Gingerbread Boys

Step 1. Refer to "Two-Sided, No-Sew Ornaments" on page 86. Make six gingerbread boy ornaments using the appliqué design from **Cookie Cutter Appliqué Patterns** on page 115.

Step 2. Trace six of each of the design details for the gingerbread boy on page 115.

Step 3. Cut appliqué film loosely around the design details traced in Step 2. Fuse traced pieces to wrong side of selected fabrics. Cut out design details, remove paper backing, and fuse to ornament fronts. Trim any extra fabrics. Glue beads for eyes and buttons in place.

Assembling the Wreath

If you wish, you can spray paint your grapevine wreath.

Step 1. Cut two 1 × 44-inch fabric strips. Tie or sew them together to make one 1 × 88-inch strip. Wrap the fabric strip around the wreath, referring to the photograph. Tie the ends of the strip together on the back of the wreath. Cut off any extra fabric.

Step 2. Make a raffia bow. Hot-glue the cinnamon sticks and the bow onto the wreath.

Step 3. Referring to the photograph, hot-glue a gingerbread boy to the bow and five gingerbread boys to the wreath.

COOKIE CUTTER APPLIQUÉ PATTERNS

Appliqué Pattern Key

——————— TRACING LINE
(Heavier line is out-
side ornament
tracing line.)

- - - - - - - - - TRACING LINE
(will be hidden behind
other fabric)

Trace two mittens.

Use mitten fabric for
main ornament fabric.

Use stocking fabric
for main ornament
fabric.

BEAD
GARLAND

Start
here.

COOKIE CUTTER APPLIQUÉ PATTERNS

Use wing fabric for
main ornament fabric.

Use reindeer fabric
for main ornament
fabric.

COOKIE CUTTER APPLIQUÉ PATTERNS

Appliqué Pattern Key

———— TRACING LINE
(Heavier line is out-
side ornament
tracing line.)

‑ ‑ ‑ ‑ TRACING LINE
(will be hidden behind
other fabric)

Add hanger here
for ornament.

FOR WALLHANGING
AND ORNAMENT

Trace entire shape
for ornament, and
use Santa suit
fabric as main
ornament fabric.

SANTA'S BAG
FOR ORNAMENT

Add hanger here
for ornament.

FOR WALLHANGING
AND ORNAMENT

Trace entire
shape for orna-
ment, and use
snowman fabric
for main
ornament fabric.

HEART FOR
CORNERS OF
WALLHANGING

Christmas Stocking Quilts

Christmas Stocking Quilts

29½"

QUILT LAYOUT

Stockings galore! You have your choice of a larger four-stocking version or a miniature eight-stocking quilt. Each one features colorful pieced stockings with appliqué details surrounded by a patchwork border. Hang these fun quilts anywhere in your home to add a country touch of holiday magic.

Big Foot

Finished Quilt: 29½ × 20 inches
Finished Block: 5 × 12 inches

Materials

FABRIC A
Use four fabrics.
Stocking Foot ⅙ yard
(6 inches) *each* of *four* fabrics

FABRIC B
Block Background ¼ yard
Lattice ⅙ yard
Outer border ⅙ yard
  TOTAL ½ yard

FABRIC C
Use four fabrics.
Stocking Top ⅛ yard
each of *four* fabrics

FABRIC D
Use four fabrics.
Stocking Accent Strip ⅛ yard
(or 1 × 3½-inch pieces)
each of *four* fabrics

FABRIC E
Half-Inch Accent Border ⅛ yard

BINDING ⅓ yard

BACKING ¾ yard

LIGHTWEIGHT BATTING ¾ yard

APPLIQUÉ DESIGNS
Several coordinated scraps

NOTIONS AND SUPPLIES
Appliqué film, nonsewable
Black, extra-fine point, permanent
  felt-tip pen

Cutting Directions

Prewash and press all of your fabrics. Using a rotary cutter, see-through ruler, and cutting mat, prepare the strips as described in the first column in the chart below. Then from those strips, cut the pieces listed in the second column. Some strips need to be cut only once, so no additional cutting information will appear in the second column. Measurements for all pieces include ¼-inch seam allowances.

	FIRST CUT		SECOND CUT	
	NO. OF STRIPS	**DIMENSIONS**	**NO. OF PIECES**	**DIMENSIONS**
FABRIC A	**Stocking Foot:** from *each* of the *four* fabrics, cut the following			
	1	4½ × 10-inch strip	1	4½ × 3½-inch piece
			1	4½ × 5½-inch piece
FABRIC B	**Block Background**			
	1	3½ × 44-inch strip	4	3½-inch squares
			4	2½-inch squares
			4	1½-inch squares
	1	2½ × 44-inch strip	4	2½ × 8½-inch pieces
	Lattice			
	2	1½ × 44-inch strips	2	1½ × 22-inch strips
			2	1½ × 14½-inch strips
	1	1 × 44-inch strip	3	1 × 12½-inch strips
	Outer Border			
	3	1½ × 44-inch strips	2	1½ × 27-inch strips
			2	1½ × 19½-inch strips
FABRIC C	**Stocking Top:** from *each* of the *four* fabrics, cut the following			
	1	3½ × 4-inch piece		
FABRIC D	**Stocking Accent Strip:** from *each* of the *four* fabrics, cut the following			
	1	1 × 3½-inch piece		
FABRIC E	**Half-Inch Accent Border**			
	2	1 × 44-inch strips	2	1 × 24-inch strips
			2	1 × 15½-inch strips
BINDING	4	2¾ × 44-inch strips		

Quick Corner Triangles

Refer to "Making Quick Corner Triangles" on page 234. You will be making four stocking blocks, one each of four different fabric combinations. Before you start sewing, coordinate the fabrics for each of the four combinations; keep track of them as you sew. Refer to the **Fabric Key** for fabric identification. Press all seams in the direction of the triangle just added.

Fabric Key

- **FABRIC A** (Stocking Foot)
- **FABRIC B** (Background)
- **FABRIC C** (Stocking Top)
- **FABRIC D** (Stocking Accent Strip)

Step 1. Sew four 2½-inch Fabric B squares to four 4½ × 5½-inch Fabric A pieces. See **Diagram 1**. Press.

DIAGRAM 1

Step 2. Sew four 3½-inch Fabric B squares to the four Step 1 units. See **Diagram 2**. Press.

DIAGRAM 2

Step 3. Sew four 1½-inch Fabric B squares to four Step 2 units. See **Diagram 3**. Press.

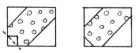

DIAGRAM 3

Making the Blocks

Review "Assembly-Line Piecing" on page 234 before you get started. Pay close attention that corner triangles are positioned as shown in the diagrams. Be sure to use ¼-inch seam allowances and press as you go in the direction indicated by the arrow in each diagram. You will be making a total of four Stocking blocks.

Step 1. Sew four 1 × 3½-inch Fabric D pieces to four 3½ × 4-inch Fabric C pieces. See **Diagram 4**. Press.

DIAGRAM 4

Step 2. Sew four 3½ × 4½-inch Fabric A pieces to the four Step 1 units, as shown in **Diagram 5**. Press.

DIAGRAM 5

Step 3. Sew four 2½ × 8½-inch Fabric B pieces to the four Step 2 units. See **Diagram 6**. Press.

DIAGRAM 6

Step 4. Sew four 4½ × 5½-inch Fabric A/B corner triangle units to

the four Step 3 units. See **Diagram 7**. Press. Your blocks should now measure 5½ × 12½ inches.

DIAGRAM 7

Lattice

Step 1. Lay out the stocking blocks in a pleasing arrangement. Keep track of your layout while sewing on the lattice.

Step 2. Sew 1 × 12½-inch Fabric B lattice strips to the right (heel) side of all but the right-hand stocking block. See **Diagram 8**. Press all seams toward the lattice.

DIAGRAM 8

Step 3. Sew together the three stocking blocks with lattice. Add the stocking block without lattice to the right end of the row. See **Diagram 9**. Press.

Step 4. Sew 1½ × 22-inch lattice strips to the quilt top and bottom. Press. Sew 1½ × 14½-inch lattice strips to the quilt sides. Press.

DIAGRAM 9

Half-Inch Accent Border

Sew 1 × 24-inch Fabric E accent border strips to the top and bottom of the quilt. Press all seams toward the accent border. Sew 1 × 15½-inch Fabric E strips to the quilt sides. Press.

Scrap Border

Step 1. Using scraps of Fabrics A, C, and D, cut several 8-inch strips. Strips should vary in width from 1¼ to 2½ inches wide. Piece them together to make an 8 × 25½-inch strip set. See **Diagram 10.** Change sewing direction with each strip sewn and press seams in one direction.

Step 2. From this strip set, cut four 1½ × 25½-inch strips, referring to the cutting lines in **Diagram 10.**

Step 3. Pin in position and sew the scrap border strips to the quilt top and bottom. Press all seams toward the accent border.

Step 4. Trim the two remaining scrap border strips to measure

1½ × 17½ inches. Pin in position and sew these scrap border strips to the quilt sides. Press.

Outer Border

Sew 1½ × 27-inch Fabric B outer border strips to the quilt top and bottom. Press all seams toward the outer border. Sew 1½ × 19½-inch Fabric B strips to the quilt sides. Press.

> ### ♥ SEW CREATIVE ♥
>
> When quilting inside each of the stockings, stitch a different pattern, such as a stripe, a grid, or circles. Look in your quilting template collection for quilting patterns that may complement the different fabric prints of your stockings.

Appliqué

Refer to "Timesaving Methods for Appliqué" on page 237 to decide which technique you will use. Quick-fuse Penstitch appliqué was the method used in the project shown. Be sure to use heavy-weight, nonsewable appliqué film for this technique. Use the **Large Stocking Appliqué Patterns** on page 125, and appliqué a design on the top of each stocking. Refer to the photograph on page 117 and the **Quilt Layout** on page 118 for placement.

Layering the Quilt

Arrange and baste together the backing, batting, and top, following the directions in "Layering the Quilt" on page 245. Trim the batting and backing to ¼ inch from the raw edge of the quilt top.

Binding the Quilt

Using the four 2¾ × 44-inch binding strips, follow the directions on page 246 for "Binding the Quilt."

Finishing Stitches

Machine or hand quilt in the seam line around the stockings. Quilt in the seam line on each side of the stocking accent strips and on each side of the accent border and scrap border. Outline the appliqué designs by quilting ¹⁄₁₆ inch away from the edge of the designs. Quilt a 1½-inch diagonal grid in the background, extending the grid into the outer border.

Festive Flourishes

Make a light-color Stocking block using the directions for the Twinkle Toes quilt on page 122, or trace the stocking shape on page 89 in Trim-a-Tree to create a special label for the back of the quilt. Or make a Twinkle Toe block, cut a piece of backing fabric, sew with right sides together, and turn. Use this as a gift tag when you wrap the quilt; the lucky recipient will receive not only a quilt but a tree ornament as well!

25½"

8"

1½"

CUTTING LINES

DIAGRAM 10

Twinkle Toes

Finished Quilt: 15½ × 16½ inches
Finished Block: 2½ × 6 inches

MINIATURE QUILT LAYOUT

Materials

FABRIC A
Use four fabrics.
Stocking Foot   ⅛ yard
each of *four* fabrics

FABRIC B
Block Background   ⅛ yard
Lattice   ⅛ yard
Binding   ⅛ yard
   TOTAL   ⅓ yard

FABRIC C
Use four fabrics.
Stocking Top   ⅛ yard
each of *four* fabrics

FABRIC D
Use four fabrics.
Stocking Accent Strip   ⅛ yard
each of *four* fabrics

BACKING   ½ yard

LIGHTWEIGHT BATTING   ½ yard

APPLIQUÉ DESIGNS
Several coordinated scraps

NOTIONS AND SUPPLIES
Appliqué film, nonsewable
Black, extra-fine point, permanent
   felt-tip pen

Cutting Directions

Prewash and press all your fabrics. Using a rotary cutter, see-through ruler, and cutting mat, prepare the strips as described in the first column in the chart below. Then from those strips, cut the pieces listed in the second column. Some strips need to be cut only once, so no additional cutting information will appear in the second column. Measurements for all pieces include ¼-inch seam allowance.

	FIRST CUT		SECOND CUT	
	NO. OF STRIPS	DIMENSIONS	NO. OF PIECES	DIMENSIONS
FABRIC A	**Stocking Foot:** from *each* of the *four* fabrics, cut the following			
	1	2½ × 11-inch strip	2	2½ × 2-inch pieces
			2	2½ × 3-inch pieces
FABRIC B	**Block Background**			
	1	2 × 44-inch strip	8	2-inch squares
			8	1½-inch squares
			8	1-inch squares
	1	1½ × 44-inch strip	8	1½ × 4½-inch pieces
	Lattice			
	3	1 × 44-inch strips	2	1 × 14-inch strips
			3	1 × 12-inch strips
			6	1 × 6½-inch strips
	Binding			
	2	1½ × 44-inch strips	2	1½ × 17-inch strips
			2	1½ × 14-inch strips

FIRST CUT		SECOND CUT	
NO. OF STRIPS	**DIMENSIONS**	**NO. OF PIECES**	**DIMENSIONS**
FABRIC C	**Stocking Top:** from *each* of the *four* fabrics, cut the following		
2	2 × 2¼-inch pieces		
FABRIC D	**Stocking Accent Strip:** from *each* of the *four* fabrics, cut the following		
2	¾ × 2-inch pieces		

Quick Corner Triangles

Refer to "Making Quick Corner Triangles" on page 234. You will be making eight Stocking blocks, two each of four different fabric combinations. Before you start sewing, coordinate the fabrics for each of the four combinations; keep track of them as you sew. Refer to the **Fabric Key** for fabric identification, and press all seams in the direction of the triangle just added.

Fabric Key

FABRIC A (Stocking Foot)
FABRIC B (Background)
FABRIC C (Stocking Top)
FABRIC D (Stocking Accent Strip)

Step 1. Sew eight 1½-inch Fabric B squares to eight 2½ × 3-inch Fabric A pieces. See **Diagram 11.** Press.

DIAGRAM 11

Step 2. Sew eight 2-inch Fabric B squares to the eight Step 2 units. See **Diagram 12.** Press.

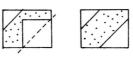

DIAGRAM 12

Step 3. Sew eight 1-inch Fabric B squares to the eight Step 3 units. See **Diagram 13.** Press.

DIAGRAM 13

Making the Blocks

Review "Assembly-Line Piecing" on page 234 before you get started. Pay close attention that the corner triangles are positioned as shown in the diagrams. Be sure to use ¼-inch seam allowances and press as you go. Follow the arrows in the diagrams for pressing direction. You will be making a total of eight Stocking blocks.

SEW SMART

When sewing a narrow ¾-inch strip, use a ¼-inch seam and then trim the seam allowance to ⅛ inch before pressing. This prevents the seam allowances from overlapping.

Step 1. Sew eight 2 × 2¼-inch Fabric C pieces to eight ¾ × 2-inch Fabric D pieces. See **Diagram 14.** Press.

2"
2¼"
¾"

DIAGRAM 14

Step 2. Sew eight 2 × 2½-inch Fabric A pieces to the eight Step 1 units. See **Diagram 15.** Press.

STEP 1 UNIT
2½"
2"

DIAGRAM 15

Step 3. Sew eight 1½ × 4½-inch Fabric B pieces to the eight Step 2 units. See **Diagram 16.** Press.

1½"
4½"
STEP 2 UNIT

DIAGRAM 16

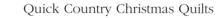

Step 4. Sew eight 2½ × 3-inch Fabric A/B corner triangle units to the eight Step 3 units, as shown in **Diagram 17**. Press. Your blocks should now measure 3 × 6½ inches.

STEP 3 UNIT

2½"

3"

DIAGRAM 17

Lattice

Step 1. Lay out the stocking blocks in a pleasing arrangement, with two rows of four blocks each. Keep track of your layout while sewing on the lattice.

Step 2. Sew 1 × 6½-inch Fabric B lattice strips to the right (heel) side of all the stocking blocks except the right-hand block from each row. See **Diagram 18**. Press all seams toward the lattice.

1"

6½"

DIAGRAM 18

Step 3. For each row, sew together the three blocks with lattice. To the right end of one row, add the block without lattice. Repeat to make two rows of four blocks. Press.

Step 4. Sew 1 × 12-inch Fabric B lattice strips to the bottom of both rows and to the top of the top row. Press seams toward the lattice. Stitch the two rows together. Press.

Step 5. Sew 1 × 14-inch Fabric B lattice strips to the sides. Press.

Scrap Border

Step 1. Using scraps of Fabrics A, C, and D, cut several 6-inch strips. The strips should vary in width from 1¼ to 2¼ inches. Piece the strips together to make a 6 × 15-inch strip set. See **Diagram 19**. Change sewing direction with each strip sewn, and press seams in one direction.

CUTTING LINES

15"

6"

1"

DIAGRAM 19

Step 2. From this strip set, cut four 1 × 15-inch strips, referring the cutting lines in **Diagram 19**.

Step 3. Trim two strips to measure 1 × 13 inches. Pin in position and sew these scrap border strips to the quilt top and bottom. Press all seams toward the lattice.

Step 4. Pin in position and sew 1 × 15-inch scrap border strips to the quilt sides. Press.

Binding

Sew 1½ × 14-inch Fabric B binding strips to the quilt top and bottom. Press all seams toward the binding. Sew 1½ × 17-inch Fabric B strips to the quilt sides. Press.

Appliqué

Refer to "Timesaving Methods for Appliqué" on page 237 to decide which technique you will use. Quick-fuse was the method used in the project shown. Be sure to use heavyweight, nonsewable appliqué film for this technique. Use the **Miniature Stocking Appliqué Patterns** on the opposite page, and appliqué a design on the top of each stocking. Refer to the photograph on page 117 for placement.

Finishing

Step 1. Position the top and backing with right sides together. Lay both pieces on top of the batting, and pin all three layers together. Trim the batting and backing to the same size as the top. Sew together, leaving a 3- to 4-inch opening for turning.

Step 2. Trim the corners, turn right side out, hand stitch the opening, and press.

Step 3. Machine or hand quilt in the seam line around each stocking, each stocking accent strip, and both sides of the scrap border. Quilt a 1-inch diagonal grid in the background.

Festive Flourishes

Gently roll up the little Twinkle Toes quilt, tie it with a piece of star garland or some other festive ribbon, and slip it inside your recipient's Christmas stocking.

MINIATURE STOCKING APPLIQUÉ PATTERNS

Appliqué Pattern Key

——————— TRACING LINE

----------- TRACING LINE
(will be hidden behind other fabric)

LARGE STOCKING APPLIQUÉ PATTERNS

Snowman Samplers

27½"

23"

LARGE SNOWMAN LAYOUT

Large Snowman Sampler

Finished Size: 27½ × 23 inches

Why venture out into the cold to make your next snowman? Stay inside at your sewing machine, where it's cozy and warm, to create one of these snowman wallhangings. Use buttons and buttonhole embroidery to embellish the large sampler or the single snowman. The miniature sampler is a breeze, thanks to quick-fuse appliqué. Have fun with these wintertime friends, but remember— no snowball fights indoors!

Festive Flourishes

Wrap the package with a "snowy" textured fabric and tie it up with a homespun plaid strip of fabric. Fray the ends so it looks like a plaid scarf. Glue a variety of black buttons onto the package.

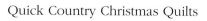

Materials and Cutting

Using a rotary cutter, see-through ruler, and cutting mat, prepare the pieces as described in the chart below. Measurements for all pieces include ¼-inch seam allowances.

	YARDAGE	CUTTING	
		NO. OF PIECES	**DIMENSIONS**
Background	¼ yard *each* of *six* different fabrics	1	6½ × 9½-inch piece (Block #1)
		1	6½ × 7-inch piece (Block #2)
		1	8 × 5-inch piece (Block #3)
		1	8 × 11½-inch piece (Block #4)
		1	6½ × 8-inch piece (Block #5)
		1	6½ × 8½-inch piece (Block #6)
Lattice	⅙ yard (6 inches; cut into four 1 × 44-inch strips)	2	1 × 21-inch strips
		2	1 × 17½-inch strips
		2	1 × 16½-inch strips
		1	1 × 8-inch strip
		2	1 × 6½-inch strips
Border	⅜ yard	4	3 × 44-inch strips
Binding	⅓ yard	4	2¾ × 44-inch strips
Backing	¾ yard		
Lightweight Batting	¾ yard		
Appliqué Pieces	⅛-yard pieces or several coordinated scraps		

Appliqué film, sewable
Embroidery floss to match appliqué fabrics
Assorted buttons and beads

Buttonhole Appliqué

The designs on the Large Snowman Sampler were designed especially to use the technique described in "Buttonhole Embroidery Appliqué" on page 240. However, you may use quick-fuse or machine appliqué if you prefer.

Step 1. Trace one of each of the six large-block snowman designs from the **Snowman Appliqué Patterns** on pages 133–139. Buttonhole embroider the designs to the center of each of the corresponding background pieces.

Step 2. Hand sew assorted buttons and beads to the snowmen for eyes, mouths, and buttons. Specifics for each design are listed with the individual appliqué designs.

SEW SMART

Be sure to use a *sewable* appliqué film for the buttonhole embroidery or machine appliqué technique. Use a heavier-weight *nonsewable* appliqué film for quick-fuse appliqué.

SEW SMART

It is easier to complete the buttonhole embroidery for each block before you assemble the wallhanging top. And that way, your blocks will be portable—you can keep them with you and work on them whenever you find a few spare minutes.

Background Assembly

Use accurate ¼-inch seam allowances, and press all seams toward the lattice after each sewing step.

Step 1. Sew a 1 × 6½-inch lattice strip between Block #1 and Block #2. See **Diagram 1.** Press.

6½"

#1   9½"

1"

#2   7"

DIAGRAM 1

Step 2. Sew the 1 × 8-inch lattice strip between Block #3 and Block #4. See **Diagram 2.** Press.

Step 3. Sew a 1 × 6½-inch lattice strip between Block #5 and Block #6. See **Diagram 3.** Press.

Step 4. Sew 1 × 16½-inch lattice strips to the sides of the Step 2 unit. See **Diagram 4.** Press.

Step 5. Sew the Step 1 unit to the left side of the Step 4 unit. Press.

Sew the Step 3 unit to the right side of the same unit. Press. See **Diagram 5.**

Step 6. Sew 1 × 21-inch lattice strips to the wallhanging top and bottom. Press.

8"

#3   5"

1"

#4   11½"

DIAGRAM 2

6½"

#5   8"

1"

#6   8½"

DIAGRAM 3

1" STEP 2 UNIT 1"

#3

16½"   #4   16½"

DIAGRAM 4

STEP 1 UNIT   STEP 4 UNIT   STEP 3 UNIT

#1   #3   #5

#2   #4   #6

DIAGRAM 5

Step 7. Sew 1 × 17½-inch lattice strips to the wallhanging sides. Press.

Border

Sew 3 × 44-inch border strips to the wallhanging top and bottom. Trim the excess and press all seams toward the border. Sew 3 × 44-inch border strips to the wallhanging sides. Trim the excess and press.

Layering the Quilt

Arrange and baste together the backing, batting, and top, following the directions in "Layering the Quilt" on page 245. Trim the batting and backing to ¼ inch from the raw edge of the quilt top.

Binding the Quilt

Using the four 2¾ × 44-inch binding strips, follow the directions in "Binding the Quilt" on page 246.

Finishing Stitches

Machine or hand quilt in the seam line around the background pieces and borders. Outline the appliqué designs by quilting 1/16 inch away from the edge of the designs. Quilt a 1½-inch diagonal grid in the border.

Miniature Snowman Sampler

Finished Size: 20 × 17 inches

Materials and Cutting

Using a rotary cutter, see-through ruler, and cutting mat, prepare the pieces as described in the chart below. Measurements for all pieces include ¼-inch seam allowances.

MINIATURE SNOWMAN LAYOUT

	YARDAGE	NO. OF PIECES	CUTTING — DIMENSIONS
Background	⅛- to ¼-yard pieces of *six* different fabrics	1	4½ × 6½-inch piece (Block #1)
		1	4½ × 5-inch piece (Block #2)
		1	5½ × 3½-inch piece (Block #3)
		1	5½ × 8-inch piece (Block #4)
		1	4½ × 5½-inch piece (Block #5)
		1	4½ × 6-inch piece (Block #6)
Lattice	⅛ yard (cut into three 1 × 44-inch strips)	2	1 × 14½-inch strips
		2	1 × 12½-inch strips
		2	1 × 11½-inch strips
		1	1 × 5½-inch strip
		2	1 × 4½-inch strips
Border	⅙ yard (6 inches; cut into two 2½ × 44-inch strips)	2	2½ × 16½-inch strips
		2	2½ × 15½-inch strips
Binding	⅛ yard (cut into two 1 × 44-inch strips)	2	1 × 19½-inch strips
		2	1 × 17½-inch strips
Backing	⅝ yard		
Lightweight Batting	⅝ yard		
Appliqué Pieces	⅛-yard pieces or several coordinated scraps		

Appliqué film, nonsewable
Black, extra-fine point, permanent felt-tip pen

Background Assembly

For this project, you will assemble the wallhanging top *before* fusing the appliqué pieces. Use accurate ¼-inch seam allowances, and press all seams toward the lattice after each sewing step.

Step 1. Sew a 1 × 4½-inch lattice strip between Block #1 and Block #2. See **Diagram 6**. Press.

DIAGRAM 6

Step 2. Sew the 1 × 5½-inch lattice strip between Block #3 and Block #4. See **Diagram 7**. Press.

DIAGRAM 7

Step 3. Sew a 1 × 4½-inch lattice strip between Block #5 and Block #6. See **Diagram 8**. Press.

DIAGRAM 8

Step 4. Sew 1 × 11½-inch lattice strips to the sides of the Step 2 unit. See **Diagram 9**. Press.

DIAGRAM 9

Step 5. Sew the Step 1 unit to the left side of the Step 4 unit. Press. Sew the Step 3 unit to the right side of the same unit. Press. See **Diagram 10.**

DIAGRAM 10

Step 6. Sew 1 × 14½-inch lattice strips to the wallhanging top and bottom. Press.

Step 7. Sew 1 × 12½-inch lattice strips to the wallhanging sides. Press.

Border

Sew 2½ × 15½-inch border strips to the wallhanging top and bottom. Press all seams toward the border. Sew 2½ × 16½-inch border strips to the wallhanging sides. Press.

Binding

Sew 1 × 19½-inch binding strips to the wallhanging top and bottom.

Press all seams toward the binding. Sew 1 × 17½-inch binding strips to the wallhanging sides. Press.

Quick-Fuse Penstitch Appliqué

Refer to "Penstitch Appliqué" on page 239.

Step 1. Trace one of each of the six miniature-block snowman designs from the **Snowman Appliqué Patterns** on pages 133–139.

Step 2. Quick-fuse appliqué the designs in the center of each corresponding background piece. Position and fuse one design at a time, using the photograph on page 126 and the **Miniature Snowman Layout** on page 130 as placement guides.

Step 3. Use the felt-tip pen to mark Penstitch details and to draw eyes, noses, and mouths.

Finishing

Step 1. Position the top and backing with right sides together. Lay both pieces on top of the batting, and pin all three layers together. Using a ¼-inch seam allowance, sew them together, leaving a 3- to 4-inch opening for turning. Trim the backing and batting to the same size as the top.

Step 2. Trim the corners, turn right side out, hand stitch the opening closed, and press.

Step 3. Machine or hand quilt in the seam line around the lattice, border, and binding. Outline the appliqué designs by quilting 1/16 inch away from the edge of the designs. Quilt a 1¼-inch diagonal grid in the border.

SINGLE SNOWMAN LAYOUT

12½"

16"

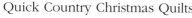

Single Snowman Wallhanging

Finished Size: 12½ × 16 inches

Materials and Cutting

Using a rotary cutter, see-through ruler, and cutting mat, prepare the pieces as described in the chart below. Measurements for all pieces include ¼-inch seam allowances.

	YARDAGE	CUTTING	
		NO. OF PIECES	**DIMENSIONS**
Background	⅓ yard	1	9 × 12½-inch piece
Accent Border	⅛ yard (cut into two 1 × 44-inch strips)	2	1 × 13½-inch strips
		2	1 × 9-inch strips
Wide Border	⅙ yard (6 inches; cut into two 2 × 44-inch strips)	2	2 × 16½-inch strips
		2	2 × 10-inch strips
Backing	½ yard		
Cotton Batting	15 × 19-inch piece		
Appliqué Pieces	⅛-yard pieces or several coordinated scraps		
Appliqué film, sewable Embroidery floss to match appliqué fabrics Assorted buttons Wooden dowel or twig for hanging			

Buttonhole Appliqué

The Single Snowman Wallhanging was designed especially to use the technique described in "Buttonhole Embroidery Appliqué" on page 240. The design was fused to the background piece and the buttonhole embroidery completed before the borders were added. You may choose quick-fuse or machine appliqué techniques if you prefer.

Step 1. Trace the snowman design for large block #4 from the **Snowman Appliqué Patterns,** shown on page 137.

Step 2. Buttonhole embroider the design to the center of the background piece. Be sure to use a *sewable* appliqué film for the buttonhole embroidery technique.

Accent Border

Sew 1 × 9-inch accent border strips to the top and bottom of the background piece. Press all seams toward the accent border. Sew 1 × 13½-inch accent border strips to the sides of the background piece. Press.

♥ SEW CREATIVE ♥

For a more "woodsy" feel, use a twig instead of a dowel to run through the hanging tabs. The twig should be 3 to 4 inches longer than the width of the quilt.

Wide Border

Sew 2 × 10-inch wide border strips to the wallhanging top and bottom. Press all seams toward the wide border. Sew 2 × 16½-inch wide border strips to the wall-hanging sides. Press.

Finishing

Step 1. To make the hanging tabs, cut one 2 × 10-inch strip of fabric from a scrap. Fold in half length-wise with wrong sides together, and press. Fold each long edge into the center fold and press again. Topstitch along the edge of both sides of the fabric strip.

Step 2. Using a ruler and rotary cutter, cut two 4½-inch pieces from the strip. Fold each piece in half so the cut ends meet. Press.

Step 3. On the right side of the wallhanging top, place the tabs ap-proximately 2½ inches in from each side and pin in position. Position the tabs with the raw edges even with the raw edge of the wallhanging. Baste the tabs into place. They will be sewn into the seam when the wallhanging is finished.

Step 4. Position the top and backing with right sides together. Lay both pieces on top of the bat-ting, and pin all three layers to-gether. Using a ¼-inch seam al-lowance, sew them together, leaving a 3- to 4-inch opening for turning. Trim the backing and bat-ting to the same size as the top.

Step 5. Trim the corners, turn right side out, hand stitch the opening, and press.

Step 6. Machine or hand quilt in the seam line around both sides of the accent border. Outline the ap-pliqué design by quilting ⅟₁₆ inch away from the edge of the design. Hand sew two ⅛-inch black but-tons to the snowman for eyes, and sew assorted buttons to the border.

MINIATURE BLOCK #3

MINIATURE BLOCK #2

Appliqué Pattern Key

———— TRACING LINE

– – – – – – – TRACING LINE
(will be hidden behind other fabric)

SNOWMAN APPLIQUÉ PATTERNS

SNOWMAN APPLIQUÉ PATTERNS

Appliqué Pattern Key

———————— TRACING LINE

- - - - - - - - TRACING LINE
(will be hidden behind
other fabric)

MINIATURE BLOCK #6

BLACK SEED
BEADS

LARGE BLOCK #2

MINIATURE BLOCK #1

MINIATURE BLOCK #4

SNOWMAN APPLIQUÉ PATTERNS

SNOWMAN APPLIQUÉ PATTERN

Appliqué Pattern Key

———————— TRACING LINE

- - - - - - - TRACING LINE
(will be hidden behind
other fabric)

¹/₈" BLACK BUTTONS

BLACK SEED
BEADS

GOLD BELL

BUTTONS

LARGE BLOCK #1

¹/₈" BLACK BUTTONS

BLACK SEED BEADS

BUTTONS

Make fringe with straight stitches, or draw with permanent pen.

LARGE BLOCK #4

SNOWMAN APPLIQUÉ PATTERN

Appliqué Pattern Key

———————— TRACING LINE

‑ ‑ ‑ ‑ ‑ ‑ ‑ TRACING LINE
(will be hidden behind other fabric)

MINIATURE BLOCK #5

SNOWMAN APPLIQUÉ PATTERNS

1/8" BLACK BEADS

BLACK SEED BEADS

LARGE BLOCK #5

LARGE BLOCK #3

BUTTON

BUTTON

BLACK
SEED
BEAD
NOSE

1/8" BLACK
BEADS

LARGE BLOCK #6

BUTTON

Draw
lines with
permanent
pen.

SNOWMAN APPLIQUÉ PATTERNS

Pine Tree Lodge

This collection of projects was designed to bring the comfort and rustic charm of a warm and cozy lodge into your home for the holidays. Let your mind wander to that rough-hewn mountain lodge amidst the tall pines as you work on these quick and easy projects.

Before you begin, take a minute to read through this checklist. These are important pointers you should keep in mind to make sure that each of your quilts is a success.

★ Be sure to read "Techniques for Quick Country Quilting," beginning on page 226. This will familiarize you with the tools you'll need; the techniques for time-saving cutting, piecing, and appliqué; and finishing instructions.

★ Check the "Festive Flourishes" box for each project to get clever and unique ideas for packaging and wrapping your gift.

★ Take advantage of the helpful hints in the "Sew Smart" boxes. Here you'll find tips for making a technique quicker or easier.

★ Prewash and press all of your fabrics. Washing will remove any sizing from the fabrics, and pressing ensures accuracy when cutting.

★ Read the step-by-step directions from start to finish, and look at all the diagrams before you cut and sew any fabric.

★ Always use a ¼-inch seam allowance, unless there is a special note that tells you a different seam allowance is required.

★ Refer to the **Fabric Key** for each project as a help in following the diagrams.

★ Pay attention to the pressing directions given in the step-by-step text and to the pressing arrows shown in the diagrams.

$\mathscr{P}$ine Tree Lodge Ornaments

Although these ornaments look as though they could have been hand stitched by the light of a kerosene lamp, you can make six of them in the same amount of time it would have taken your grandmother to make one, thanks to today's quick-cutting and quick-piecing techniques.

Button Ornament

Finished Size: 2½ inches square

Making the Ornaments

Throughout this section, refer to the **Fabric Key** to identify the fabric placements in the diagrams. It's a good idea to review "Assembly-Line Piecing" on page 234 before you get started. It's more efficient to do the same step for each ornament at the same time than to piece an entire ornament together at one time. Be sure to use ¼-inch seam allowances and press as you go. Follow the arrows in the diagrams for pressing direction. You will be making six ornaments.

Fabric Key

FABRIC A
(Center Square)

FABRIC B
(Borders)

FABRIC C
(Corner Squares)

Materials and Cutting

(for six ornaments)

Using a rotary cutter, see-through ruler, and cutting mat, prepare the pieces as described in the chart below. Measurements for all pieces include ¼-inch seam allowances.

	YARDAGE	CUTTING	
		NO. OF PIECES	**DIMENSIONS**
Fabric A Center Square	⅛ yard	1	2 × 15-inch strip
Fabric B Backing	⅙ yard (6 inches)	6	3-inch squares
Border		1	2 × 15-inch strip
		2	1 × 15-inch strips
Fabric C Corner Squares	⅛ yard	2	1 × 15-inch strips

1 yard jute for hangers
Smooth stuffing, like polyester fiberfill (not shredded foam)
Six assorted buttons, approximately ¾-inch diameter
Crochet thread

Step 1. Sew one 1 × 15-inch Fabric B strip to each side of one 2 × 15-inch Fabric A strip. Press seams toward Fabric B. Use a rotary cutter and ruler to cut six 3 × 2-inch pieces from this strip set. See **Diagram 1.**

DIAGRAM 1

Step 2. Sew one 1 × 15-inch Fabric C strip to each side of one 2 × 15-inch Fabric B strip. Press seams toward Fabric B. Use a rotary cutter and ruler to cut twelve 3 × 1-inch pieces from this strip set. See **Diagram 2.**

DIAGRAM 2

Step 3. Sew the twelve 3 × 1-inch Fabric B/C units to the top and bottom of six 3 × 2-inch Fabric A/B units. See **Diagram 3.** Press seams toward the Fabric B/C units.

DIAGRAM 3

Step 4. Cut six 5-inch pieces of jute for hangers. Make a loop and center it along the top of the pieced ornament, positioning the cut ends of the jute even with the raw edges of the ornament. Pin and baste in place. See **Diagram 4.**

DIAGRAM 4

Step 5. Position the ornament front and the 3-inch backing square with right sides together.

Pin and sew them together, leaving an opening at the bottom for turning. Trim the corners, turn right side out, and press. Stuff lightly with polyester fiberfill. Slip

stitch the opening closed.

Step 6. Center a button on the front of the ornament. Starting and ending in front, sew the button in

place through all the layers with one strand of crochet thread. Tie the ends of the thread in a knot on the top of the button. Trim threads to ¼ inch.

Pine Tree Ornament

Finished Size: 3 × 4 inches

Materials and Cutting

Using a rotary cutter, see-through ruler, and cutting mat, prepare the pieces as described in the chart below. Measurements for all pieces

include ¼-inch seam allowances. **Note:** The fabrics and supplies listed below will make several ornaments. If you plan to make just one, this is a good project to use up your scraps! The cutting and directions given are for making one ornament.

	YARDAGE	NO. OF PIECES	CUTTING — DIMENSIONS
Fabric A Tree	⅛ yard	2	1½ × 2½-inch pieces
Fabric B Background	⅛ yard	4	1½-inch squares
		2	1½ × 1¼-inch pieces
Fabric C Trunk	⅛ yard	1	1 × 1½-inch piece
Border	⅛ yard		**Before You Cut:** Cut the backing piece first.
		2	1 × 4½-inch squares
		2	1 × 2½-inch pieces
Backing		1	3½ × 4½-inch piece

⅔ yard jute for hanger
Smooth stuffing, like polyester fiberfill (not shredded foam)
Four assorted buttons, ⅜- to ½-inch diameter
Glue

Quick Corner Triangles

Refer to "Making Quick Corner Triangles" on page 234 for how to make corner triangle units. Refer to the **Fabric Key,** and press in the direction of the triangle just added. For clarity, seam allowances are shown in the diagrams.

Fabric Key

FABRIC A
(Tree)

FABRIC B
(Background)

FABRIC C
(Trunk)

Step 1. Sew two 1½-inch Fabric B squares to two 1½ × 2½-inch Fabric A pieces. See **Diagram 5.** Press.

DIAGRAM 5

Step 2. Sew two additional 1½-inch Fabric B squares to the opposite end of the Fabric A/B corner traingle units. See **Diagram 6.** Press.

DIAGRAM 6

Assembling the Tree

Be sure to use accurate ¼-inch seam allowances and press as you go. Follow the arrows in the diagrams for pressing direction.

Step 1. Sew the two Fabric A/B corner triangle units together. See **Diagram 7.** Press.

DIAGRAM 7

Step 2. Sew one 1¼ × 1½-inch Fabric B piece to each side of one 1 × 1½-inch Fabric C piece. See **Diagram 8.** Press.

DIAGRAM 8

Step 3. Sew the Step 1 unit to the Step 2 unit. See **Diagram 9.** Press.

DIAGRAM 9

Assembling the Ornament

Step 1. Sew 1 × 2½-inch border strips to the top and bottom of the tree. Press seams toward the border. Sew 1 × 4½-inch border strips to the sides. Press.

Step 2. Cut two 12-inch pieces of jute for hangers. Pin each piece in place on the border seam, with the cut edges even with the top of the ornament. See **Diagram 10.** Baste the jute in place.

DIAGRAM 10

Step 3. Position the ornament front and the 3½ × 4½-inch backing piece with right sides together. Pin and sew them together, leaving an opening at the bottom for turning. Trim the corners, turn right side out, and press. Stuff lightly with polyester fiberfill. Slip stitch the opening closed.

Step 4. Glue a button on each corner. Tie the jute in a loose bow for the hanger.

Festive Flourishes

Line a rustic basket with a homespun plaid, and fill it with an assortment of ornaments. Mix in some pinecones and potpourri. Or for the hiker or backpacker on your list, include an assortment of these ornaments with a gift of a trail guide, some woolly hiking socks, or a subscription to *Backpacker* magazine.

Country Cotton Ornaments

Add a handcrafted, homespun touch to your Christmas tree with ornaments made using cotton batting. They're so quick and fun that you can easily make them all on a Saturday afternoon (perhaps with a holiday video like *White Christmas* to help set the mood!). The designs include a woolly mitten, cozy cottage, plaid Christmas tree, Mr. Moon, striped stocking, and fanciful fish. Finish them with a running stitch of black embroidery floss and then trim. What could be easier?

Materials (for one ornament)

ORNAMENT FRONT AND BACK   ⅛- to ¼-yard pieces
Note: Fabric requirements vary between two 3 × 5-inch and two 5 × 7-inch pieces.

APPLIQUÉ DESIGN DETAILS
Several coordinated scraps or ⅛-yard pieces

COTTON BATTING
5 × 7-inch piece
Note: I prefer Warm and Natural cotton batting.

NOTIONS AND SUPPLIES
Appliqué film, sewable
Black embroidery floss
Assorted buttons, ⅛- to ⅝-inch diameter

Making the Ornaments

Use the **Ornament Appliqué Patterns** on pages 148–149.

Step 1. Cut the ornament front and back fabric and the batting into pieces, from 3 × 5 inches to 5 × 7 inches, depending on which ornament you are making.

Step 2. On the paper side of sewable appliqué film, trace around the entire outside edge (heavier line) of the ornament design.

Step 3. Cut the appliqué film loosely around the traced ornament design. See **Diagram 1**.

DIAGRAM 1

Step 4. Fuse the traced pattern to the wrong side of the fabric that will be the front of the ornament. Cut the traced pattern out, cutting on the drawn line. See **Diagram 2.** Remove the paper backing from these pieces. A thin fusing film will remain on the fabric.

DIAGRAM 2

Step 5. Fuse the ornament front to the cotton batting.

Step 6. Trace the design details (heel, toe, heart, fins, door, windows, roof, moon) for the ornament you have selected onto the paper side of sewable appliqué film. Cut the appliqué film loosely around the traced design details and fuse to the wrong side of selected design detail fabrics. Cut

out the design details, remove the paper backing, and fuse to the ornament fronts.

Step 7. Position the ornament front (now fused to the batting) on top of the wrong side of the ornament back fabric. Pin together. Using two strands of black embroidery floss, hand sew the layers together with a running stitch. The stitches should be approximately ¼ inch long and ⅛ inch from the edge of the ornament front.

Step 8. Trim the batting and ornament backing to the same shape as the ornament front.

Decorative Touches

Additional design details can be added by gluing buttons to some of the ornaments. You may substitute fabric pieces for buttons if you prefer. Use the photograph on the opposite page or the **Ornament Appliqué Patterns** on pages 148–149 as placement guides.

• **Tree:** Glue five buttons (¼- to ⅜-inch diameter) to the tree.

• **Stocking:** Glue three buttons (approximately ¼-inch diameter) to the top of the stocking.

• **House:** Add a running stitch around the roof edge.

• **Fish:** Glue on a ⅛-inch black button for an eye.

• **Mitten:** Glue a button (approximately ⅜-inch diameter) in the middle of the heart.

Hangers

Thread a needle with a 5-inch length of two strands of black embroidery floss. Pull through the top of the ornament. Tie the loose ends in a knot.

Festive Flourishes

A basket brimming with these handmade ornaments would be a welcome gift to someone who's just starting out and doesn't have a collection of Christmas trimmings yet.

Or make a welcoming holiday wreath that a new neighbor or good friend can use from year to year. Find a 16- to 18-inch-diameter artificial pine wreath. Make a set of ornaments, and attach them to the wreath. Tie bows onto the wreath branches to fill in the spaces between the ornaments, making the bows from narrow grosgrain ribbons or thin strips torn from homespun fabrics. For a wreath that jingles with holiday spirit, attach tiny bells to the ends of the bows.

ORNAMENT APPLIQUÉ PATTERNS

BUTTON

BUTTONS

ORNAMENT APPLIQUÉ PATTERNS

Appliqué Pattern Key

———— TRACING LINE
(Heavier line is outside ornament tracing line.)

BUTTONS

BUTTON

Rustic Twig Ornaments

These easy, no-sew twig ornaments have the look of primitive, handcrafted folk art that's so popular now. They give you the perfect chance to use up scraps of fabric you've been saving. Fuse them to thin cardboard, and embellish with twigs, beads, and raffia hangers.

Finished Size: 3 × 4 inches

Materials (for one ornament)

BACKGROUND FABRIC
Two 4 × 5-inch scraps

APPLIQUÉ PIECES
Several coordinated scraps

NOTIONS AND SUPPLIES
Appliqué film, nonsewable
One 4 × 5-inch piece of light-
  weight cardboard
Two 5-inch twigs and two 4-inch
  twigs
Black seed beads
Black quilting thread
Hot-glue gun or tacky glue
Black, extra-fine point, permanent
  felt-tip pen
8 inches of raffia

Making the Ornaments

Refer to "Quick-Fuse Appliqué" on page 238.

Step 1. Fuse 4 × 5-inch fabric pieces to both sides of the 4 × 5-inch lightweight cardboard. Fuse one side, turn it over and fuse the second side. Trim the cardboard-and-fabric piece to 3 × 4 inches, using a cork-backed steel-edge ruler and razor blade or an X-Acto knife.

SEW SMART

If you have old rotary blades that are too dull for fabric but still sharp enough to cut cardboard, you could use them with a see-through ruler to cut the cardboard.

Step 2. Trace the desired appliqué design, using the **Twig Ornament Appliqué Patterns** on the opposite page.

Step 3. Quick-fuse appliqué the design in the center of the background piece.

Decorative Touches

• **Duck:** Glue on a black seed bead for the eye.

• **Fish:** Fuse black quilting thread behind heads for fishing line. Glue on a black seed bead for each eye.

• **Deer:** Glue on two black seed beads for eyes and one black seed bead for a nose.

• **Fisherman in Canoe:** Using a permanent felt-tip pen, draw a dot for the fisherman's eye and a straight line for a fishing line.

• **Moose:** Glue on a black seed bead for the eye.

Finishing

Step 1. Glue dry twigs to the edges of the ornament to form a frame.

Step 2. Glue a raffia loop to the center top of the back of the ornament to form a hanger.

Appliqué Pattern Key

———————— TRACING LINE

- - - - - - - - TRACING LINE
(will be hidden behind other fabric)

Fishing line is fused behind fish heads.

Draw line with felt-tip pen.

TWIG ORNAMENT APPLIQUÉ PATTERNS

Christmas Cabin Tree Skirt

31"

TOP

31"

BOTTOM

TREE SKIRT LAYOUT

All the cozy charm of celebrating Christmas in a toasty warm cabin in the woods is captured in this simple-to-make tree skirt. One look at the plaid cabins and it's easy to imagine smoke curling out of the chimneys on a cold winter night. A friendly visiting moose, tall pine, and sliver of moon complete the mood. A border of crisp patchwork points adds just the right touch to frame your Christmas tree.

Finished Size: 31 inches square

Materials

Obvious directional prints are not recommended for borders and binding.

FABRIC A

Patchwork Points Border
(dark color)   ¼ yard

FABRIC B

Background   ⅞ yard
Patchwork Points Border
(light color)   ¼ yard
  TOTAL   1⅛ yards

FABRIC C

Accent Border   ⅙ yard (6 inches)
Corner Squares   ⅛ yard
  TOTAL   ⅙ yard

BINDING   ⅝ yard

BACKING   1 yard

COTTON FLANNEL   1 yard

APPLIQUÉ PIECES

Several coordinated scraps or ⅛- to ¼-yard pieces
Note: The cabins, roofs, and trees require the width of ¼-yard pieces.

NOTIONS AND SUPPLIES

Appliqué film, nonsewable
Bias binding, for center hole (optional)

Cutting Directions

Prewash and press all of your fabrics. Using a rotary cutter, see-through ruler, and cutting mat, prepare the strips as described in the first column in the chart below. Then from those strips, cut the pieces listed in the second column. Some strips need to be cut only once, so no additional cutting information will appear in the second column. Measurements for all pieces include ¼-inch seam allowances.

	FIRST CUT		SECOND CUT	
	NO. OF STRIPS	DIMENSIONS	NO. OF PIECES	DIMENSIONS
FABRIC A	**Patchwork Points Border (dark color)**			
	3	2 × 44-inch strips	36	2 × 3½-inch pieces
FABRIC B	**Background**			
	1	26½-inch square		
	Patchwork Points Border (light color)			
	4	2 × 44-inch strips	72	2-inch squares
FABRIC C	**Before You Cut:** Cut the four 2-inch corner squares first.			
	Corner Squares			
	4	2-inch squares		
	Accent Border			
	2	1 × 27½-inch strips		
	2	1 × 26½-inch strips		

Cutting the Binding

Refer to the **Cutting Diagram for Binding** on page 156. First cut a 1¾ × 16-inch bias strip from the corner of the fabric. Then cut the remaining fabric into six 2¾-inch-wide binding strips.

Note: If you are using purchased bias binding for the center hole binding, then you need to cut only five 2¾ × 44-inch binding strips.

Marking the Background

Before beginning the assembly, the center hole and the back opening must be marked on the 26½-inch background square.

Step 1. Fold the background square in half, with wrong sides together, and press. Fold the piece in half again to form a square. Press again. The center of the background piece is where the two pressed lines meet.

Step 2. Trace the **Circle Template** on page 158 onto template plastic or heavy paper, and cut it out.

Step 3. Place the circle at the folded corner of the square, lining up the center crosshairs with two adjacent folded edges of the square. See **Diagram 1.** Trace around the outer edge of the circle, using a sharp pencil. This marks the cutting line for the center hole. Mark along one of the fold lines from the center to the outer edge. This marks the cutting line for the back opening. **Do not cut yet.** These cutting lines are marked only at this point. (You won't actually make these cuts until you add binding to the completed tree skirt.)

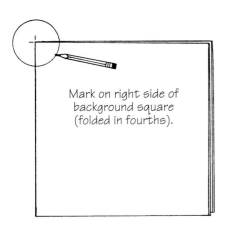

Mark on right side of background square (folded in fourths).

DIAGRAM 1

Half-Inch Accent Border

Sew 1 × 26½-inch Fabric C accent border strips to the top and bottom of the 26½-inch background square. Press all seams toward the accent border. Sew 1 × 27½-inch Fabric C strips to the sides. Press.

Quick Corner Triangles

Refer to "Making Quick Corner Triangles" on page 234 and review "Assembly-Line Piecing" on page 234. You will be making 36 corner triangle units. Refer to the **Fabric Key,** and press seam allowances in the direction of the triangle just added. For clarity, seam allowances are shown in the diagrams.

Fabric Key

▨ FABRIC A

▢ FABRIC B

Step 1. Sew thirty-six 2-inch Fabric B squares to thirty-six 2 × 3½-inch Fabric A pieces. See **Diagram 2.** Press.

3½"

2"

DIAGRAM 2

Step 2. Sew 36 additional 2-inch Fabric B squares to the opposite end of the Fabric A/B corner triangle units. See **Diagram 3.** Press.

DIAGRAM 3

Patchwork Points Border

Step 1. Using the photograph on page 152 and the **Tree Skirt Layout** on page 153 as placement guides, sew the corner triangle units together in four strips, with nine triangle units in each strip. Press all seams in the same direction.

Step 2. Fit, pin in position, and sew the border strips to the tree skirt top and bottom. Press seams toward the accent border.

SEW SMART

To fit the patchwork points border to the tree skirt, measure the border strips against the tree skirt top and bottom. Take in or let out a few seams by 1/16 inch or less to make them fit the tree skirt. After the top and bottom borders are sewn on, add corner squares to the side strips and check them against the sides of the tree skirt. Adjust the same way, if necessary.

Step 3. Sew 2-inch Fabric C corner squares to the ends of the two remaining border strips. Press seams toward the corner squares.

Step 4. Fit, pin, and sew the borders to the tree skirt sides. Press.

Appliqué

Refer to "Quick-Fuse Appliqué" on page 238.

Step 1. Trace three sets of appliqué designs for the tree skirt, using the **Tree Skirt Appliqué Patterns** on pages 157–158.

Step 2. Fuse the designs to the top (front) and side edges of the background square. Begin by centering the cabin approximately 1¼ inches above the accent border. Position and fuse one design grouping at a time. Use the **Tree Skirt Layout** on page 153 and the photograph on page 152 as placement guides. Add Penstitches if you like.

Layering the Tree Skirt

Arrange and baste the backing, cotton flannel, and tree skirt top together, following the directions in "Layering the Quilt" on page 245. Trim the flannel and backing to ¼ inch from the raw edge of the tree skirt top.

Binding the Tree Skirt

The technique for binding the tree skirt is similar to the one for binding a quilt. Read through the general directions in "Binding the Quilt" on page 246 to familiarize yourself with the technique. Specific directions for the tree skirt are given here. Always use ¼-inch seam allowances and press all seams toward the binding.

Step 1. Press all six 2¾-inch binding strips (five strips if using purchased binding for the center hole) in half lengthwise, with the wrong sides together.

Step 2. For the top and bottom edges, align the raw edges of the two longest binding strips with the raw edge of the border on the tree skirt. Sew ¼ inch from the tree skirt edge, going through all layers of the tree skirt. Trim the excess binding, and press.

Step 3. Make the back opening by cutting through the tree skirt on the previously marked line from the bottom edge of the tree skirt to the center hole. You will be cutting through the binding on the bottom edge. Cut out the center hole as marked, cutting through all layers.

Step 4. For the binding on the center hole, press the 1¾ × 16-inch bias binding strip in half, with wrong sides together. (Or use purchased binding.) Align the raw edges of the binding with the edge of the center hole. Sew, easing the bias binding around the curve. Trim the excess binding even with the cut edges of the opening, and press.

Step 5. Align the raw edges of two additional binding strips with the edge of the border on each side of the tree skirt. Sew binding in place, trim the excess binding, and press.

Step 6. Use the remaining binding strips to bind the edges of the back opening. (If you cut only five binding strips, cut the last one in half to make two 2¾ × 22-inch strips.) Align the raw edges of each binding strip with the raw edges of each side of the opening. Sew in place, trim the excess binding, and press. See **Diagram 4.**

FRONT OF TREE SKIRT

BINDING

Sew binding strips to each side of opening and press out.

DIAGRAM 4

Step 7. Fold the binding over the edges to the back, folding the top and bottom bindings first. Press, and pin in position. See **Diagram 5.** Fold the side bindings to the back, press, and pin in position.

TOP

BACK OF TREE SKIRT

BOTTOM

Fold top and bottom binding to back, press, and pin.

DIAGRAM 5

Step 8. Fold the center hole binding to the back, press, and pin in position. See **Diagram 6.** Fold the side and back opening binding to the back, press, and pin in position. See **Diagram 7.** Hand stitch all bindings in place. The finished center hole binding will measure ¼ inch, and all the other bindings will measure ½ inch.

BACK

Fold center hole binding to back, press, and pin.

DIAGRAM 6

BACK OF TREE SKIRT

Fold side and back opening binding to back, press, and pin.

DIAGRAM 7

Finishing Stitches

Machine or hand quilt in the seam line on both sides of the accent border. Outline the appliqué designs by quilting ¹⁄₁₆ inch away from the edges of the designs. Quilt a 1½-inch diagonal grid in the background. Quilt in the seam line of the patchwork points and corner

Festive Flourishes

Wrap the tree skirt in plain-color paper onto which you've fused many moose designs and some stars using the appliqué patterns. Tie off with a raffia bow.

11"

SELVAGE

11"

1¾"

16"

2¾" 2¾" 2¾" 2¾" 2¾" 2¾"

44"

SELVAGE

CUTTING DIAGRAM FOR BINDING

TREE SKIRT APPLIQUÉ PATTERNS

Appliqué Pattern Key

_____ TRACING LINE

- - - - - - TRACING LINE
(will be hidden behind
other fabric)

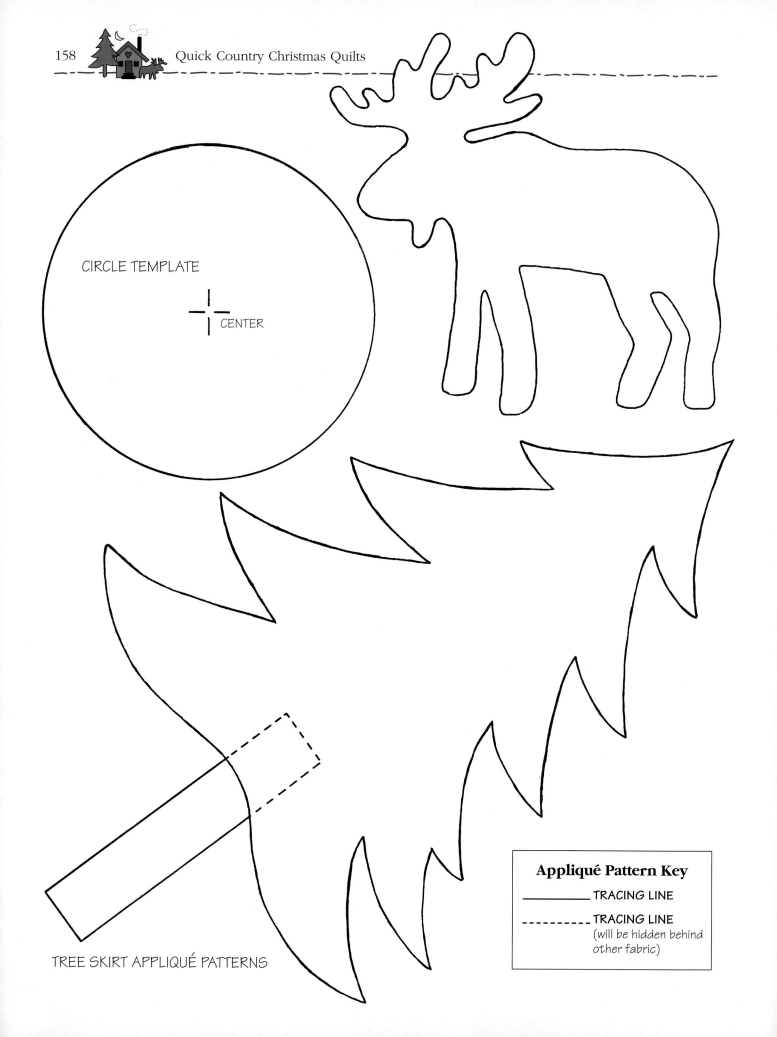

CIRCLE TEMPLATE

CENTER

Appliqué Pattern Key

_____ TRACING LINE

- - - - - - - - - TRACING LINE
(will be hidden behind other fabric)

TREE SKIRT APPLIQUÉ PATTERNS

Mantel Tree Quilt

Mantel Tree Quilt

Finished Quilt: 45 × 25 inches
Finished Block: 8 × 7 inches

45"

25"

QUILT LAYOUT

Add a touch of the pine forest to your mantel with this woodsy grouping of eight pine trees surrounded by a scrap border. This quilt can make the mantel the focal point of your room. Arrange sprigs of greenery and pinecones nearby to add the look and scent of the real thing.

Materials

Note: The yardages stated below allow for extra fabric from which to make the scrap border.

FABRIC A
Use four fabrics.
Tree   ¼ yard
each of *four* fabrics

FABRIC B
Block Background   ⅝ yard

FABRIC C
Trunk   ⅙ yard (6 inches)

FABRIC D
Lattice   ⅜ yard
Binding   ⅓ yard
 TOTAL   ¾ yard

FABRIC E
Corner Squares   ⅛ yard
Half-Inch Accent Border ⅛ yard
 TOTAL   ⅓ yard

BACKING   1⅜ yards

LIGHTWEIGHT
BATTING   1⅜ yards

Cutting Directions

Prewash and press all of your fabrics. Using a rotary cutter, see-through ruler, and cutting mat, prepare the strips as described in the first column in the chart below. Then from those strips, cut the pieces listed in the second column. Some strips need to be cut only once, so no additional cutting information will appear in the second column. Measurements for all pieces include ¼-inch seam allowances.

	FIRST CUT		SECOND CUT	
	NO. OF STRIPS	DIMENSIONS	NO. OF PIECES	DIMENSIONS
FABRIC A	**Tree:** from *each* of the *four* fabrics, cut the following			
	1	2½ × 44-inch strip	2	2½ × 8½-inch pieces
			2	2½ × 6½-inch pieces
			2	2½ × 4½-inch pieces
FABRIC B	**Block Background**			
	4	2½ × 44-inch strips	64	2½-inch squares
	3	1½ × 44-inch strips	16	1½ × 3½-inch pieces
			16	1½ × 2½-inch pieces
FABRIC C	**Trunk**			
	1	1½ × 44-inch strip	8	1½ × 2½-inch pieces
FABRIC D	**Lattice**			
	1	8½ × 44-inch strip	1	7½ × 18-inch piece
			12	8½ × 1½-inch strips
	Binding			
	Before You Cut: From *two* of the 44-inch strips, cut the pieces as directed in the second column. The remaining two strips require no further cutting.			
	4	2¾ × 44-inch strips	2	2¾ × 30-inch strips
			2	2¾ × 10-inch strips
FABRIC E	**Corner Squares**			
	1	1½ × 44-inch strip	1	1½ × 18-inch strip
			1	1½ × 9-inch strip
	Half-Inch Accent Border			
	3	1 × 44-inch strips		

Making the Tree Blocks

These tree blocks are identical to the tree blocks in Yuletide Tables. Follow all the directions in "Quick Corner Triangles" and "Making the Blocks" for the Tablecloth in Yuletide Tables, beginning on page 69. You will be making a total of eight tree blocks, two each of the four different Fabric As.

Lattice

Step 1. Lay out your blocks in a pleasing arrangement of two rows with four blocks each. Keep track of your layout while sewing on the lattice. Refer to the **Fabric Key** for fabric identification.

Fabric Key

FABRIC A
(Tree)

FABRIC B
(Background)

FABRIC C
(Trunk)

FABRIC D
(Lattice)

FABRIC E
(Corner Square)

Step 2. Sew 1½ × 8½-inch Fabric D lattice strips to the top of all eight blocks. See **Diagram 1.** Press all seams toward the lattice.

DIAGRAM 1

Step 3. Sew the blocks with lattice together to make four sets of two blocks each. See **Diagram 2.** Press.

Step 4. Sew 1½ × 8½-inch lattice strips to the bottom of the four Step 3 units. See **Diagram 3.** Press.

DIAGRAM 2

DIAGRAM 3

Step 5. Sew the 1½ × 18-inch Fabric E strip to the 7½ × 18-inch Fabric D lattice piece. See **Diagram 4.** Press the seam toward the lattice. Cut the strip set into halves (approximately 9 inches each).

DIAGRAM 4

Step 6. Resew the halves together to make a 17½ × 9-inch strip set. See **Diagram 5.** Press.

DIAGRAM 5

Step 7. Sew the 1½ × 9-inch Fabric E strip to the right side of the Step 6 strip set. See **Diagram 6.** Press.

DIAGRAM 6

Step 8. Using a rotary cutter and ruler, cut five 1½ × 17½-inch lattice strips from this strip set. See **Diagram 7.**

DIAGRAM 7

Step 9. Matching seams, pin in position and sew four lattice strips to the left side of the four Step 4 units. See **Diagram 8.** Press.

DIAGRAM 8

Step 10. Referring to the **Quilt Layout** on page 160, pin and sew the four Step 9 units together. Press. Pin and sew the remaining lattice strip to the right side of the quilt top. Press.

Half-Inch Accent Border

Sew 1 × 44-inch Fabric E accent border strips to the top and bottom of the quilt. Trim the excess and press all seams toward the border. Cut the remaining 1 × 44-inch Fabric E border strip in half. Sew the 1 × 22-inch strips to the quilt sides. Trim the excess and press.

Scrap Border

Before cutting the scrap border strips, it's a good idea to read "Pieced Borders" on page 243. You will need a total of 13 to 16 strips to make your border: 6 to 8 Fabric A strips, 2 Fabric B strips, 2 Fabric C strips, 2 Fabric D strips, and 1 or 2 Fabric E strips. These strips should vary in width from 1½ to 3½ inches and should all be 23 inches long.

Step 1. Sew the scrap border strips together to make a 24½ × 23-inch strip set, alternating the colors. See **Diagram 9.** Change sewing direction with each strip sewn, and press the seams in one direction. Cut six 3½ × 24½-inch strip sets, referring to the cutting lines.

DIAGRAM 9

Step 2. For the top and bottom borders, sew four of these strips together in pairs to make two 3½ × 48½-inch strips. Pin and sew

the scrap border strips to the top and bottom of the quilt. Trim the excess length. Press all seams toward the accent border.

Step 3. Pin and sew the two remaining 3½ × 24½-inch border strips to the quilt sides. Press.

Machine stitch around the quilt a scant ¼ inch from the edge to keep the seams of the scrap border from coming apart before the edges are bound.

Layering the Quilt

Arrange and baste the backing, batting, and top together, following the directions in "Layering the Quilt" on page 245. Trim the batting and backing to ¼ inch from the raw edge of the quilt top.

Binding the Quilt

Follow the directions in "Binding the Quilt" on page 246. For the top and bottom bindings, sew the 2¾ × 10-inch Fabric D binding strips to one end of each of the two 2¾ × 44-inch Fabric D strips, to make two approximately 2¾ × 54-inch binding strips. Use the 2¾ × 30-inch Fabric D strips for the sides.

Finishing Stitches

Machine or hand quilt in the seam line around each tree. Quilt a vertical line in the center of each tree and in each of the "branches" in the tree. See **Diagram 10.** Quilt vertical lines 1 inch apart in the block background. Quilt in the seam line along each side of the lattice, corner squares, accent border, and each piece of the scrap border. Quilt trees, moons, and *X*s in some of the larger pieces of the scrap border, using the **Tree** and **Moon Quilting Patterns** on this page.

DIAGRAM 10

Festive Flourishes

Candlelight adds warmth and a magical glow to all your holiday decorations. A selection of candles in holiday colors given with the Mantel Tree Quilt would make a very special gift for a very special person.

MOON QUILTING PATTERN

TREE QUILTING PATTERN

Pine Tree Lodge Stockings and Pillows

CABIN STOCKING LAYOUT

Hang rustic cabin-in-the-woods or pine tree stockings from the mantel. Then spread Christmas charm throughout the room with matching pillows for the sofa, overstuffed easy chair, or recliner. Won't Santa be impressed! Just make sure he doesn't get too comfortable... you may find him asleep in your living room on Christmas morning!

Cabin Stocking

Finished Size: 11¼ × 19 inches

Materials

Obvious directional prints are not recommended.

FABRIC A

Cabin, Top Border, and Bottom
    Accent Strip   ⅛ yard

FABRIC B

Background   ⅛ yard

FABRIC C

Roof, Top Accent Strip, Lower
    Stocking, Stocking Back,
    and Hanging Tab   ⅜ yard

FABRIC D

Door   2 × 3-inch scrap

FABRIC E

Windows   1½ × 4-inch scrap

FABRIC F

Tree   3 × 8-inch scrap

FABRIC G

Trunk   1½ × 3-inch scrap

FABRIC H

Patchwork Points Border
    (dark color)   ⅛ yard

FABRIC I

Patchwork Points Border
    (light color)   ⅛ yard

MUSLIN BACKING   ⅜ yard

COTTON FLANNEL   ⅜ yard

LINING   ⅜ yard

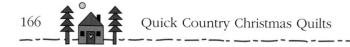

Cutting Directions

Prewash and press all of your fabrics. Using a rotary cutter, see-through ruler, and cutting mat, prepare the strips as described in the first column in the chart below. Then from those strips, cut the pieces listed in the second column. Some strips need to be cut only once, so no additional cutting information will appear in the second column. Measurements for all pieces include ¼-inch seam allowances.

	FIRST CUT		SECOND CUT	
	NO. OF STRIPS	**DIMENSIONS**	**NO. OF PIECES**	**DIMENSIONS**
FABRIC A	Cabin			
	1	1½ × 44-inch strip	1	1½ × 5½-inch piece
			2	1½ × 2½-inch pieces
			2	1½-inch squares
			2	1½ × 1-inch pieces
	Top Border			
	1	2 × 8½-inch piece		
	Bottom Accent Strip			
	1	1 × 8½-inch piece		
FABRIC B	Background			
	1	3 × 44-inch strip	2	3-inch squares
			8	1½-inch squares
			2	1¼ × 2½-inch pieces
			2	1 × 6½-inch pieces
			1	1 × 5½-inch piece
FABRIC C	Roof, Top Accent Strip, and Hanging Tab			
	Before You Cut: Cut an 8½-inch square from Fabric C first and cut these pieces from that square. The remaining yardage will be used for the lower stocking and stocking back.			
	1	8½-inch square	1	3 × 5½-inch piece (Roof)
			1	1 × 8½-inch piece (Top Accent Strip)
			1	1 × 5-inch piece (Hanging Tab)
FABRIC D	Door			
	1	1½ × 2½-inch piece		
FABRIC E	Windows			
	2	1 × 1½-inch pieces		
FABRIC F	Tree			
	4	2½ × 1½-inch pieces		

	FIRST CUT		SECOND CUT	
	NO. OF STRIPS	DIMENSIONS	NO. OF PIECES	DIMENSIONS
FABRIC G	Trunk			
	1	1 × 2½-inch piece		
FABRIC H	Patchwork Points Border (dark color)			
	1	1½ × 44-inch strip	8	1½ × 2½-inch pieces
FABRIC I	Patchwork Points Border (light color)			
	1	1½ × 44-inch strip	16	1½-inch squares
MUSLIN	1	13½ × 22-inch piece		
FLANNEL	1	13½ × 22-inch piece		

Quick Corner Triangles

Refer to "Making Quick Corner Triangles" on page 234 for how to make corner triangle units. Refer to the **Fabric Key,** and press in the direction of the triangle just added. For clarity, seam allowances are shown in the diagrams.

Fabric Key

FABRIC A (Cabin)
FABRIC B (Background)
FABRIC C (Roof)
FABRIC D (Door)
FABRIC E (Windows)
FABRIC F (Tree)
FABRIC G (Trunk)

Step 1. Sew one 3-inch Fabric B square to one 3 × 5½-inch Fabric C piece. See **Diagram 1.** Press.

Step 2. Sew an additional 3-inch Fabric B square to the opposite end of the Step 1 unit. See **Diagram 2.** Press.

5½"
3"

DIAGRAM 1

DIAGRAM 2

Step 3. Sew four 1½-inch Fabric B squares to four 1½ × 2½-inch Fabric F pieces, as shown in **Diagram 3.** Press.

2½"
1½"

DIAGRAM 3

Step 4. Sew four additional 1½-inch Fabric B squares to the opposite end of the Step 3 units. See **Diagram 4.** Press.

DIAGRAM 4

Making the Block

Pay close attention that the corner triangle units are positioned the same as shown in the diagrams. Be sure to use accurate ¼-inch seam allowances and press as you go. Follow the arrows in the diagrams for pressing direction.

Cabin

Step 1. Sew two 1 × 1½-inch Fabric A pieces to two 1 × 1½-inch Fabric E pieces, as shown in **Diagram 5.** Press.

1"   1"
1½"   1½"
←

DIAGRAM 5

Step 2. Sew two 1½-inch Fabric A squares to the two Step 1 units. See **Diagram 6.** Press.

1½"
STEP 1 UNIT   1½"
→

DIAGRAM 6

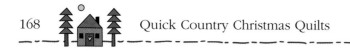

Step 3. Sew one 1½ × 2½-inch Fabric A piece to the bottom of one Step 2 unit, as shown in **Diagram 7.** Press. Rotate the remaining Step 2 unit 180 degrees, and sew the remaining 1½ × 2½ Fabric A piece to the bottom. Press.

DIAGRAM 7

Step 4. Sew one Step 3 unit to each side of one 1½ × 2½-inch Fabric D piece. See **Diagram 8.** Press.

DIAGRAM 8

Step 5. Sew one 1½ × 5½-inch Fabric A piece to the top of the Step 4 unit. See **Diagram 9.** Press.

DIAGRAM 9

Step 6. Sew one 3 × 5½-inch Fabric B/C corner triangle unit to the top of the Step 5 unit. See **Diagram 10.** Press.

DIAGRAM 10

Step 7. Sew one 1 × 5½-inch Fabric B piece to the top of the Step 6 unit. See **Diagram 11.** Press.

DIAGRAM 11

Step 8. Sew one 1 × 6½-inch Fabric B piece to each side of the Step 7 unit. See **Diagram 12.** Press. The Cabin block should now measure 6½ inches square.

DIAGRAM 12

Tree

Step 1. Sew four 1½ × 2½-inch Fabric B/F corner triangle units together, as shown in **Diagram 13.** Press all seams toward the top triangle unit.

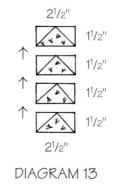

DIAGRAM 13

Step 2. Sew one 1¼ × 2½-inch Fabric B piece to each side of one

1 × 2½ Fabric G piece. See **Diagram 14.** Press.

DIAGRAM 14

Step 3. Sew the Step 1 unit to the Step 2 unit. See **Diagram 15.** Press. The Tree block should now measure 2½ × 6½ inches.

DIAGRAM 15

Assembling the Block

Sew the Tree block to the left side of the Cabin block. See **Diagram 16.** Press the seam toward the Cabin block. The Tree/Cabin block should now measure 8½ × 6½ inches.

DIAGRAM 16

Patchwork Points Border

Refer to "Making Quick Corner Triangles" on page 234 for how to make corner triangle units. Refer to the **Fabric Key** for fabric identification, and press in the direction of the triangle just added.

Fabric Key

FABRIC H
(Dark Color)

FABRIC I
(Light Color)

Step 1. Sew eight 1½-inch Fabric I squares to eight 1½ × 2½-inch Fabric H pieces. See **Diagram 17.** Press.

2½"

1½"

DIAGRAM 17

Step 2. Sew eight additional 1½-inch Fabric I squares to the opposite end of the Fabric H/I corner triangle units from Step 1. See **Diagram 18.** Press.

DIAGRAM 18

Step 3. Sew the Fabric H/I corner triangle units together to make two patchwork points border strips of four corner triangle units each, as shown in **Diagram 19.** Press all seams in the same direction.

2½" 2½" 2½" 2½"

1½" 1½"

← ← ←

DIAGRAM 19

Assembling the Stocking Front

Step 1. Fit, pin in position, and sew the patchwork points border strips to the top and bottom of the Tree/Cabin block. See **Diagram 20.** Press seams toward the block.

DIAGRAM 20

SEW SMART

Measure the patchwork points border strips against the top and bottom of the Cabin/Tree block. If necessary, take in or let out a few seams by 1/16 inch or less to make them fit the block.

Step 2. Sew the 2 × 8½-inch Fabric A strip to the top of the Step 1 unit. Press the seam toward Fabric A.

Step 3. Sew the 1 × 8½-inch Fabric C strip to the top of the Step 2 unit. Press the seam toward Fabric C.

Step 4. Sew the 1 × 8½-inch Fabric A strip to the bottom of the Step 3 unit. Press the seam toward Fabric A.

Step 5. Trace the **Lower Stocking Pattern** on pages 178–179 onto tracing paper or interfacing to make a pattern. Place the pattern on the right side of Fabric C and cut a lower stocking piece.

Step 6. Sew the lower stocking piece to the Step 4 unit. Press seam toward the Step 4 unit. Your stocking front is now complete.

Layering and Quilting

Step 1. Lay the pressed muslin on the bottom (right side down), the flannel in the middle, and the stocking front on top (right side up). Make sure everything is centered and that the muslin and flannel are flat. The muslin and flannel should extend ¾ to 1 inch beyond all edges of the stocking front. Hand baste around the raw edges of the stocking front to hold the layers together.

Step 2. Machine or hand quilt in the seam line around the cabin, tree, cabin door, windows, all borders, and all patchwork points. Quilt a chimney on the right side of the cabin roof in the background. Quilt in the horizontal seam lines in the cabin. Quilt horizontal lines across the cabin in the center of each piece to simulate logs or siding. Quilt a 1½-inch diagonal grid in the stocking toe and wide top border.

Step 3. Trim the muslin and flannel even with the raw edge of the stocking front.

Stocking Assembly

Step 1. Place the stocking front against the back with right sides together. Cut one stocking back, using the completed stocking front as a pattern. Fold the lining fabric with right sides together. Use the stocking front as a pattern and cut two stocking lining pieces.

Step 2. With right sides together, sew the stocking front to the front lining along the top edge. See **Diagram 21.** Press the seam open.

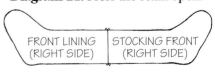

FRONT LINING
(RIGHT SIDE)

STOCKING FRONT
(RIGHT SIDE)

DIAGRAM 21

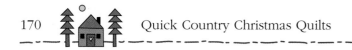

Step 3. To make the hanging tab, fold the 1 × 5-inch Fabric C piece in half lengthwise, with wrong sides together, and press. Fold each long edge into the center fold and press again. See **Diagram 22.** Topstitch along the double folded edge through all thicknesses.

DOUBLE FOLD

FOLD

DIAGRAM 22

Step 4. Fold the hanging tab in half, and baste to the right side of the stocking back. Position it ½ inch from the raw edge on the heel side of the stocking. See **Diagram 23.** With right sides to-

gether, sew the stocking back to the back lining along the top edge. Press the seam open.

STOCKING BACK (RIGHT SIDE OF FABRIC)

DIAGRAM 23

Step 5. Position the stocking front and lining on the stocking back and lining, with right sides together. See **Diagram 24.** Pin all outside edges. Sew together, leaving a 3- to 4-inch opening for turning in the lining. Clip all curves. Turn and press. Hand stitch the opening.

Step 6. Stuff lining into the stocking and press.

STOCKING BACK   BACK LINING

STOCKING FRONT (WRONG SIDE)   FRONT LINING (WRONG SIDE)

Leave open for turning.

DIAGRAM 24

Festive Flourishes

Fill this stocking with Lincoln Logs to surprise a child or anyone who's a child at heart.

Pine Tree Stocking

Finished Size: 11¼ × 19 inches

PINE TREE STOCKING LAYOUT

Materials

Obvious directional prints are not recommended.

FABRIC A

Use four fabrics.
Tree and Borders   ⅛ yard *each* of *four* fabrics (or one 3 × 5-inch scrap each of three fabric As and one 3½ × 14-inch scrap of a fourth fabric A)
Note: The two border strips are cut from the fourth Fabric A.

FABRIC B

Background   ⅛ yard

FABRIC C

Trunks   One 3 × 4-inch scrap

FABRIC D

Top Accent Strip, Lower Stocking, Hanging Tab, and Stocking Back   ⅜ yard

FABRIC H

Patchwork Points Border (dark color)   ⅛ yard

FABRIC I

Patchwork Points Border (light color)   ⅛ yard

MUSLIN BACKING   ⅜ yard

COTTON FLANNEL   ⅜ yard

LINING   ⅜ yard

Cutting Directions

Prewash and press all of your fabrics. Using a rotary cutter, see-through ruler, and cutting mat, prepare the strips as described in the first column in the chart below. Then from those strips, cut the pieces listed in the second column. Some strips need to be cut only once, so no additional cutting information will appear in the second column. Measurements for all pieces include ¼-inch seam allowances.

	FIRST CUT		SECOND CUT	
	NO. OF STRIPS	DIMENSIONS	NO. OF PIECES	DIMENSIONS
FABRIC A	**Trees:** from *each* of the *four* fabrics, cut the following			
	1	2½ × 4½-inch piece		
	Borders: from *one* of the *four* fabrics, cut the following			
	1	2 × 8½-inch piece (Top Border)		
	1	1 × 8½-inch piece (Bottom Accent)		
FABRIC B	**Background**			
	1	2½ × 44-inch strip	8	2½-inch squares
			4	2½ × 2¼-inch pieces
FABRIC C	**Trunks**			
	2	1 × 2½-inch pieces		
FABRIC D	**Note:** Cut the pieces as described below. The remaining yardage will be used for the lower stocking and the stocking back.			
	Top Accent Strip			
	1	1 × 8½-inch piece		
	Hanging Tab			
	1	1 × 5-inch piece		
FABRIC H	**Patchwork Points Border (dark color)**			
	1	1½ × 44-inch strip	8	1½ × 2½-inch pieces
FABRIC I	**Patchwork Points Border (light color)**			
	1	1½ × 44-inch strip	16	1½-inch squares
MUSLIN	1	13½ × 22-inch piece		
FLANNEL	1	13½ × 22-inch piece		

Before You Begin

Many of the assembly directions for the Pine Tree Stocking are the same as those given for the Cabin Stocking. Throughout these directions, you will be referred back to the Cabin Stocking for steps that are identical.

Quick Corner Triangles

Refer to "Making Quick Corner Triangles" on page 234 for how to make corner triangle units. You will be making four corner triangle units, one each of the four different Fabric As. Refer to the **Fabric Key,** and press in the direction of the triangle just added. For clarity, seam allowances are shown in the diagrams.

Fabric Key

FABRIC A (Trees)
FABRIC B (Background)
FABRIC C (Trunks)

Step 1. Sew four 2½-inch Fabric B squares to four 2½ × 4½-inch Fabric A pieces. See **Diagram 25.** Press.

4½"
2½"

DIAGRAM 25

Step 2. Sew four additional 2½-inch Fabric B squares to the opposite end of the Fabric A/B corner triangle units from Step 1. See **Diagram 26.** Press.

DIAGRAM 26

Assembling the Block

Pay close attention that the corner triangles are positioned the same as shown in the diagrams. Be sure to use accurate ¼-inch seam allowances and press as you go. Follow the arrows in the diagrams for pressing direction.

Step 1. Sew the 2½ × 4½-inch Fabric A/B corner triangle units together in pairs to make two tree units. See **Diagram 27.** Press.

4½"
2½"
2½"

DIAGRAM 27

Step 2. Sew two 2¼ × 2½-inch Fabric B pieces to each side of two 1 × 2½-inch Fabric C pieces, as shown in **Diagram 28.** Press.

2¼" 1" 2¼"
2½"   2½"

DIAGRAM 28

Step 3. Sew two Step 2 units to two Step 1 units. See **Diagram 29.** Press.

STEP 1 UNIT
STEP 2 UNIT

DIAGRAM 29

Step 4. Sew the two Step 3 units together. See **Diagram 30.** Press. The tree block should now measure 8½ × 6½ inches.

STEP 3 UNIT   STEP 3 UNIT

DIAGRAM 30

Patchwork Borders

To make these border strips, refer to "Patchwork Points Border" for the Cabin Stocking, on page 168, and follow the directions there. Fit, pin in position, and sew the patchwork point strips to the top and bottom of the Tree block, as shown in **Diagram 31.** Press seams toward the block.

DIAGRAM 31

Assembling the Front

Step 1. Sew the 2 × 8½-inch Fabric A strip to the top of the Tree block. Press the seam toward Fabric A.

Step 2. Sew the 1 × 8½-inch Fabric D strip to the top of the Step 1 unit. Press the seam toward Fabric D.

Step 3. Sew the 1 × 8½-inch Fabric A strip to the bottom of the Step 2 unit. Press the seam toward Fabric A.

Step 4. Trace the **Lower Stocking Pattern** on pages 178–179 onto tracing paper or interfacing to make a pattern. Place the pattern on the right side of Fabric D and cut a lower stocking piece.

Step 5. Sew the lower stocking piece to the Step 3 unit. Press toward the Step 3 unit. Your stocking front is now complete.

Finishing

Step 1. Follow Step 1 of "Layering and Quilting" for the Cabin Stocking on page 169.

Step 2. Machine or hand quilt ¼ inch from the pine trees, tree trunks, and background seams. Quilt in the seam line of the patchwork points, borders, and accent strips. Quilt a 1½-inch diagonal grid in the lower stocking, and wide top border.

Step 3. Trim the muslin and flannel layers so that they are even with the raw edge of the stocking front.

Step 4. Refer to "Stocking Assembly" for the Cabin Stocking, on page 169, and follow the directions there to assemble the stocking.

Cabin Pillow

Finished Size: 13 × 11 inches

Materials
Obvious directional prints are not recommended.

FABRIC A
Cabin — ⅛ yard

FABRIC B
Background — ⅙ yard (6 inches)

FABRIC C
Roof — 4 × 6-inch scrap

FABRIC D
Door — 2 × 3-inch scrap

FABRIC E
Windows — 1½ × 4-inch scrap

FABRIC F
Tree and Binding — ⅛ yard

FABRIC G
Trunk — 1½ × 3-inch scrap

FABRIC H
Patchwork Points Border (dark color) — ⅛ yard

FABRIC I
Patchwork Points Border (light color) — ⅛ yard

PILLOW BACK — ½ yard

MUSLIN LINING — ½ yard

BATTING — ½ yard

NOTIONS AND SUPPLIES
One 1-pound bag of smooth stuffing, like polyester fiberfill (not shredded foam)

Cutting Directions

Prewash and press all of your fabrics. Using a rotary cutter, see-through ruler, and cutting mat, prepare the strips as described in the first column in the chart below. Then from those strips, cut the pieces listed in the second column. Some strips need to be cut only once, so no additional cutting information will appear in the second column. Measurements for all pieces include ¼-inch seam allowances.

	FIRST CUT		SECOND CUT	
	NO. OF STRIPS	**DIMENSIONS**	**NO. OF PIECES**	**DIMENSIONS**
FABRIC A	Cabin			
	1	1½ × 44-inch strip	1	1½ × 5½-inch piece
			2	1½ × 2½-inch pieces
			2	1½-inch squares
			2	1½ × 1-inch pieces
FABRIC B	Background			
	Before You Cut: Cut the 1½ × 44-inch strip first.			
	1	1½ × 44-inch strip	4	1½ × 8½-inch pieces
	2	3-inch squares		

(continued)

Cabin Pillow
Cutting Chart—
Continued

	FIRST CUT		SECOND CUT	
	NO. OF STRIPS	DIMENSIONS	NO. OF PIECES	DIMENSIONS
FABRIC B (continued)	8	1½-inch squares		
	2	1¼ × 2½-inch pieces		
	2	1 × 6½-inch pieces		
	1	1 × 5½-inch piece		
FABRIC C	**Roof**			
	1	3 × 5½-inch piece		
FABRIC D	**Door**			
	1	1½ × 2½-inch piece		
FABRIC E	**Windows**			
	2	1 × 1½-inch pieces		
FABRIC F	**Tree**			
	1	1½ × 10-inch strip	4	1½ × 2½-inch pieces
	Binding			
	2	1 × 44-inch strips	2	1 × 12½-inch strips
			2	1 × 11½-inch strips
FABRIC G	**Trunk**			
	1	1 × 2½-inch piece		
FABRIC H	**Patchwork Points Border (dark color)**			
	1	2½ × 44-inch strip	18	2½ × 1½-inch pieces
			4	1½-inch squares
FABRIC I	**Patchwork Points Border (light color)**			
	2	1½ × 44-inch strips	40	1½-inch squares
PILLOW BACK	2	9 × 11½-inch pieces		
MUSLIN LINING	1	14 × 17-inch piece		
BATTING	1	14 × 17-inch piece		
	2	10½ × 12½ pieces (for pillow form)		

CABIN PILLOW LAYOUT

13"

11"

Making the Cabin Block

To make the Cabin block for the pillow, refer to "Quick Corner Triangles" and "Making the Block" for the Cabin Stocking, beginning on page 167.

Background Border

Sew 1½ × 8½-inch Fabric B strips to the top and bottom of the block. Press all seams toward the border. Sew 1½ × 8½-inch Fabric B strips to the sides of the block. Press.

Patchwork Points Border

Refer to "Making Quick Corner Triangles" on page 234 for how to make corner triangle units. Refer to the **Fabric Key** for fabric identification, and press in the direction of the triangle just added.

Fabric Key

FABRIC H
(Dark Color)

FABRIC I
(Light Color)

Step 1. Sew eighteen 1½-inch Fabric I squares to eighteen 2½ × 1½-inch Fabric H pieces. See **Diagram 32.** Press.

2½"

1½"

DIAGRAM 32

Step 2. Sew eighteen additional 1½-inch Fabric I squares to the opposite end of the Step 1 units. See **Diagram 33.** Press.

DIAGRAM 33

Step 3. Sew four 1½-inch Fabric I squares to four 1½-inch Fabric H squares, as shown in **Diagram 34.** Press the seam toward Fabric H.

1½"

1½"

DIAGRAM 34

Step 4. Sew the 1½ × 2½-inch Fabric H/I corner triangle units together in two strips of four triangle units each for the top and bottom borders and two strips of five triangle units each for the side borders. See **Diagram 35.** Press all seams in the same direction in each strip.

1½"   2½"   2½"   2½"   2½"   1½"

DIAGRAM 35

Step 5. For the top and bottom border strips, add 1½-inch-square Fabric H/I corner triangle units to each end of the two strips of four units. See **Diagram 36.** Press.

DIAGRAM 36

Step 6. Fit, pin in position, and sew the patchwork point strips from Step 5 to the top and bottom of the Cabin block. Press seams toward the background border.

SEW SMART

Measure the patchwork points border strips against the top and bottom of the Cabin block. If necessary, take in or let out a few seams by ¹⁄₁₆ inch or less to make them fit the block.

Step 7. Fit, pin in position, and sew the five-unit patchwork point strips to the sides of the Cabin block. Press.

Binding

Sew 1 × 12½-inch binding strips to the pillow top and bottom. Press all seams toward the binding. Sew 1 × 11½-inch binding strips to the pillow sides. Press.

Layering the Pillow Top

Arrange and baste together the muslin lining, the 14 × 17-inch batting piece, and the pillow top, following the directions in "Layering the Quilt" on page 245.

Finishing Stitches

Machine or hand quilt in the seam line around the door and windows. Quilt ¼ inch away from the seam around the cabin, pine tree, and trunk, and quilt a chimney on the right side of the roof in the background. Quilt in the horizontal seam lines in the cabin. Quilt horizontal lines across the cabin in the center of each piece to simulate logs or siding. Quilt a mirror image of the patchwork points in the one-inch background border. Quilt in the seam line of the inside points (Fabric H) of the patchwork points border. *Do not quilt in the seam line next to the binding.*

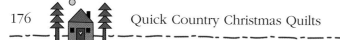
Making the Pillow Back

Step 1. On one long edge of one pillow back piece, fold under ¼ inch to the wrong side. Press. Fold again ½ inch to the wrong side. Press. Topstitch along the folded edge to make a hem. Repeat for second pillow back piece.

Step 2. With right sides up, lay one pillow back piece over the second piece so the hemmed edges overlap 3 inches. Baste the pieces together at the top and bottom where they overlap. See **Diagram 37.** The pillow back should now measure 13½ × 11½ inches.

DIAGRAM 37

Finishing the Pillow

Step 1. With right sides together, sew the quilted pillow front to the back, using a ¼-inch seam allowance. Trim the batting and the muslin lining even with the edges of the pillow top and backing. Trim the corners, turn right side out, and press.

Step 2. To create the look of piping, machine stitch in the seam line between the binding and the background border.

Step 3. Refer to "Making Custom-Fit Pillow Forms" on page 178, and follow all directions there. Insert the pillow form through the opening in the back of the pillow. **Note:** Because of the topstitching in the seam line of the binding, the finished size of the pillow form should be 12 × 10 inches.

Pine Tree Pillow

Finished Size: 13 × 11 inches

PINE TREE PILLOW LAYOUT

Materials

Obvious directional prints are not recommended.

FABRIC A
Use four fabrics.
Trees   One 3 × 5-inch scrap
               each of *four* fabrics

FABRIC B
Background   ⅙ yard (6 inches)

FABRIC C
Trunks   One 3 × 4-inch scrap

FABRIC H
Patchwork Points Border
   (dark color)   ⅛ yard

FABRIC I
Patchwork Points Border
   (light color)   ⅛ yard

BINDING   ⅛ yard

PILLOW BACK   ½ yard

BATTING   ½ yard

MUSLIN LINING   ½ yard

NOTIONS AND SUPPLIES
One 1-pound bag of smooth
   stuffing, like polyester fiberfill

Cutting Directions

Prewash and press all of your fabrics. Using a rotary cutter, see-through ruler, and cutting mat, prepare the strips as described in the first column in the chart on the opposite page. Then from those strips, cut the pieces listed in the second column. Some strips need to be cut only once, so no additional cutting information will appear in the second column. Measurements for all pieces include ¼-inch seam allowances.

Making the Pillow Top

The Tree block for the pillow is identical to the one made for the Pine Tree Stocking. Refer to "Quick Corner Triangles" and "Assembling the Block" on page 172, and follow the directions. Refer to "Background Border" through "Layering the Pillow Top" for the Cabin Pillow on page 175.

Finishing Stitches

Machine or hand quilt ¼ inch from the pine trees, tree trunks, and background seams. Quilt in the seam line of the background border and the inside points (Fabric H) of the patchwork points border. Quilt a mirror image of the

	FIRST CUT		SECOND CUT	
	NO. OF STRIPS	**DIMENSIONS**	**NO. OF PIECES**	**DIMENSIONS**
FABRIC A	**Trees:** from *each* of the *four* fabrics, cut the following			
	1	2½ × 4½-inch piece		
FABRIC B	**Background**			
	1	2½ × 44-inch strip	8	2½-inch squares
			4	2½ × 2¼-inch pieces
	1	1½ × 44-inch strip	4	1½ × 8½-inch pieces
FABRIC C	**Trunks**			
	2	1 × 2½-inch pieces		
FABRIC H	**Patchwork Points Border (dark color)**			
	1	2½ × 44-inch strip	18	2½ × 1½-inch pieces
			4	1½-inch squares
FABRIC I	**Patchwork Points Border (light color)**			
	2	1½ × 44-inch strips	40	1½-inch squares
BINDING	2	1 × 44-inch strips	2	1 × 12½-inch strips
			2	1 × 11½-inch strips
PILLOW BACK	2	9 × 11½-inch pieces		
BATTING	1	14 × 17-inch piece		
	2	10½ × 12½-inch pieces (for pillow form)		
MUSLIN LINING	1	14 × 17-inch piece		

patchwork points in the background border. *Do not quilt in the seam line next to the binding.*

Finishing the Pillow

Refer to "Making the Pillow Back" and "Finishing the Pillow" for the Cabin Pillow on the opposite page. Follow all steps in those sections.

Festive Flourishes

Wrap the pillow up with a good book and encourage the receiver to curl up in the corner of the sofa with the pillow and read. Or enclose a bag of woodsy, pine-scented potpourri. Tie a sprig of pine greenery or holly and a miniature log cabin tree ornament in with the ribbon on the package.

LOWER STOCKING PATTERN SECTION A

MAKING CUSTOM-FIT PILLOW FORMS

The secret to an attractive finished pillow is a pillow form that
fits perfectly inside the pillow top.
This cannot always be achieved
with standard-size pillow forms,
but you can easily make your own.

All you need is some polyester
batting or needlepunch and a
1-pound bag of smooth stuffing,
such as polyester fiberfill (not
shredded foam). The amount of
batting or needlepunch you will
need is listed with each pillow
project.

Step 1. Take the finished size of
your pillow and add ½ inch to
those measurements. Cut two
pieces of batting or needlepunch
to those dimensions. For ex-

ample, in the Cabin and Pine Tree
pillows, the size of the pillow form
should be 12 × 10 inches, so you
will need to cut two pieces of
batting, each 12½ × 10½ inches.

Step 2. Using a ¼-inch seam allowance, sew the two pieces of
batting together, leaving a 3- to
4-inch opening for turning. Turn
them so the seam allowances are
on the inside.

Step 3. Fill the pillow form with
stuffing until it reaches the desired firmness. Hand stitch the
opening closed.

Step 4. Slip the custom-made
pillow form into the opening of your
pillow. It should be a perfect fit!

Match dots with Lower Stocking Pattern Section B.

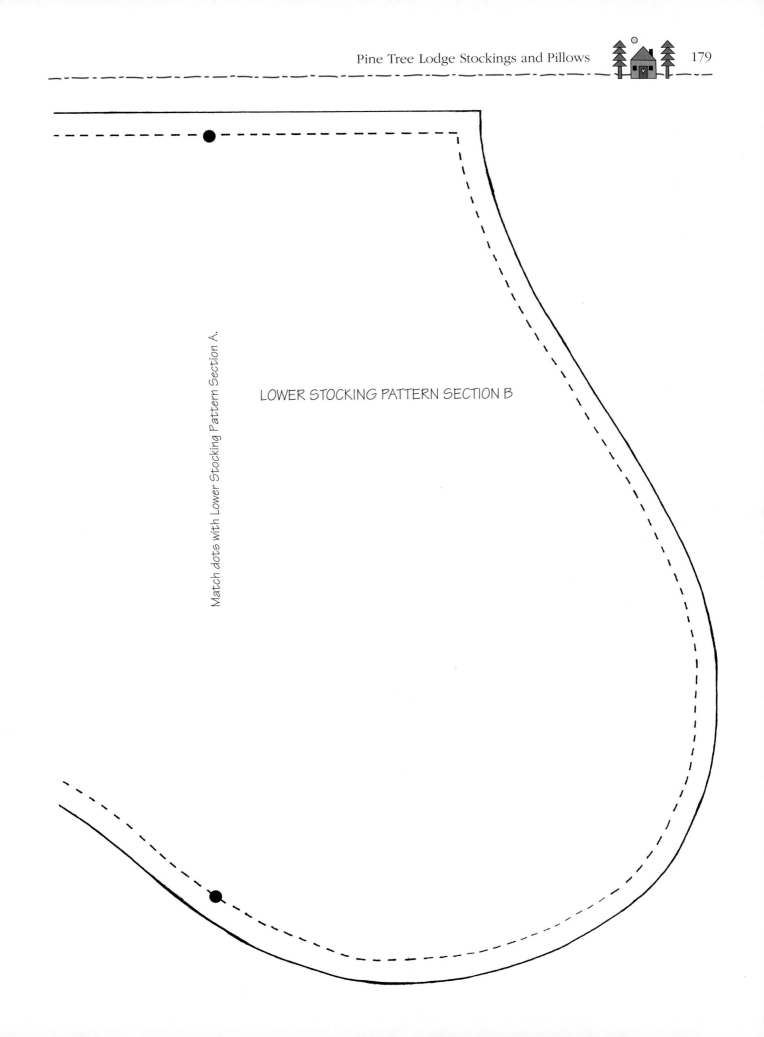

LOWER STOCKING PATTERN SECTION B

Match dots with Lower Stocking Pattern Section A.

©Debbie Mumm

In the Nick of Time
Gifts to Make in a Weekend

Need a quick gift? Check out these projects, and you'll find something to make no matter how busy your holiday schedule is. Going to a dinner party? You'll never go empty-handed after seeing how quick and easy these hostess gifts are. Stumped on what to give to a favorite teacher or the men in your life? Set aside a weekend to create these almost-instant gifts that are as much fun to make as they are to receive.

Before you begin, take a minute to read through this checklist. These are important pointers you should keep in mind to make sure that each of your quilts is a success.

★ Be sure to read "Techniques for Quick Country Quilting," beginning on page 226. This will familiarize you with the tools you'll need; the techniques for time-saving cutting, piecing, and appliqué; and finishing instructions.

★ Check the "Festive Flourishes" box for each project to get clever and unique ideas for packaging and wrapping your gift.

★ Take advantage of the helpful hints in the "Sew Smart" boxes. There you'll find tips for making a technique quicker or easier.

★ Prewash and press all of your fabrics. Washing will remove any sizing from the fabrics, and pressing ensures accuracy when cutting.

★ Read the step-by-step directions from start to finish, and look at all the diagrams before you cut and sew any fabric.

★ Always use a ¼-inch seam allowance, unless there is a special note that tells you a different seam allowance is required.

★ Refer to the **Fabric Key** for each project as a help in following the diagrams.

★ Pay attention to the pressing directions given in the step-by-step text and to the pressing arrows shown in the diagrams.

Field and Stream

33"

DUCK WALLHANGING LAYOUT

25"

Duck Wallhanging

Finished Size: 33 × 25 inches
Finished Block: 12 × 8 inches

Materials

Obvious directional prints are not recommended.

FABRIC A

Duck and Border	⅜ yard

FABRIC B

Block Background and Border	½ yard
Lattice	¼ yard
TOTAL	¾ yard

FABRIC C

Wing and Border	⅓ yard

FABRIC D

Tail	⅛ yard
Half-Inch Accent Border	⅛ yard
TOTAL	¼ yard

FABRIC E

Beak and Corner Squares	⅛ yard

BINDING ⅓ yard

BACKING ⅞ yard

LIGHTWEIGHT BATTING ⅞ yard

NOTIONS AND SUPPLIES

Four ⅜-inch buttons for eyes

Surprise your favorite outdoorsy person with a wallhanging for the den or office. Choose four delightful ducks or three troutlike fish, surrounded by a sawtooth border for a rustic effect. And just for fun, stitch up a coordinating "catch of the day"—these stuffed fish *never* get away! Capturing the great outdoors couldn't be easier! (You can piece each of these quilt tops in a weekend, but allow enough extra time to quilt them before the holidays get too hectic.)

Cutting Directions

Prewash and press all of your fabrics. Using a rotary cutter, see-through ruler, and cutting mat, prepare the strips as described in the first column in the chart below. Then from those strips, cut the pieces listed in the second column. Some portions of the quilt need to be cut only once, so no additional cutting information will appear in the second column. Measurements for all pieces include ¼-inch seam allowances.

	FIRST CUT		SECOND CUT	
	NO. OF STRIPS	DIMENSIONS	NO. OF PIECES	DIMENSIONS
FABRIC A	Duck and Border			
	Before You Cut: Cut the 8½ × 19-inch piece for the Border from the 44-inch strip first.			
	1	8½ × 44-inch strip	1	8½ × 19-inch piece
			4	8½ × 2½-inch pieces
			12	1½-inch squares
	1	3½ × 44-inch strip	4	3½-inch squares
			4	2½-inch squares
FABRIC B	Block Background and Border			
	1	8½ × 44-inch strip	2	8½ × 19-inch pieces
	3	2½ × 44-inch strips	4	2½ × 10½-inch pieces
			4	2½ × 8½-inch pieces
			4	2½ × 4½-inch pieces
			8	2½-inch squares
			4	1½-inch squares
	Lattice			
	4	1½ × 44-inch strips	3	1½ × 25½-inch strips
			2	1½ × 19½-inch strips
			2	1½ × 8½-inch strips
FABRIC C	Wing and Border			
	1	8½ × 44-inch strip	1	8½ × 19-inch piece
			4	8½ × 4½-inch pieces

	FIRST CUT		SECOND CUT	
	NO. OF STRIPS	**DIMENSIONS**	**NO. OF PIECES**	**DIMENSIONS**
FABRIC D	**Tail**			
	4	2½-inch squares		
	Half-Inch Accent Border			
	Before You Cut: From *one* of the 44-inch strips, cut the pieces as directed in the second column. The remaining two strips require no further cutting.			
	3	1 × 44-inch strips	2	1 × 22-inch strips
FABRIC E	**Beak**			
	4	2½-inch squares		
	Corner Squares			
	4	2½-inch squares		
BINDING	4	2¾ × 44-inch strips		

Quick Corner Triangles

Refer to "Making Quick Corner Triangles" on page 234. You will be making four identical Duck blocks. Use the assembly-line method (see page 234) to make the corner triangle units for all four blocks. Refer to the **Fabric Key** for fabric identification, and press in the direction of the triangle just added.

Fabric Key

FABRIC A (Duck)
FABRIC B (Background)
FABRIC C (Wing)
FABRIC D (Tail)
FABRIC E (Beak)

Step 1. Sew four 2½-inch Fabric E squares to four 2½ × 8½-inch Fabric B pieces. See **Diagram 1.** Press.

8½"

2½"

DIAGRAM 1

Step 2. Sew four 1½-inch Fabric A squares to four 2½ × 10½-inch Fabric B pieces. See **Diagram 2.** Press.

10½"

2½"

DIAGRAM 2

Step 3. Sew four 1½-inch Fabric A squares to four 4½ × 8½-inch Fabric C pieces, as shown in **Diagram 3.** Press.

8½"

4½"

DIAGRAM 3

Step 4. Sew four additional 1½-inch Fabric A squares to the four Step 3 units. See **Diagram 4.** Press.

DIAGRAM 4

Step 5. Sew four 3½-inch Fabric A squares to four Step 4 units. See **Diagram 5.** Press.

DIAGRAM 5

Step 6. Sew four 1½-inch Fabric B squares to the four Step 5 units. See **Diagram 6.** Press.

DIAGRAM 6

Step 7. Sew four 2½-inch Fabric D squares to four 2½ × 4½-inch Fabric B pieces. See **Diagram 7.** Press.

DIAGRAM 7

Step 8. Sew four 2½-inch Fabric B squares to four 2½ × 8½-inch Fabric A pieces. See **Diagram 8.** Press.

DIAGRAM 8

Step 9. Sew four additional 2½-inch Fabric B squares to the Step 8 units, as shown in **Diagram 9.** Press.

DIAGRAM 9

Assembling the Blocks

Throughout this section, refer to the **Fabric Key** on page 185 to identify the fabric placements in the diagrams. Also, it's a good idea to review "Assembly-Line Piecing" on page 234 before you get started. It's more efficient to do the same step for each block at the same time than to piece an entire block together at one time. Pay close attention that the corner triangles are positioned the same as shown in the diagrams. Be sure to use accurate ¼-inch seam allowances and press as you go. Follow the arrows in the diagrams for pressing direction. You will be making a total of four Duck blocks.

Step 1. Sew four 2½-inch Fabric A squares to four 2½ × 8½-inch Fabric B/E corner triangle units. See **Diagram 10.** Press.

DIAGRAM 10

Step 2. Sew four Step 1 units to four 2½ × 10½-inch Fabric A/B corner triangle units. See **Diagram 11.** Press.

DIAGRAM 11

Step 3. Sew four 4½ × 8½-inch Fabric A/B/C corner triangle units to four 2½ × 4½-inch Fabric B/D corner triangle units. See **Diagram 12.** Press.

DIAGRAM 12

Step 4. Sew four Step 2 units to four Step 3 units, as shown in **Diagram 13.** Press.

DIAGRAM 13

Step 5. Sew four 2½ × 8½-inch Fabric A/B corner triangle units to four Step 4 units. See **Diagram 14.** Press. Your blocks should now measure 12½ × 8½ inches.

DIAGRAM 14

♥ **SEW CREATIVE** ♥

Instead of making the quilt, make each block into a pillow, and breathe a sigh of relief that you've taken care of four favorite men on your Christmas list!

Lattice

Step 1. Sew the 1½ × 8½-inch Fabric B lattice strips to the right side of two blocks. Press all seams toward the lattice. See **Diagram 15.** Sew a block to the right side of each of those lattice strips to make two rows of two ducks each. See **Diagram 16.** Press.

DIAGRAM 15

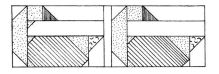

DIAGRAM 16

Step 2. Sew one 1½ × 25½-inch Fabric B lattice strip to the bottom of each row of blocks. Press all seams toward the lattice. Sew the two rows together. Press.

Step 3. Sew a 1½ × 25½-inch Fabric B lattice strip to the top of the quilt. Press. Sew 1½ × 19½-inch lattice strips to the quilt sides. Press.

Half-Inch Accent Border

Step 1. Sew 1 × 44-inch Fabric D accent border strips to the quilt top and bottom. Trim the excess and press all seams toward the accent border.

Step 2. Sew 1 × 22-inch Fabric D strips to the quilt sides. Trim the excess and press.

Speedy Triangles

Step 1. Refer to "Making Speedy Triangles" on page 232 for how to mark, sew, and cut triangle sets for the border. Position an 8½ × 19-inch piece of each of Fabrics A and B with right sides together. Draw a grid of twelve 2⅞-inch squares. Mark on the wrong side of the lighter fabric. See **Diagram 17.**

19"

8½"   2⅞"

DIAGRAM 17

Step 2. After sewing and cutting are complete, press all seams toward Fabric A. You will have made twenty-four 2½-inch triangle sets.

Step 3. Position the 8½ × 19-inch pieces of Fabrics B and C with right sides together, and repeat Steps 1 and 2.

Sawtooth Border

Step 1. Take all 48 triangle sets and lay them out around the edge of the quilt top. Alternating colors, lay 14 triangle sets across both the top and bottom of the quilt and 10 triangle sets on each side. Use the photograph on page 182 and the **Duck Wallhanging Layout** on page 183 as placement guides. Keep track of this layout when you sew.

Step 2. For the top and bottom borders, sew two rows of 14 triangle sets each. Press all seams in the same direction for both rows.

SEW SMART

Measure the border strips against the quilt top and bottom. Take in or let out a few seams by ¹⁄₁₆ inch if necessary to make them fit the quilt top. After the top and bottom borders are sewn on, check the side strips against the sides of the quilt and adjust the same way if necessary.

Step 3. Fit, pin in position, and sew the border strips to the quilt top and bottom. Press seams toward the accent border.

Step 4. For the side borders, sew two rows of ten triangle sets each. Press all seams in the same direction for both rows.

Step 5. Sew 2½-inch Fabric E corner squares to each end of these two border strips. Press seams toward the corner squares.

Step 6. Pin and sew the border strips to the quilt sides. Press.

Layering the Quilt

Arrange and baste the backing, batting, and top together, following directions in "Layering the Quilt" on page 245. Trim the batting and backing to ¼ inch from the raw edge of the quilt top.

Binding the Quilt

Using the four 2¾ × 44-inch binding strips, follow the directions in "Binding the Quilt" on page 246.

Finishing Stitches

Machine or hand quilt in the seam line around each duck. Quilt a scallop design in the bodies and wings. Quilt in the seam line around the beaks and tails and around the half-inch accent border. Quilt a 1½-inch diagonal grid in the background, and quilt in the seam line around each triangle in the border. Sew a ⅜-inch button to each duck for an eye.

Festive Flourishes

Include a selection of fishing lures and hooks, a subscription to an outdoors magazine, a fishing pole, or a tackle box to add an extra-special touch to your gift.

Fish Wallhanging

Finished Size: 19 × 25 inches
Finished Block: 11 × 5 inches

FISH WALLHANGING LAYOUT

Materials

Obvious directional prints are not recommended.

FABRIC A
Use three fabrics.
Body and Corner Squares   ⅛ yard
                    each of *three* fabrics

FABRIC B
Block Background
    and Border   ½ yard
Lattice   ⅙ yard (6 inches)
    TOTAL   ⅝ yard

FABRIC C
Use three fabrics.
Head, Tail, and Border   ¼ yard
                    each of *three* fabrics

FABRIC D
Use three fabrics.
Fins   ⅛ yard

FABRIC E
Half-Inch Accent Border   ⅛ yard

(You may want to buy an extra ⅛ yard of one of your Fabric As for the Half-Inch Accent Border.)

BINDING   ¼ yard

BACKING   ⅔ yard

LIGHTWEIGHT BATTING   ⅔ yard

NOTIONS AND SUPPLIES
Three ⅜-inch buttons for eyes

Cutting Directions

Prewash and press all of your fabrics. Using a rotary cutter, see-through ruler, and cutting mat, prepare the strips as described in the first column in the chart below. Then from those strips, cut the pieces listed in the second column. Some portions of the quilt need to be cut only once, so no additional cutting information will appear in the second column.

	FIRST CUT		SECOND CUT	
	NO. OF STRIPS	**DIMENSIONS**	**NO. OF PIECES**	**DIMENSIONS**
FABRIC A	**Body:** from *each* of the *three* fabrics, cut the following			
	1	3½ × 6½-inch piece		
	1	2½-inch square		
	Corner Squares: from *one* Fabric A, cut the following			
	4	2½-inch squares		
FABRIC B	**Border**			
	1	8 × 44-inch strip	3	8 × 11-inch pieces
	Background			
	1	2½ × 44-inch strip	6	2½-inch squares
			3	2½ × 1½-inch pieces
	2	1½ × 44-inch strips	3	1½ × 5½-inch pieces
			6	1½ × 3½-inch pieces
			24	1½-inch squares

	FIRST CUT		SECOND CUT	
	NO. OF STRIPS	**DIMENSIONS**	**NO. OF PIECES**	**DIMENSIONS**
FABRIC B	Lattice			
	3	1½ × 44-inch strips	2	1½ × 19½-inch strips
			4	1½ × 11½-inch strips
FABRIC C	**Border:** from *each* of the *three* fabrics, cut the following			
	1	8 × 11-inch piece		
	Head and Tail: from *each* of the *three* fabrics, cut the following			
	1	2½ × 5½-inch piece		
	1	2½ × 3½-inch piece		
	1	1½ × 3½-inch piece		
FABRIC D	**Fins:** from *each* of the *three* fabrics, cut the following			
	1	1½ × 4½-inch piece		
	2	1½-inch squares		
FABRIC E	**Half-Inch Accent Border**			
	2	1 × 44-inch strips	2	1 × 20½-inch strips
			2	1 × 13½-inch strips
BINDING	**Before you cut:** From *one* of the 44-inch strips, cut the pieces as directed in the second column. The remaining two strips require no further cutting.			
	3	2¾ × 44-inch strips	2	2¾ × 22-inch strips

Quick Corner Triangles

Refer to "Making Quick Corner Triangles" on page 234 for how to make corner triangle units. You will be making three blocks, each one using a different Fabric A, C, and D combination. Before you start sewing, coordinate the fabrics for each of the three combinations. Keep track of the combinations as you sew the quick corner triangle units. Use the assembly-line method to make the same corner triangle pieces for all three blocks. Refer to the **Fabric Key** for fabric identification, and press in the direction of the triangle just added.

Fabric Key

FABRIC A
(Body)

FABRIC B
(Background)

FABRIC C
(Head and Tail)

FABRIC D
(Fins)

Step 1. Sew three 1½-inch Fabric B squares to three 2½ × 3½-inch Fabric C pieces. See **Diagram 18.** Press.

3½"
2½"

DIAGRAM 18

Step 2. Sew three additional 1½-inch Fabric B squares to the three Step 1 units, as shown in **Diagram 19.** Press.

DIAGRAM 19

Step 3. Sew three 2½-inch Fabric A squares to the three Step 2 units. See **Diagram 20.** Press.

DIAGRAM 20

Step 4. Sew three 1½-inch Fabric B squares to three 1½ × 3½-inch Fabric C pieces. See **Diagram 21.** Press.

DIAGRAM 21

Step 5. Sew three 1½-inch Fabric D squares to three 1½ × 3½-inch Fabric B pieces. See **Diagram 22.** Press.

DIAGRAM 22

Step 6. Sew three 1½-inch Fabric B squares to three 1½ × 4½-inch Fabric D pieces. See **Diagram 23.** Press.

DIAGRAM 23

Step 7. Sew three additional 1½-inch Fabric B squares to the three Step 6 units, as shown in **Diagram 24.** Press.

DIAGRAM 24

Step 8. Sew three 1½-inch Fabric B squares to three 3½ × 6½-inch Fabric A pieces. See **Diagram 25.** Press.

DIAGRAM 25

Step 9. Sew three additional 1½-inch Fabric B squares to the three Step 8 units. See **Diagram 26.** Press.

DIAGRAM 26

Step 10. Sew three 1½-inch Fabric D squares to three 1½ × 5½-inch Fabric B pieces. See **Diagram 27.** Press.

DIAGRAM 27

Step 11. Sew three 2½-inch Fabric B squares to three 2½ × 5½-inch Fabric C pieces. Press seams toward Fabric C. See **Diagram 28.**

DIAGRAM 28

Step 12. Sew three additional 2½-inch Fabric B squares to the three Step 11 units. Press seams toward Fabric C. See **Diagram 29.**

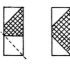

DIAGRAM 29

Assembling the Blocks

Throughout this section, refer to the **Fabric Key** on page 189 to identify the fabric placements in the diagrams. Also, review "Assembly-Line Piecing" on page 234 before you begin. It's more efficient to do the same step for each block at the same time than to piece an entire block together at one time. Pay close attention that the corner triangles are positioned the same as shown in the diagrams. Be sure to use accurate ¼-inch seam allowances and press as you go. Follow the arrows in each diagram for pressing direction. You will be making a total of three Fish blocks. Remember to keep track of your fabric combinations as you sew.

SEW SMART

It may be helpful to lay out the pieces that will make up one block to help you visualize how they go together.

Step 1. Sew three 1½ × 3½-inch Fabric B pieces to three 2½ × 3½-inch Fabric A/B/C corner triangle units. See **Diagram 30.** Press.

DIAGRAM 30

Step 2. Sew three Step 1 units to three 1½ × 3½-inch Fabric B/C corner triangle units. See **Diagram 31.** Press.

DIAGRAM 31

Step 3. Sew three Step 2 units to three 1½ × 3½-inch Fabric B/D corner triangle units. See **Diagram 32.** Press.

DIAGRAM 32

Step 4. Sew three 1½ × 4½-inch Fabric B/D corner triangle units to three 1½ × 2½-inch Fabric B pieces. See **Diagram 33.** Press.

DIAGRAM 33

Step 5. Sew three Step 4 units to three 3½ × 6½-inch Fabric A/B corner triangle units. See **Diagram 34.** Press.

DIAGRAM 34

Step 6. Sew three 1½ × 5½-inch Fabric B/D corner triangle units to three 1½-inch Fabric B squares. See **Diagram 35.** Press.

DIAGRAM 35

Step 7. Sew the three Step 5 units to the three Step 6 units. See **Diagram 36.** Press.

Step 8. Sew the three Step 3 units to the three Step 7 units. See **Diagram 37.** Press.

DIAGRAM 36

DIAGRAM 37

Step 9. Sew three 2½ × 5½-inch Fabric B/C corner triangle units to the three Step 8 units. See **Diagram 38.** Press. Your blocks should now measure 11½ × 5½ inches.

DIAGRAM 38

Lattice

Step 1. Lay out your blocks in a pleasing arrangement. Keep track of your layout while sewing on the lattice.

Step 2. Sew 1½ × 11½-inch Fabric B lattice strips to the top of all three blocks and to the bottom of the bottom block. See **Diagram 39.** Press all seams toward the lattice.

DIAGRAM 39

Step 3. Stitch the three blocks together. Press. Refer to the **Fish Wallhanging Layout** on page 188.

Step 4. Sew 1½ × 19½-inch Fabric B lattice strips to the sides. Press.

Half-Inch Accent Border

Step 1. Sew 1 × 13½-inch Fabric E accent border strips to the quilt top and bottom. Press all seams toward the accent border.

Step 2. Sew 1 × 20½-inch Fabric E strips to the quilt sides. Press.

Speedy Triangles

Step 1. Refer to "Making Speedy Triangles" on page 232 for how to mark, sew, and cut triangle sets for the border. Position an 8 × 11-inch piece of each of Fabrics B and C with right sides together. Draw a grid of six 2⅞-inch squares. Mark on the wrong side of the lighter fabric. See **Diagram 40.**

FABRICS B AND C

DIAGRAM 40

Step 2. After sewing and cutting are complete, press all seams toward Fabric C. You will have made twelve 2½-inch triangle sets.

Step 3. Position the remaining 8 × 11-inch pieces of Fabrics B and C with right sides together, and repeat Steps 1 and 2. You will have made a total of 36 triangle sets, 12 of each Fabric C. You will use 34 of these triangle sets to make the border.

Sawtooth Border

Step 1. Take 34 triangle sets and lay them out around the edge of the quilt top. Alternating colors, lay 7 triangle sets across both the top and bottom of the quilt and 10 triangle sets on each side. Use the photograph on page 182 and the **Fish Wallhanging Layout** on page 188 as placement guides. Keep track of this layout when you sew.

Step 2. For the top and bottom borders, sew two rows of seven triangle sets each. Press all seams in the same direction for both rows.

Step 3. Fit, pin in position, and sew the border strips to the quilt top and bottom. See "Sew Smart" on page 187 for help in fitting the border. Press seams toward the accent border.

Step 4. For the side borders, sew two rows of ten triangle sets each. Press all seams in the same direction for both rows.

Step 5. Sew 2½-inch Fabric A corner squares to each end of these two border strips. Press seams toward the corner squares.

Step 6. Pin and sew the border strips to the quilt sides. Press.

Layering the Quilt

Arrange and baste the backing, batting, and top together, following directions in "Layering the Quilt" on page 245. Trim the batting and backing to ¼ inch from the raw edge of the quilt top.

Binding the Quilt

Using the two 2¾ × 22-inch binding strips for the top and bottom and the two 2¾ × 44-inch strips for the sides, follow the directions in "Binding the Quilt" on page 246.

Finishing Stitches

Machine or hand quilt in the seam line around each fish, around the half-inch accent border, and around each triangle in the border. Quilt an upside-down scallop shape to form waves on the background fabric. Follow the fabric patterns for quilting on the fish bodies. Sew a ⅜-inch button to each fish for an eye.

Stuffed Fish

Materials (for one fish)

Two 4 × 8-inch pieces of fabric for the body
One 2 × 6-inch piece of fabric for the fins
Smooth stuffing (like polyester fiberfill)
Thread to match fish fabric
Two ⅜-inch buttons for eyes

Making the Fish

Step 1. Make a template of the large or small **Fish Pattern** on the opposite page.

Step 2. Put two 4 × 8-inch pieces of your selected fabric with wrong sides together. With a pencil, trace around the fish onto the right side of the fabric, leaving at least ¼ inch around all edges of the template. This is your sewing line.

Step 3. For the fins, cut three 1½-inch fabric squares for the small fish or three 2-inch squares for the large fish. With wrong sides together, press the squares in half diagonally. See **Diagram 41.**

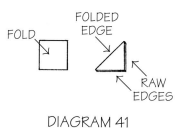

FOLD
FOLDED EDGE
RAW EDGES

DIAGRAM 41

Step 4. Using the marks on the pattern as a guide, position the fins between the layers of fabric, with the folded edge of each fin toward the head of the fish. Pin in place. Be sure to position them far enough into the seam allowance so that they will be securely sewn in.

Step 5. Using a small straight stitch and thread that matches the fish fabric, start sewing where marked on the pattern. Continue to sew all the way around the fish on the marked line, stopping where indicated. Use the opening to stuff the fish.

Step 6. After stuffing, pin the opening closed and topstitch across the opening with your sewing machine.

Step 7. Trim ¼ inch away from the seam line all the way around the fish. Separate the two layers of fabric and trim one layer at a time where the fins are sewn in. Be careful not to accidently trim away the fins!

Step 8. Sew a button to each side of the fish to give it eyes.

"CATCH OF THE DAY" WALL DECORATION

The fun Stuffed Fish are sure to please the fishing enthusiast on your list. Make several of them in different sizes for an impressive catch, even when the real ones get away.

Materials

3 large Stuffed Fish
2 small Stuffed Fish
Fabric scrap, 3 × 44 inches
2 yards of heavyweight
   natural jute
1 package of raffia (1 to
   1½ yards)

For the wall decoration shown in the photograph on page 182, make three large and two small fish. Cut two 1-yard lengths of heavyweight jute. Position two fish on one piece of jute and three on the other. Using a hot-glue gun, glue the jute to the back of each fish head.

From the fabric scrap, tear one 1¼ × 44-inch strip of fabric. Gather the fabric strip and the raffia together and tie an 8-inch bow, leaving the ends to hang down loose. Tie the pieces of jute together and attach the bow. You may need to trim the ends of the fabric, raffia, and jute. Hang your fish wherever you want to show off your catch!

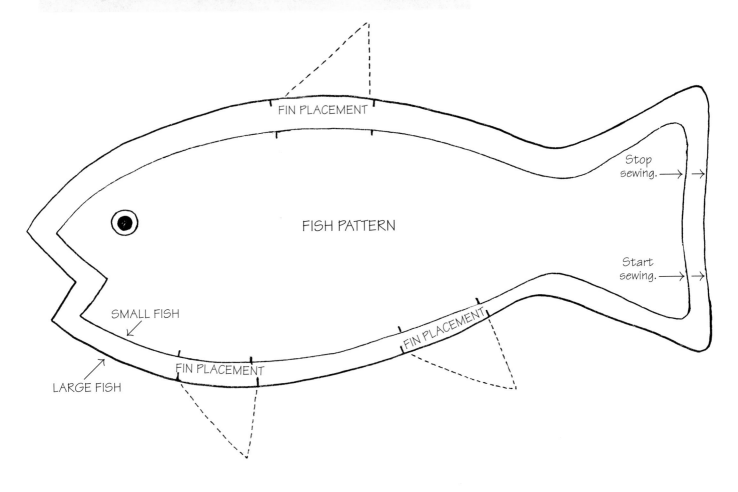

FIN PLACEMENT

Stop sewing. → →

FISH PATTERN

Start sewing. → →

SMALL FISH

LARGE FISH

FIN PLACEMENT

FIN PLACEMENT

Holiday Hostess Set

APRON

When you're the holiday hostess, play the part in style by wearing this charming apron made of Christmas fabrics and a patchwork Wreath block. Use the coordinating hot pad to protect your table under hot dishes. If you're the guest, or if you have a dedicated cook on your Christmas list, make this as a lovely gift set.

Hostess Apron

Materials

Obvious directional prints are not recommended for the wreath block.

FABRIC A

Wreath and Corner Squares	⅛ yard
Pocket and Pocket Lining	⅙ yard
	(6 inches)
TOTAL	⅓ yard

FABRIC B

Block Background	⅛ yard

FABRIC C

Border, Trim, and Bow	⅙ yard
Bib Lining	⅓ yard
TOTAL	½ yard

FABRIC D

Apron Skirt, Waistband, and Neck Straps	1⅛ yards

FABRIC E

Skirt Lining	⅞ yard

NOTIONS AND SUPPLIES

16 assorted red buttons
⅝ yard of ½-inch-wide ribbon for bow (optional substitute for fabric bow)

Cutting Directions

Prewash and press all of your fabrics. Using a rotary cutter, see-through ruler, and cutting mat, prepare the strips as described in the first column in the chart below. Then from those strips, cut the pieces listed in the second column. Some strips need to be cut only once, so no additional cutting information will appear in the second column. Measurements for all pieces include ¼-inch seam allowances.

SEW SMART

If you're making the Hostess Apron *and* the Hot Pad, cut one 1½ × 44-inch strip from Fabric C into two 1½ × 22-inch strips for the bows.

FIRST CUT		SECOND CUT	
NO. OF STRIPS	DIMENSIONS	NO. OF PIECES	DIMENSIONS
FABRIC A	**Wreath and Corner Squares**		
1	3½ × 44-inch strip	4	3½-inch squares
		4	2½-inch squares
		4	1½-inch squares (Corner Squares)
	Pocket		
1	4½ × 5½-inch piece		
	Pocket Lining		
1	5½-inch square		
FABRIC B	**Block Background**		
1	2½ × 44-inch strip	1	2½ × 4½-inch piece
		4	2½-inch squares
		2	2½ × 1½-inch pieces
		4	1½-inch squares
FABRIC C	**Border and Trim**		
2	1½ × 44-inch strips	1	1½ × 30½-inch strip (Apron Trim)
		4	1½ × 8½-inch strips (Block Border)
		1	1½ × 5½-inch strip (Pocket Trim)
	Bow		
1	1½ × 22-inch strip		
	Bib Lining		
1	10½-inch square		

FIRST CUT			SECOND CUT	
NO. OF STRIPS	DIMENSIONS		NO. OF PIECES	DIMENSIONS
FABRIC D	Apron Skirt, Waistband, and Neck Straps			
	Before You Cut: Cut the following pieces in the order listed.			
1	24½ × 30½-inch piece (Apron Skirt)			
4	1½ × 44-inch strips (Waistband)			
2	2½ × 24½-inch strips (Neck Straps)			
FABRIC E	Skirt Lining			
1	30½ × 25½-inch piece			

Quick Corner Triangles

Refer to "Making Quick Corner Triangles" on page 234 for how to make corner triangle units. You will be making one Wreath block. Use the assembly-line method (see page 234) to make the corner triangle units. Refer to the **Fabric Key** for fabric identification, and press seams in the direction of the triangle just added.

Fabric Key

FABRIC A (Wreath)

FABRIC B (Background)

FABRIC C (Apron, Pocket Trim)

SEW SMART

When making the apron and the hot pad, you will save time by using assembly-line piecing to make both Wreath blocks at the same time.

Step 1. Sew four 2½-inch Fabric B squares to four 3½-inch Fabric A squares. See **Diagram 1.** Press.

DIAGRAM 1

Step 2. Sew four 1½-inch Fabric B squares to four 3½-inch Fabric A/B corner triangle units. See **Diagram 2.** Press.

DIAGRAM 2

Assembling the Block

Pay close attention that the corner triangles are positioned as shown in the diagrams. Be sure to use accurate ¼-inch seam allowances and press as you go. Follow the arrows in the diagrams for pressing direction.

Step 1. Sew two 2½-inch Fabric A squares to two 1½ × 2½-inch

Fabric B pieces, as shown in **Diagram 3.** Press.

DIAGRAM 3

Step 2. Sew one 3½-inch Fabric A/B corner triangle unit to each side of two Step 1 units. See **Diagram 4.** Press.

DIAGRAM 4

Step 3. Sew one 2½-inch Fabric A square to each side of one 2½ × 4½-inch Fabric B piece. See **Diagram 5.** Press.

DIAGRAM 5

Step 4. Sew the Step 2 units to the top and bottom of the Step 3 unit. See **Diagram 6.** Press. The block should now measure 8½ inches square.

STEP 2 UNIT

STEP 3 UNIT

STEP 2 UNIT

DIAGRAM 6

Border

Step 1. Sew 1½ × 8½-inch Fabric C border strips to the top and bottom of the block. Press all seams toward the border.

Step 2. Sew 1½-inch Fabric A corner squares to each end of the remaining two 1½ × 8½-inch Fabric C strips. Press.

Step 3. Pin and sew the border strips to the sides of the block. Press.

Attaching the Neck Straps

Step 1. Fold each 2½ × 24½-inch Fabric D neck strap strip in half lengthwise, with right sides together. Using an accurate ¼-inch seam allowance, sew along the long side and one short side on each of the two straps. Trim the corners, turn each strap right side out, and press.

Step 2. Pin the straps in place, with the raw edge even with the top edge of the bib. The outside edge of each strap should line up with the seam of the corner square on each side of the block. See **Diagram 7.** Baste the straps in place. They will be sewn into the seam when the bib is finished.

DIAGRAM 7

Finishing the Bib

Position the bib front and the 10½-inch Fabric C square with right sides together. Pin the pieces together along the two sides and the top edge. Sew them together, leaving the bottom edge open. Trim the corners and turn the bib right side out. Press. Refer to the photograph on page 194 for placement ideas, then position 16 red buttons on the Wreath block and hand sew in place. Baste the bottom edge of the bib together.

Pocket

Step 1. Sew the 1½ × 5½-inch Fabric C pocket trim strip to the 4½ × 5½-inch Fabric A piece. Press the seam toward trim.

Step 2. Accurately trace and cut out the **Pocket Guide** on page 201 to make a pocket template. Position the pocket template on the pocket, with the raw edges of the sides and bottom even with the template. With a pencil, mark angled corners on the pocket. Cut off the two corners on the marked lines. Mark and cut off two corners on the 5½-inch Fabric A pocket lining square in the same manner.

Step 3. With right sides together, sew the pocket to the pocket lining, leaving an opening in the bottom

edge for turning. Trim the corners, turn it right side out, and press. Slip stitch the opening. The finished pocket should now measure 5 × 5 inches. See **Diagram 8.**

5"

5"

DIAGRAM 8

Step 4. Pin the pocket in position on the apron skirt. Position it 3 inches down from the 30½-inch raw edge at the top of the apron skirt and 4¼ inches from the right side of the apron skirt. (Note that the right side as you'd wear it would be the *left* side as you're working on it.) Topstitch the pocket in place, leaving the top edge open.

Skirt

Step 1. Sew the 1½ × 30½-inch Fabric C strip to the bottom of the 24½ × 30½-inch Fabric D piece. Press the seam toward the trim. The skirt should now measure 25½ × 30½ inches.

Step 2. Position the skirt front and the 25½ × 30½ Fabric E lining piece with right sides together. Pin the pieces together along the two sides and the bottom edge. Sew them together, leaving the top edge open. Trim the corners and turn the skirt right side out. Press.

Step 3. Topstitch approximately ¼ inch from the edge of the sides and bottom edge of the skirt. Baste the raw edges of the skirt and lining together on the upper edge of the skirt.

Step 4. Mark the center top of the skirt. Machine baste ¼ and ⅛ inch from the raw edge along the top of the skirt. To gather, pull up the bobbin threads. The top edge of the skirt needs to measure approximately 16 inches after gathering.

Attaching the Waistband

Step 1. Trim the selvage edges from each end of the four 1½ × 44-inch Fabric D strips.

Step 2. Sew the strips together in pairs along the short edges, to make two (approximately) 1½ × 88-inch strips. Press the seams open. One of these strips will be the waistband, and the other strip will be the waistband lining.

Step 3. With a pencil, make a small mark in the seam allowance 8 inches from each side of the center seam on both long edges of the waistband. With right sides together, pin the gathered skirt to the waistband, matching centers and using the pencil marks as guides for the side edges of the skirt. Line up the raw edge of the skirt top with the raw edge of the waistband. See **Diagram 9**. Baste the skirt in place, using a ¼-inch seam allowance.

Step 4. With right sides together, pin the waistband lining to the waistband. (The apron skirt will be sandwiched between the waistband and the waistband lining.) Using a continuous ¼-inch seam,

sew the waistband lining to the waistband. Referring to **Diagram 10**, start sewing at the dot on the waistband next to the left edge of the skirt. Stop sewing at the dot at the right edge of the skirt. Be sure to leave an opening between the two marks. Trim the corners, turn the waistband right side out, and press.

Attaching the Bib

Step 1. Position the bib on the apron waistband by matching the center of the bib to the center of the waistband, with right sides together. (Note that the opening will be wider than the bib.) Using a ¼-inch seam allowance, sew the bib in place. Press the seam toward the waistband.

Step 2. Press the seam allowance under ¼ inch on the unfinished portion of the waistband lining. Hand stitch this to the waistband and bib.

Fabric Bow

To make a fabric bow, fold the 1½ × 22-inch Fabric C strip in half lengthwise with right sides together. Using a ¼-inch seam allowance, sew along the long side of the strip. Turn right side out and press. Turn in ¼ inch on each end of the strip, and hand stitch the ends closed. Tie the strip into a bow and hand sew it in place at the top of the wreath, using the photograph on page 194 as a placement guide. A quick and easy alternative to making a fabric bow is to use a ribbon bow instead.

SEW SMART

Using a bow whip or loop turner will make turning the long, narrow tube of fabric for the bow much easier! See "Quilting by Mail" on page 250 for ordering information.

DIAGRAM 9

DIAGRAM 10

Hot Pad

Finished Size: 10 inches square

Materials

Obvious directional prints are not recommended.

FABRIC A
Wreath and Corner Squares ⅛ yard

FABRIC B
Block Background ⅛ yard

FABRIC C
Border and Bow ⅛ yard
Backing ⅓ yard
or one 12-inch square
TOTAL ½ yard

THERMAL FLEECE
⅓ yard or two 12-inch squares

NOTIONS AND SUPPLIES
⅝ yard ribbon for bow (optional substitute for fabric bow)

Cutting Directions

Prewash and press all of your fabrics. Using a rotary cutter, see-through ruler, and cutting mat, prepare the strips as described in the first column in the chart below. Then from those strips, cut the pieces listed in the second column. Some strips need to be cut only once, so no additional cutting information will appear in the second column. Measurements for all pieces include ¼-inch seam allowances.

	FIRST CUT		SECOND CUT	
	NO. OF STRIPS	DIMENSIONS	NO. OF PIECES	DIMENSIONS
FABRIC A	**Wreath and Corner Squares**			
	1	3½ × 44-inch strip	4	3½-inch squares
			4	2½-inch squares
			4	1½-inch squares (Corner Squares)
FABRIC B	**Block Background**			
	1	2½ × 44-inch strip	1	2½ × 4½-inch piece
			4	2½-inch squares
			2	2½ × 1½-inch pieces
			4	1½-inch squares
FABRIC C	**Border**			
	1	1½ × 44-inch strip	4	1½ × 8½-inch strips
	Bow			
	1	1½ × 22-inch strip		
	Backing			
	1	12-inch square		
THERMAL FLEECE	2	12-inch squares		

10"

10"

HOT PAD

Assembling the Hot Pad

Step 1. Refer to the instructions under "Quick Corner Triangles," "Assembling the Block," and "Border" for the Hostess Apron, beginning on page 197. Follow all the steps in those sections to make one Wreath block.

Step 2. Position the block and backing with right sides together. Lay both pieces on top of the two squares of thermal fleece and pin all three layers together. (A double thickness of the thermal fleece will ensure better heat protection for your tabletop.) Sew them together, leaving a 3- to 4-inch opening for turning. Trim the fleece and backing to the same size as the top.

Step 3. Trim the corners, turn right side out, hand stitch the opening, and press.

Step 4. Machine or hand quilt in the seam line around the wreath.

Step 5. You have the option of trimming the hot pad with a fabric bow or a ribbon bow. Refer to "Fabric Bow" for the Hostess Apron on page 199.

Festive Flourishes

At the next holiday potluck dinner you attend, carry your hot dish with the wreath Hot Pad. Leave the Hot Pad with your hostess as a special gift of thanks.

POCKET GUIDE

Gifts for the Hostess

COASTER PATTERN

Coasters

Finished Size: 3½ inches square

A Saturday afternoon is all it takes to whip up several of these darling gifts so that you'll always be prepared with something handmade to give hostesses of the holiday parties you attend. Choose from a festive set of vinyl-covered coasters, charming lid covers for jars of goodies, a fabric wine bag, an appliquéd fabric sack to dress up a holiday gift plant, or a jauntily decorated paper gift bag. What a nice way to say "Thank you!"

Festive Flourishes

Fill jars with a variety of goodies such as cookies, candies, homemade preserves, gourmet popcorn, dried fruits, or nuts. Or fill a jar with golf tees for the family golfer, an assortment of buttons or spools of threads for your favorite seamstress, or colored pencils for a budding artist.

★

The Potted Plant Gift Bag can dress up an artificial tree or lovely potted poinsettia and is guaranteed to make your gift even more special! You may want to decorate the plant itself with fabric bows, garlands, or raffia.

Materials and Cutting
(for four coasters)

Using a rotary cutter, see-through ruler, and cutting mat, prepare the pieces as described in the chart below. Measurements for all pieces include ¼-inch seam allowances.

	YARDAGE		CUTTING	
			NO. OF PIECES	DIMENSIONS
Base	⅓ yard		4	5½-inch squares
Backing			4	6-inch squares
Background	⅙ yard (6 inches)		1	4 × 20-inch strip
Appliqué Pieces	Several coordinated scraps			
⅓ yard appliqué film, nonsewable, cut into four 5-inch squares and one 3½ x 17-inch strip ⅓ yard Heat n Bond iron-on flexible vinyl				

Making the Coasters

Step 1. Make a template, using the **Coaster Pattern** on page 203. The template resembles a small square picture frame with rounded corners.

Step 2. Fuse 5-inch appliqué film squares to the wrong sides of the four 5½-inch coaster base squares. Peel away the backing papers.

Step 3. Position the 6-inch backing fabric squares and coaster bases from Step 2 with wrong sides together (the fusing film will be in the middle), with the coaster bases on top. *Do not fuse* them together at this point. (Repeated applications of heat tend to weaken the fusing ability of the appliqué film.)

Step 4. Using the inside edge of the template, trace four background shapes onto the paper side of the 3½ × 17-inch strip of appliqué film. Fuse the marked appliqué film to the wrong side of the 4 × 20-inch background fabric strip. Cut out the background

pieces. Remove the paper backing from each piece. Position one in the center of each coaster base. *Do not fuse yet.*

Step 5. Refer to "Quick-Fuse Appliqué" on page 238. Trace the house, snowman, and ginger-bread boy designs from the **Stocking Sampler Appliqué Designs** on pages 99–105. In addition, trace the Santa appliqué design using the **Coaster Pattern** on page 203. Center the appliqué designs on the background pieces. When the appliqué design is in place, fuse all the layers together at once.

Applying the Vinyl

Step 1. Cut the iron-on vinyl into eight 5½-inch squares. For each coaster, peel one of these squares from the paper backing. Place the vinyl sticky-side down on the coaster front. Smooth it out with your hands. Since your vinyl square is smaller than the coaster base, be sure it is centered.

Repeat the process for the back of the coaster.

Step 2. Place the vinyl's protective paper with the shiny side toward the coaster on both sides. Starting on the coaster front, glide the iron over the paper with medium pressure for six to eight seconds. Turn the coaster over and iron again. Carefully remove the paper from both sides.

SEW SMART

Make sure your iron is set on a *medium* temperature. Too much heat will melt the appliqué film, which will cause the layers to separate.

Step 3. Center the template on top of the coaster. Trace around the outside edge of the template with a ballpoint pen. Using sharp scissors, trim the coaster on the line drawn.

Jar Lid Covers

Materials

APPLIQUÉ BACKGROUND
¼ yard

APPLIQUÉ PIECES
Coordinated scraps

NOTIONS AND SUPPLIES
Appliqué film, nonsewable
Jute, raffia, or fabric scraps for
    tying a bow

Appliqué

You will have enough fabrics to
make several jar lid covers. The directions are for making one.

Step 1. Cut a background square
that is 3 to 4 inches larger than the
jar lid. Pink the edges.

Pinked edges can be
made with either pinking
shears or a rotary cutter. Both
Olfa and Fiskars now have
pinking blades available for
their cutters.

Step 2. Refer to "Quick-Fuse
Appliqué" on page 238. Trace the
gingerbread boy or Christmas

stocking design from the
Appliqué Ornament Patterns
on pages 88–89. Center it on the
background piece and fuse it in
place.

Step 3. Embellish the gingerbread
boy or stocking, as described on
pages 86–87.

Step 4. Tie the fabric square over
the jar lid with jute, raffia, or a
pinked strip of fabric.

SEW SMART

Hold the fabric in place
on the jar lid with a rubber
band while tying the bow.

Gift Bag

Finished Size: 8 × 10½ inches

Materials

APPLIQUÉ BACKGROUND
¼ yard or 7½ × 9½-inch piece

APPLIQUÉ PIECES
Several coordinated scraps

NOTIONS AND SUPPLIES
8 × 10½-inch brown kraft
    shopping bag with handles
Appliqué film, nonsewable
Raffia
4 assorted buttons (½ to ¾ inch)
Three ³⁄₁₆-inch black buttons
7 black seed beads for embellishing
Note: If your crafts shop doesn't
    carry shopping bags, see
    "Quilting by Mail" on page 250
    for ordering information.

Appliqué

Step 1. Refer to "Quick-Fuse
Appliqué" on page 238. Trace the

snowman design for Block #1 from
the **Snowman Appliqué
Patterns** on pages 134–135.

Step 2. Cut a 7 × 9-inch piece of
appliqué film. Fuse it to the back
of the 7½ × 9½-inch background
fabric piece. Trim this layered
piece down to 6½ × 8½ inches.
Remove the paper backing.

Step 3. Quick-fuse the background piece and snowman design onto the bag front. Center
the design approximately 1 inch
from the top edge of the bag.
Position and fuse the entire design all at one time.

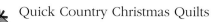

Finishing

Tie several strands of raffia in a bow. Hot-glue the bow to the center top of the bag front, above the snowman. Glue a button at each corner of the background piece.

Glue on black seed beads for eyes and mouth. Glue three $\frac{3}{16}$-inch black buttons on Mr. Snowman's front.

Potted Plant Gift Bag

Finished Size: 12 × 10 inches

Materials

BAG FABRIC $\frac{3}{8}$ yard

APPLIQUÉ PIECES AND FABRIC TIE
Several coordinated scraps

NOTIONS AND SUPPLIES
Appliqué film, nonsewable

Making the Bag

This plant gift bag fits a pot that is 4½ inches tall and 6 inches wide at the top. You may need to adjust the cutting dimensions given to fit the pot size you have selected.

Step 1. Cut the bag fabric to 12½ × 22 inches.

Step 2. Make a narrow hem on both 12½-inch edges of the fabric piece. Fold ¼ inch to the wrong side, fold another ¼ inch to the wrong side, and stitch along the folded edge.

Step 3. Fold the bag fabric in half, with right sides together, to make a 12½ × 10½-inch bag. Pin and sew a ¼-inch seam on each side. See **Diagram 1.** Press so that a crease forms across the bottom of the bag.

HEMMED EDGES

FOLD

DIAGRAM 1

Step 4. To square the corners, line up one side seam to be directly on top of the crease in the bottom of the bag, forming a triangle. Draw a line across the point. See **Diagram 2.** The line should be perpendicular to the seam and 4½ inches long. Machine stitch on the line. Repeat for the other corner.

4½"

STITCHING LINE

SIDE SEAM

HEMMED EDGES

DIAGRAM 2

Step 5. Trim off the triangle points, leaving a ¼-inch seam. See **Diagram 3.** Turn the bag right side out and press. The bag will now have a rectangular base.

TRIM

Leave ¼" seam allowance.

DIAGRAM 3

Appliqué

Step 1. Refer to "Quick-Fuse Appliqué" on page 238. Trace the snowman design for Block #6 from the **Snowman Appliqué Patterns** on pages 134–135.

Step 2. Cut a 5-inch square of appliqué film. Fuse it to the wrong side of the 5½-inch-square background fabric. Trim it to 4¼ × 4 inches. Remove the paper backing.

Step 3. Center the background piece ¾ inch from the bottom of the bag. Position the snowman on top of the background piece, and fuse it in place on the bag.

Finishing

To make a fabric ribbon, cut a ½ × 44-inch strip of fabric with pinked edges. Place a potted plant in the gift bag, and loosely tie the top of the bag shut with the fabric ribbon. You can place the tie around the rim or just above the rim of the pot.

Wine Bottle Gift Bag

Finished Size: 5¼ × 14½ inches

Materials

BAG FABRIC ⅓ yard

FABRIC TIE ⅛ yard
or one 2 × 22-inch scrap

APPLIQUÉ DESIGNS
Several coordinated scraps

NOTIONS AND SUPPLIES
Appliqué film, nonsewable

Making the Bag

Step 1. Cut the bag fabric to 11 × 17 inches.

Step 2. Make a hem on one of the 11-inch edges of the fabric piece. Fold ¼ inch to the wrong side and press. Fold the same edge 2 inches to the wrong side and press. Stitch along the first folded edge. The fabric piece should now measure 11 × 14¾ inches.

Step 3. Fold the fabric piece in half lengthwise, with right sides to-

gether. Pin and sew ¼-inch seams along the bottom and side edges. See **Diagram 4.** Clip the corners, turn right side out, and press.

DIAGRAM 4

Appliqué

Step 1. Refer to "Quick-Fuse Appliqué" on page 238. Trace the **Santa Appliqué Pattern** on this page.

Step 2. Quick-fuse appliqué Santa to the front of the bag. Position and fuse the entire design at one time.

Finishing

Make a fabric ribbon by cutting a 1 × 22-inch strip of fabric with pinked edges. Place the bottle of wine in the bag and tie the fabric ribbon around the neck of the bottle.

❤ SEW CREATIVE ❤

Look for a more glitzy fabric and add some silver or gold dazzling ribbon or decorations to make your Wine Bottle Gift Bag suitable for a bottle of champagne to give the hostess for a New Year's Eve celebration.

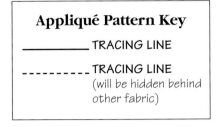

Appliqué Pattern Key	
———————	TRACING LINE
- - - - - - - - -	TRACING LINE (will be hidden behind other fabric)

SANTA APPLIQUÉ PATTERN

Teacher's Pet

Share your quilting talents with a special teacher with this quaint apple quilt. Apples are a decorating staple of country decor, though, so don't limit these ideas to teachers only. For extra credit, wrap your quilt in a gift bag that can double as a lunch bag.

Mini-Apple Quilt

Finished Size: 19 × 16½ inches

Materials and Cutting

Using a rotary cutter, see-through ruler, and cutting mat, prepare the pieces as described in the chart below. Measurements for all pieces include ¼-inch seam allowances. Obvious directional prints are not recommended for the lattice, borders, and binding.

	YARDAGE		CUTTING	
		NO. OF PIECES	**DIMENSIONS**	
Background	¼ yard		**Before You Cut:** Cut one 4½ × 44-inch strip.	
		6	4½ × 5½-inch pieces	
Four-Patch		1	1½ × 15-inch strip	
Lattice	¼ yard		**Before You Cut:** Cut three 1 × 44-inch strips.	
		3	1 × 13½-inch strips	
		2	1 × 12-inch strips	
		4	1 × 5½-inch strips	
Four-Patch		1	1½ × 15-inch strip	
Binding			**Before You Cut:** Cut two 1 × 44-inch strips.	
		2	1 × 18½-inch strips	
		2	1 × 17-inch strips	
Border	⅙ yard (6 inches; cut into two 2½ × 44-inch strips)	2	2½ × 14½-inch strips	
		2	2½ × 12-inch strips	
Backing	⅝ yard	1	20½ × 23-inch piece	
Lightweight Batting	⅝ yard	1	20½ × 23-inch piece	
Appliqué Pieces	Several coordinated scraps			
Appliqué film, nonsewable				

QUILT LAYOUT

19"

16½"

Background and Lattice

Use accurate ¼-inch seam allowances, and press all seams toward the lattice after each step.

Step 1. Sew 1 × 5½-inch lattice strips to each side of two 4½ × 5½-inch background pieces. See **Diagram 1.** Press.

1" 4½" 1"

5½" 5½"

DIAGRAM 1

Step 2. Sew 4½ × 5½-inch background pieces to each side of the Step 1 units to make two rows of three blocks each. See **Diagram 2.** Press.

4½" STEP 1 UNIT 4½"

5½" 5½"

DIAGRAM 2

Step 3. Sew one 1 × 13½-inch lattice strip to the top of each row and to the bottom of the bottom row. Press. Sew the two rows together and press.

Step 4. Sew 1 × 12-inch lattice strips to the sides of the quilt. Press.

Four-Patch Squares

Step 1. Sew together the 1½ × 15-inch Four-Patch strips, one each of two different fabrics, as shown in **Diagram 3.** Press the seam toward the darker fabric. Cut this strip set into eight 2½ × 1½-inch pieces.

2½"

1½"

15"

CUTTING LINES

DIAGRAM 3

Step 2. Sew these pieces together into four sets of two pieces each, making four 2½-inch Four-Patch squares. See **Diagram 4.** Press.

2½"

2½"

DIAGRAM 4

Border and Binding

Step 1. Sew 2½ × 14½-inch border strips to the quilt top and bottom. Press all seams toward the border.

Step 2. Sew 2½-inch Four-Patch squares to each end of two 2½ × 12-inch border strips. Press.

Step 3. Pin and sew the borders to the quilt sides. Press.

Step 4. Sew 1 × 18½-inch binding strips to the quilt top and bottom. Press all seams toward the binding. Sew 1 × 16-inch binding strips to the quilt sides. Press.

Appliqué

Step 1. Refer to "Quick-Fuse Appliqué" on page 238. Trace six apples, using the **Apple Appliqué Pattern** on the opposite page.

Step 2. Position and fuse one apple at a time in the center of each background piece, using the photograph on page 208 as a placement guide.

Finishing

Step 1. Position the top and backing with right sides together. Lay both pieces on top of the batting, and pin all three layers together. Sew together, leaving a 3- to 4-inch opening for turning. Trim the batting and backing to the same size as the top.

Step 2. Trim the corners, turn right side out, hand stitch the opening, and press.

Step 3. Machine or hand quilt in the seam line around the lattice, borders, and binding. Outline the appliqué designs by quilting ⅟₁₆ inch away from the edge of the designs. Quilt a leaf design along the border and diagonal lines through the center of the Four-Patch squares.

Lunch Bag

Materials

APPLIQUÉ PIECES
Several coordinated scraps
Note: The blackboard and frame require 7-inch squares.

NOTIONS AND SUPPLIES
8 × 10½-inch brown kraft shopping bag with handles
Appliqué film, nonsewable
Raffia

Appliqué

Step 1. Refer to "Quick-Fuse Appliqué" on page 238. Trace the blackboard, frame, and apple, using the **Lunchbag Appliqué Pattern** and the **Apple Appliqué Pattern** on this page.

Step 2. Fuse the entire design on the bag all at one time. Tie several strands of raffia to the bag handle.

Festive Flourishes

Decorate Teacher's gift package with an apple ornament and an apple peeler all tied in a raffia bow. Or fuse apples to a package wrapped in brown kraft paper. Either way, Teacher will be absolutely delighted! Include a gift certificate from a bookstore to add to Teacher's library. The Lunch Bag can double as a great gift bag for giving Teacher the quilt. A nice red, juicy apple inside the bag would be a fun treat as well.

LUNCH BAG APPLIQUÉ PATTERN

Appliqué Pattern Key
_____ TRACING LINE
- - - - - TRACING LINE
(will be hidden behind other fabric)

APPLE APPLIQUÉ PATTERN

Tooltime

11"

22½"

BANNER LAYOUT

Tooltime Banner

Finished Size: 11 × 22½ inches

Festive Flourishes

Give him that tool box he's been asking for, and inside, surprise him with his own work apron! Tuck some small specialty items in the pockets of the apron, or tie them onto the package. You could even hot-glue some spare nuts, bolts, and screws onto the outside of the package, along with some particularly graceful tendrils of wood shavings.

Here's a perfect gift to sew for the men on your list who would rather get tools than ties. This fun banner with all the basics from the toolbox goes together quickly and easily. The apron is practical and useful—just right for a down-to-earth, nuts-and-bolts kind of guy! You'll have as much fun making these as the guys will have receiving them!

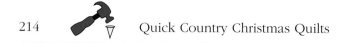

Materials and Cutting

Using a rotary cutter, see-through ruler, and cutting mat, prepare the pieces as described in the chart below. Measurements for all pieces include ¼-inch seam allowances. Obvious directional prints are not recommended.

	YARDAGE		CUTTING
		NO. OF PIECES	**DIMENSIONS**
Background	¼ yard (cut into two 3½ × 44-inch strips)	1	3 × 10½-inch piece
		4	3½ × 7-inch pieces
		4	3½-inch squares
Large Triangle	⅙ yard (6 inches)	1	triangle (use the Triangle Template on page 218)
Hanging Tabs		1	2 × 20-inch strip
Lattice	⅙ yard (cut into four 1 × 44-inch strips)	5	1 × 10½-inch strips
		2	1 × 7-inch strips
		3	1 × 3½-inch strips
Binding		2	1 × 22-inch strips
		2	1 × 12-inch strips
Backing	⅜ yard	1	13½ × 25-inch piece
Lightweight Batting	⅜ yard	1	13½ × 25-inch piece
Appliqué Pieces	⅛-yard pieces or several coordinated scraps		

Appliqué film, nonsewable
12-inch wooden ruler
5½-inch-long fine wire (optional)

Background Assembly

Use accurate ¼-inch seam allowances, and press all seams toward the lattice after each step.

Step 1. Sew a 1 × 3½-inch lattice strip between a 3½ × 7-inch background piece and a 3½-inch background square. See **Diagram 1.** Press.

Step 2. Sew a 1 × 3½-inch lattice strip between two 3½-inch background squares, as shown in **Diagram 2.** Press.

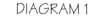

DIAGRAM 1

DIAGRAM 2

Step 3. Sew 1 × 7-inch lattice strips to each side of the Step 2 unit. See **Diagram 3.** Press.

DIAGRAM 3

Step 4. Sew a 3½ × 7-inch background piece to each side of the Step 3 unit. See **Diagram 4.** Press.

DIAGRAM 4

Step 5. Sew a 1 × 3½-inch lattice strip between a 3½-inch background square and a 3½ × 7-inch background piece. See **Diagram 5.** Press.

DIAGRAM 5

Step 6. Sew 1 × 10½-inch lattice strips to the top and bottom of the 3½ × 10½-inch background piece, as shown in **Diagram 6.**

DIAGRAM 6

Step 7. Sew 1 × 10½-inch lattice strips to the bottom of the units from Steps 1, 4, and 5. See **Diagram 7.** Press.

DIAGRAM 7

Step 8. Sew the rows together. Press. Sew the triangle to the bottom of the rows, as shown in **Diagram 7.** Press.

Binding

Step 1. Sew a 1 × 12-inch binding strip to the left side of the triangle end. See **Diagram 8.** Press. Trim the excess.

DIAGRAM 8

Step 2. Sew a 1 × 12-inch binding strip to the right side of the triangle end. See **Diagram 8.** Press. Trim the excess.

Step 3. Sew 1 × 22-inch binding strips to the sides of the banner. Press. Trim the excess.

Appliqué

Step 1. Refer to "Quick-Fuse Appliqué" on page 238. Trace one of each of the appliqué designs, using the **Tooltime Appliqué Patterns** on pages 216–218.

Step 2. Quick-fuse appliqué the designs in the center of each corresponding background piece. Position and fuse one design at a time. Use the photograph on page 212 as a placement guide.

Step 3. Make a handle for the paint can using a 5½-inch piece of fine wire. Make a loop on each end and hand sew them in place on each side of the paint can. Refer to the photograph on page 212. The handle can also be drawn in place using a black, extra-fine point, permanent felt-tip pen.

Finishing

Step 1. To make the hanging tabs, fold the 2 × 20-inch strip of fabric in half lengthwise, with wrong sides together, and press. Fold each long edge into the center and press again. Topstitch along the edge of both long sides of the fabric strip.

Step 2. Using a ruler and a rotary cutter, cut three 6-inch pieces from this strip. Fold each piece in half so the cut ends meet. Press.

Step 3. On the right side of the banner top, space the tabs evenly across the top of the banner. Position the tabs with the raw edges even with the raw edge of the banner. Pin and then baste the tabs in place. They will be sewn into the seam when the banner is finished.

Step 4. Position the top and backing with right sides together. Lay both pieces on top of the batting and pin all three layers together. Using a ¼-inch seam allowance, sew together, leaving a 3- to 4-inch opening for turning. Trim the backing and batting to the same size as the top.

Step 5. Trim the corners, turn right side out, hand stitch the opening, and press.

Step 6. Machine or hand quilt in the seam line around the lattice and binding. Outline the appliqué designs by quilting 1⁄16 inch away from the edge of the designs. Beginning in the center, quilt 1-inch vertical lines in the bottom triangle.

Step 7. Paint or stain a 12-inch wooden ruler and insert it through the tabs.

Tooltime Apron

Materials

PURCHASED DENIM OR CANVAS APRON

APPLIQUÉ PIECES

Several coordinated scraps or ⅛-yard pieces

NOTIONS AND SUPPLIES

Appliqué film, sewable

Appliqué

Step 1. Refer to "Quick-Fuse Appliqué" on page 238 and "Machine Appliqué" on page 239. Trace one of each of the hammer, paintbrush, large and small screwdrivers, and "Tooltime" appliqué designs, using the **Tooltime Appliqué Patterns** on pages 216–218.

Step 2. Using a sewable appliqué film, fuse the appliqué designs in a pleasing arrangement on the front of your purchased apron. Refer to the photograph on page 212 for placement.

Step 3. Machine appliqué the designs in place.

TOOLTIME APPLIQUÉ PATTERNS

Cut with pinking shears.

Appliqué Pattern Key

——————— TRACING LINE

- - - - - - - TRACING LINE (will be hidden behind other fabric)

TOOLTIME APPLIQUÉ PATTERNS

Appliqué Pattern Key

——————— TRACING LINE

- - - - - - - TRACING LINE
(will be hidden behind other fabric)

TOOLTIME APPLIQUÉ PATTERNS

TRIANGLE TEMPLATE

Hearts and Buttons

Hearts and Buttons

14½"

16"

QUILT LAYOUT

Miniature Heart Quilt

Finished Quilt: 14½ × 16 inches
Finished Block: 4 × 3 inches

Materials

FABRIC A

Use six fabrics.	
Hearts	⅛ yard
	each of *six* fabrics

FABRIC B

Background	⅛ yard
	(6 inches)
Lattice	⅛ yard
TOTAL	¼ yard

FABRIC C

Half-Inch Accent Border	⅛ yard
Binding	⅛ yard
TOTAL	¼ yard

FABRIC D

Wide Border	⅛ yard

BACKING	½ yard

LIGHTWEIGHT BATTING	½ yard

Just about any of the women on your gift list would be delighted to find one of these stylish projects under the tree on Christmas morning. The Miniature Heart Quilt is just right for filling a small nook or cranny or for displaying on a dresser. The coordinating Sachet can be tucked into the drawer. Just for fun, make an embellished tie, button pin, and earrings, as shown on page 225. They're so easy—better make one of each for yourself, too!

Cutting Directions

Prewash and press all of your fabrics. Using a rotary cutter, see-through ruler, and cutting mat, prepare the strips as described in the first column in the chart below. Then from those strips, cut the pieces listed in the second column. Some strips need to be cut only once, so no additional cutting information will appear in the second column. Measurements for all pieces include ¼-inch seam allowances.

	FIRST CUT		SECOND CUT	
	NO. OF STRIPS	**DIMENSIONS**	**NO. OF PIECES**	**DIMENSIONS**
FABRIC A	**Hearts:** from *each* of the *six* fabrics, cut the following			
	1	2½ × 44-inch strip	1	2½ × 4½-inch piece
			2	2½ × 1½-inch pieces
FABRIC B	**Background**			
	1	2½ × 44-inch strip	12	2½-inch squares
	1	1½ × 44-inch strip	24	1½-inch squares
	Lattice			
	2	1 × 44-inch strips	2	1 × 11½-inch strips
			4	1 × 9-inch strips
			3	1 × 3½-inch strips
FABRIC C	**Half-Inch Accent Border**			
	2	1 × 44-inch strips	2	1 × 12½-inch strips
			2	1 × 10-inch strips
	Binding			
	2	1 × 44-inch strips	2	1 × 15½-inch strips
			2	1 × 14-inch strips
FABRIC D	**Wide Border**			
	2	2 × 44-inch strips	2	2 × 15½-inch strips
			2	2 × 11-inch strips
BACKING	1	17 × 19-inch piece		
BATTING	1	17 × 19-inch piece		

Quick Corner Triangles

Refer to "Making Quick Corner Triangles" on page 234 for how to make corner triangle units. You will be making six Heart blocks, one each of six different fabric As. Refer to the **Fabric Key**, and press in the direction of the triangle just added.

Fabric Key

 FABRIC A
(Hearts)

☐ FABRIC B
(Background)

Step 1. Sew twelve 1½-inch Fabric B squares to twelve 1½ × 2½-inch Fabric A pieces. See **Diagram 1** for proper placement. Press.

DIAGRAM 1

Step 2. Sew 12 additional 1½-inch Fabric B squares to the 12 Step 1 units. See **Diagram 2.** Press.

DIAGRAM 2

Step 3. Sew six 2½-inch Fabric B squares to six 4½ × 2½-inch Fabric A pieces. See **Diagram 3.** Press.

DIAGRAM 3

Step 4. Sew six additional 2½-inch Fabric B squares to the six Step 3 units, as shown in **Diagram 4.** Press.

DIAGRAM 4

Making the Heart Blocks

Review "Assembly-Line Piecing" on page 234 before you get started. It's more efficient to do the same step for each block at the same time than to piece an entire block together at one time. Pay close attention that the corner triangles are positioned the same as shown in the diagrams. Be sure to use accurate ¼-inch seam allowances and press as you go. Follow the arrows in the diagrams for pressing direction. You will be making a total of six Heart blocks.

Step 1. Sew six 1½ × 2½-inch Fabric A/B corner triangle units to the other six 1½ × 2½-inch Fabric A/B corner triangle units. See **Diagram 5.** Press.

DIAGRAM 5

Step 2. Sew six 2½ × 4½-inch Fabric A/B corner triangle units to the six Step 1 units. See **Diagram 6.** Press. The blocks should now measure 4½ × 3½ inches.

DIAGRAM 6

Lattice

Step 1. Lay out the Heart blocks in a pleasing arrangement in three rows of two blocks each. Keep track of your layout while sewing on the lattice, and press all seams toward the lattice.

Step 2. Sew a 1 × 3½-inch Fabric B strip between the two Heart blocks from each of the three rows. See **Diagram 7.** Press.

DIAGRAM 7

Step 3. Sew 1 × 9-inch Fabric B strips to the bottom of all three rows and to the top of the top row. Press. Sew the three rows together. Press.

Step 4. Sew 1 × 11½-inch Fabric B strips to the sides. Press.

Half-Inch Accent Border

Sew 1 × 10-inch Fabric C accent border strips to the top and bottom of the quilt. Press all seams toward the accent border. Sew 1 × 12½-inch Fabric C strips to the quilt sides. Press.

Wide Border

Sew 2 × 11-inch Fabric D wide border strips to the top and bottom of the quilt. Press all seams toward the wide border. Sew 2 × 15½-inch Fabric D strips to the quilt sides. Press.

Binding

Sew 1 × 14-inch Fabric C binding strips to the quilt top and bottom.

Press all seams toward the binding. Sew 1 × 15½-inch Fabric C strips to the quilt sides. Press.

Finishing

Step 1. Position the top and backing with right sides together. Lay both pieces on top of the bat-ting, and pin all three layers to-gether. Sew them together, leaving a 3- to 4-inch opening for turning. Trim the batting and backing to the same size as the top.

Step 2. Trim the corners, turn right side out, hand stitch the opening, and press.

Step 3. Machine or hand quilt in the seam line around the hearts, borders, and binding. Use a pur-chased quilting template, if you like, to quilt an interlocking circle design in the background. Quilt a 1¼-inch diagonal grid in the wide border.

Sachet

Finished Size: 4 × 7½ inches

Materials

FABRIC A

Heart and Top Band ⅛ yard

FABRIC B

Background ⅙ yard (6 inches)

NOTIONS AND SUPPLIES

⅝ yard of ribbon for bow (or one ⅝ × 22-inch strip of coordinating fabric)
Potpourri

Cutting Directions

Prewash and press all of your fab-rics. Using a rotary cutter, see-through ruler, and cutting mat, pre-pare the strips as described in the first column in the chart below. Then from those strips, cut the pieces listed in the second column. Some strips need to be cut only once, so no additional cut-ting information will appear in the second column. Measurements for all pieces include ¼-inch seam al-lowances.

	FIRST CUT		SECOND CUT	
	NO. OF STRIPS	DIMENSIONS	NO. OF PIECES	DIMENSIONS
FABRIC A	**Heart and Top Band**			
	1	2½ × 44-inch strip	1	1½ × 8½-inch piece
			1	2½ × 4½-inch piece
			2	2½ × 1½-inch pieces
FABRIC B	**Background**			
	1	4½ × 44-inch strip	1	4½ × 7½-inch piece
			1	4½ × 3½-inch piece
			1	4½ × 1½-inch piece
			2	2½-inch squares
			4	1½-inch squares

SACHET LAYOUT

Making the Heart Block

Refer to "Quick Corner Triangles" and "Making the Heart Blocks" for the Miniature Heart Quilt on page 222. Follow all the steps in those sections. Since you will be making only one Heart block for each Sachet, the numbers will change from twelve to two and from six to one.

SEW SMART

If you plan on making several sachets as gifts, make all of the Heart blocks at once, using assembly-line piecing (see page 234).

Assembling the Sachet

Use accurate ¼-inch seam allowances, and press seams in the direction indicated in each diagram.

Fabric Key

▨ FABRIC A (Hearts)

☐ FABRIC B (Background)

Step 1. Sew the 3½ × 4½-inch Fabric B piece to the top of the Heart block. See **Diagram 8.** Press.

4½"
3½"
3½"
4½"

DIAGRAM 8

Step 2. Sew the 1½ × 4½-inch Fabric B piece to the Step 1 unit. See **Diagram 9.** Press.

STEP 1 UNIT
1½"
4½"

DIAGRAM 9

Step 3. Sew the 4½ × 7½-inch Fabric B piece to the left side of the Step 2 unit. See **Diagram 10.** Press.

4½"
7½"
STEP 2 UNIT

DIAGRAM 10

Step 4. Sew the 1½ × 8½-inch Fabric A piece to the top of the

Step 3 unit. See **Diagram 11.** Press the seam toward Fabric A.

8½"
1½"
STEP 3 UNIT

DIAGRAM 11

Step 5. Press under ¼ inch on the long unfinished edge of the top band. Press the band in half lengthwise, with wrong sides together. The pressed edge should barely cover the stitching line from Step 4. Baste in position. Topstitch the band on the front side of the sachet.

Step 6. Fold the sachet so that right sides are together, and stitch the side and bottom seams. Trim the corners, turn right side out, and press. Fill to the top of the heart with your favorite potpourri. Tie a ribbon or fabric strip around the top to close.

Festive Flourishes

Make the sachet bag, but use it to hold the Button Pin and Earrings. Along with the gift, give a bag of scented potpourri to fill the bag after the jewelry is removed.

Button Pin and Earrings

Bags of buttons are available in bulk through the mail-order sources listed in "Quilting by Mail" on page 250. A good place to look for deals on jars or bags of buttons is at weekend yard sales and secondhand stores. (Look for the metal base pieces, pin backs, and earring backs at a craft or jewelry supply store.)

Materials

Assorted buttons, ¼ to 1 inch
Base piece *or* large button
Pin back
Earring backs
Hot-glue gun

Button Pin

Using a hot-glue gun, glue buttons in a pleasing arrangement on top of the base piece or large button. Refer to the photograph on this page for placement ideas. Glue the pin back to the back side of the base piece.

Earrings

Using a hot-glue gun, glue matching buttons to the earring backs.

Embellished Tie for Her

Scour the secondhand stores for ties and buttons, and put them together with your fabric scraps to create a unique fashion statement like one you'd find in a specialty boutique.

Materials

Purchased tie
Coordinated fabric scraps
Appliqué film
Assorted buttons, ⅜ to ¾ inch

Appliqué

Step 1. Refer to "Quick-Fuse Appliqué" on page 238. Trace three of each of the hearts from the **Heart Appliqué Patterns** on this page.

Step 2. Quick-fuse the hearts to the tie, refering to the photograph on this page for placement.

Step 3. Hand sew a button in the center of each fused heart. Hand sew assorted buttons to the tie.

HEART APPLIQUE
PATTERNS

Techniques for Quick Country Quilting

In these chapters you'll find all the details you'll need for making the quilt projects
in this book. "Timesaving Methods for Cutting and Piecing" on page 228 highlights the
speedy cutting and sewing techniques I incorporate into all of my projects. In
"Timesaving Methods for Appliqué" on page 237, you'll learn my Penstitch appliqué
technique, as well as other shortcut methods. "Putting It All Together" on page 242 takes
you from the finished quilt top through the final phase of quilting and binding.
Here's a handy checklist of pointers on how to use this section of the book.

★ Before you make your first project, take the time to
read these chapters. They don't take long to read, and
it's a good way to familiarize yourself with all the techniques that appear in the projects.

★ Be sure to check "What You'll Need for Cutting and
Piecing" on page 228 and "What You'll Need for
Appliqué" on page 237. You may want to take this book
with you to the quilt shop in case you have any questions
about one or more of the items you need to purchase.

★ Once you are actually working on a project, be
sure to flip back to these chapters when you need to
refresh your memory about the specific details of a
certain technique. The techniques can apply to any
quilt you're making.

★ Watch for "Sew Smart" and "Sew Creative" tips
throughout the chapters and project directions. These
are handy hints and creative ideas you can use as you
make your projects.

Timesaving Methods for Cutting and Piecing

Timesaving methods for cutting and piecing have opened up the world of quiltmaking to many people who would not otherwise have attempted even a simple beginner's project. It's wonderful to see so much quilting and creativity result from the use of easy-to-master tools and techniques.

In this chapter, I'll list all the tools and supplies you'll need to get started quilting and explain in detail how to use them. Investing in the appropriate tools and learning the techniques will ensure that your projects go together quickly and accurately. I'll also explain simple sewing techniques that will help you piece your quilt together in no time flat! Be sure to read and understand this chapter before you start any of the projects, and refer back to these pages whenever you need a refresher on any details of the techniques for cutting and piecing.

What You'll Need for Cutting and Piecing

Here's a rundown of items you should have before you begin a project.

Sewing Machine: You'll need a sewing machine that does a good, reliable straight stitch. All the bells, whistles, and stitches of sophisticated machines aren't necessary for basic piecing. Just keep your machine clean, oiled, and in good working condition.

Rotary Cutter: This simple tool has sparked a quiltmaking renaissance. With it, you can cut quilt pieces much more quickly and accurately than with scissors. You can cut four or more layers of fabric at once without marking the fabric or using a template.

Rotary cutters are readily available in quilt shops, in fabric stores, and through mail-order catalogs. Select the larger-size cutter—its bigger blade will give you more control and will last longer. (By

the way, a rotary cutter works comfortably whether you're left- or right-handed.) Be sure to purchase a cutting mat as well. You should never use a rotary cutter without one.

Cutting Mat: The cutting mat is the surface on which you lay your fabric before cutting. It's essential to use this with your rotary cutter. The mat protects the tabletop on which you are cutting as well as the blade of your cutter. Its surface also helps keep your fabric from slipping. Most mats are "self-healing," meaning you won't see the cutting lines in the surface. Under normal use, these mats will last for many years.

Get the largest size mat you have room for. The 24 × 36-inch mat is an all-around good size. If your mat is small, you will end up moving your fabric all the time while cutting. A cutting mat will warp when exposed to any heat sources, so be sure to store it flat and out of sunlight, and don't set anything hot on it.

See-Through Ruler: The third essential element in your trio of quick-cutting tools is a special rigid plastic, see-through ruler to use with your rotary cutter and cutting mat. There are lots of shapes and sizes of rulers on the market now, but to start out, I recommend a 6 × 24-inch ruler with ⅛-inch increments and a 45 degree angle line marked on it.

Pen: For drawing the Speedy Triangle grids, you will need a fine- or medium-point ballpoint pen or a fine or extra-fine point, permanent felt-tip pen.

Sewing Thread: Use a good-quality thread for piecing. When you're investing your time and fabrics in a project, you want to make certain that your thread will not compromise your efforts. Use a light neutral color, such as beige or gray, when piecing light fabrics, and a dark neutral, such as dark gray, when piecing dark fabrics.

Iron, Ironing Board, and Towel: Use your iron on the cotton setting and keep the ironing surface clean. For precise pressing of your pieces, position a thick terry cloth towel on top of your ironing board. Set your ironing board next to your sewing machine and position it at the same height as your sewing machine table. This saves on steps between your machine and ironing board. You can also use the ironing board as a work surface to keep your fabric pieces organized. (See "Precise Pressing" on page 235.)

Seam Ripper: There are times when nothing but a sharp seam ripper will do. The tiny, sharp point can rip out stitches much more effectively and carefully than the tips of scissor blades. When fitting checkerboard and scrap borders to the quilt, a seam ripper is the perfect tool to remove extra border pieces.

Scissors: Most fabric cutting for the projects is done with the rotary cutter, but you still need a good, sharp pair of fabric scissors at hand for cutting threads and trimming the backing fabric.

Color and Fabric

A trip to the fabric store can be a little overwhelming with all the beautiful fabrics available now. If you're like me, you'll probably want just about every one! To help you focus on what you need, here's a handy list of points to keep in mind.

Visual Texture: Visual variety is the spice of life. . . and quiltmaking. Choose fabrics from different categories of print, such as geometric, pictorial, circular or swirly, abstract, plaids and stripes, florals, leafy prints, paisleys, and subtle textures. A nice medley of visual textures will enhance the look of your quilt.

Contrast: Make sure there is good contrast between the fabrics you choose for the blocks, background, and borders.

Scale: Vary the scale of the prints you choose by incorporating small, medium, and large ones. Mixing different-size prints together will really enliven the mix and create a more visually stimulating quilt.

Value: Value is the darkness or lightness of a color. Determine where you want to place light, medium, and dark fabrics in your project.

Multicolor Prints: You can often start with a multicolor print and use the colors in that print to select the other fabrics for the quilt.

Directional Prints: I've noted in the projects where directional prints are not recommended. Be sure to consider how the print will look in the block or project once it's cut. If it's subtle, it may be fine, but it could be distracting if it veers off in many directions.

Rich versus Bright: Choose either deep, rich shades or bright colors for a project. For a warm,

Country Colors for Christmas

In all the Christmas projects throughout this book, you'll probably notice a trend in the colors I use to create an old-fashioned country Christmas look and feel. The key to this "antiquey" look is the combination of dark, rich colors with warm naturals and tans.

The reds and greens are deep, rich, and fully saturated with color. The reds are a little closer to burgundy than a bright red, and I would describe it as a turkey red or barn red. The green is more of a hunter or forest green.

I have used light to medium tans instead of white for background fabrics. Dark tans and medium browns create that old-fashioned sepia tone that really enhances the warm, aged look of the projects. Just make sure there is enough contrast between your block fabrics or appliqué shapes and the background fabric, so that the design will stand out. (See the brown tones used in the Gingerbread Boy wallhanging on page 106.)

Black is the perfect accent to red, green, brown, and tan, and reinforces the dark country color scheme.

When combining several fabrics of the same color together in a quilt, be sure to pick a variety of visual textures—a variety of different types of prints with different shapes. And be sure to vary the scale of the prints by choosing some small, medium, and large prints.

Don't be afraid to substitute different colors to create your own Christmas look. If you want a more formal look, think about adding rich and dressy-looking golds, purples, or blues to the reds and blacks. If Victorian is your style, try substituting some pinks for the reds and teals for the greens. For a brighter, more contemporary feel, choose bright, true reds, clear kelly greens, and yellowy golds, and combine these with white backgrounds. Even more than the design, the colors and fabrics you choose will really determine the look and style of your quilt.

country folk-art look, I use the deeper, richer shades that are saturated with color and don't include any brights. Bright, bold colors can be very successful and will give you a cheerful look, but I don't recommend mixing and matching here.

Have fun and enjoy! Be flexible and open to experimenting with color. Try fabrics and combinations you normally wouldn't use. Relax and don't worry! You may surprise yourself!

Accuracy Counts!

Accuracy begins with prewashing your fabrics and pressing out all the wrinkles before cutting. When you do start cutting, be certain that you line your ruler up precisely with the edges of your fabric. Do not use the thick lines on your cutting mat for precise cutting. Cut your pieces carefully and they will stitch up beautifully. To achieve precise piecing, take your time, be patient, and make sure to have exact ¼-inch seam allowances. Press as you sew to make sure seams lie flat as you assemble your block. When you add it all up, accurate cutting, piecing, and pressing will bring 100 percent accurate results.

The Basics of Rotary Cutting

If this is the first time you will be using a rotary cutter, cutting mat, and see-through ruler, read through these directions carefully. Then practice on scrap fabrics before you cut into your project fabric.

Precise cutting is the first step in precision sewing. Take your time to measure and cut your strips and pieces accurately. All rotary cutting dimensions include ¼-inch seam allowances.

A work surface that is kitchen-counter height will be easiest on your back and bring you closer to your work. Lay your cutting mat on your work surface.

Making the Cut

Step 1. Most 44-inch-wide fabric comes off the bolt folded in half with selvage to selvage (finished edge) to measure approximately 22 inches wide. (If you have washed your fabric, refold selvage to selvage.) Make sure the fabric is straight and then fold again, bringing the fold up to the selvages. It will now be four layers thick and approximately 11 inches wide. Refer to **Diagram 1.** Position the folded fabric so that the edge

with the selvages is facing away from you and the double-folded edge is facing toward you. Again be very careful that the fabric is straight. From this folded length of fabric, you can now start to cut your strips.

In the project directions, the dimension for the first strip cut is often 44 inches long. Don't worry if your fabric is only 42 or 43 inches. This variance has been considered in the yardage and cutting dimensions. If your fabric is *less* than 42 inches, you may occasionally need to cut an extra strip and may need to purchase extra yardage.

DIAGRAM 1

Step 2. Use your see-through ruler as a cutting guide. Align one of the horizontal lines of the ruler with the double-folded edge of the fabric so the ruler is square with the fabric. See **Diagram 2.** Using some pressure, hold the ruler in position and use the rotary cutter to trim off the uneven edges on the right end of the fabric. Make sure you've cut through all four layers. You should now have a perfectly straight edge of fabric.

DIAGRAM 2

Step 3. Rotate your fabric so that the end you have trimmed is on your left. All of the cutting of strips and pieces for your quilt will be made measuring from this trimmed end of fabric. To move your fabric into the correct position, simply rotate your cutting mat. If you pick up the fabric, you'll risk messing up the four layers.

If you're left-handed, as I am, you will find it more comfortable to measure and make your cuts from the right end of the folded fabric. In that case, simply reverse the directions given in Steps 2 and 3. Trim off uneven edges on the left end of the fabric in Step 2 and rotate the fabric so the trimmed edges are on your right in Step 3. (When you look at the diagrams, keep in mind that they are drawn for right-handers.)

Sew-Safe Rotary Cutting

✂ Always retract the blade whenever you set your cutter down, and keep it out of reach of children. The blade is extremely sharp.

✂ For the most control, always stand when cutting. You'll have a straight perspective on your work and can exert more pressure with less effort. A counter-height cutting surface is best.

✂ Always cut away from your body. If you cut toward yourself, your elbow runs into your side, causing the loss of a smooth cutting movement. You also risk slipping and cutting yourself.

✂ Keep fingers from getting too close to the edge of the ruler when cutting.

✂ To prevent your ruler from sliding, hold it with flexed fingers. The ruler will slip more easily if your palm is flat on the ruler.

✂ Cut only on a cutting mat intended for rotary cutting.

✂ If your cutter begins skipping, it's time for a new blade. Don't put off replacing too long or you'll run the risk of mistakes and less-than-accurate cutting.

✂ Wrap cardboard and then tape around blades before you dispose of them. (You can use the packaging from the replacement blade for this.)

✂ Clean and oil your rotary cutter occasionally and after lengthy cutting sessions. Pay close attention when disassembling your cutter so you can reassemble it properly.

✂ Use the rotary cutter only on cotton fabrics (polyester battings and fabrics will dull your blade).

Step 4. Use the horizontal lines on your ruler as your point of reference as you make the next cuts. From the edge of the ruler, going across one of these lines, find the width of the first strip you want to cut. For example, if the strip is 2½ inches wide by 44 inches long, find 2½ inches from the edge of your ruler. Align the 2½-inch line on the ruler with the straight edge of the fabric. See **Diagram 3.** To make sure your ruler is lined up perfectly straight, look for the 2½-inch mark on two or three of the lines that cross the ruler. These marks should also lie directly over the straight edge of the fabric. When the ruler is lined up perfectly with the fabric edge, hold it in position and cut.

Cut.

DIAGRAM 3

SEW SMART

Here are some no-slip tricks to keep your ruler from sliding as you cut:

• Adhere masking tape to the underside of the ruler.

• Fasten sandpaper dots to the underside of the ruler.

• Purchase fabric grips to apply to your ruler.

• Add dabs of rubber cement to the ruler and let them dry.

Step 5. After cutting the strips, many of the projects then require you to cut pieces from those strips. If you're cutting several pieces that are the same size, you can leave your strip folded either in quarters or in half so you can cut more than one piece at a time. Lay the ruler on top of the strip. Line up one of the horizontal lines on your ruler with the long edge of your strip. Trim off one end of the strip to square and straighten the edge of the fabric. For fabric folded in quarters, trim the end with one fold and the selvages; for fabric folded in half, trim the end with the selvages. See **Diagrams** 4 and **5.** Rotate the fabric so this cut end is on the left, as described in Step 3. Following the cutting procedure explained in Step 4, cut the pieces as specified in the project. See **Diagram 6.** In some cases you may be cutting several different size pieces from one strip. Cut the largest pieces first and then the smaller pieces.

DIAGRAM 4

DIAGRAM 5

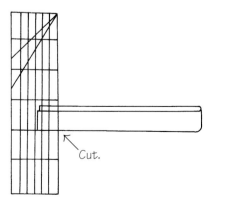

DIAGRAM 6

Making Speedy Triangles

A triangle set consists of two triangles sewn together to make a square. The traditional method for preparing these units is to cut two individual triangles, then stitch them together. I use a quick-sew method of constructing several triangle sets at one time. Read through the step-by-step directions below for details on this quick and easy technique. Refer to each specific project for fabric color, fabric size, and grid size.

Accuracy is critical in every step of making triangle sets (marking, cutting, sewing, and pressing). If you don't pay close attention, you can alter the size of your triangle set, making piecing the blocks together more difficult.

SEW SMART

Always double-check your measurements before you cut. There's a lot of wisdom in the old saying, "Measure twice, cut once."

Marking, Sewing, and Cutting Speedy Triangles

Step 1. Line up and position your selected fabrics with right sides together.

Step 2. To mark the grid, you need a ballpoint pen (or extra-fine point felt-tip pen), a see-through ruler, and good light. The specific project will list the size of the squares in the grid and how many squares to include in your grid. For an example, let's say our pattern requires a grid of eight 2⅞-inch squares. You should draw the grid on the wrong side of the lightest fabric.

Step 3. Line your ruler approximately ½ to 1 inch from the lengthwise edge of your fabric and draw a line. The size of fabric pieces used for the Speedy Triangles allows a ½- to 1-inch margin of fabric all the way around the grid.

Step 4. Rotate your fabric and line up your ruler to draw a second line exactly 2⅞ inches from the first line. Align your ruler with the second line to draw a third line exactly 2⅞ inches from the second line.

Step 5. To draw perpendicular lines to make the squares, rotate your fabric a quarter turn. Line up one of the horizontal lines on your ruler with one of the lines drawn on your fabric to square your ruler. Draw your first perpendicular line about ½ to 1 inch from the edge of the fabric.

Step 6. Rotate your fabric and line your ruler up to draw a second line exactly 2⅞ inches from the first perpendicular line. Align your ruler with the second line to draw a third line 2⅞ inches away. Repeat two more times to draw a fourth and fifth line. Your grid is now complete.

Step 7. The next step is to draw diagonal lines that will exactly intersect the corners of the squares. Drop the point of your pen exactly on the corners you will intersect and then butt the ruler up to the pen. You will need to shift the pen back and forth between those points until you get your ruler lined up so that the line you draw will precisely intersect the corners. Refer to **Diagram 7.**

DIAGRAM 7

Step 8. Now you're ready to sew. Using a ¼-inch seam allowance, stitch along *both* sides of each diagonal line. Use the edge of your presser foot as a ¼-inch guide, or draw a line ¼ inch away from both sides of the pen lines if your presser foot isn't exactly ¼ inch.

To speed up your stitching, start sewing above the grid line marked on the top left square. See **Diagram 8.** (If you've drawn the diagonal lines in the opposite direction from the diagram, start sewing on the lower left square.) Sew a ¼-inch seam along the diagonal line, and stop sewing when you're a few stitches past the second grid line you cross. Stop stitching and put your needle in the up position. Turn your piece of fabric around, and continue sewing the other direction on the opposite side of the diagonal line. (When you turn your fabric, you will pull threads through your machine and bobbin. This thread will hang loose between where you stopped and started sewing.) After you have passed the top grid mark by a few stitches, stop sewing again, pull the threads across, turn the fabric, and start stitching down the second upper left square. Do this continuous sewing until you've stitched along both sides of all the diagonal lines in your grid. When you're done

sewing, you should have a piece of fabric that looks like **Diagram 9.**

DIAGRAM 8

DIAGRAM 9

Troubleshooting Speedy Triangles

Dilemma: The finished triangle sets aren't perfectly square.

✁ Did you mark your grid accurately?

✁ Were the diagonal lines connected exactly across the corners?

✁ Did you tug them out of whack while pressing? Try gently finger-pressing the triangle sets open before using the iron.

✁ Try using fewer squares per grid.

Dilemma: The size of the triangle sets varies slightly from set to set.

✁ Did you mark your grid accurately?

✁ Did you sew with an accurate ¼-inch seam?

✁ Did you cut exactly along the pen lines?

✁ Did you fail to open the seams fully when pressing the sets open?

Dilemma: Little "tails" of fabric (the seam allowance) stick out on the sides.

✁ If you find these distracting, trim off the seam allowance carefully so it is even with the sides of the square.

Step 9. Use your rotary cutter and ruler to cut along all the pen lines. On many of the points of the triangles, a couple of stitches will remain, as shown in the triangle set in **Diagram 10.** Just open up the triangle set with a gentle tug, and the stitches will pull out. Do not tug with force, or you can stretch your triangle set out of shape. Based on our example, you will have made a total of sixteen 2½-inch triangle sets. Each square from the grid you drew makes two triangle sets.

DIAGRAM 10

Step 10. Gently press open the triangle sets. See the individual projects for which direction to press the seam allowances. Triangle sets should be right side up while pressing. Your finished sets should look like the one in **Diagram 11.**

DIAGRAM 11

Making Quick Corner Triangles

Quick corner triangles is a technique I use to simplify the construction of pieces with triangles in one or more corners. They are formed by simply sewing fabric squares to other squares and rectangles. As many as four corner triangles may be sewn to one piece of fabric.

Step 1. With a pencil, draw a diagonal line from corner to corner on the wrong side of the fabric square that will form the triangle. This will be your sewing line. See **Diagram 12.**

DIAGRAM 12

Step 2. With right sides together, place the square on the corresponding piece. Matching raw edges, pin in place and sew on the drawn diagonal line.

Step 3. Trim off excess fabric, leaving a ¼-inch seam allowance. See **Diagram 13.** Press all seams toward the triangle, except when otherwise indicated.

Use assembly-line piecing as described below to make enough of the same corner triangle units for all blocks. Sew all the sets for each step. Cut threads, trim, and press toward the triangle.

Follow the project directions carefully, and be sure to measure each piece after adding the corner triangle.

Trim ¼" away from sewing line.   FINISHED CORNER TRIANGLE UNIT

DIAGRAM 13

Assembly-Line Piecing

For the quickest piecing, you need to apply the principles of an assembly line to your sewing. By repeating the same step over and over, your piecing can go much more quickly and efficiently. You will assemble the blocks one step at a time, repeating the same step for each block at the same time. Instead of finishing the blocks one by one, you will finish the blocks all at the same time.

Let's say you are working on a quilt that has 12 blocks. The first step calls for you to sew together two triangle sets. You repeat this step of sewing the triangle sets 12 times (once for each block). If the next step calls for you to sew a rectangle to the triangle set units, you repeat that step 12 times. As you proceed through the rest of the assembly steps, repeating each step 12 times, all of your blocks will take shape at the same time and will be completed all together.

Besides speeding up your piecing, the assembly-line technique will help keep you organized. You think once, repeat the step for the number of blocks in the quilt, and then move on to the next step.

Continuous-Seam Technique

Assembly-line piecing and the continous-seam technique (also called laundry-line piecing) go hand in hand. Any time you are using the assembly-line method to piece your blocks or sew a series of strips or pieces, you can use the continuous-seam method of sewing them together.

Line up all the same pieces for the first step for each block next to your sewing machine. With right sides together, stitch the first two pieces together. Instead of removing those pieces from under the presser foot and clipping the threads, keep them where they are. Butt the next set of pieces directly behind the set you have just sewn, and continue sewing.

Precise Pressing

✂ Always press following each sewing step. Put the tip of your iron right on the seam line on the right side of your fabrics. Come straight down on your fabric, and be careful not to stretch your fabric out of shape by moving the iron with too much force across your fabrics. I prefer to use a steam iron on the cotton setting.

✂ Look for the arrows on the piecing diagrams for pressing directions for each step. Following these arrows will ensure that your seams will lie flat.

✂ The surface of your ironing board is very hard. To make a more forgiving surface for pressing, lay a terry cloth towel on your ironing board. It will provide a cushion to absorb the indentations your seam allowances would make on the front of your quilt block and top. The nap of the towel helps prevent distortion of your fabrics when pressing.

Add each set without breaking your seam until you have joined all the sets together. (The hardest part about learning this technique is to overcome the natural tendency to want to clip the threads.) Begin and end your stitching with a piece of scrap fabric, and you'll eliminate a mound of thread clippings next to your sewing machine.

You will end up with a long chain of pieces joined together by thread. See **Diagram 14.** Take this chain to your ironing board and press, following the directions for pressing given in the project text. Once you've pressed the seams, you can clip the threads that join all the pieces.

DIAGRAM 14

SEW SMART

When you're matching two pieces or rows together, if one is slightly shorter than the other, lay the shorter piece on top. Fit and pin them together and the bottom piece should ease to fit the top piece. The motion of the feed dogs helps to ease in a little extra length.

Precise Piecing

An exact ¼-inch seam allowance is the foundation for accurate piecing. Check your sewing machine to make sure you can get an accurate ¼-inch seam allowance. Do this test: Cut a double-thickness scrap of fabric with your rotary cutter to get a perfectly straight edge. Line the edge of your scrap with the edge of the presser foot, and sew several inches. Using a seam gauge, measure from the edge of the fabric strip to the stitching line. If this is not exactly ¼ inch, start making adjustments until you find just where to align your fabric with the presser foot to achieve a perfect ¼-inch seam allowance.

Mark the throat plate on your sewing machine with masking tape exactly ¼ inch from the center of the needle. Be sure to make a test after your tape is positioned. If you adhere a few layers of tape, the tape will create a ridge for your fabric to glide along while you sew.

Enlarging a Wall Quilt to Fit a Bed

Nearly all of the quilts in this book are intended to be hung on a wall. However, you may fall in love with one of the designs and decide that you would like to expand it to fit a bed. Here's how I suggest you adapt a smaller quilt to fit a bed.

Step 1. Look up the dimensions of the finished block for the quilt you want to enlarge.

Step 2. Measure the top of your bed. Knowing the finished block size, determine how many blocks it will take to cover the mattress top. Don't forget to include the measurement for the lattice. You could increase the width of the lattice so you wouldn't need to make so many blocks. (When you figure the yardage for the lattice strips, make sure you measure so they're ½ inch wider than the finished size you desire.) Once you have determined how many blocks you will need, refigure the yardage required to make the new number of blocks.

Step 3. Measure from the top of the mattress down the side of the bed (toward the floor). Add two or three borders to the sides of the quilt to acquire that needed length.

Step 4. Draw the bed quilt with borders on graph paper. Use a scale of one square per inch. This important step will help you determine your fabric requirements for the lattice, borders, backing, and batting. (You'll need a calculator, too!) It will also help you visualize your project. When it comes time to translate your drawing into yards of fabric, keep in mind that most cotton fabrics run 42 to 44 inches wide. The width of the fabric is crucial in determining how much you need for the lattice, borders, and backing. If you do your figuring based on a 42-inch width and find out when you get to the fabric store that the fabric you want happens to be narrower or perhaps even wider, you will need to do some refiguring.

If you have problems acheiving a perfect ¼-inch seam allowance on your machine, you may want to look for a specialty foot that measures exactly ¼ inch from the needle to the edge of the presser foot. Check with your sewing machine manufacturer to see if such a foot is made for your model. If not, there is a universal foot called the "little foot" that can be adapted to most machines. (See "Quilting by Mail" on page 250 for ordering information.)

When you start a project, try to finish it on the same sewing machine that you started with. If you're using a special foot, such as a walking foot or little foot, be sure to use it for the entire project.

Speedy Strips

With this basic and very easy technique, you will be able to assemble complex-looking quilt blocks and create checkerboards or multicolored patchwork or scrap borders in no time flat. For an example, look at the Cookie Cutter Christmas Wallhangings on page 106.

The unit assembled using the speedy strip technique is called a strip set. The directions for each project will tell you the number of strips to cut and which fabrics to use to create the required strip sets.

To make a checkerboard, patchwork, or scrap border, sew the strips together along the long edges, alternating the fabrics as directed. As you add each strip, always pause to press the seam. The general rule for pressing is to press seams toward the darkest fabric or all in the same direction. Change sewing direction with each strip. It will help avoid the warping that can occur when sewing several long strips together.

Once you have joined together all the strips, you will have created a large strip set. The directions will then tell you to cut this strip set in half or in thirds and to resew the sections end to end. From this final strip set, you will cut the narrow strips that form the border. (See "Pieced Borders" on page 243 for more details on making scrap, patchwork, and checkerboard borders.)

SEW SMART

Use colored pencils to color in the squares in the Fabric Key to match the colors you're using in the project. You could also color in the piecing diagrams to make it even easier to follow.

Timesaving Methods for Appliqué

Even the most exquisite appliqué started out simply as cut-out shapes of fabric to be applied to a background fabric. In the past, a quilter's only option for fastening these fabric pieces onto the background was to use a needle to turn under the raw edges of the appliquéd pieces and then stitch or embroider them by hand. Many quilts are still made this way, and they are certainly very traditional and beautiful, but they are also very time-consuming.

The techniques and tools have changed over time, and new products have been developed. There are computerized sewing machines to finish the edges with fancy stitches, appliqué film to hold fabric pieces in position while we sew them, tear-away paper to stabilize fabrics to keep them from puckering, and thread made especially for machine embroidery. Plus, I've developed a great technique—quick-fuse Penstitch appliqué—you don't even need to finish the edges with sewing. All of these advances in tools and techniques mean you can create a lovely appliqué project in a mere fraction of the time it takes using traditional methods.

Many of the appliqué projects I've included in this book are designed for the quick-fuse Penstitch technique, but there are some in which I will suggest other possibilities. In this section, I've included complete directions for several appliqué methods, so feel free to choose your technique. Just be aware of the limitations of each method and decide whether it is appropriate for the specific appliqué design you have in mind.

As a general guide, designs with very small pieces should only use the quick-fuse Penstitch appliqué technique. Designs with larger pieces may be done with machine appliqué, buttonhole embroidery, or hand appliqué.

What You'll Need for Appliqué

The supplies you'll need for just about any method of appliqué are included here. Use this checklist when you're planning your project to make certain you'll have everything on hand that you need.

Sewing Machine: In addition to straight stitching for piecing backgrounds and borders, your machine should do a nice, even satin stitch for machine appliqué. Some machines have decorative stitches that are fun to use with appliqué.

Sewing Thread: For machine appliqué, use a thread that is specifically meant for machine embroidery or a good-quality, all-purpose thread. For hand appliqué, use a good-quality sewing thread. The thread color should match the appliqué fabric.

Needles for Appliqué: I prefer quilting needles for hand appliqué, but some people like to use sharps. Sharps are longer needles with a larger eye than the betweens you use for quilting.

Straight Pins: More delicate pins, such as glass-head appliqué pins, are easier to use for appliqué.

Rotary Cutter, Cutting Mat, and See-Through Ruler: For appliqué projects, these are used mainly for cutting background pieces, borders, and binding strips. For more details on these tools, see page 228.

Scissors: Use good-quality scissors or a pair of appliqué scissors for cutting designs out of appliqué film. These scissors need to be sharp, but I don't recommend using a really expensive pair of scissors for this.

Iron, Ironing Board, and Towel: See page 228 for a discussion of these items. I don't recommend using an automatic shut-off iron when working with quick-fuse appliqué. It may drive you crazy!

Appliqué Film: Nearly all of the appliqué projects in this book are perfectly suited for appliqué film. This paper-backed fusible webbing is sold in precut packets or on bolts at most fabric and quilting stores. There are both heavyweight and lightweight types. If you plan to do machine appliqué or buttonhole embroidery, use a lighter weight, *sewable* appliqué film. For quick-fuse appliqué and projects with edges that will not be sewn, use a heavier weight, *nonsewable* appliqué film. Appliqué film replaces laborious hand stitching; a simple stroke of the iron fuses pieces of fabric in place on a background.

Tear-Away Paper: Use tear-away paper (sold with interfacings under names like Stitch-N-Tear) as a stabilizer behind the background fabric when doing machine appliqué. This keeps your fabrics from puckering.

Extra-Fine Point, Permanent Felt-Tip Pen: For Penstitch appliqué, use this type of pen to draw stitches. You can also use it to add details such as eyes, noses, mouths, and buttons to various appliqué designs.

Embroidery Floss: Embroidery floss is used for adding details such as noses, eyes, and mouths to some of the appliqué designs. Choose a floss color that works well for the details you are adding.

Embroidery floss is also used for the buttonhole embroidery hand appliqué technique. Use black for an old-fashioned look, or coordinate embroidery floss color with your appliqué fabrics.

Light Table: If you do a lot of appliqué, you might want to consider an inexpensive, lightweight, portable light table that is now available and made just for quilters' needs. It is useful for tracing appliqué designs onto appliqué film or tracing quilting designs onto quilt tops. It's not an essential item, but it would make a terrific addition to your stock of quilting aids. (For ordering information, see "Quilting by Mail" on page 250.)

Quick-Fuse Appliqué

For Penstitch, machine, and buttonhole appliqué, you will need to fuse your appliqué pieces onto a background. The quickest and easiest way to do this is to use appliqué film. If you plan to machine or buttonhole appliqué afterward, be sure to use a sewable, lightweight appliqué film. For Penstitch appliqué and other projects that will not be sewn, use a heavier weight, nonsewable film.

Step 1. Trace each of the parts of the selected appliqué design individually onto the paper side of the appliqué film. Since you can see through the film, you can lay it directly over the design in the book and trace it. Remember, your design will be the mirror image of what you see on the book page, but it will be in the same position as the finished project in the photograph. If you want to reverse this, first trace the design from the book onto a piece of white paper using a dark felt-tip pen. Turn the paper over so the lines you've traced are facing down. Retrace the design onto the side of the paper that is facing up, again using the felt-tip pen. From this second tracing, transfer the design onto the appliqué film. Keep in mind that letters *must* be traced in reverse.

Step 2. Using sharp paper scissors, cut loosely around the traced designs on the appliqué film, as shown in **Diagram 1.** Do not cut along the lines at this point.

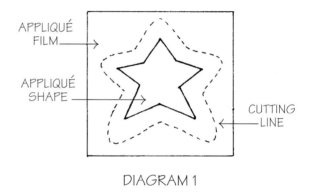

APPLIQUÉ FILM →

APPLIQUÉ SHAPE →

← CUTTING LINE

DIAGRAM 1

Step 3. Before you fuse, check the manufacturer's instructions for the proper iron setting to use with that brand of appliqué film. Fuse each piece of appliqué film to the *wrong* side of your selected fabrics. Place the appliqué film with the paper side up and the webbing side against your fabric.

Step 4. When all the pieces are fused, cut out the appliqué shapes following the tracing lines. See **Diagram 2.** Remove the paper backing from the appliqué film. A thin fusing film will remain on the wrong side of the fabric.

WRONG SIDE OF FABRIC

Cut on tracing line.

DIAGRAM 2

Step 5. Arrange and center all the pieces of the appliqué design on the background fabric. Remember to allow ¼ inch for seam allowances on the edges of background fabric if the project directs you to appliqué before piecing. Refer to the appliqué patterns as you position the pieces; the dotted lines will indicate where certain pieces should be placed underneath others. When everything is arranged, fuse the pieces in position with your iron. After the fabric is fused to the background, you can leave it as is or choose the appliqué technique you prefer: Penstitch, machine appliqué, or buttonhole embroidery.

Penstitch Appliqué

I developed this technique for small projects to give the look of appliqué without having to spend a lot of time. Penstitch is a pseudo-stitch done with an extra-fine point, permanent felt-tip pen. After you quick-fuse the appliqué pieces to the background fabric, use the pen to draw in stitches along the edges of the appliqué. Since there is no real stitching, the fusing is what holds the appliqué pieces in place. It's great if you want quick results. After all, the pen is much quicker than the needle!

Use this technique in smaller projects that have a lot of detail but won't have a lot of stress put on them. I wouldn't recommend Penstitch for items like pillows and baby bibs that will be handled a lot or that will need to be laundered frequently. But for other projects like wallhangings or ornaments, Penstitch is perfect.

Once the edges of the appliquéd pieces are held in position with the appliqué film, you can then finish them with Penstitch. Make the stitches along the outer edges of the appliqué shapes. The idea is to have them resemble a running stitch. Working about ¹⁄₁₆ inch from the outer edge of the appliqué pieces, draw lines about ¹⁄₁₆ inch long on the appliqué fabric. See **Diagram 3** for an example.

DIAGRAM 3

For larger appliqué pieces, you can make your running Penstitch "stitches" a little longer, with more space between them. For very small pieces, make your "stitches" shorter, with less space between them.

Special Tips for Quick-Fuse and Penstitch Appliqué

✂ If you are using quick-fuse appliqué (without any stitching) on sweatshirts or other washables, be sure to prewash *all* of your fabrics. Also, prewash sweatshirts two or three times to remove all the sizing and any finish on the fabric. Use one of the heavyweight appliqué films, such as Heat n Bond, if you won't be stitching them at all. When laundering is necessary for the finished shirt, do so very gently. Hand washing would be best. Expect quick-fused wearables to have a lifetime of a season or two.

✂ Laundering is NOT recommended for quick-fuse and Penstitch wallhangings, ornaments, and other projects. Treat them with a stain protector, such as Scotchgard, to help keep them clean.

✂ Use a muffin tin or tray to segregate and organize all the appliqué pieces for the different blocks or designs.

✂ Because your fingers may be a little awkward and clumsy, use a straight pin to move all your pieces into place.

✂ Lay out your appliqué pieces on the ironing board. That way you can avoid moving them once you have them arranged.

✂ With very dark fabrics, skip the Penstitch. Your pen lines won't show.

✂ If the edges of your appliquéd piece ever lift up, don't worry! Just re-press them back in position with your iron.

✂ After fusing, check your iron for residue and use iron cleaner as needed. Keep a towel on your ironing board to protect both the ironing board surface and any clothing that may be ironed afterward!

Machine Appliqué

After fusing the appliqué pieces in place, you can outline the edges with a machine embroidery stitch.

This technique may be your best choice for projects you'd like to launder and for those with larger pieces. Spend some time with practice fabrics before starting your project.

Step 1. Fuse all the appliqué pieces in place on the background fabric, following the steps given in "Quick-Fuse Appliqué" on page 238.

Step 2. Use tear-away paper as a stabilizer underneath the machine stitches. Cut a piece of the paper large enough to cover the area you'll be stitching. Hold or pin the tear-away paper to the *wrong* side of the background fabric in the stitching areas. This keeps your fabrics from puckering when you do your appliqué stitching.

Step 3. Use a neutral-color bobbin thread for all of the appliqué. Coordinate several thread colors to match the various appliqué fabric colors. Use these for the top threads, changing them as needed as you work on the appliqué. For best results, use machine embroidery thread.

Step 4. To get a good appliqué stitch, select a satin stitch at about 80 stitches per inch. Use buttonhole tension so that the top thread is looser than the bobbin thread. Use an appliqué foot if your machine has one. Be sure to practice on test fabric to adjust your machine settings to exactly where you want them.

SEW SMART

Fused appliqué can be removed if necessary. Set your iron at the same setting as for fusing. Hold the iron on the piece for the same amount of time, then lift up a corner of the piece. You may need to use a straight pin to help lift the corner. Peel the piece off. Don't worry if there is some residue left; the replacement piece will cover that.

Step 5. Stitch along all the edges of each appliqué piece. First appliqué along the edges of the pieces that go underneath other appliqué pieces. Don't stitch along edges that will be hidden under other pieces.

(This will help eliminate bulk.) Change top thread color as necessary. When you're all finished, pull away the paper from the back side of the fabric.

Buttonhole Embroidery Appliqué

Although this technique does call for hand stitching, it is fairly simple and it gives a very traditional, old-fashioned look to your quilt. Buttonhole embroidery is best suited to appliqué projects with relatively large, simple pieces. If the appliqué pieces are too small or there are too many small pieces, Penstitch appliqué may be a better choice. Be sure to use a lightweight appliqué film.

After you have fused the appliqué design to the background fabric, outline the edges of the appliqué pieces with the buttonhole stitch done in embroidery floss. Use an assortment of different floss colors to coordinate with the appliqué fabrics, or use one color throughout (black can be quite effective).

Use two to three strands of embroidery floss, and refer to **Diagram 4** for guidance on how to do the stitch. For very small pieces, use one strand of floss.

DIAGRAM 4

Hand Appliqué

In some of the appliqué projects in the book, you could choose the option of hand appliqué. Two basic methods are described below.

Quick-and-Easy Hand Appliqué

For larger, relatively simple shapes like hearts or apples, this technique is a quicker alternative to the laborious, needle-turning hand appliqué method that our grandmothers used.

Step 1. For this example, let's assume we're making an appliquéd heart. First, make a heart template. Then, put two pieces of your selected fabric with right sides together. With a pen, trace around the heart template onto the wrong side of the fabric.

Step 2. Holding the two pieces of fabric together, cut ¼ inch outside the traced line. Stitch all the way around the heart shape on the traced line. Clip the curves and trim the seam allowance down to ⅛ inch, as shown in **Diagram 5.**

STITCHING LINE

Trim seam allowance.

DIAGRAM 5

Step 3. Slit the back of the heart and turn it right side out. Use a blunt but pointy object (like a knitting needle) to smooth out the seams and create smooth curves. Press flat.

Step 4. Pin the heart in position, baste, and hand stitch it in place. You may want to cut out the fabric behind the appliqué to eliminate the extra bulk.

Freezer Paper Appliqué

Like the technique described above, freezer paper appliqué works best with larger, simpler shapes. It is a great way to create nice, smooth curves on appliqué pieces.

Step 1. Trace the appliqué design from the book onto freezer paper and cut out the shape for each piece.

Step 2. Using the freezer paper shape as your pattern, cut out the fabric piece, adding ¼ inch all the way around. See **Diagram 6.**

Step 3. Lay the freezer paper on top of the wrong side of the fabric piece. The waxy side of the freezer paper should be facing up.

Step 4. Fold the ¼-inch seam allowance of fabric up and over the edge of the freezer paper shape, referring to **Diagram 6.** Curves and corners will need to be clipped. Use the tip of your iron to press the seam allowances to the waxy side of the freezer paper. The heat will fuse the edges of the fabric in position, creating a perfect appliqué shape.

RIGHT SIDE OF FABRIC

FREEZER PAPER SHAPE

DIAGRAM 6

Step 5. Leaving the freezer paper in place for now, pin the appliqué in position and hand stitch it in place.

Step 6. Cut out the fabric behind the appliqué piece (leaving a ¼-inch seam allowance) and remove the freezer paper, as shown in **Diagram 7.** Press.

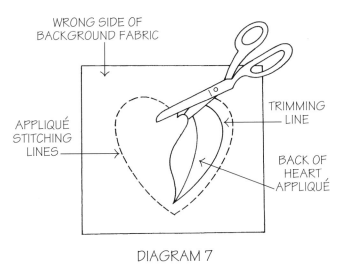

WRONG SIDE OF BACKGROUND FABRIC

TRIMMING LINE

APPLIQUÉ STITCHING LINES

BACK OF HEART APPLIQUÉ

DIAGRAM 7

Putting It All Together

Once your blocks are pieced or appliquéd, you are ready to join them together to make the quilt. In this chapter, I'll give you general pointers on everything from attaching the lattice to hanging the quilt to make the process of going from blocks to finished quilt nearly foolproof.

Lattice

Lattice strips are the "glue" that holds the individual quilt blocks together, defining and enhancing the overall quilt design. The lattice includes the strips of fabric that go between and around each of the blocks. (See **Diagram 1**.) In most cases, the lattice fabric I choose is the same as the background of the blocks. If you use a contrasting fabric instead, the lattice will act more like a frame around each block. For a smooth, flat quilt top, always press as you sew, and press all the seams toward the lattice.

DIAGRAM 1

Trimming the Blocks

Before sewing on the lattice strips, compare the size of your blocks. They should all be about the same size (within about ⅛ to ¼ inch). If they are not, you may need to do a *little* trimming with your rotary cutter to make them more similar. Do not trim your blocks unless it is really necessary.

Matching the Lattice to the Blocks

Before cutting your strips for the lattice, measure the height of the finished blocks. This measurement should be the same as the length you cut the lattice strips that go between the blocks. If you cut the lattice strips before the blocks were done and find they are too long, trim the excess lattice. If the lattice strips are less than ¼ inch too short, center the lattice strip along the side of the block. If the lattice strips are *more* than ¼ inch short, cut new strips and match the block dimensions.

Overcoming Uneven Edges

When sewing lattice strips to your blocks, lay the strips on top of the blocks with right sides together. The edge of your block may not have a perfectly straight edge (not uncommon with pieced blocks), but your lattice strip will (since you were able to cut perfectly straight with a rotary cutter). Use the lattice strip as your sewing guide for your ¼-inch seam allowance, and adjust the inconsistent edges of your quilt block as needed.

If you have triangles in your blocks, you may want to try sewing with the block on top. You'll be able to see just where the points of the blocks are so you don't cut them off with your sewing or make your stitching too far away from the points in your block.

Borders

The borders are the strips that go around the joined blocks and lattice. Think of a piece of matted and framed artwork: Without the mat between the art and the frame, the total effect could be much less dramatic. The same thing is true for quilts—think of the borders as the mats and the binding as the frame.

In many of the projects, the first border I've used outlines the blocks with a thin strip (frequently about ½ inch wide), using an accent color from the quilt blocks. This border sets off the quilt top.

The second border is usually a wider border that picks up one of the main colors or fabrics of the quilt.

A print fabric that incorporates many of the quilt colors often works well. In many of the projects, I combine several of the quilt fabrics into pieced borders, often including the background fabric to tie it all together.

Plain Borders

A plain border, made of strips of just one fabric, is obviously the simplest to sew. However, it can be more difficult to find just the right fabric to tie your quilt project together. (Consider adding corner squares to your border if you feel you need to pull another color into the border.) Basically, you sew strips to the quilt top and bottom and then to the sides. (In some projects I specify to add border strips to the sides first.) As you sew, be sure to press all seams toward the border.

Pieced Borders

There are a number of different types of pieced borders throughout the book. They may all look difficult and time-consuming, but looks can be deceiving! Using your rotary cutter and the speedy strip technique, you can put these together in no time at all. A checkerboard border consists of two colors, a light and a dark, and can be one or more rows. As you can see in the Yuletide Tables projects on page 66, checkerboards add a delightful touch to the design. Patchwork borders add a unifying look. They consist of many of the fabrics in the quilt, and each piece is the same size. See March of the Toy Soldiers on page 54 for an effective patchwork border. A scrap border is not literally made of scraps, but from all the fabrics in the quilt. The pieces are of varying widths. It adds a scrappy look but serves to pull all the pieces of the quilt together. See the Mantel Tree Quilt on page 159.

With the exception of patchwork points borders and sawtooth borders, pieced borders always start with a strip set made using the speedy strip technique described on page 236. Below are some helpful guidelines for scrap borders, patchwork borders, and checkerboard borders. The piecing and fitting of these borders is the same; only the cutting of strips and strip sets is different. In each project you will find the necessary yardages, as well as specific cutting and sewing requirements. Specific directions for other borders are given in each project. Also see "Hints on Fitting Pieced Borders" on page 244.

Step 1. Arrange all the strips in a pleasing order and sew them together side by side along the long edges. As you sew, press all the seams in the same direction. The project directions may have you cut this strip set in half (or sometimes in thirds), as in **Diagram 2A.** Resew the

halves together and cut again. See **Diagram 2B.** In the example shown, the strip set is cut and resewn twice before the border strips are finally cut in **Diagram 2C.**

DIAGRAM 2

Step 2. Fit and sew the border to the quilt top and bottom (or sides first if indicated in the directions), raw edge to raw edge. Use a seam ripper to remove excess strips to make sure there's a perfect fit. Press seams toward the border.

Step 3. Fit and sew the border to the sides of the quilt. Press seams toward the border.

Choosing the Best Batting

Once the quilt top is complete, with all the borders sewn on, you are ready to prepare the other two layers, the batting and the backing. There are a variety of quilt battings on the market, made of different materials and in different sizes and thicknesses. How can you tell what is the best choice for your project?

Since most of my quilts are used for wallhangings, I prefer a thin, lightweight, polyester batting. This batting is thinner than standard batting and enhances the country look of the quilts (something a thicker, puffier batting wouldn't do).

Loft

Loft is the term used to describe the thickness of the batting. A thin, lightweight batting with a low loft will give you a flatter quilt. It is also the easiest to slide a quilting needle through. No matter which thickness you choose, a good-quality batting will have an even loft. There shouldn't be thick and thin spots. And it should not pull apart too easily. Always look for good-quality products.

Hints on Fitting Pieced Borders

✂ Count the pieces in the border. With the exception of scrap borders, there should be the same number in each of the top and bottom border strips. The same should be true for the side border strips; each of those two borders should contain an equal number of pieces. (But the side borders don't have to match the top and bottom borders.)

✂ The border will have a fair amount of give and can be stretched to fit an extra ¼ to ⅜ inch if necessary. You can stretch your strip by tugging on it gently while you press it with your iron. Be careful not to overstretch, however.

✂ If your border needs to be adjusted more than ¼ to ⅜ inch, I suggest making your adjustments by taking in or letting out a few of the seam allowances. For example, let's say a scrap or patchwork border strip is ¾ inch too long. You can remove one 1-inch piece and stretch the remaining border ¼ inch to perfectly match the side of the quilt. For another example, assume that a border strip is ½ inch too long. You can reasonably expect to take in a seam by 1⁄16 inch without disrupting the overall look of the border. To "swallow" the excess ½ inch, you would need to take in eight seam allowances by 1⁄16 inch each.

✂ Because the pieced border will stretch, always pin it in position before sewing it to the quilt top. Press all the seams away from the border.

Content

Batting is made of cotton, polyester, or a blend of both. With traditional cotton batting, each row of quilting had to be no farther than an inch apart, or the cotton fibers would separate and bunch up. That's a lot of quilting! There are some cotton battings available now, though, that allow for rows of quilting stitches to be up to 8 inches apart. Some people find that cotton is harder to hand quilt than polyester. However, in its favor, cotton batting does give a very flat, traditional look to your quilt. With polyester batting, there is no minimum amount of quilting and the needle slides through the batting easily. One drawback to polyester batting is that the fibers can often work through the grain of the fabric, creating "batting stubble" or "bearding" on the surface of your quilt. The cotton/polyester blend battings promise to give you the best of both worlds—the easy quilting of polyester (without migrating fibers) plus the more traditional appearance of cotton.

Marking the Quilt Top

In every project I recommend ways to quilt the design to add some nice finishing details. It's usually easiest to mark the quilting design onto the quilt top before you layer it with the batting and backing fabric.

Choosing Your Marker

New, improved products are always being developed, so get in the habit of checking the displays at your quilt shop or the pages in the quilting supply catalogs. I like to use a sharpened, hard-lead pencil for marking. If you have an electric pencil sharpener, you can keep a white chalk pencil sharp enough to mark neat lines on darker fabrics. Always mark lightly and do a test on scrap fabric first to make sure that you can clean away any lines that remain after quilting.

Making a Template

I have suggested quilting patterns for some of the projects, but if you want to quilt a different design, you can make your own template or purchase a ready-made plastic template. To make your own, buy a sheet of template plastic (available from your favorite quilt-supply shop or through mail-order catalogs). Look for medium-weight, see-through plastic. Lay the sheet of plastic over the template pattern you have chosen. With a permanent felt-tip pen, trace the design onto the plastic. Cut it out with a craft knife or paper scissors. Your template is now ready for tracing.

Marking a Grid Pattern

Many of the projects in this book suggest quilting a grid on the background fabric. Your see-through ruler can make this marking quite easy. There should be a 45 degree angle marked on your ruler. Using that as your reference, mark your first line at a 45 degree angle to the horizontal seam lines of the quilt. (See **Diagram 3.**) Then continue to mark lines across your quilt in regular increments, as recommended by the project directions. Next, align the 45 degree angle on your ruler with one of the vertical seam lines of the quilt, and mark your grid lines in the other direction. These intersecting lines will form a grid that you can use to quilt in nice, straight lines.

45° 60°

DIAGRAM 3

Outline Quilting

For outlining the shapes in your quilt designs, there are two options. You can quilt "in the ditch," which means you add a line of stitches directly next to a seam line or along the outline of an appliqué shape. This sort of quilting requires no marking. Quilting in the ditch works best when you quilt along the seam line on the side that does not have the seam allowance. If you try to quilt through the seam allowance, you'll be creating extra work for yourself as you push the needle through two extra layers of fabric. Another option is to outline your design ¼ inch from the seam line. If you do this, I recommend using quilter's ¼-inch masking tape. This will save you from having to mark all the quilting lines on your design. Just position strips of tape around the parts of the design you want to outline, and use the edge of the tape as your quilting guide. Lift up the tape and reuse it until the stickiness is gone. Do not leave the masking tape on your fabric for long periods of time; some sticky residue may remain on the fabric.

Layering the Quilt

Now it's time to turn your quilt top into a quilt. By this point, you should have selected your batting, and your quilting lines should be marked on the quilt top. Purchase the backing fabric if you haven't already done so. Your next task is to layer these and baste them all together. (For all these steps, refer to **Diagram 4**.)

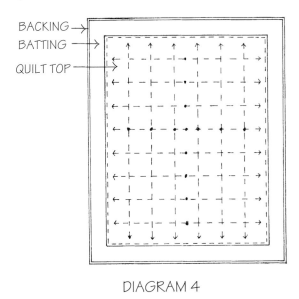

DIAGRAM 4

Step 1. Cut the batting and backing pieces 4 to 6 inches larger than the quilt top.

Step 2. Press the quilt top and backing. Find a large work area, like the dining room table or the floor. Lay the backing piece down first with the right side facing down. Lay the batting on top of the backing and smooth it out. Then place the quilt top (face up) on top. Make sure everything is centered and that the backing, batting, and quilt top are flat.

Step 3. The backing and batting should extend 2 to 3 inches beyond the quilt top on all four sides. Since some shifting will take place during basting, this extra margin of backing and batting will come in handy.

Step 4. To keep the layers in place as you baste, pin them together. Place a pin every 6 inches in vertical and horizontal rows. Begin basting in the center and work out to the outer edges of the quilt. Baste vertically and horizontally, forming a 3- to 4-inch grid. If you're tempted to skimp on this basting—don't! An adequate amount of basting is critical to keep the layers flat while you are quilting. Last, baste or pin completely around the outer edge of the quilt top.

Basting Hints

Here are some tips for making basting easier.

- Use longer needles than you normally use for hand stitching, such as sharps or darning needles. They are easier to handle for this type of stitching and can make the basting go more quickly.

- Thread several needles with extra-long lengths of thread before you begin and have them handy.

- Take long stitches, about ½ to 1 inch long.

- Divide your quilt into quarters for basting. Work in one quarter at a time, basting from the center to the outer edges. This will save wear and tear on your knees and back since you won't have to shift from one part of the quilt to another.

- Keep one hand underneath while you're basting to make sure your backing remains smooth and flat. Before tying off the thread after doing a row of basting, smooth the top and backing with your hand to make sure you haven't slightly gathered the fabric during your stitching.

- When you're doing your final bit of basting along the outside edges of the quilt, baste inside the ¼-inch seam line. When you sew on the binding, this line of basting won't be visible, saving you from having to rip out the basting threads.

Binding the Quilt

For the wall-size projects in this book that you will be hand quilting, it's okay to add the binding to the quilt before doing the actual quilting. Since the binding finishes the raw edges, it gives your quilt a finished look even before you've done your quilting. If you will be machine quilting or working on larger projects, I suggest you quilt *before* binding.

Step 1. Cut the binding strips as indicated for each project. Press the strips in half with wrong sides together.

Step 2. Trim the batting and backing to within ¼ or ¾ inch of the top, as directed in the individual projects.

Step 3. Align the raw edges of the binding with the front edge of the quilt top and bottom. Pin the binding strips in place. Sew ¼ inch from the quilt edge, being sure to catch all the layers of the quilt. Also, make sure the weight of the quilt is supported by your sewing table. Trim the excess binding and press the seams toward the binding. (Some quilt projects may specify that you sew the bindings to the sides first, then the top and bottom.)

Step 4. Align the raw edges of the binding with the edges of the quilt sides. Repeat the sewing and pressing directions given in Step 3. Your quilt should now look like the one shown in **Diagram 5.**

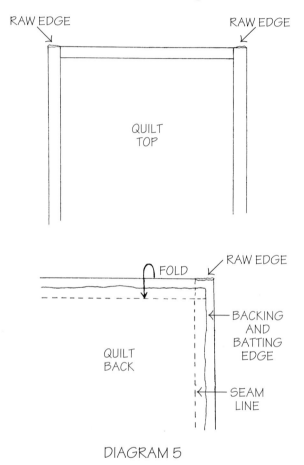

DIAGRAM 5

Step 5. Bring the top and bottom bindings around to the back. Fold in half so that the outer folded edge of the binding meets the seam line, as shown in **Diagram 6.** Press and pin in position.

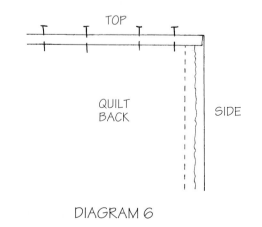

DIAGRAM 6

Step 6. Fold the side bindings around to the back so that the outer folded edges meet the seam line. Press. Pin in position and hand stitch all the way around the binding. Stitch closed the little opening at all four corners, as shown in **Diagram 7.**

DIAGRAM 7

Helpful Hints for Attaching Binding

Be careful not to stretch the binding when sewing it onto the quilt. When sewing through several layers, the top layer is pushed forward, and that can stretch and warp your binding. To prevent this from happening:

✂ Increase the stitch length on your sewing machine (it should look about average or a little longer than average in length).

✂ Don't skimp on pins when you're attaching the binding to the quilt. Use enough to be sure it is held securely in place while you're stitching.

✂ Sew at a slow pace. If you sew too quickly, it is easy to lose the extra control you need to make sure the binding goes on smoothly.

✂ Use a walking foot or an even feed attachment if you have one for your machine. It feeds all the layers through at the same rate.

Finishing Small Appliqué Projects

Some of the small appliqué projects direct you to use a self-binding method. You layer the top and backing with right sides together on top of the batting, stitch (leaving an opening), turn right side out, and hand stitch the opening closed. For these projects, consider using the same fabric for the backing that you use for the binding. That way, the backing fabric won't stand

out if it sneaks around to the front.

Another option for projects with self binding is to sew all the way around the wallhanging edge without leaving an opening for turning. Cut a 2- to 2½-inch slit through the backing and batting and turn right side out. To seal up the slit, hand sew it together, make a quilt label, and stitch it over the opening. Because you avoid hand stitching the opening in your binding, it will make a nice, smooth edge all the way around your wallhanging. (See "Quilt Labels" on page 249.)

How to Quilt

The quilting I recommend for each project serves the dual function of holding the batting in place between the quilt top and backing and adding decorative stitching. Since my projects are not heavily quilted, hand stitching is much less time-consuming than you might expect. If you're in a real hurry, however, you can always let your sewing machine do the quilting.

Tools for Hand Quilting

The supplies necessary for hand quilting are minimal. Here's a checklist of tools you'll need to have.

Quilting Needles: These are also called betweens. If you are a beginning quilter, I suggest starting with a package of needles that carries an assortment of sizes. Size 10 is a commonly used size and is the needle I prefer. The larger the number, the smaller the needle.

Quilting Thread: Always be sure to use extra-strong thread made especially for quilting. Choose a quilting thread color that coordinates with the background fabric color if you want the background to recede. If you want the background to be more active, use a contrasting color of thread. For a special design feature that you want to stand out (like a heart), contrasting thread will show up more.

Thimble: This is another tool that may require some trial and error before you settle on one you like. I really prefer the leather thimbles. Look for one with elastic (it stays on your finger better), a slit for your fingernail, and extra reinforcement at the fingertip. These leather thimbles can be very comfortable to wear and not too cumbersome.

Quilting Hoop or Frame: Hoops or frames hold the three layers taut and smooth while you are quilting. Some people find it easier to make small, evenly spaced stitches when quilting in a hoop. There's also less likelihood that the fabric will pucker or wrinkle under the stitching. Since the projects in the book are relatively small, you don't need a hoop much larger than lap size.

Quilting by Hand

Hand quilting is similar to playing the piano—the more you do it, the better your fingers get. Good quilting stitches are small and even. At first, you should concentrate on even stitches; as you gain experience, your stitches will naturally become smaller.

Step 1. Cut a length of quilting thread (approximately 18 inches), thread the needle, and knot one end.

Step 2. About 1 inch from the point where you want to begin stitching, insert the needle through the top layer of fabric. See **Diagram 8.** Bring it up right where you want to take the first stitch, and pull on the thread until the knot rests against the surface of the fabric. With a gentle tug, pull on the thread to pop the knot through the fabric. The knot will stay securely anchored in the batting beneath the quilt top, hidden out of sight. Whenever you need to start a new piece of thread, repeat this procedure for burying the knot.

DIAGRAM 8

Step 3. The quilting stitch is a series of running stitches made along the lines of the quilting design you have marked. I would encourage you to practice "stacking" your stitches on the needle right from the start. This technique, once you get the hang of it, allows you to make many small, nicely aligned stitches at a time and makes the quilting go more quickly.

To stack your stitches, push just the tip of the needle down through the three layers, using the finger with the thimble on your top hand, as shown in **Diagram 9.** As soon as your finger on the underside feels the needle come through, rock it up again toward the surface. (Simultaneously press down on the head of the needle with the thimble finger and push up against the needle tip with a finger on the underside.) When the needle tip pokes through the top surface, push it down again, then rock it back through the top. You may start by stacking two stitches, then find as you get more practice you can stack four or five comfortably. Once you've stacked your stitches, pull it through the fabric using the thumb and forefinger of your top hand. Pull the thread taut, but don't pull it too tight, or the fabric will pucker. See **Diagram 10.**

DIAGRAM 9

DIAGRAM 10

If you have trouble pulling the needle through the fabric after you've stacked the stitches on it, reach for a needle grabber. These round circles of thin rubber wrap around the needle to give you a good grip. They're inexpensive and available at most sewing and quilting shops. In a pinch, you can use a deflated rubber balloon instead.

Step 4. To end a line of stitching, bring the needle up where you want to stop. Wrap the thread around the end of the needle two or three times. Pull the needle through these circles of thread to form a knot. Push the needle back down through the top of the quilt and pull it up about ½ inch away. Tug on the thread to pop the knot through the top of the fabric and bury it in the batting layer, as shown in **Diagram 11.** Pull on the thread slightly and clip it close to the surface of the quilt. The end should disappear back beneath the quilt top.

DIAGRAM 11

Quilting by Machine

Letting your sewing machine do the quilting can be a quick solution (especially if you're in a last-minute rush to get your holiday gifts done), but it is not necessarily easier than hand quilting. Just like hand stitching, machine quilting takes some practice. A walking foot or an even feed attachment is great for machine quilting. It can help avoid the problem of having the three layers bunch up.

Machine quilting works best on smaller projects, like the appliqué wallhangings, where you quilt in the ditch along the borders. These straight quilting lines are a good match for machine stitching. If you are trying machine quilting for the first time, keep in mind that the smaller the project, the easier it will be.

The layering process is the same as for hand quilting—you sandwich the backing, batting, and quilt top together. However, instead of hand basting the quilt, you can use safety pins to hold the layers together while you stitch. Position the safety pins so they won't get in the way of where you plan to quilt. Do all the quilting *before* you add the binding (unless it has a self binding).

Step 1. Coordinate the thread color with the quilt top or use clear nylon monofilament thread. Coordinate the bobbin thread with the backing fabric. (If you're using clear nylon thread, you must use regular sewing thread in the bobbin.) Never use hand-quilting thread for machine quilting.

Step 2. Set your machine for normal straight stitching. You may want to increase the stitch length for stitching through the three layers. Starting in the center of the quilt and working out toward the edges, machine stitch in the ditch (right next to the seam lines) to outline the block designs and borders.

Hanging Your Wall Quilts

Using fabric hanging tabs and a wooden dowel is my favorite way to hang wall quilts. But it is not the only way. Here are some possibilities.

Sleeve: Create a sleeve or "tube" of fabric that will run the entire width of your quilt. Cut the strip approximately 5 inches wide by the width of the quilt. With right sides together, fold the strip in half lengthwise and sew the length of the strip. Turn the sleeve right side out and press. Hand stitch the sleeve to the back of your quilt and run a wooden dowel through it.

Hidden Fabric Tabs: For smaller projects, you can use three or four hanging tabs on the back of your wall quilt instead of a sleeve. Cut 1½ × 2½-inch pieces of fabric. Fold them in half, right sides together, and stitch. Turn them right side out. Space the tabs evenly across the top of the quilt back, right under the binding. Hand stitch them in place, turning under ¼ inch on each end and stitching across the top and bottom of the tabs. Slip a ½-inch-diameter wooden dowel through the tabs. It should be cut ½ inch shorter than the width of the quilt.

Manufactured Wooden Quilt Grippers: Keep an eye open in quilt shops and home decor shops for ready-made hangers especially designed for quilts. These usually come in a variety of widths to accommodate different quilt sizes. They usually grip the top of the quilt and run the entire width of the quilt. Make sure the one you choose is free of wood stain to keep your quilt safe from fiber-damaging chemicals. For a mail-order source, see "Quilting by Mail" on page 250.

Decorative Bars and Rods: Find an attractive towel bar meant for the bathroom and hang it in a spot where you'd like to show off a quilt. Decorative curtain rods with interesting finials can also be used.

Cafe Curtain Rods: Purchase cafe curtain rods, the hanging hardware, and the rings that clip to the curtains. Attach the rod to the wall, put the clips on your quilt, and slide it onto the curtain rod.

Quilt Labels

It's a very special touch to add a label with your name, the name of the quilt, the year you made it, and where you made it. This will make it easier for family historians to identify who made that wonderful quilt! You may also want to consider adding other information, such as what inspired you to make the quilt or what important events were going on in the world when you were stitching it.

When handwriting your label, use an extra-fine point, permanent felt-tip pen to do your marking. For an even more personal look, fuse onto the label a simple motif that ties in with your quilt theme. (See "Quick-Fuse Appliqué" on page 238.)

To attach the label to the back of your quilt, use your preferred appliqué method.

Santa Sampler
Made by Elizabeth Ross
Merry Christmas!

Kent, Ohio   1995

Quilting by Mail

Clotilde, Inc.
2 Sew Smart Way B8031
Stevens Point, WI 54481-8031
(800) 772-2891
Sewing notions and quilting supplies, including the "little foot" presser foot, Heat n Bond appliqué film, thimbles, see-through rulers, rotary cutters, cutting mats, pins, needles, permanent markers, and charms for embellishment

DeCuyper Trading Co.
815 LaSalle Drive
Little Rock, AR 72211
(501) 221-3094
Stoneware buttons

Gay Bowles Sales, Inc.
P.O. Box 1060
Janesville, Wisconsin 53547
(608) 754-9466
Call or write for retail source of Mill Hill antique glass beads and other glass seed beads.

Keepsake Quilting
Route 25B
P.O. Box 1618
Centre Harbor, NH 03226-1618
(800) 525-8086
Quilting supplies and notions, including fabrics, patterns, quilt kits, permanent markers, "little foot" presser foot, pins, thimbles, templates, quilting frames and hoops, and cotton, polyester, and wool battings

Mumm's the Word
2900 North Nevada
Spokane, WA 99207-2760
(509) 482-0210
Fax (509) 482-2036
$7\frac{1}{4} \times 9\frac{1}{8}$-inch kraft bags with handles; specify brown or white. For $\frac{1}{2}$ dozen: $5.00; for 1 dozen: $10.00. (Add $3.75 shipping and handling; $4.75 outside United States.)

Also available from Mumm's the Word:

Country Fabric Line
Designed by Debbie Mumm
Six fat-quarter pieces (18 × 22 inches) $13.00. (Add $3.50 shipping and handling; $5.00 outside United States.)

Write to Mumm's the Word for a brochure of Debbie Mumm's other patterns and stationery products.

Nancy's Notions
P.O. Box 683
Beaver Dam, WI 53916-0683
(800) 833-0690
Sewing notions and supplies, including the Narrow Loop Turner by Dritz

Quilts and Other Comforts
Box 4100
Golden, CO 80402-4100
(800) 881-6624
Notions and supplies for quilters, including coordinated fabric packs, patterns, quilt kits, thimbles for collectors, pins, needles, permanent markers, and quilting hoops and frames

Sew Special
9823 Old Winery Place
Suite 12, Department MTH3
Sacramento, CA 95827
(916) 361-2086
Bulk buttons, wooden buttons, small wooden spools, wooden thimbles, and miniature scissors and sewing machines for embellishment

Specialty Distributors
P.O. Box 19
Logan, UT 84323-0019
(801) 752-3446
Bow whip

Credits

Photography Locations

The cover photograph and the photograph of Santa Claus were taken in the home of Kim and Jeff Finnegan in Phillipsburg, New Jersey. The editors thank them for letting our crew and Santa Claus into their beautifully restored home. Photographs were also taken there of the following projects: Holiday Hostess Set, Field and Stream, Pine Tree Lodge Christmas Cabin Tree Skirt, and Pine Tree Lodge Stockings and Pillows.

The balance of the photographs in the book were taken at:

The Bucksville House
4501 Durham Road, Route 412
Kintnersville, PA 18930
(610) 847-8948

This bed-and-breakfast inn is also a registered historical landmark in Bucks County, Pennsylvania. Special thanks to owners Barbara and Joe Szollosi for welcoming yet another photo shoot among the wonderful collection of antiques in their exquisite inn.

Furniture for Cover Photo

The furniture for the cover photo was generously loaned by:

Karen and Mark Carter
Carter Furniture
Route 611
Ottsville, PA 18942